CELEBRATING 1895

The Centenary of Cinema

The National Museum of Photography, Film &
Television is part of The National Museum of
Science and Industry.

CELEBRATING 1895

The Centenary of Cinema

Edited by John Fullerton

John Libbey

LONDON · PARIS · ROME · SYDNEY

NATIONAL MUSEUM
PHOTOGRAPHY · FILM · TELEVISION

PICTUREVILLE · BRADFORD

Cataloguing in Publication Data

CELEBRATING 1895
The Centenary of Cinema

1. Motion pictures. 2. Motion pictures – History.
3. Technology in motion pictures. 4. Motion picture audiences.
5. Popular culture. I. Fullerton, John, 1949–. II. Celebrating 1895
(1995: National Museum of Photography, Film & Television, Bradford (England))

791.43

ISBN: 1 86462 015 3 (Hardback)

Published by

John Libbey & Company Pty Ltd, Level 10, 15–17 Young Street, Sydney, NSW 2000, Australia.
Telephone: +61 (0)2 9251 4099 Fax: +61 (0)2 9251 4428
e-mail: jlsydney@mpx.com.au

John Libbey & Company Ltd, 13 Smiths Yard, Summerley Street, London SW18 4HR,
England; John Libbey Eurotext Ltd, 127 avenue de la République, 92120 Montrouge, France.
John Libbey/C.I.C. s.r.l., via Lazzaro Spallanzani 11, 00161 Rome, Italy.

Printed in Malaysia by Nanyang-Vivar Printing, 48000 Rawang, Selangor Darul Ehsan.

1895

Contents

1895

Foreword

DEPENDING ON WHERE YOU LIVE in the world – and on your views of what constituted the first cinema performance – the centenary of cinema was celebrated in different years. In Europe, 1995 was the official centenary year, with due homage paid to the Lumières. In Britain it was 1996, marking the centenary of the first performances in London and throughout the country. However, the National Museum of Photography, Film & Television chose to take an international perspective and began its year of exhibitions and events celebrating the centenary of cinema in June 1995, with a conference devoted to film before 1920.

Celebrating 1895 was organised jointly by the National Museum of Photography, Film & Television and the University of Derby, with financial assistance from Christie's (South Kensington), and took place at the National Museum of Photography, Film & Television, Bradford from 16–19 June 1995. During those four action-packed days, over sixty papers covering aspects as diverse as national cinema, genre, reception studies, technology, propaganda, and museums and archives were presented to delegates from fifteen countries.

This volume brings a selection of those papers to a wider audience. In his preface, John Fullerton explains the rationale behind the choice. As in all selections, there are regrets about what has been passed over or not been available for some reason, but I believe that these papers truly reflect the range and quality of all those presented throughout the conference. Furthermore, they encapsulate the stimulating spirit of those four days at Bradford so kindly remarked on by many delegates during and after the conference. I hope that this same spirit will be transmitted to those readers who were not able to attend *Celebrating 1895*.

Michael Harvey

Chair, *Celebrating 1895* Steering Committee

1895

Acknowledgements

WE WOULD LIKE TO THANK all those whose work before, during and after *Celebrating 1895* contributed so much to the success of the conference. Paul Spehr, Luke McKernan, Richard McLoughlin and Cine Chimera for outstanding film screenings. David Robinson for his witty and erudite speech at the Gala Dinner, and our guests of honour, Rachael Low and John Barnes for gracing us with their presence. We would also like to thank our keynote speakers and those speakers who took part in the symposium on early European cinema: Richard Abel, Thomas Elsaesser, Tom Gunning, Martin Loiperdinger, Charles Musser, Jan Olsson, Kristin Thompson and Yuri Tsivian. Without their support, the conference would never have become a reality. The truly formidable conference administration team of Mary Pagnamenta, Alleynn Wilkinson and Nicola Morrison. The National Museum of Photography, Film & Television's ever-resourceful technical staff of Jennifer Beyer, Tony Cutts, Duncan McGregor and Alan Noble, led by Martin Oliver and Dick Vaughan. Those other members of Museum staff for their help in ways too numerous to mention: Bob Cox, Paul Goodman, Colin Harding, Imelda Kay, Glenn Kefford, Brian McCann, Lorna Mills, Mary Murphy, Koshek Parekh, Jo Price, Janet Quereshi, Jane Parkin, Roger Taylor, Paul Thompson, John Trenouth and Lynn Worsley. And finally, those colleagues on the Steering and Programme Committees whose wisdom guided us through the complex process of organising an international conference: Susannah Daley, Steve Edwards, Anne Fleming, Nigel Hamilton, John Hawkridge, Stanley Mitchell, Simon Popple, Anna Scrine, Tony Sweeney and Philip Taylor.

Michael Harvey and John Fullerton

1895

Introduction

John Fullerton

Department of Cinema Studies, Stockholm University, 105 21 Stockholm, Sweden

AS HISTORIANS, we are probably obsessed with establishing origins, no more so than in a year in which the centenary of cinema was celebrated. The decision to hold a conference at the National Museum of Photography, Film & Television may be traced, no doubt, to some 'founding moment' of discussion between Michael Harvey and I when I taught at the University of Derby. Equally, the origins of the conference may be sought in the 1978 FIAF conference at Brighton, which event has stood as figurative birthplace for so many historians of early cinema formed in the 'new film history' mould. Just such a sense of moment infused delegates attending the Bradford conference, a sense of 'collective origin' which Tom Gunning noted in his conference closing remarks when he observed that the Bradford conference had been the most important early cinema conference since Brighton. Making a selection of papers for publication from a conference of that significance would never be an easy task, and, with over sixty papers presented, the final selection could not include all those papers I would have liked to publish. However, brought together here are presentations which reflect the breadth of interest represented at the conference and the sense of occasion that inspired delegates throughout four memorable days in June 1995; a celebration indeed.

In the first part of the collection, 'Inscribing a New Technology', I have brought together papers that discuss the reception of film as new technology or characterise institutional agendas that were developed for the preservation of the medium. Michael Harvey provides an overview of the history and interpretation of the cinematographic collection of the National Museum of Photography, Film & Television from the original loan in 1913 of apparatus by Robert W. Paul to the Science Museum, London to the Museum's current acquisitions policy. In outlining a chronology for the Polish inventor Kazimierz Prószyński, Marek Hendrykowski details the activity of an early pioneer who has been overlooked in accounts in the West relating to the development of Polish cinematography. A concern for the ways in which historical representation may articulate absence as much as presence informs the presentation by Simon Popple who, characterising the historiography concerned with the development of film technology in Britain before 1913, discusses the ways in which acquisition at the Science Museum responded to an implicit agenda. The desire to go beyond linear or teleological accounts for explaining technological innovation also characterises the presentation by Deac Rossell. Adopting a sociotechnical approach and developing Charles Musser's concept of a history of screen practice, Rossell argues that the medium of film in the period up to 1904 should be regarded more as an extension of magic lantern culture than an autonomous screen

1895

practice. The ways in which the inauguration of a new medium was conceptualised also informs the contribution by Elżbieta Ostrowska who, discussing the early film theory of Karol Irzykowski, provides insight into the ways in which a new technology was understood to reconfigure the human sensorium. In providing an overview of Irzykowski's theory, Ostrowska brings a major early theorist of cinema to our attention.

The second part of the collection, 'Exhibition and Audiences', draws together a number of papers that challenge current understanding of the exhibition context. The close relation of production to exhibition and reception as mediated by the trade press forms the concern of Richard Abel's discussion of changes in French–American relations in the period 1908–16. Examining the ways in which a company as strong as Pathé in the 1900s responded to the challenge of US film in the mid-1910s, Abel proposes that changes in narrative content responded to new market demands which may have reflected a significant increase in the number of women attending the cinema in France in the early years of the First World War. An interest in the role of women in the exhibition context also informs Vanessa Toulmin's study of show women in travelling exhibition in Britain before the First World War. Toulmin details the ways in which film was interspersed with live acts, and provides an overview of the way in which film was exhibited in the showground context. The importance of the exhibition context in determining production also provides focus for Mats Björkin's study of the production output of Orientaliska Teatern, a Swedish exhibition concern that turned to production in 1911–12. Discussing the close association of film with consumer culture, Björkin assesses the ways in which the company unsuccessfully tried to capitalise upon one of Sweden's major cultural assets, August Strindberg. Alan Burton's examination of the ways in which film was used by left activists in Britain demonstrates the potential for worker education that the new medium was seen to represent. In discussing the Consumer Co-operative Movement, Burton details the type of films that were exhibited and produced by the Movement in Britain, and

provides an account of the ways in which films were programmed to advance the educational objectives of the Movement. The concern with establishing a hitherto occluded history is also central to the strategy that William Uricchio and Roberta E. Pearson adopt in examining the nickelodeon period in New York. Noting that in the absence of other sources, the archival record established by the social elite of a given period constitutes the only available 'facts' at the disposal of the historian, Uricchio and Pearson argue for reading period evidence 'against the grain' in an attempt to attain a perspective that more properly represents the experience of marginalised social groups. The call for a historiography that can represent the dynamics of historical process also finds advocacy in Nicholas Hiley's discussion of the British cinema audience before 1920. Drawing upon a social history of film exhibition, Hiley argues that the type of history that accords priority to the medium should make way for one that more fully represents the ways in which the medium was transformed by the intervention of the audience.

Early film and its relation to popular culture forms the organising principle for the third part of the collection. In a paper that examines the depiction of Hispanics and other races and ethnicities in US film before 1920, Gary D. Keller and Estela Keller discuss the almost static perpetuation of Hispanic stereotyping from nineteenth-century popular literature through to film in the early twentieth century. Although their discussion evidences strong continuity between the traditions of popular literature and film, Keller and Keller also indicate ways in which popular fictions began to redefine notions of the public domain. A similar crossover between popular literature and film is the subject of Peter Krämer's study of the Bad Boy figure in literature, newspaper comic strips, and turn-of-the-century US film. Krämer's argument is that gender stereotyping was not only central to the processes by which tensions between the public and domestic sphere could be played out, but that bad boy films, staging their pranks for the benefit of primarily middle-class males in the vaudeville audience, represented a social class that was not only different to that featured in newspaper comic strips, but one which became crucial to the development of the nickelodeon and the one-reel 'headline' or 'feature' film. The relation between film and the popular stage provides focus for Stephen Johnson's study of the Tom Show tradition in Edwin S. Porter's *Uncle Tom's Cabin*. Comparing the film translation of Stowe's novel with a near-contemporary stage production by William Brady, Johnson concludes that Porter's film was probably an authentic if rather old-fashioned and highly condensed example of the Tom Show, while Brady's production addressed an audience which, disdaining the Tom Show tradition, relished the sense of childhood nostalgia that the production induced. Contemporary perceptions of a new technology characterise the concerns of the last two contributors in this section. Contrasting the reception accorded X-Ray photography in the British popular and photographic press with that which attended the exhibition of cinematography in 1896, Richard Crangle examines popular discourses relating to the 'New Photography' at the end of the nineteenth century, and characterises the function and attraction these new apparatuses of vision were perceived to represent. Taking issue with the concept of shock and distraction which has characterised recent discussion of modernity, Casper Tybjerg documents the sense of exhilaration that new technologies were perceived to represent in discourses as diverse as journalism, autobiography and scenario manuals for the aspiring freelance writer of *sensationsfilm*.

The fourth part of the collection is concerned with the ways in which the new medium threw into disarray earlier definitions of the public and private spheres. The film reform movement provides focus for Karen J. Kenkel's discussion of film exhibition, cultural representation, and the notion of the mass audience in Wilhelmine Germany. Arguing that the politics of the film reform movement were essentially conservative and nationalist in ideology, Kenkel demonstrates that the exclusion of the mass audience from German culture and politics made it difficult, in the post-First World War period, to reconcile the notion of national identity with the modern, mass cultural landscape of Weimar Germany. The interrelation of the public and domestic spheres is central to Constance Balides' examination of the conjunction of Fordism with the regulation of the domestic sphere in the US during the 1910s. While DeMille's *The Cheat* is usually associated with a culture that valorised consumption, Balides demonstrates that the film may also be understood as an articulation of a Fordist agenda through its presentation of the dilemma of the modern woman not only in economic terms, but in terms that bound her to the efficient management of the domestic sphere. The regulation and control of representations of the public and domestic sphere forms the focus for Stephen Bottomore's discussion of the ways in which monarchs responded to the introduction of film into the royal domestic sphere. Bottomore describes how different monarchs sought to control their representation in the medium, and identifies in what ways cultural codes and proxemics were challenged by the ways in which a new medium was used. Debates concerning modernity and tradition also inform Andrew Higson's discussion of heritage discourses in British film before 1920. Identifying key practices, Higson characterises the ways in which British cinema variously responded to the attractionist aesthetic of display in framing discourses concerned with patriotism, the cult of the national hero, or the adaptation of 'national literature', so inscribing modernity and tradition – heritage discourse – in a new medium. The ways in which the American Museum of Natural History sought to reconcile the conflicting values of anthropological rigour with pleasurable display forms the focus for Alison Griffiths' investigation of the ways in which a public institution policed the encounter between scientific discourse and film whose claim to scientific objectivity was perceived to be compromised through the association of the medium with entertainment. The ways in which the context of reception may frame audience interpretation is also central to Frank Gray's discussion of James Williamson's *China Mission – Bluejackets to the Rescue* (1900) in which cartoon illustration contemporary with the period of the Boxer Rebellion is identified as an important intertext for reconstructing the historical reception of Williamson's film. A similar per-

1895

spective informs Clodualdo del Mondo's discussion of the Spanish–American conflict in the Philippines where, to understand history as the figuration of colonised space, actualities and film re-enactments are contrasted with a variety of source material, including the exhibition of over 1200 Filipino natives at the 1904 St. Louis World's Fair, to envision historical consciousness.

In the final part of the collection, accounts relating to the formal development of the medium are reconsidered. Discussing narrative structure in early classical cinema, Kristin Thompson examines the ways in which the industry sought to stabilise the production of screenplays for the new narrative feature film through the publication of scenario manuals. Thompson's analysis of selected US films from the 1910s and from the last twenty years demonstrates that the mainstream feature film observes remarkable structural consistency in its organisation of action into three or, more typically in the case of post-classical film, four acts. Jan Olsson focuses attention on extant screenplays, rather than scenario manuals, for his discussion of narration in Swedish film in the 1910s. Central to Olsson's argument is that censorship records and screenplays provide insight into the ways in which close shots were understood in the 1910s. As in the case of the formal development of the medium in the US, Olsson proposes that 1917 represents a key year for developments relating to filmic narration. In discussing pictorial styles of acting, Ben Brewster and Lea Jacobs examine the importance of the nineteenth-century stage acting tradition to European film in the 1910s. Discussing the ways in which poses and attitudes were used to manage the stage picture rather than articulate a system of conventionalised meaning, Brewster and Jacobs

demonstrate that pictorialism in film acting was employed to orchestrate key dramatic moments. Reflecting on developments in recent German film historiography, Thomas Elsaesser elaborates an approach to narrative space that takes into account the ways in which the variety theatre principle not only structured the film programme, but also framed spectators' registers of reference. From this perspective, Elsaesser argues that transformations in narrative space responded to the interplay of collective and individual modes of spectatorship, which perception would seem to indicate that the ways in which reception history, genre study and formal analysis interrelate may form a fruitful agenda for future investigation.

Celebrating 1895 focuses, then, on the study of early cinema in the context of advancing and refining some of the paradigms available to us for studying the medium. What becomes evident, however, from this collection of essays is not so much the ground that has been covered as the terrain that remains to be revealed, let alone charted. From these essays, perhaps the most pressing area of concern remains the interrelation of reception and the formal development of the medium. In this context, the ways in which colour, sound and music were used to structure affect are major concerns that await further investigation. But also evident is the work that needs to be done on mapping mentalities and specifying the modalities of historical reception. Central to this project, I would argue, is the investigation of a lacuna that seems almost endemic to the field: the interrelation of form and reception in non-fiction film with those of fiction film. If this collection of conference papers can in some small way frame future investigations, it will have more than achieved its objectives.

1895

Contributors

Richard Abel teaches cinema studies and cultural studies in the English Department at Drake University. His books as author and editor include *French Cinema: The First Wave, 1915–1929* (1984), *French Film Theory and Criticism, 1907–1939: A History/Anthology* (1988), *The Ciné Goes to Town: French Cinema, 1896–1914* (1994), *Silent Film* (1996) and, forthcoming, *The 'Red Rooster' Scare, or the Americanization of Early American Cinema*.

Constance Balides is Assistant Professor in the Department of Communication, Tulane University. She has contributed to *Screen* and *Camera Obscura*, and is author of, forthcoming, *Making Dust in the Archives*.

Mats Björkin is a doctoral candidate in the Department of Cinema Studies, Stockholm University, where he is completing a dissertation on Swedish cinema in the 1920s. He has published in *Aura: Filmvetenskaplig tidskrift*.

Stephen Bottomore is a freelance writer on early cinema. He has contributed to *Film History*, *Sight and Sound*, and *Historical Journal of Film, Radio and Television*, and is the author of *I Want to See This Annie Mattygraph – A Cartoon History of the Coming of the Movies* (1996).

Ben Brewster is Assistant Director of the Wisconsin Center for Film and Theater Research, University of Wisconsin – Madison. He has published in *Screen* and *Cinema Journal*, and is co-author with Lea Jacobs of *Theatre to Cinema: Stage Pictorialism and the Early Feature Film* (1997).

Alan Burton teaches Media Studies at De Montfort University, Leicester. His books include *The People's Cinema: Film and the Co-operative Movement* (1994) and *The British Co-operative Movement Film Catalogue* (1997).

Richard Crangle is Assistant Director of the Bill Douglas Centre for the History of Cinema and Popular Culture, University of Exeter. He has contributed to *Le Cinéma au tournant du siècle/Cinema at the Turn of the Century* (1997).

Clodualdo del Mundo, Jr. is Professor in the Department of Communication at De La Salle University, and is also a screenwriter.

Thomas Elsaesser is Professor of Film and Television Studies at the University of Amsterdam, and Visiting Professor in the Department of Media Studies at the University of Bergen. His books as author and editor include *New German Cinema: A History* (1989), *Early Cinema:*

1895

Space Frame Narrative (1990), *Writing for the Medium: Television in Transition* (1994), *Hoogste Tijd voor een speelfilm* (1995), *A Second Life: German Cinema's First Decades* (1996) and *Fassbinder's Germany* (1996).

Frank Gray is Curator of the South East Film and Video Archive, and teaches art and media history in the School of Historical and Critical Studies, University of Brighton. In 1996, he edited the collection of essays, *The Hove Pioneers and the Arrival of Cinema*.

Alison Griffiths is a doctoral candidate in the Department of Cinema Studies, New York University, where she is completing a dissertation on the origins of ethnographic film. Her work has appeared in *Visual Anthropological Review* and *Wide Angle*, and she has contributed to *Dressing in Feathers: The Construction of the Indian in American Popular Culture*.

Michael Harvey is Curator of Cinematography at the National Museum of Photography, Film & Television, Bradford, and was Chair of the Steering Committee and member of the Programme Committee for *Celebrating 1895: An International Conference on Film before 1920*.

Marek Hendrykowski is Professor of Cinema Studies at Adam Mickiewicz University, Poznan. He has published widely on film, and is co-author with Malgorzata Hendrykowska of *Film in Poznan, 1896–1996* (1996).

Andrew Higson teaches Film Studies at the University of East Anglia and is Chair of the Film Studies Sector. He has contributed to *Film and the First World War* (1995), and his books include *Waving the Flag: Constructing a National Cinema in Britain* (1995) and, as editor, *Dissolving Views: Key Writing on British Cinema* (1996).

Nicholas Hiley is Head of Information at the British Universities Film and Video Council, London. He has published in *Historical Journal of Film, Radio and Television*, and has contributed to *Researcher's Guide to British Newsreels, III* (1993), *Film and the First World War* (1995) and the 1993 reprint of Geoffrey Malins' *How I Filmed the War*.

Lea Jacobs is Associate Professor at the University of Wisconsin – Madison, and is co-author with Ben Brewster of *Theatre to Cinema: Stage Pictorialism and the Early Feature Film* (1997).

Stephen Johnson teaches Film Studies, Theatre History, Acting and Directing in the School of Art, Drama and Music at McMaster University. He has contributed to *Nineteenth Century Theatre*, and is co-editor of *Theatre Research in Canada/Recherches théâtrales au Canada*.

Estela Keller is retired. She is a specialist in Mesoamerican anthropology.

Gary D. Keller is Regents' Professor and Director of the Hispanic Research Center, Arizona State University. He has contributed to *The Hispanic-American Almanac* (1993), *The Hispanic-American Almanac: From Columbus to Corporate America* (1994), and *Bilingual Review/Revista Bilingüe*, and his books include *Hispanics and United States Film: An Overview and Handbook* (1994) and *A Biographical Handbook of Hispanics and United States Film* (1997).

Karen J. Kenkel is Assistant Professor in the German Studies Department, Stanford University, where she is currently completing a book on the German ideology of the masses from the Enlightenment to Fascism.

Peter Krämer teaches American Film in the Department of American Studies, Keele University.

He has contributed to *Screen*, *The Velvet Light Trap* and *Theatre History Studies*, and is currently researching the early stage and film career of Buster Keaton.

Jan Olsson is Professor of Cinema Studies at Stockholm University. His books as author and editor include *Från Filmljud till Ljudfilm: Samtida Experiment med Odödlig Teater, Sjungande Bilder och Edisons Kinetophon 1903–1914* (1986), *Sensationer från en Bakgård: Frans Lundberg som Biografägare och Filmproducent i Malmö och Köpenhamn* (1988) and *I Offentlighetens Ljus: Stumfilmens Affischer, Kritisker, Stjärnor och Musik* (1990), and he has contributed to *I Musernas Tjänst: Studier i konstarternas interrelationer* (1993), *Filmen 100 År: Några glimtar ur de rörliga bildernas historia* (1996), and *Aura: Filmvetenskaplig tidskrift*, of which he is editor.

Elżbieta Ostrowska teaches in the Department of Audiovisual Culture at the University of Lodz, and is a contributor to *Z problemow analizy i interpretacji filmu* (*Problems of Film Analysis and Interpretation*, 1996).

Roberta E. Pearson teaches Mass Communications at the Centre for Journalism Studies, University of Wales, Cardiff. She is the author of *Eloquent Gestures: The Transformation of Performance Style in the Griffith Biograph Films* (1992), and co-author with William Uricchio of *Reframing Culture: The Case of the Vitagraph Quality Films* (1993) and, forthcoming, *The Nickel Madness: The Struggle over New York's Nickelodeons, 1906–1913*.

Simon Popple teaches History of Film and Visual Media at Manchester Metropolitan University. He has contributed to *Photographica World*, *Film History*, *Cinema: The Beginnings and the Future* (1996), and *Cinema in Britain: The First 100 Years* (1996), and is co-author with Colin Harding of *In the Kingdom of the Shadows: A Companion to Early Cinema* (1996) and, forthcoming, *'Chambers of Light': A Companion to Nineteenth Century British Photography*.

Deac Rossell is Visiting Fellow, Goldsmiths College, University of London, UK, and a freelance writer on pre- and early cinema. A contributor to *Archivos de la Cinemateca*, *KINtop*, *Film History*, *Wir Wunderkinder. 100 Jahre Filmproduktion in Niedersachsen* (1995), *Who's Who of Victorian Cinema* (1996), and *Servants of Light: A History of the Magic Lantern* (1997), his books include *Ottomar Anschütz and his Electrical Wonder* (1997), *'Living Pictures': The Origins of the Cinema* (1997) and a forthcoming study of the life and work of Ernst Kohlrausch.

Kristin Thompson is an Honorary Fellow in the Department of Communication Arts at the University of Wisconsin – Madison. The author of numerous articles in anthologies and journals, her books as author include *Eisenstein's Ivan the Terrible* (1981), *Exporting Entertainment: America's Place in World Film Markets, 1907–1934* (1985), *Breaking the Glass Armor: Neoformalist Film Analysis* (1988), *Wooster Proposes, Jeeves Disposes; or, Le Mot Juste* (1992), with David Bordwell, *Film Art: An Introduction* (fifth edition, 1996) and *Film History: An Introduction* (1994), and with David Bordwell and Janet Staiger, *The Classical Hollywood Cinema: Film Style and Mode of Production to 1960* (1985).

Vanessa Toulmin is Assistant Director of the National Fairground Archive, University Library, University of Sheffield, and has contributed to *Film History* and *Picture House*.

Casper Tybjerg is Assistant Professor in the Department of Film and Media Studies, University of Copenhagen. He has contributed to *Schwarzer Traum und weisse Sklavin: Deutsch-dänische Filmbeziehungen 1910–1930* (1994) and *A Second Life: German Cinema's First Decades* (1996).

1895

William Uricchio is Professor of Film and Television History at Utrecht University. He has published numerous articles in anthologies and journals, and is co-author with Roberta E. Pearson of *Reframing Culture: The Case of the Vitagraph Quality Films* (1993) and, forthcoming, *The Nickel Madness: The Struggle over New York's Nickelodeons, 1906–1913.*

1895

1

Inscribing a new technology

The Cinematography Collection of the National Museum of Photography, Film & Television

Michael Harvey

Curator of Cinematography, National Museum of Photography, Film & Television, Bradford, UK

LIKE MOST MUSEUM COLLECTIONS, the nature of the cinematography collection of the National Museum of Photography, Film & Television has been shaped by the institution that houses it, the individual interests of the curators who have had charge of its care and development, and their relationship with collectors, donors and the collections of other institutions.

The National Museum of Photography, Film & Television (NMPFT) opened on 16 June 1983, after seventeen months intensive work by a team of Science Museum curators, design and technical staff, led by the Museum's first Head, Colin Ford. As a member of that team and one of the first curators specifically appointed to the National Museum of Photography, Film & Television, I remember how conscious we were that all the Museum owned was on display in the galleries: we had no collection of our own. This perception, though, ignored the reality that we were a part – albeit the latest – of a huge national institution more than 130 years old with existing photography and cinematography collections over which we then had no control – an institutional anomaly that was eventually changed.

The Science Museum's origins are rooted in that triumphal expression of Britain's industrial and political power, the Great Exhibition of 1851. After the Exhibition closed, it was decided to use its profits to establish a museum in London that had two major aims: to increase the means of industrial education and to extend the influence of science and art upon productive industry. The South Kensington Museum, as it was then known, was opened by Queen Victoria in 1857 and was housed in temporary buildings for the first forty years of its existence.

In 1874, a Royal Commission set up to examine the state of scientific instruction in Britain proposed that a collection of physical and mechanical instruments should be created out of the scientific collections of the South Kensington Museum, its science and educational department and of the Patent Museum.

1895

Fig. 1. *Robert W. Paul's Theatrograph Projector No. 2 Mark 1, 1896. Paul (1869–1943) first demonstrated his Theatrograph projector at Finsbury Technical College, London on 20 February 1896, the same day as the preview showing of the Lumière Cinématographe at the Polytechnic Institution, London. This is the second, improved model, patented on 2 March 1896, which sold for £80. Over a hundred were produced. The lamphouse, spool and driving handle are replicas made by the Science Museum workshops in the 1930s exactly to the original patent specification. [National Museum of Photography, Film & Television cinematography collection.]*

Thus, already we see the beginnings of the division between science and art that underlies both the perception of the history of the media that this Museum represents, and the nature and content of our collection. This took place over eighty years before the scientist and novelist C.P. Snow drew attention to the split in the nature of British culture in his famous 'Two Cultures' lecture at Cambridge in 1959.

By 1885, the division between art and science was formally recognised when part of the South Kensington Museum was designated the 'Science Museum'. Twelve years later, a Parliamentary Select Committee appointed to examine the state of British museums recommended that the science and art sections of the museum should be split and housed in separate purpose-built accommodation. The

Government made £800,000 available to fund the development of the two museums.

The art museum moved ahead relatively quickly. Queen Victoria laid the foundation stone for the Victoria and Albert Museum in 1899 and it was opened ten years later. The Science Museum had to wait longer for permanent premises and it was not until 1913, two years after the report of another committee, the Bell Committee, that building began. The Science Museum was opened in 1928 and still only two-thirds of the original building programme has been completed.

The cinematography collection came into existence in 1913 with the loan (later converted into a donation) of six objects by the British cinema pioneer, Robert W. Paul. The Museum already had a photographic collection, founded in the 1870s as part of the Department of Chemistry, and the cinematography collection was established within that department. Paul's gifts to the Museum included his Theatrograph No. 2 Mark 1 projector and the camera and tripod with panning head, with which it is thought that Paul filmed the 1897 Diamond Jubilee procession.[1]

After this auspicious start, there was little progress, as the First World War intervened and the collection was closed until 1919. Even after it was reopened, there was scant activity until 1922 when the Museum acquired the massive Will Day collection on loan. Will Day, described in *The Kinematograph Yearbook* as a 'professional cyclist, pioneer motorist, aeronaut and entertainer ... Vice-President [of the] Magician's Club and first patentee with J.L. Baird of television',[2] was one of the pioneers of the British film industry. He had started by showing 'animated pictures' in 1898 as a young man of twenty-five. Day amassed a collection of over 500 items, mainly with the purpose of demonstrating that cinema was a British invention and William Friese-Greene was its inventor. The Day collection included a huge amount of pre-cinema material, such as the Rudge Phantascope Lantern, and early cinema apparatus, including equipment associated with Trewey's first Cinématographe shows in Paris and at the Polytechnic Institution in London.

This was indeed a rich collection but, ulti-

1895

mately, it inhibited the development of the Science Museum's own holdings. It was assumed that the loan would eventually be converted into a purchase or donation and thus there was no need to collect similar objects. The Day collection went on display in the Science Museum in 1924 and remained there until the Second World War when, along with the rest of the collections, it was closed.

However, there were significant objects collected in the inter-war period. Robert Paul made further donations and a considerable body of material, ranging from cameras and projectors to film samples, came from the Prestwich Company and the engineer and camera designer Arthur Newman of Newman-Sinclair fame. Perhaps the most important acquisitions were two cameras by Louis Le Prince. With the 1888 single-lens camera, he made what are possibly the earliest motion picture sequences, in Leeds in October 1888, at almost the same time that his compatriot, Etienne-Jules Marey, succeeded in a similar accomplishment using his Chronophotographe. The Le Prince cameras were donated by his daughter Marie Le Prince.[3] The Museum also acquired a huge body of material from Charles Urban, mostly relating to the Kinemacolor process and to the Urban company

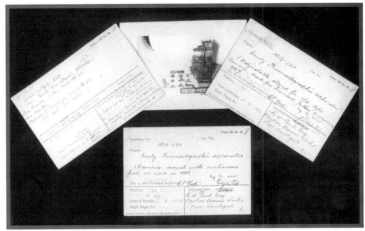

– the objects became part of the cinematography collection while the photographs and printed material were lodged with the Science Museum Library.

Nevertheless, collecting in those inter-war years remained slow: just forty-two inventory records, mostly relating to single objects, cover the period 1921–30 and sixty account for the years 1931–40. Even from the end of the Second World War until 1960, there are only just over a hundred inventory records – one relates to an Edison Kinetoscope, one of two Edison machines in the collection (the other is a Kinetophone, purchased in 1930 for £6) and five list film clips and cameras, including the Birtac, presented by Birt Acres in 1946.

In 1949, the collection became part of the new Department of Chemistry and Photography under the curatorial control of Alexander Barclay. During his time as Keeper he had to deal with the greatest crisis in the history of the cinematography collection: the loss of the Will Day material in 1959. Day (and after his death in 1936, his heirs) had been attempting to sell his collection since the 1930s and, despite the combined efforts of the Science Museum and the British Film Institute, the asking price of £10,000 could not be raised in this country. Instead, the collection was sold to Henri Langlois, who used it as the basis for the Musée du Cinéma in Paris. In 1959, the entire Science Museum's purchase grant (the fund out of which it buys objects for its

Fig. 2. Accession cards, known as 'Forms 100', for four of the six items originally lent by Robert W. Paul to the Science Museum in 1913. These cards give the date of their accession, 5 April 1913, and record that the loan was later converted into a donation. The card for the Theatrograph projector (top left) shows that the pedestal was a later donation on 17 March 1930 and that parts of the apparatus are replicas or non-original. [National Museum of Photography, Film & Television cinematography collection.]

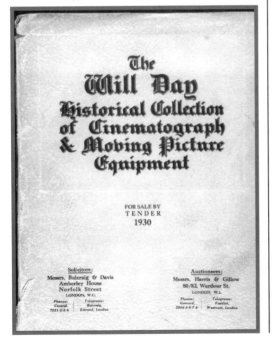

Fig. 3. Cover of the catalogue offering the Will Day collection for sale, 1930.

Fig. 4. *The Will Day collection on display at the Science Museum in the 1920s.*

Fig. 5. *The single-lens camera devised by Louis Aimé Augustin Le Prince (1842– 1890?), said to have been used in 1888 to take moving picture sequences at his father-in-law's house at Round-hay, Leeds and of Leeds Bridge. This is possibly the second of two single-lens cameras designed by Le Prince. The lower of the two lenses is the taking lens and the upper is the viewfinder. The lens assembly could be moved for focusing, using the lever on the right. The camera body was made by Frederic Mason, a local joiner, the metal parts were cast at Le Prince's father-in-law's firm, Whitley Partners, Leeds and fitted by Le Prince's assistant, James W Longley. [National Museum of Photography, Film & Television cinematography collection.]*

Fig. 6. *A section copied from a paper print of a film taken in the garden of the Whitley family house in Roundhay, a suburb of Leeds, by Louis Aimé Augustin Le Prince using his single-lens camera. Le Prince's son, Adolphe, who appears in this sequence, stated that it was shot in early October 1888 as it shows Mrs Sarah Whitley, Le Prince's mother-in-law, who died on 24 October that year. The other subjects are Joseph Whitley and Miss Harriet Hartley. They are all plainly having fun walking round in circles, keeping within the area framed by the camera. [National Museum of Photography, Film & Television cinematography collection.]*

collections) amounted to £2,000 – a twentieth of that of the Tate Gallery or the Victoria and Albert Museum and one-fiftieth of that awarded to the National Gallery. The vast discrepancy in purchase grant not only reflects the relative values of art and technical objects on the open market but also explains why the majority of objects acquired by the Science Museum are donations – in the cinematography collection this accounts for around 60 per cent over its entire history.

This statistic reveals not just the Museum's dependence on donation but also the largely passive nature of the acquisition process; in this situation the curator simply has to wait for what turns up or courts individuals or companies in the hope that they will donate objects by which they wish to be remembered by posterity. This is not to say that curators

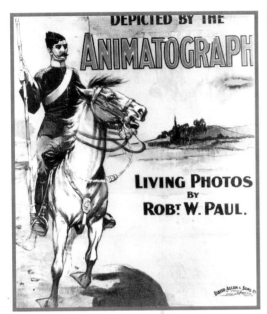

Fig. 7. *Poster for the Alhambra Theatre of Varieties, Leicester Square, London, 1896/7 where Robert W. Paul presented film shows using his Theatrograph projector, re-named the Animatograph specifically for that venue. Originally part of the Kodak Museum collection, it now forms part of the National Museum of Photography, Film & Television cinematography collection.*

Fig. 8. *William Friese-Greene. Analysis of movement experiment, undated. Printed from the original glass-plate negative in the National Museum of Photography, Film & Television cinematography collection.*

Fig. 9. *Birtac combined camera and projector, 1898. Designed by Birt Acres (1854–1918), this was the first British apparatus designed for amateur use. It used 17.5 mm film, produced by slitting standard 35 mm nitrate film in half. Its carrying case was designed so that, by opening flaps to expose the lens and viewfinder, the camera could be operated secretly. This was presented by Birt Acres to the Science Museum in 1946. [National Museum of Photography, Film & Television cinematography collection.]*

did not exercise considerable judgement over what they collected: indeed those early curators enjoyed a degree of power over their collections that is inconceivable today. Keepers in charge of departments acquired what they wished, only seeking permission from the Director when there was a particularly large acquisition or a call on the purchase grant.

Though there was no formal acquisitions policy for the cinematography collection, it is possible to see how collecting fell within the general philosophy espoused by Colonel Henry Lyons, Director of the Science Museum from 1920–30. In a report, delivered at the Museum's Association Conference in 1924 he asserted that:

> The objects which are exhibited in a technical museum differ fundamentally from those in an art museum since they are shown on account of their utility and not for their beauty or attractiveness, as those in an art collection. Each one has been designed for the purpose of performing specific operations more efficiently than heretofore and so in their assembly they represent the steps by which progress has been made, and show the gradual development of instruments, machines, etc.[4]

This is an attitude rooted in a nineteenth-cen-

Fig. 10.
Hand-coloured nineteenth-century magic lantern slide, one of hundreds in the National Museum of Photography, Film & Television cinematography collection.

the cinematography collection was broadened the scale of collecting remained modest. When David Thomas became Keeper of Museum Services in 1973, John Ward took over the day-to-day running of the photography and cinematography collections, curating the two galleries devoted to the subjects at the Science Museum which opened in 1979. On Dr Thomas's retirement in 1987, John Ward became responsible for the collection until 1989 when it became the National Museum of Photography, Film & Television's responsibility.

The limitations of the technological approach towards film in the Science Museum were thrown into relief as early as 1933 by the formation of another national institution, the British Film Institute (BFI). Funded by the same government department as the national museums, the BFI took a broader cultural stance towards the history of film which has been widely disseminated and more influential amongst media teachers and students than the technological view of the medium's history (another example of the 'Two Cultures' split?). Until the emergence of 'high-tech' special effects and computer animation, the role of technology in film production and its influence on style and content was largely ignored in critical practice.

If this implies a 'failure' of the collection to make its mark and of film technology historians to advance their cause within the media studies field – partly, I suspect, because the two sets of people do not speak the same language – it also highlights the inability of either institution to present a comprehensive overview of the film medium. This began to change in the 1980s with a broadening of the approach of both institutions. The BFI opened the Museum of the Moving Image (MOMI) in 1988 with many displays presenting the technological history of film. The Science Museum appointed Colin Ford, Keeper of Film and Photography at the National Portrait Gallery, to create the National Museum of Photography, Film & Television. Colin Ford's earlier experience was in theatre and film (as Deputy Curator of the National Film Archive in the 1960s he had produced the original proposal for MOMI). Subsequently, other curators who came from the media rather than

tury concept of technological progress which ignores social, economic or philosophical concerns: in other words, the wider world of ideas. I quote it, not to criticise but to illustrate its influence on successive Science Museum curators' attitudes to their collections until the 1970s. Throughout those years, the cinematography collection remained almost entirely a collection of technological artefacts with little associated material, except for technical manuals. There were few examples of film or magic lantern slides or posters. Nor was there any documentation or paraphernalia associated with the film production process.

In 1961, Dr David Thomas joined the Science Museum as Assistant Keeper in the Department of Chemistry where he assumed responsibility for the photography and cinematography collections. He was instrumental in curating the ground-breaking exhibition 'From Today Painting is Dead' at the Victoria and Albert Museum in 1972 and also drew up the original proposal for a National Museum of Photography in 1977. During his term of curatorship, the photography collection expanded considerably but whilst the scope of

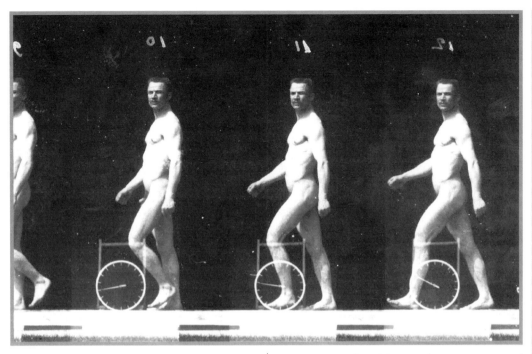

Fig. 11. *Some frames from a Chronophotographe film taken by Etienne Jules Marey, 1891. Printed from one of a number of Chronophotographe negative films in the National Museum of Photography, Film & Television cinematography collection, it shows a naked man walking. This example shows evidence of frames overlapping.*

a traditional museum background were appointed and this has had a direct impact on the development of the Museum's collections.

When the National Museum of Photography, Film & Television was established in the 1980s, a radical reappraisal of the purpose of museums, and their funding, was taking place. Pressured by the reductions in government grant-in-aid, museums were forced to become more market-oriented. They had to make themselves attractive to potential sponsors and audiences in a way that had never been required before. The old-style curators, absolute monarchs of their collections, disappeared – to be replaced by a more corporately-responsible attitude to collecting and collection management. Ironically, curators have had less time for their collections as they busied themselves with burgeoning public programmes and the expansion of visitor attractions, while responding to the pressures of customer service and public accountability. Museums even began questioning whether there was a need for collections at all, given that the costs of storage, security and conservation were an increasing drain on decreasing resources.

Here, at the National Museum of Photography, Film & Television we were – and still are

– involved in that debate. It has not prevented us from developing our collections but we have established a mechanism which ensures that all acquisitions are considered within the overall Museum context. Each curator must present a case for every acquisition before a board of their peers and Head of Museum. The written case is then filed with other details of the acquisition so that future curators and Museum management will understand the reasons for acquiring the artefact.

One of the positive by-products of this process is that curators become increasingly aware of how their speciality relates to those of colleagues: an important aspect in a world of converging technologies and especially where the borders of one collection impinge on those of another. A simple example is the work of the film stills photographer. Since the mid-1980s we have collected the work of individual film stills photographers, such as Cornel Lucas, Bob Willoughby, Eric Gray and Ken Danvers. Though acquired by the Curator of Cinematography, these photographs reside and are cared for within the photographs collection.

In the 1980s, there were two large acquisitions which profoundly altered the complexion of the cinematography collection. In 1983, Kodak Limited offered their museum at Harrow to the Science Museum and it was completely redisplayed at Bradford in newly-built galleries, opened in 1989. Originally established in 1927, the Kodak Museum comprises not only an extensive collection of Kodak photographic and ciné apparatus but also an important collection of professional ciné equipment gathered by another distinguished pioneer, Arthur Kingston. That went some way towards filling the gap left by the loss of the Will Day collection.

The second important acquisition was John Burgoyne-Johnson's Buckingham Movie Museum in 1989. Consisting of over five hundred items of mainly amateur film equipment, it filled most of the gaps in that area not represented in the Science Museum and Kodak collections and took the story of amateur film equipment up to the early 1980s and the beginning of home video.

During the first six years of the National Museum of Photography, Film & Television, the Science Museum photography and cinematography collections continued to grow independently of Bradford. In 1989, the National Museum of Photography, Film & Television assumed the management of those collections, with the Head of Film Development, Rod Varley, becoming responsible for the cinematography collection. Thus, what we hold is effectively a collection of collections – a combination of Science Museum, Kodak Museum, Buckingham Movie Museum and National Museum of Photography, Film & Television collections acquired under different rationales. We were aware that the collection contained some duplication and in 1994 undertook a study to examine precisely what we possessed and to work towards a coherent philosophy for our collections in photography, film and television.

Before we could map what was already in our collections, we constructed a classification model based on an assessment of what our collections should contain if the three media in our title were to be represented fairly and accurately. This forced us to examine our view of the history of the media and the criteria that we should apply. To some extent, part of this work had already been started by the

Science Museum. In the National Museum of Science and Industry (NMSI)'s *Acquisition and Disposal Policy, April 1992 – March 1995* general acquisition criteria had been established. It makes an interesting comparison with the ideas of Colonel Lyons, seventy years earlier:

> Objects acquired by the NMSI are collected to represent the development of the main streams of the Western Tradition in Science, Technology and Medicine from 1700 to the present, except in specifically defined areas. Within the Western Tradition artifacts are acquired to illustrate one or more of the following overlapping themes of interest:
>
> • the development of theory
>
> • the development of practice
>
> • the processes of discovery and invention
>
> • the processes of innovation and diffusion
>
> • the relationship to economics
>
> • the relationship to society and social issues
>
> • a particular aspect currently in the public eye
>
> • association with particularly important events, individuals, groups of people or institutions.[5]

With a couple of exceptions, these criteria are broad-based and readily applicable to our collections; they had moved on significantly from Lyons's concept of merely charting technological progress.

There were existing classification systems for the Science Museum cinematography collection and for the Kodak Museum. By combining the two and enlarging the categories to include areas such as lighting and sound, computer control equipment, special effects equipment and models, we arrived at twenty-one categories with various sub-divisions that we considered gave a fair reflection of the history and practice of film. We then looked at the content of the cinematography collection – some 12,000 objects – measuring

1895

it against these categories and evaluating its strengths and weaknesses.

As we suspected, we found that the collection was strong in pre-cinema and early cinema artefacts, becoming progressively weaker as we moved into the 1930s and the sound era. The one exception to this was the collection of amateur equipment. The level of duplication was surprisingly low. The way forward for the development of the collection was clear: we should concentrate mainly on strengthening our representation of professional practice over the past sixty years.

Interestingly, this conclusion had much in common with the main thrust of the NMSI acquisition policy that accorded greatest priority to contemporary (i.e. post-1960) acquisition. In the NMSI's latest policy document, which published acquisition policies for this Museum for the first time, we have attempted a definition of what we collect:

> The NMPFT acquires artefacts to represent the past, present and future evolution of photography, film and television as both technological and aesthetic components of human culture. The history and contemporary nature of the media involved require that acquisition is undertaken internationally.
>
> In the pursuit of its mission, the NMPFT documents the application, impact and mechanics of these media using images, objects, printed materials and ephemera illustrating professional and amateur working practice and final product. In so doing, the NMPFT endeavours to place these items within their economic, cultural and aesthetic contexts.[6]

When it comes to the cinematography collection the scope is further defined:

> This subject represents the evolution of the means of recording and showing moving images in a photographic form. It embraces the pre-history of cinematography, which ranges from optical toys and magic lanterns to pioneer work in motion studies and the audio-visual field such as slide-tape and multivision. It aims to record, by means of associated contextual material how the processes of film production and dissemination, both profes-

Fig. 12. *Vinten HS300 High Speed Camera, 1938. This was the first high speed camera capable of reaching 300 frames per second using an intermittent mechanism. The Vinten company started in 1909 by making Kinemacolor projectors for Charles Urban. Subsequently, the firm was associated with instrumentation and military reconnaissance cameras, and camera mounts. Today, it is a leading manufacturer of film and television dollies and cranes. [National Museum of Photography, Film & Television cinematography collection.]*

sional and amateur have developed, particularly in Britain. Whilst not concerned with the collection and preservation of film, it includes a range of film samples to demonstrate process and format; and representative examples of film footage to illustrate the production process.[7]

This is impersonal language but we have tried to be precise and unambiguous. The definition recognises that it is primarily a technological collection but that there must be a range of supporting material without which the technology and its applications cannot be understood. It observes the boundaries between the collection and that of the National Film and Television Archive.

Later in the document, we outlined development priorities that included objectives such as the broadening of the collection to represent post-war production technology and practices; and research into the development of working practices in British film production, building upon the Museum's programme of *Script to Screen* interviews with production personnel, first instituted in 1985.

In the period since the Acquisition Policy was published, only some of these development priorities have been realised. For instance, we have acquired a VistaVision camera used on many of the Bond films and which was used to shoot Marlon Brando's only film as director, *Cool Hand Luke* (1967); we have also added more recent camera equipment and the very first Dolby Stereo sound camera, used at Elstree. In addition, we have acquired the photographs used to plan the various elements of the 'parting of the Red Sea' sequence in *The Ten Commandments* (1956). Recently, with the aid of the Heritage Lottery Fund, we have purchased the collection of objects, drawings and photographs associated with the work of the pioneering Hammer special effects make-up artists Phil Leakey and Roy Ashton. However, other aims, such as research, remain a long-term commitment to be accommodated within the other demands of the institution, such as the development of exhibitions and the extension to and refurbishment of the Museum, planned to be completed in 1999.

Since it opened, one of the Museum's main tenets has been that visual artefacts should be exhibited alongside the equipment that made them: in this way we attempt to bridge the divide between science and art. But even this ignored a fundamental point. It is not technology but human beings, using their intellectual, artistic and craft skills, who create photographs, films and television programmes. And human beings design the technology that is used for making photographs, films and television programmes. Their ideas and motives are often complex, the products of different cultures, different epochs. The aim of the collection must be to reflect this human dimension. So now we do not just collect objects but also, wherever possible, the associated material that will help interpret, understand and communicate the subjects which the National Museum of Photography, Film & Television represents.

Notes

1. See John Barnes, *The Beginnings of Cinema in England* (Newton Abbot, David and Charles, 1976), 50–55 for a fuller description of the equipment.
2. *The Kinematograph Yearbook* (London, Kinematograph Publications Limited, 1934), 266.
3. See Simon Popple, 'Louis Le Prince', *Photographica World* 66 (September 1993): 33–37 for a fuller discussion of the cameras.
4. Quoted in *Museums Journal* (vol. 31, April 1931), 39.
5. *The National Museum of Science & Industry Acquisition and Disposal Policy, April 1992 – March 1995*, (London, Science Museum, 1992), 4.
6. *The National Museum of Science & Industry Acquisition and Disposal Policy, April 1995 – March 1998*, (London, Science Museum, 1995), 96.
7. *Ibid,* 104.

1895

Kazimierz Prószyński and the origins of Polish cinematography

Marek Hendrykowski
Adam Mickiewicz University, Poznań, Poland

POLISH CINEMATOGRAPHY at the end of the nineteenth century? Contemporary historians of early cinema from the West, even those who are well-informed about the film output of Eastern European countries, commonly associate Poland's contribution to the development of world cinematography with Bolesław Matuszewski and his two famous publications, 'Une nouvelle source de l'Histoire' and 'La photographie animée' published, respectively, in March and August 1898 in Paris.[1]

Apart from him, there is another very important reason to talk about the Polish contribution to the development of cinematography in the years leading up to 1914: specifically, the work of the scientist, inventor and pioneer of Polish cinematography, Kazimierz Prószyński. He is a forgotten inventor, yet one who should be remembered on the occasion of the centennial of cinema.[2] My aim is not to set any kind of precedence (which is always difficult to establish in the development of cinematography), but to bring to general attention the contribution Prószyński made to research and development in the art of moving pictures.

In the light of his inventions, Kazimierz Prószyński should not be regarded as just one more little-known figure from the history of early Polish cinematography. After all, he shot the earliest Polish moving pictures on celluloid with a camera of his own construction in 1895. He also shot *Powrót Birbanta* (Return of a Rake) in 1902 (Fig. 1), the first Polish narrative film with actors, and acquired an international reputation for his achievements.[3]

Even if we are sceptical or critical of his inventions, his achievements were, in their day, universally regarded as important in the development of film technology. These include research into an intermittent mechanism for film projection, the design and construction of a lightweight camera in 1909, the 'Aeroskop' (Fig. 2), and the design and construction of a combined camera-projector apparatus in 1912, the 'Oko' (Fig. 3). During the celebration of the centenary of cinema, we should recall this person without whom the history of the development of film technology in Europe would be incomplete.

Who was Kazimierz Prószyński? He was born on 4 April 1875 in Warsaw. His grandfather,

1895

Stanisław Antoni Prószyński, the owner of a photographic firm, was sent to Siberia for anti-czarist activities in the National Uprising of 1863–64. As for Kazimierz's father, Konrad Prószyński, he managed to escape from Siberia to Poland where, as a young man, he settled in Warsaw. A born patriot and organiser of the secret Towarzystwo Oświaty Narodowej (National Education Society) in 1875, Konrad Prószyński had a life-long passion for furthering the education of the working classes. Under the pseudonym of Kazimierz Promyk, he wrote manuals that developed a modern method for helping the self-educated to read and write, and edited *Obrazkowa nauka czytania i pisania* (*How to Read and Write Through Pictures*) which had a broad and popular readership that extended far beyond his native country. The British Government awarded Kazimierz Promyk a special prize of £1000 for his innovative learning methods at the International Congress of People's Education in London. Over the years prestigious British awards and recognition became a distinctive feature of the Prószyński family: in 1913 Kazimierz Prószyński (aka Kazimir Prószyński or Casimir de Prószyński) was awarded the Golden Medal during the International Kinematograph Exhibition held at Olympia, London,[4] and in 1920 he was made a Fellow of the Royal Photographic Society.

How did Prószyński become a pioneer of cinematography? From his early years he showed interest in technology and a passion for science. Through constructing various machines and mechanisms, he acquired considerable knowledge and experience in the field of mechanics. Like his grandfather, Kazimierz was passionately fond of photography, and was particularly interested in developments in the field of moving pictures. He would carefully scrutinise notes in newspapers about the achievements of Marey, Demenÿ, Muybridge, and others. His memoirs relate that when he was sixteen years old, he watched a demonstration in Warsaw of the Electrotachyscope by the German inventor, Ottomar Anschütz. Prószyński wrote that this show led him to think more seriously about 'living photography, about the cinematograph'.[5]

After he had completed his grammar-school education in 1894, Kazimierz went to study at the École Supérieure Polytechnique in Liège, Belgium.[6] Contact with the world of science and the opportunity for seeing the latest achievements in recording and projecting moving images fired Prószyński to construct a cinematographic apparatus of his own. He called it the 'Pleograf'. Prószyński used a special kind of celluloid film with a frame dimension of 45 x 38 mm, perforations which included several small holes between the frames, and an innovatory mechanism for transporting the film. He completed the construction of a prototype 'Pleograf' in 1895 after his return to Warsaw from Liège.

Prószyński was not alone in his research in Poland. In the nineteenth century, Warsaw constituted an important centre for photographic art. Karol Beyer (1818–1877), considered to be the forefather of Polish art photography, taught many assistants in his studio. One of them was Konrad Brandel (1838–1920), an instrument-maker and inventor who, in 1889, obtained the patent for his 'Fotorewolwer'.[7] Similarly, Ottomar Anschütz, born in 1846 in Leszno, was an apprentice in Maksymilian Fajans' Warsaw photo-workshop where he met Stanisław Jurkowski, a Polish instrument-maker, who presented his Electrotachyscope to the Warsaw public in 1891.[8] Between 1893 and 1896, a number of Polish inventors designed apparatuses for creating and projecting moving pictures. Piotr Lebiedziński (1860–1934), an engineer co-operating with Jan and Józef Popławski, constructed an apparatus known as the 'Zooskop Uniwersalny'. In the 1890s this camera was used to shoot several cinematographic scenes. What seriously limited the dissemination of their invention was the fact that the camera only recorded scenes of a maximum duration of 30 seconds on glass plates, not on celluloid. Bolesław Matuszewski,[9] joint owner of the Warsaw-Paris photographic firm of Lux-Sigismond et Comp., started to produce his first films in 1896 in Warsaw. If we add to this circle of inventors the name of Jan Szczepanik, the precursor of colour photography, sound film, and television, we begin to build up a picture of Warsaw as a city active in the development

Fig. 2. *Aersocope camera with pneumatic cylinders and stirrup pump.*

Fig. 3. *Oko camera-projector.*

of cinematography at the end of the nineteenth century.

Through constructing the 'Pleograf' camera, Kazimierz Prószyński found himself in the company of an exclusive group of pioneers. His achievements in the development of cinematography include:

> *1891–1895:* design and construction of a pioneer cinematographic apparatus, the 'Pleograf';

> *1895–1898:* construction of an improved version of the 'Pleograf', the 'Biopleograf' which partially eliminated flicker, and employed two lenses and two positive film strips;[10]

1895

1898: elaboration of a concept of the 'Telefoto', a device for sending photographic images over a distance;

1899: construction of an amateur version of the 'Pleograf' using a sub-standard film gauge with one perforation between the frames;

1899: innovation of a stereoscope apparatus, the 'Stereos', completed and demonstrated at the Muzeum Przemysłu i Rolnictwa, Warsaw;

1900–03: production (from 1901 by Towarzystwo Udziałowe Pleograf company) of numerous films, both documentaries (footage of the Ambulance Service, horse races, scenes of Warsaw and Vilnius) and narrative films such as *Powrót Birbanta* (Return of a Rake, 1902), a film farce with professional actors,[11] considered to be the first Polish narrative film;[12]

1903: the use of a trick film to accompany The Ride of the Valkyries in a production of Richard Wagner's *Die Walküre* at Teatr Wielki, Warsaw;

1906: an improved version of the 'Pleograf', a camera-projector with the 'greifer' film transportation mechanism, patented in the same year as the device was patented in Belgium, France and Britain;[13]

1907: elaboration of the 'Kinofon' method of moving picture and sound synchronisation by pneumatic compression, a method patented in Germany and Britain;[14]

1904–09: completion of research into flicker-free projection, and the construction of the first film projector with additional diaphragm and a three-blade intermittent, patented in Paris, 7 June 1909;[15]

1907–10: construction of the 'Aeroskop', a camera that employed a gyroscope for steady, hand-held filming, driven by a mechanism using compressed air supplied by a stirrup pump. Application for a French patent was filed on 22 January 1909; the patent was granted on 26 March 1910;[16]

1909–12: construction of the 'Oko', a combined camera-projector apparatus for amateur use. The apparatus was designed to transport 12 cm-wide film horizontally with the frames distributed on a round disc. The 'Oko' was granted a British patent in December 1912,[17] and an improved version was demonstrated to members of the Royal Photographic Society in London on 20 January 1914;[18]

1913: Kazimierz Prószyński shot two sound films produced by The Warwick Trading Co. using the 'Kinofon' and sound synchronisation system he designed, *Ave Maria*, and *The Soothing Influence of Music on Nerves;*[19]

1914–15: Prószyński constructed the first aerial cinematographic camera for the Royal Ministry of War.

As the above chronology demonstrates, Kazimierz Prószyński's construction of the 'Pleograf' and the 'Aeroskop', and his invention of an intermittent mechanism indicate that he was no ordinary inventor. As a pioneer of cinematography, he demonstrated imagination and flair for solving difficult technical problems. His ingenious solutions place him amongst the first rank of cinematographic inventors and designers.

He remained faithful to his great passion for cinematography till the end of his life. Deported by the Nazis during the Warsaw Uprising in August 1944, Prószyński was taken first to Gross-Rosen concentration camp and then to Mauthausen. On his last journey, Prószyński took the 'Oko' apparatus and outlines of other projects with him. In all likelihood, the 'Oko' apparatus which Prószyński took with him is the one now held in the collection of the Science Museum in London. The great inventor did not live to see the Liberation. He died as prisoner number 129997 in Mauthausen concentration camp, at the age of 70, on 13 March 1945.

Notes

1. Bolesław (Boleslas) Matuszewski, 'Une nouvelle source de l'Histoire: Création d'un Dépôt de Cinématographie historique', Paris, March 1898; 'La photographie animée, ce qu'elle est, ce qu'elle doit être', Paris, August 1898.

2. For further reading on Kazimierz Prószyński, see Marian Dabrowski, 'Kazimierz Prószyński', *Tygodnik Ilustrowany* (1913): 23; F.A. Talbot, *Moving Pictures*, London 1912; Władysław Banaszkiewicz, Witold Witczak, *Historia Filmu Polskiego, vol. 1: 1895–1929*, Warsaw 1966; Władysław Jewsiewicki, *Kazimierz Prószyński*, Warsaw 1974.

3. See R. B. Foster, *Hopwood's Living Pictures*, London 1915; Fritz Schmidt, *Kompendium der praktischen Photographie*, Leipzig 1916; Paul F. Liesegang, *Wissenschaftliche Kinematographie*, Leipzig 1920.

4. Olympia International Kinematographic Exhibition, London 1913: 'This year the Aeroscope was awarded first prize, gold medal'.

5. Kazimierz Prószyński, 'Ze wspomnień wynalazcy', *Kinoświat* 7 (1929): 3–4.

6. Prószyński commenced his studies at the École Supérieure Polytechnique in Liège in 1894 and graduated as an engineer in 1908.

7. Brandel's 'Fotorewolwer' was granted a Russian patent (priwilegija, number 11515) by Diepartamient Torgowli i Manufaktur, Moscow in 1889.

8. Małgorzata Hendrykowska and Marek Hendrykowski, *Film w Poznaniu, 1896–1945*, Poznań, 1990, 14–18.

9. Bolesław Matuszewski's brother, the professional photographer Zygmunt Matuszewski, must have been an outstanding figure in his profession for his work received an award for high quality at the Paris Exhibition of 1900.

10. The first public exhibition of the films made with the improved version of the 'Pleograf' (the 'Kinematograf uniwersalny' or the 'Biopleograf') took place in the Museum of Industry and Agriculture, Warsaw in June 1898. The presentation was reported by the Warsaw newspaper, *Kurier Codzienny* (1898), 182.

11. Two professional actors, Władysław Neubelt (from Warsaw People's Theatre) and Kazimierz Junosza-Stępowski (a leading actor in pre-War Polish cinema) acted in *Return of a Rake: Amusing Adventures of a Gentleman After a Holiday Binge*.

12. For details concerning Prószyński's films, see Małgorzata Hendrykowska, *Śladami tamtych cieni: Film w kulturze polskiej przełomu stuleci 1895–1914*, 281–282.

13. Application for Belgian patent number 190959 filed 15 March 1906, application for French patent number 365077 filed 10 April 1906, application for British patent number 12072 filed 23 May 1906.

14. German patent number 207366, application for British patent number 22415 filed 22 October 1908; see also R. B. Foster, *Hopwood's Living Pictures*, London 1915.

15. 'Problème de vision cinématographique sans scintillements. Note de M. Casimir de Prószyński, présentée par M. Albert Dastre', *Comptes rendus hebdomadaires des séances de l'Académie des Sciences*, vol. CXLVIII, no. 23 (7 June 1909, Paris 1909), 1544–1546.

16. 'Application du gyroscope et de l'air comprimé à la prise des vues cinématographiques. Note de M. Casimir Prószyński présentée par M. Gabriel Lippmann', *Comptes rendus hebdomadaires des séances de l'Académie des Sciences*, vol. CLI, no. 26 (27 December 1910, Paris 1910), 1342–1344. The 'Aeroskop', the first lightweight camera (weighing only 6 kilos), was employed by newsreel companies (eg Warwick Bioscope Chronicle, Gaumont Graphic, Gaumont British News) and by travelling cinematographers such as Cherry Kearton, Paul J. Rainey and others ('Revolution in cinematography. The Aeroscope. The camera that does it. Total weight 14 lbs (including film). Size 12 inches x 8 ½ inches. No tripod or stand required. The Aeroscope Camera, invented by C. de Prószyński, is driven by compressed air. As supplied to Paul J. Rainey, esq. and exclusively by Cherry Kearton, esq. […]', commercial leaflet for the Aeroscope Camera, London 1911). Newman and Sinclair Ltd, the well-known British firm, put the camera into production on 22 June 1911, and Prószyński himself shot a newsreel of the coronation of King George V. In a later modified version (1912–13), the pneumatic drive mechanism was replaced by an electric motor powered by a battery. This version of the 'Aeroskop' was demonstrated by Prószyński and Newman at the Royal Photographic Society, London on 13 February 1913, see Kazimir Prószyński, 'On the principles and problems involved in

the design of the 'Aeroscope' cinematograph camera', *The Photographic Journal* (March 1913): 106–109. See also 'The amateur cinema camera', *The Photographic Journal* 2 (1914): 91–98; special report from London demonstration of the 'Aeroscope' camera, *The Bioscope*, vol. XVIII, 327 (16 January 1913).

17. Application for a British patent for the 'Oko' apparatus, number 29417, filed 20 December 1912.

18. A prototype was built in 1915. In November 1919, after returning from the USA, Prószyński put the 'Oko' into production. A joint stock company was established to manufacture the 'Oko', but the company was later taken over by the Centralna Europejska Wytwórnia Kinematografu Amatorskiego, Warsaw. The company closed down in 1925 after the production of only 100 units.

19. In the USA Prószyński continued his experiments with sound film, and shot a film of a Fritz Kreisler concert in 1918.

'Cinema Wasn't Invented, It Growed': Technological Film Historiography Before 1913

Simon Popple

Department of History of Art & Design, Manchester Metropolitan University, Manchester M15 6BG, UK

THIS ESSAY EXAMINES the various sources of early technological film historiography in Britain before 1913. The significance of this date is to be found in the establishment of the Science Museum's Collection 18 – Cinematography. This collection, administered by the National Museum of Photography, Film & Television, has become the nation's largest technological cinematography collection. The foundation of such a collection, later augmented by the National Film Archive and its various off-shoots, marked a process by which these histories became progressively institutionalised. What particularly interested me was the status of these complex histories before such a demonstrable process occurred, which histories they inhabited before the history of early cinema became absorbed into institutional agendas, and to what extent, if any, they prefigure the resultant institutional models.

The process of institutionalisation was clearly in evidence from the outset within the Science Museum and explains many of the collec-tion's current deficiencies. The institution's own history dictated that it collect scientific and technological materials, ignoring the ar-tistic and cultural products of its many collections. That role was assumed by the Victoria and Albert Museum, which did not collect film or cinema ephemera. Despite a concerted attempt by that arch self-publicist R.W. Paul, the cultural product of cinema, the film was not systematically collected in Brit-ain until after the Second World War. As a direct correlative, the subsequent histories of early British cinema are predominantly reli-ant on narrow, nationally biased institutions, challenged only by a small group of important private collections.[1]

All such institutions naturally become the focus for the generation of histories of the collections they hold, communicating them through their varying functions: exhibition, publication, education and their status as research archives. They have consequently articulated quite specific notions of early Brit-ish cinema history. The key factor in this

1895

process is the notion of the status of the institution and its holdings, and how the inevitable notion of hierarchy translates into a canon of objects and personalities which historically represent the essence of early British cinema. Because of the undeniable technological bias attached to the Science Museum's Cinematography collection, its presentation of early British cinema history has, until recent years, been narrow and relatively shallow with emphasis given to the age-old debate about the primacy of invention of cinema, a debate grounded in empirical evidence and valorising the technological artifact.[2] Within this context perhaps one issue characterises the problem: the relative contributions of two men, R.W. Paul and Birt Acres. Their competing claims about who achieved what and when has, in a sense, come to symbolise the way in which early British cinema has been conducted for the best part of a century. Their very public feud, which one can follow in the pages of the *British Journal of Photography*[3] was based on the issue of invention, with important consequences in terms of patent revenue. Of the two, Paul was perhaps most concerned with the prestige associated with the vindication of these claims, and what more logical and visible means of ensuring that history afforded him his dues than to lodge the evidence within a national institution, the Science Museum. This he attempted to do from May 1897 onwards, with his first letter to the Secretary of the Science Museum:

Sir,

I have three instruments which were the original experimental models of the Animatographe, which I shall be pleased to present to the Museum for deposit in the patent branch, if they can be accepted. Awaiting the favour of your reply, I am, sir,

your obedient servant

Robert Paul[4]

In essence, this type of debate is predicated on a linear historical model, concerned with getting from A to Z, from the lens to the Cinématographe, via the medium of technological advancement, usually at the behest of

a series of talented and selfless men of science. The more recent shift towards seeking linkage with the other dimensions of cinema history, its economy, aesthetic and audience have begun to replace this mode of explication. Yet why did these technologically biased methods of describing the historical process of cinema's evolution arise? And are they positioned solely within the archives and institutions which have supported this interpretation? Or do they, as I believe, go further than the origins of these particular institutions in the early part of this century, and beyond the immediate history of cinema itself?

Part of the solution lies in the very nature of cinema's status as a mongrel technology. The notion of bricolage is useful in understanding the various chemical, optical and engineering advances which constitute cinema, but are not its only history or series of competing histories. It is perhaps understandable that linear technological models evolved in order to contain such a complex mesh of histories. But it does not explain the lack of cultural or economic histories until more recent years. For if cinema is a mongrel technology it has also a mongrel economy and aesthetic. It is quite apparent that if one interrogates the pre-institutional historiography of early British cinema before 1913, all these facets are present and excite heated commentary. Cinema as a fledgling institution is clearly positioned within existing debates, markets and practices as well as forging new contexts.[5] The other probable explanation for the reliance on technologically biased early cinema histories was the climate of scientific rationalism, the status of technology and the ascendency of empirical histories. This climate forged institutions such as the Science Museum as well as setting the tone of their own exhibitions and scholarship. The tensions generated between the historical dynamic and museological practices evolved and strengthened a specific linear thesis of technological change, common not just to cinema, but nearly every other technology covered by the institution. If we accept that such a linear, technologically determinist pattern has dominated the collecting, display and scholarship associated with the institution,

1895

then it would seem logical to apportion some of the responsibility to the scholar-curators responsible for forming the collection. Yet, ignoring all the financial and institutional constraints placed upon them, these scholar-curators were, arguably, replicating a historical model laid down for them by the bulk of pre-1913 literature, and even before the foundation of their own institution in 1871. If we consider pre-1913 technological literature relating to the cinema, this linearity is very strongly evident. Are these fledgling histories, however, as insular as their institutional counterparts? More recent historians have consciously sought to broaden the parameters of their study, to consider the relation between the technology of the medium and its aesthetic, audience and economic concerns. What is central to this debate is the process of technological change and the very nature of invention, or more accurately, bricolage. Cinema is by no means unique in possessing a complex technological history, one which is neither clear nor discrete. Indeed, one of the defining factors of a distinctive technology is the development of a new set of critical and descriptive idioms, idioms which separate it from the mass of complementary technologies and scientific principles from which it arose. The origins of technological film history perfectly demonstrate this idiomatic development.

Contemporary accounts of the invention and growth of cinema form the basis of most early film histories, and in themselves represent the first film histories proper. If we consider the coverage of the first year of the arrival of cinema in Britain in 1896 through several publications including the *British Journal of Photography* (*BJP*), *The Optical Magic Lantern Journal and Photographic Enlarger* (*OMLJ*) we can chart the impact of the 'new' medium. What is immediately discernible is an uncertainty as to how to classify cinema, and the tendency to represent it as an adaptation of pre-existing technologies, and thus to judge it by existing conventions. What is also implicit is that, as a consequence, cinema is regarded as belonging to pre-existing technologies such as those of photography and the magic lantern, and hence their histories. Cinema is regarded as a linear improvement on the capabilities of the technologies from which it has emerged. Such adopted critical and historiographic orientations overlay technical and scientific issues which have evolved into a theory of technological change best characterised as determinist. In this mode, technological and scientific advances facilitate aesthetic development and entail sociological consequences. For example, the development of editing techniques and the impact on narrative form, attributed to Porter and Hepworth, are perceived to derive from the basic ability to splice lengths of film together, and the growing spool capacity of cinematographic cameras. The aesthetic impetus and sociological consequences are secondary. However the question of causation, i.e. what triggers technological advances is not considered in this formative period nor is the relation of technology to aesthetics discussed. Our current readings take account of these factors, but in this pre-1913 period the overwhelming thesis suggests that technology and science developed in a logical, empirical and, above all, linear manner. Another consequence of this model of technological change is the high esteem in which technology is held, and the tendency to regard all developments as positive. Another factor introduced into this model of technological change was the role played by scientists and inventors in what has become termed 'the great man' theory of history.[6]

The tendency to see cinema's invention and subsequent development as the result of the brilliance and sacrifice of a small group of dedicated men led immediately to the personalisation of history, and the proliferation of biographical histories fuelled by the desire to establish and capitalise upon the primacy of invention. Once the initial novelty of cinema and the cinematic had begun to recede, arguably by the end of 1896,[7] the commercial imperative became the primary concern of the specialist journals. Both the *BJP* and the *OMLJ*, along with *The Era* began to focus more and more on the actual technology of the medium, providing full reviews of equipment. The October issue of the *OMLJ* carried an illustrated review of the new Wrench Cinematograph of which the following extract forms an introduction:

1895

For the past year the making of apparatus to show the effects spoken of (animated pictures) has practically been a monopoly, and prices ranging from £100 and upwards have been asked and obtained for them. Such prices are now, however, a thing of the past, and owing to the announcement made in ours and other columns, the lantern world has been set on edge on hearing that Mr Wrench, wholesale optician, of Grey's Inn Rd, had taken out a patent and was hard at work making a complete outfit to retail for £36. We have had an opportunity of trying Mr Wrench's apparatus, and were surprised at the quietness with which it worked, the sound being similar to that made by a sewing machine. It works with great smoothness, is quickly charged with a new film, the projected picture is particularly steady, and leaves nothing to be desired.[8]

Apart from the relative inexpense of the apparatus, the key reference in this extract, and a very common one in these types of review, is to the quality of the images. Such reviews became the staple fare in terms of cinema coverage until around 1900 when these journals began to carry not only film advertising but film synopses.

Another emerging phenomenon was the appearance of essays and, in one case, an extended series of histories of the moving image. In February 1897 the *OMLJ* carried a notice of a lecture delivered at the Camera Club by W.J. Coles entitled 'The History and Development of the Cinematograph',[9] followed in June by an article entitled 'Animated Pictures' by Edmund A. Robins. In this article, Robins provides what can be regarded as the standard linear account adopted by film historians and curators for the next seventy years. Importantly, these accounts in themselves evolved from pre-cinematic histories of the magic lantern and optical toys, as well as a host of publications on the phenomenon of persistence of vision.[10] Robbins is not alone, nor was he perhaps the first to have done so, but it is a typical example of the type of approach adopted in the late 1890s:

There is much difficulty in assigning an actual inventor, or a precise date to the first attempt at reproduction of the very varied movements of animated and inanimated objects, and to show that the idea is not of recent origin, the following verse of Titus Lucretius Carus, in his work 'De Rerum Nature', book iv, verse 766, published between 99–65 B.C., certainly presents the idea of a series of movements.

Do not thou moreover wonder that the images appear to move.
And appear in one order and time their legs and arms to use.
For one disappears, and instead of it appears another
Arranged in another way, and now appears each gesture to alter.
For you must understand that this takes place in the quickest of time.[11]

In common with other writers the article begins with an attempt to preface the consideration of the technological/scientific chronology by linking the appearance of cinema with the earliest possible moving images, making a conceptual if not a scientific connection between the two. In this case, the author has chosen to use a much-quoted classical reference,[12] but others referred to prehistoric cave paintings. Terry Ramsaye, writing in 1925, devotes the whole preface to 'A Million and One Nights' to his very particular impression of the development of visual and aural cultures.[13] Two other articles of this period follow the same developmental pattern, the first of which by A. Lomax was published in August 1896:

The introduction of the Edison Kinetoscope has undoubtedly caused special attention to be given to instruments of this class, and which are known under many and diverse names. The general principles upon which they are all constructed is practically the same, and is very very old – as age is taken in these rapid times.[14]

The second by Charles Jenkins in July 1898:

There is one thing that has probably impressed itself upon those who have studied the subject, i.e. that the moving picture machines which have been so widely exploited during the past two years are the culmination of a very long series of experiments. The sensational

1895

appearance of these machines in a relatively perfect form has given rise to the general impression that they were something new under the sun, a sort of minerva birth of inventive genius; but like all notable achievements in mechanism the animated picture machine has a long line of predecessors, and the difficult problem of recording and reproducing motion has not yielded without much preliminary fumbling.[15]

Both, in common with Robbins, allude to the classical origins of the moving image, and then proceed to elaborate almost identical chronologies taking a direct route through the development of optical sciences, lens technology, the theory of persistence of vision, chronophotography, and then through their preferred series of pioneers which almost always include Muybridge, Marey, Edison, Paul and the Lumières. Integral technologies such as photography, or the development of essential materials such as celluloid are often fitted into these early accounts. But what is most interesting from a historiographic perspective is how these narratives are constructed, and how the evaluation of technologies and their mentors are handled. The areas of focus within these accounts are naturally different, the perspectives as diverse as the authors themselves, but the raw subject matter of explaining the technological evolution of cinema is constant. In all three accounts there is a broadly similar approach to explaining the course of scientific/technological development; namely, that it occurred primarily as a result of a few dedicated men of science. The goal of animated pictures was not seen as motivated by commercial imperatives, even in Edison's case, but more as a prestigious, almost selfless quest in its own right. All three authors present the narrative as a logical progression of experiments foreshadowed by the key individuals involved. Even Jenkins, who was himself integrally involved in the first successful screenings in the US, ignores the commercial pressures upon those involved.[16] These accounts serve to reiterate the primacy of technology and scientific advances which are by and large unsullied, in the mind of the authors, by external financial and sociological factors.

They also display a uniform impression about the relationship between human endeavour and scientific progress; that it is one of self-perpetuating sacrifice. Above all, these early accounts served to frame the future representations of cinema's history, and particularly that of cinema technology. Because of the heavy reliance on a linear narrative account and the canonisation of those involved, particularly in the area of primacy of invention, the twin phenomena of technological determinism and the 'Great Man' theory became the standard modes of technological cinema history. One might readily expect these early histories to lack a comprehension of the broader issues and debates which were to evolve alongside the development of cinema, and to centre more on the issues of how and by whom cinema was developed. This specific orientation was particularly suited to the medium of technological/scientific history, and was to remain the focus of debates within this strand of cinema history. This basic template was developed through a series of longer and more complex histories presented not only within standard historical formats but also within instructional, advertising and incidental contexts, including the press and popular journals.[17] These publications fall into roughly four categories: medium-specific histories, instructional publications, advertising catalogues, and incidental publications including magic lantern, fairground and theatrical journals. A brief examination of these groups confirms their common linear approach, despite their multifarious readership.

Medium-specific histories

The first of these was a self-published work by Charles Francis Jenkins entitled *Animated Pictures. An Exposition of the Historical Development of Chronophotography, Its Present Scientific Applications and Future Possibilities, and of the Methods and Apparatus Employed in the Entertainment of Large Audiences by Means of Projecting Lanterns to Give the Appearance of Objects in Motion*. Despite the long title, this 1898 publication was little more than an expanded version of the article published earlier that year.[18] The following

1895

year saw what was the first major history, Henry Vaux Hopwood's *Living Pictures: Their History, Photo-Reproduction and Practical Working, with a Digest of British Patents and Annotated Bibliography*.[19] Hopwood provided a detailed, linear consideration of the evolution of cinema, accompanied by what became the standard patent reference for film historians as well as a comprehensive bibliography relating to photography, optics and the persistence of vision. The next major publication appeared in 1912 with Frederick Talbot's *Moving Pictures. How They are Made and Worked*.[20] This work is particularly interesting as it is justified by a desire to make the link between cinema technology and the moving image.

> The marvellous, universal popularity of moving pictures is my reason for writing this volume. A vast industry has been established of which the great majority of picture palace patrons have no idea, and the moment appears timely to describe the many branches of the art.[21]

Talbot also considers, within an historical framework, how films are produced, from the manufacture of celluloid, through production, processing, editing and screening. This approach distinguishes it from other contemporary guides to the art and production of films by virtue of the historical component, and by the complex introduction it provides to pre- and early cinema. Talbot firstly considers the nature of the moving image which he initially grounds in the development of photography:

> From the day when it was found possible (by the aid of sunlight) to fix a permanent image of an object upon a sensitised surface, inventors steadily applied their ingenuity to the problem of instantaneous photography. In other words, they strove to realise the possibility of photographing movement.[22]

However, rather than develop a narrative beginning with photographic reproduction, Talbot reverts to the more traditional device of rooting the concept of cinema in the distant past:

> The idea of producing apparent animation by means of pictures is by no means new, the origin of the most primitive form of moving picture device is lost in the mists of antiquity; but it is certain that long before photography was conceived animated pictures were in vogue, and constituted a source of infinite amusement among children.[23]

He then develops a straightforward narrative through optical toys, their basis in the theory of the persistence of vision, photography, chronophotography and primary inventors. The treatment of invention is again based primarily on the patience and ingenuity of the individuals involved, and the attitude to the process of invention is logical and scientific in basis. Where there is development in the complexity of the narrative is in the acceptance of the differing circumstances of particular inventions, and the recognition, although not explicitly articulated, that the cinema in its broadest sense is industrially based. This is a major departure from previous commentators in that it recognises that the cinema has an important economic dynamic, and that the basis and impetus for future developments will be conditioned by a broader range of factors than the will and insight of individuals working to their own ends. The tendency to concentrate on the individual inventors rather than the major corporation with an advanced research capability, enjoyed in embryo by Edison, was perhaps due to the fact that most of the original players, R.W. Paul, William Friese-Greene and G.A. Smith, were still very much at the forefront of the industry in Britain.

Instructional publications

The first major guide to the use of the film camera and projector was provided by Cecil Hepworth in 1897 entitled *Animated Photography. The ABC of the Cinematograph. A Simple and Thorough Guide to the Projection of Living Photographs, with Notes on the Production of Cinematograph Negatives*.[24] The book, besides being a practical guide to cinematography and exhibition, also contains an historical foreword which again mirrors the linear pattern adopted by contemporary writers, centring on the pioneering work of Muybridge and Edison. The book is naturally tentative about the long-term future develop-

1895

ment of cinema, but Hepworth is at pains to anticipate rapid qualitative improvements. This pattern continued, the publications evolving to cover new technical advances. *The Modern Bioscope Operator*[25] published in 1911 is typical in this respect, being prefaced once again with a condensed history, which in this case is appreciative of the tendency to seek the antecedence of cinema:

> The origins of the moving picture, like that of gunpowder, is lost in mystery; and the more we trace the history backwards to try and arrive at its real start, the more difficult it is to know where to stop. The fact is, that the moving picture, as we have it at the present day, contains such a remarkable number of inventions, and is composed of, and dependent upon, so many scientific facts and principles, that a treatise several volumes in length would be required to deal completely with the subject.[26]

The usual pattern then follows, but what is interesting is that a more sophisticated, historiographic perspective is alluded to in the introduction. The anonymous author has at least seen the necessity in moving the historical parameters closer to home. Also, for one of the first times, the relationship between diverse scientific elements is recognised, a sort of primitive statement of the concept of bricolage.

Advertising catalogues

A large proportion of advertising literature contained brief technological histories of a given product; for example, the 'Supplementary List of Improved Apparatus for Optical Projection'[27] issued by R.W. Paul in 1904 which contains his own account entitled 'The Development of the Animatograph'.

Incidental publications

This category contains two types of publication; firstly, scientific histories/accounts and, secondly, theatrical and fairground journals relating to the use of cinema within differing aesthetic contexts such as magic, pantomime and illusion. The majority of publications in the first group relate to histories of chronophotography in which cinema is seen as the logical consequence of experiments in sequential photography. One of the most prolific writers and contributors to the science was Etienne-Jules Marey who published *The History of Chronophotography* in 1901.[28]

The second group relates to histories and practical guides in which cinema is utilised in a different aesthetic/cultural context, i.e. within another entertainment medium such as theatre. These sources are particularly interesting as they treat the development of cinema within a non-scientific/technological context. Albert Hopkins' *Magic Stage Illusions and Scientific Diversion, including Trick Photography*, published in 1897, contains a brief history of the moving image, taking as its origins chronophotography and the work of Edison. However, the technological aspects of cinema are given second place to potential uses to which it is suited within the theatre.[29]

These publications were directly and indirectly establishing the pattern and parameters of concern within technological film history within Britain, and prefigured the larger, survey histories which began to emerged in the mid-1920s.[30] The template which these histories established was given wider currency through the institutions which increasingly came to dominate collection and research. This process was by no means unconscious. In 1952, the Science Museum's advisory council instituted a policy review for the whole Museum, covering the scope and purposes the Museum should serve.[31] The resultant document contains a clear recognition of the historical component of the institution, and demonstrates that it had the power to shape and create specific histories of scientific and technological development through a variety of media. Yet it has only been in the past couple of years that the collection has been evaluated contextually and exhibited. This re-evaluation has happily coincided with the broader re-evaluation taking place within the study of early cinema triggered by the Brighton FIAF Conference and continued by this conference.

1895

Notes

1. The Will Day collection and the Barnes collection.

2. This is evidenced by various attempts to credit individuals such as Louis Le Prince and William Friese-Greene with the invention of cinema.

3. Their public feud can be followed in the letter pages of the *British Journal of Photography* throughout 1896.

4. R.W. Paul, letter to the Science Museum, 15 May 1897.

5. For a discussion of these issues, see S. Popple,' The Diffuse Beam: Cinema and Change' in C. Williams (ed) *Cinema: The Beginnings and the Future* (Westminster University Press, 1996), 97–107.

6. Allen, R. and Gomery, D. *Film History – Theory and Practice* (A Knopf, NY, 1985), 51.

7. This is evidenced by a fall in the price of apparatus and films.

8. *The Optical Magic Lantern Journal and Photographic Enlarger* (October 1896), 168.

9. *Ibid*, February 1897, p. 23, History of the Cinematographs, – on the 18th ult. an instructive paper was read by Mr W.J. Coles, on the 'History of and Development of the Cinematograph' at the Camera Club, Charing Cross Road, W.

10. See Hecht, H. *Pre-Cinema – An Encyclopedia and Annotated Bibliography of the Moving Image Before 1896* (London, BFI), 1994.

11. Robins, A. 'History and Development of the Cinematograph', *OMLJ* (June 1897): 99.

12. Also in Theisen, E. 'The Depiction of Motion Prior to the Advent of the Screen', *SMPTE* (January 1933).

13. Ramsaye develops a thesis which places the evolution of moving images in the basis of primitive pictographic languages.

14. Lomax, A. 'Kinetoscopes and Their Lanterns' *OMLJ* (August 1896): 132.

15. Jenkins, C. 'Animated Pictures', *The Photographic Times*, 7 (July 1898): XXX.

16. Hecht, *op. cit.*, p. 403.

17. For a selection of these accounts, see C. Harding and S. Popple, *In The Kingdom of Shadows* (Cygnus Arts Press,1996).

18. Jenkins, *op. cit.*

19. Hopwood, H. *Living Pictures* (London, 1899).

20. Talbot, F. A. *Moving Pictures* (London, 1912).

21. *Ibid.*, p.7 (Intro).

22. *Ibid.*, p.1 (Intro).

23. *Ibid.*, p.10.

24. Hepworth, C. *ABC of the Cinematograph* (London, 1897).

25. *The Modern Bioscope Operator* (London, 1911).

26. *Ibid.*, p. 1.

27. Paul, R.W. *Supplementary List of Improved Apparatus For Optical Projection* (London, 1904).

28. Marey, J. *The History of Chronophotography* (Washington, 1901).

29. For an account of Devant's use of Pauls' Animatograph, see Barnouw, E. *The Magician and the Cinema* (Oxford, 1981).

30. For example, Terry Ramsaye's *A Million and One Nights*.

31. Purposes the Science Museum should serve. The Science Museum should bring before the public, in a pleasing and intelligible form, the principles and practices of science within the museum's field, the applications of these sciences to the arts and industries, and the total effect upon the life of man. This is to be achieved by the exhibition of scientific instruments, apparatus, machines and any objects or representations that may contribute to these purposes, and also by the provision of information concerning the collections. *Report of the Advisory Council of the Science Museum*, 1950, p. 1.

Double Think: The Cinema and Magic Lantern Culture

Deac Rossell

Visiting Fellow, Goldsmiths College, University of London, UK

THE DISCUSSION OF CINEMA and magic lantern culture in this paper forms a small portion of a larger ongoing investigation into the early years of film that looks at the invention and beginnings of the cinema with the help of new methodologies in the history of technology, in particular recent theories of the sociology of the history of technology elaborated by Wiebe E. Bijker, Trevor J. Pinch, and Thomas P. Hughes.[1]

In preparing my just-published chronology of cinema in the years 1889–1896, *The New Thing with the Long Name, and the Old Thing with the Name that Isn't Much Shorter,*[2] I quickly came to recognise that there are still many unresolved mysteries about the appearance of the cinema in the late nineteenth century, and that most of the work in this area that has been done to date rests on a very shaky foundation made up of dubious assumptions, hidden agendas, and outright misrepresentation of the data.[3] The most pervasive honest error in accounts of the invention of cinema is a conceptual one, which comes from the blithe use of *ex post facto* reasoning. This habit argues from the later development of narrative film style and a vertically integrated industrial setting retrospectively back into the period of invention in a hopeless quest to define the 'first' source (in more modern work, *sources*) that

somehow embody all of the later characteristics of the movies, and establish a single moment or artifact from which they may be derived.[4] This futile quest alone has drastically obscured our understanding of the invention of the cinema in the late nineteenth century. When, as so often, the argument is combined with a linear model of technological development, the result is the implicit assumption that the movies of Griffith and Feuillade and Pastrone were the inevitable outcome of the discovery of a viable method of reproducing natural motion on the screen in front of an audience. As a result we also lose contact with those subsequent distinguishing characteristics that make narrative cinema a unique medium of its own. In this paper, I would like to propose an alternative to this linear model of the invention of motion pictures, and to examine more closely some alternative influences on the early cinema, using in this short study examples drawn from the relationship of the cinema to magic lantern culture.

First, let me summarise some of the principles involved in contemporary work in the history of technology, particularly in the sociology of the history of technology as defined by the authors noted above. In abandoning both the defects of a linear model of technological development and the fallacy of looking at the

1895

beginnings of the cinema through the rear-view-mirror of its later evolution, we need to look at any technological artifact symmetrically, and not asymmetrically. That is, since no technological artifact is inevitable, or is the only possible solution to a particular problem, we must examine not only 'successful' artifacts, but also 'failed' artifacts with an equal care and precision if we are to have any answer at all to the question: why did this particular artifact succeed? Since there are always a number of possible solutions to a technological problem – and the period of the invention of the cinema is particularly replete with examples – we need to look in detail at the social groups of users, inventors, promoters, manufacturers, exhibitors, audiences and commentators to see what individual, separate, and sometimes conflicting stakes they had in an artifact, and what influences they brought to the individual technological solutions required to achieve moving pictures.

For example, one of the enduring problems of early cinema was the attempt to overcome flicker on the screen, an irritant to showmen, audiences and inventors alike caused by the interruption of the light source from the projector by the shutter whilst the film band was advanced from one frame to the next. Solutions to the problem were aggravated by the strain put on the celluloid film by the tensions of starting and stopping each frame mechanically at the projector gate, combined with the mechanical problems of synchronously gearing the film transport and shutter apparatus. The wide variety of early intermittent movements used at the birth of the cinema were designed to ameliorate one or another element of this problem, for which an adequate solution did not appear until after 1902[5] for mechanical intermittents. But an alternative line of development was not only possible but also suggested from the very beginning in the 1890s: a continuously moving film band with the necessary intermittent projection of each frame provided by interrupting the optical path of the light – instead of interrupting the physical movement of the film band – by interposing revolving or alternating prisms or mirrors. Indeed, this alternate technology had the cinema's most substantively successful public antecedent, in Emile Reynaud's 12,800

presentations of the Théâtre Optique at the Musée Grevin that began in October 1892. And optical solutions to intermittent projection had the additional advantage of providing practical assistance in the solution of several other persistent difficulties in early film exhibition, such as the inordinate wear and scratching of films which degraded the image for both audiences and showmen, causing films to be rapidly unusable, and the constant breakage caused by mechanical inertia and by tensioning problems that frequently interrupted showings and degraded film prints.

Why did optical solutions to the problem of intermittent projection 'fail', and why did mechanical ones, with their very evident drawbacks, 'succeed' – and thereby themselves contribute strongly to the very retarded development of cinematic institutions in the period 1898–1902? We can begin to answer this question only by examining the artifacts of early cinema, of intermittent projection, symmetrically. The historical literature as it stands discusses optical solutions only before December 1895, where they are considered as faltering experiments on the road to successful screen projection, as if mechanical intermittents were the inevitable and only possible solution to the issue.[6] Even the Lumière brothers, whose work is perhaps the most intensively studied and voluminously published among all cinema inventors, fall prey to this historical asymmetry: two devices with continuously moving film and quite different optical intermittent movements developed by Auguste and Louis Lumière in 1898 and by the Lumière Company in 1902 are nowhere discussed in any of the writings on this important firm from Lyons.[7]

Perhaps one part of the answer can be found in the concept of the interpretive flexibility of a technological artifact. As suggested by Bijker and Pinch,[8] a given artifact has different meanings for different social groups, who attach a meaning to it in the light of their own experiences, goals, and needs. Some photographers considered the cinema to be a new kind of portrait photography, and like Ottomar Anschütz and later Georges Demeny proposed its use for 'living portraits'.[9] Magic lantern exhibitors considered moving pictures to be the final culmination of two generations of ever more elaborate mechanisms for quickly changing slides and/or invisibly dissolving from scene to scene.[10] Importantly, the interpretive flexibility of an artifact is not limited to how social groups attach meaning to the artifact, but it also recognises that there is flexibility in how the artifact is designed, and that social groups of non-engineers can influence that design. The influence of lanternists on the technological artifacts of the cinema can be seen in mechanisms like Cecil Wray's Kineoptoscope, intended to fit in the standard slide stage of a normal magic lantern. The quick inclusion of lightweight and simple cinema apparatus in the offerings of magic lantern supply firms like Riley Brothers in England and Eduard Liesegang Co. in Germany, amongst many others, encouraged the development of particularly portable and elegantly concise apparatus clearly intended as an adjunct to the magic lantern.[11] Each of these separate interpretations of the meaning of the cinema had a traceable influence on the technological design of individual artifacts, on their usage in the marketplace and on their longevity as a part of the overall institution of the cinema.

Here, I want to introduce Bijker's concept of the technological frame. He defines a technological frame as 'the concepts and techniques employed by a community in its problem solving',[12] specifying that problem solving is a broadly inclusive concept which encompasses the recognition of what counts as a problem as well as the strategies available for solving the problem, making a technological frame 'a combination of current theories, tacit knowledge, engineering practise ... goals, and handling and using practice'.[13] Inclusion in a technological frame is not limited only to inventors, engineers or scientists, but is extended to all social groups with a stake in the artifact: it applies to the *interaction* of the various forces that determine technological construction, and *clarifies* both how technology structures the social environment and how the social environment structures an artifact's design.

Using a technological frame can give us a clue about how mechanical projection systems, with all of their drawbacks, dominated the early days of the cinema. Among the early

user groups gathered around the new artifact, who formed a primary market and first circle of negotiants for the cinema, were inventors and mechanics, fairground showmen, variety and theatrical impresarios, magic lanternists, lecturers, photographers, magicians, lantern and photographic manufacturers and suppliers, and photographic journalists. Debatably, the social group of professional travelling magic lanternists *may* have been the largest of these groups; undoubtedly a major part of the experience of many members of all of these groups was familiarity with the technical operations of the magic lantern, its use in the projection of images, its manipulation as an instrument of showmanship, and the magic lantern culture that surrounded it.

As has been noted, magic lantern technology had been edging toward ever-faster, smoother, and more elaborate representations of fluid motion since the 1860s.[14] To see a quiet country mill wheel slowly turning in the late autumn, to see winter approaching, the snow falling as the mill wheel stills, the outbreak of spring at the mill pond with a flock of swans proceeding across the fresh water and gracefully bending their elegant necks for food – to describe only one of the most widely-known dissolving slide sets of the last third of the nineteenth century – is to recognise that the invention of the cinema was inevitable. For all of these lantern practitioners, the lantern represented centuries of solid evolution of a finely tuned optical instrument. For everyone included in this technological frame, the problem of motion was primarily a mechanical one: an optical device for the projection of images already existed in a well-proven form.[15] It is not surprising, then, that a high value was placed on developing a mechanical device which could be used in conjunction with a proven optical pathway that included highly evolved powerful light sources and sharp projection lenses capable of providing a bright image for audiences in large halls and venues.

I would argue here that the magic lantern was not so much a 'precursor' of the cinema, as it was the environment into which the cinema was born, the *milieu* which nursed it through its extended period of invention to about 1903, the institution which provided its early

1895

business practices,[16] and the medium with which the cinema coexisted for about two decades, not achieving its 'independence' as a separate medium (through its own venues, its own specialist personnel, its own aesthetic language, its own economic institutions, its own themes and subjects for films) until well after the turn of the new century. As Henry V. Hopwood wrote in 1899: a film for projecting a living picture is nothing more, after all, than a multiple lantern slide.[17]

* * *

Magic lantern culture and the concept of the technological frame are also helpful in analysing some otherwise problematic phenomena in early filmmaking practice. In his article '"Primitive" Cinema: A Frame-up? Or The Trick's on Us',[18] Tom Gunning presents an account of the 'splice of substitution' in the work of Georges Méliès. Examining this 'hidden' splice in relation to his concept of non-continuous editing in early film, Gunning comments that, 'This discovery of a previously unperceived process of film cutting raises enormous problems of definitions for the film historian'.[19] From Gunning's point of view, reaching back into early cinema and exploring its uniquenesses from his awareness of the later development of classical editing and its practise of 'invisible cutting', the Méliès 'splice of substitution' does indeed present problems. But not quite in the way that Gunning states when he comments Méliès' splice shows that 'early filmmakers were concerned with issues that traditionally they are thought to have ignored, those of precise continuity of action over a splice'.[20] I would contend, instead, that at the time of making *Le bourreau Turc* (The Terrible Turkish Executioner) in 1904, Gunning's exemplar for Méliès' regular editing practice with the 'splice of substitution', Méliès had little or no engagement with the idea of narrative continuity across a splice – as evidenced in others of his 1904 productions like *La damnation du Docteur Faust* (Faust and Marguerite) or *Le voyage à travers l'impossible* (The Impossible Voyage). In his relation to the cinema, Méliès would have a high inclusion in a technological frame of magicians who were early users of animated pictures, a position that would include strong prohibition against 'giving

away the trick'. But for our discussion, it is Méliès' inclusion in a technological frame of magic lantern culture that is more interesting: in *Le bourreau Turc* Méliès is reproducing the two hundred year old transformation effect of a slipping slide. Along with a jumping figure or a juggler, severed heads and transforming heads probably accounted for by far the largest number of these comic illusions, whose proper manipulation by the lanternist was itself a practised and refined art of showmanship which required adeptness and skill so as not to 'give away the trick' and to produce on the screen an instantaneous and surprising effect. The traditions of this basic illusion were so firmly and fully established for both showmen and audiences by the time of Méliès, especially against the still tentative and unsettling concept of spatial continuity across the splice, that his film must be read as having a high inclusion in a technological frame of magic lantern culture, rather than as an aberrant problem derived from the retrospective importation of a narrative film aesthetic.

The audience, too, if we include them in relation to the same technological frame, would have been thoroughly familiar with the effect, a shared experience across both magic lantern culture and the new film culture that again argues for an analytical perspective that Charles Musser has called 'a history of screen practice'.[21] From this vantage point we can legitimately ask why Méliès chose to bring forth yet another version of an age-old comic scene in this new medium, when in doing so he needed to spend a considerable amount of time and trouble in technically manipulating his camera, negative, and prints to hide the origins of his trick and invent his 'splice of substitution'. Only part of the answer comes from the often-cited rationale of the economies of permanently fixing an elaborate stage effect on film and then inexpensively reproducing it again and again. In this case, the cinema provided Méliès with a technological development that allowed a continuous repetition and variation of transformations within one scene that were not possible with the magic lantern. Where an expertly handled slipping slide could sever a single head or a single group of heads in a single motion and make a single substitution, *Le bourreau Turc* (The Terrible Turkish Executioner) severs four individually moving heads with a single blow, each of which is separately animated and then separately restored, before the victims turn on the executioner himself and cut him in half as well. Reassembling himself, the executioner flees the stage, pursued by his erstwhile victims. In the film, the essential 'trick' appears six times, a set of variations beyond the capabilities of the lantern, and this elaboration negotiates a space between familiarity and freshness for its audiences.

Another, earlier example of films existing within the established magic lantern frame might be taken from the Lumière film *Barque sortant du port* (Boat Leaving Harbour) of 1896, about which Dai Vaughn has written so eloquently.[22] Vaughn's articulate examination of the many resonances of this title which, in his words, 'begins without purpose and ends without conclusion',[23] begs the question of the film's aesthetic origins; his celebration of the film's spontaneity, and his use of spontaneity as the decisive factor in why 'we consider Lumière cinema and Edison not'[24] is insufficient all the way back to that most spontaneous of Edison productions, *Fred Ott's Sneeze*. The fragment of reality represented by *Barque sortant du port* is directly derived from panoramic magic lantern slipping slides – distinct from quickly moved transformation slipping slides – that were used in magic lantern shows throughout the nineteenth century to represent views of various types of boats and ships entering and leaving harbours, fleets back from naval engagements, and depictions of harbour scenes. With its seemingly randomly-chosen framing, complete lack of any tensions or compositions against the edges of the frame, and wholly incomplete 'action' of rowing out of the harbour, Lumière's film, which 'begins without purpose and ends without conclusion', is constructed as a familiar static slide thrown upon the screen,[25] this time using the apparatus of a moving film band to reconstitute, in today's jargon, the 'full motion graphics' of the exertions of the rowers against wind and waves. It is 'an attachment to any standard lantern'

again mediating for its audiences a representational space between the comfortably familiar and the dynamically new; it is on the basis of this negotiation that the first cinema audiences were so startled, as both Vaughn and many contemporary reporters noted, by the gentle fluttering of background leaves on trees, and other non-central 'inessential' details of the first films. Today, even as scholars watching early films, these 'non-central' movements are not a primary or pre-emptive call on our attention as they were for contemporary audiences, and we need to make a conscious effort to reach back in time to see them; yet they were noticeable, shocking, attention-grabbing for an audience with a high inclusion in a technological frame of magic lantern culture, where motion was not at all the new experience, but where motion had always been centralised and limited, presented within the repetitive limitations of a mechanical lantern slide. Cinema did not bring motion to the screen; it brought the duration of motion, it brought the elaboration and variation of motion, it brought an unlimited motion of nature, of the natural world, that astonished audiences and was so often noted in press reports of early film showings.[26]

From 1896 to 1904, from *Bargue sortant du port* to *Le bourreau Turc*, the resonance of magic lantern culture is vividly present. So it is also for the Lumières in their design of an optical intermittent projection movement in mid-1902. The period of invention of the cinema does not end in 1895, as suggested by Georges Sadoul in the first part of his classic *Histoire général du cinéma*. The magic lantern was not a precursor of the cinema; rather, the cinema was in its beginnings an extension of the magic lantern, one which later outgrew the lantern's technical boundaries and aesthetic vocabulary to speak with its own voice and develop its own technical artifacts. We can find out how much later only by deserting the linear model of the early development of the cinema, by abandoning retrospective importations of later developments, and by examining the period symmetrically and with historical precision.

1895

Notes

1. See: Wiebe E. Bijker, Thomas P. Hughes, and Trevor J. Pinch (eds), *The Social Construction of Technological Systems. New Directions in the Sociology and History of Technology* (Cambridge: The MIT Press, 1987) and especially the articles 'The Social Construction of Bakelite: Toward a Theory of Invention', by Wiebe E. Bijker (pp 159–187); 'The Social Construction of Facts and Artifacts: or How the Sociology of Science and the Sociology of Technology Might Benefit Each Other', by Trevor J. Pinch and Wiebe E. Bijker (pp. 17–50); and 'The Evolution of Large Technological Systems', by Thomas P. Hughes (pp. 51–82). See also: Thomas P. Hughes, *Networks of Power: Electrification in Western Society, 1880–1930* (Baltimore: The Johns Hopkins University Press, 1983); Wiebe E. Bijker, *Of Bicycles, Bakelites and Bulbs. Toward a Theory of Sociotechnical Change* (Cambridge: The MIT Press, 1995); and Wiebe E. Bijker and John Law (eds), *Shaping Technology/Building Society. Studies in Sociotechnical Change* (Cambridge: The MIT Press, 1992). For a further elaboration of my approach since this paper was delivered, and an indication of its usefulness across the entire span of the beginnings of moving pictures, see Deac Rossell, *Living Pictures. The Origins of the Cinema* (Albany: State University of New York Press, 1998).

2. Deac Rossell, '"The New Thing with the Long Name and the Old Thing with the Name that Isn't Much Shorter": A Cinema Chronology, 1889–1896', *Film History*, vol. 7, no. 2 (Special Issue), (Summer 1995): 115–236.

3. For one example, as recent as April 1995, see Jacques Rittaud-Hutinet, *Les frères Lumière. L'invention du cinéma*. (Paris, 1995: Editions Flammarion). This is Rittaud-Hutinet's fourth book on the Lumières over a period of twenty years, apart from numerous articles. In this centennial publication he mis-states both the dates and contents of their French patent for the Cinématographe of 13 February 1895; distorts the factual history of the Edison Kinetoscope in France and its influence on the Lumière invention; ignores the prior public projections of both Max Skladanowsky in Berlin and the Lathams in America; misrepresents the first work of Georges Méliès; and makes numerous other errors. For an insightful and perceptive review, see Laurent Mannoni, 'baisse un peu l'abat-Jour ...', *La Quinzaine littéraire*, no. 668 (30 April 1995), 28.

4. These attempts still plague otherwise sane film historians: at a press conference for the 100th Anniversary of the cinema packed with over 1300 film journalists from around the world, and hosted by the Minister of Culture and the Cinémathéque française, among others, the filmmaker and respected historian Bertrand Tavernier declared in his most forceful manner that the sole, true, original inventors of the cinema were Auguste and Louis Lumière, contending that 'Edison with his peep-show kinetoscope is the precursor of television. Pick any date you like for the Centennial of television, and you can celebrate the work of Thomas Alva Edison. The true inventors of the cinema are Auguste and Louis Lumière and the birth of the cinema was on 28 December 1895.' The author was present at this event, and witnessed the strenuous arguments that ensued both during and after the press conference, along with Tavernier's unrelenting pursuit of his most original thesis.

5. The solution around which this problem was resolved was the introduction of the three-bladed shutter, still in use today. By interrupting the light from the projector not just whilst the film band was being moved from frame to frame (necessary at speeds under about 40 frames per second to prevent blurring of the image on the screen while the image was in motion), but also interrupting the steady light on the screen during the projection of the image at rest in the projection gate, the variation in light intensity is evened out, resulting in a (at first seemingly paradoxical) great reduction or complete loss of flicker in the image on the screen. The three-bladed shutter was developed by Theodor Pätzold for his own Messter projector, and brought into Messter's production by Max Gliewe with the Model XI apparatus manufactured from 1902; in that same year John A. Pross patented a three-bladed shutter in the United States on behalf of the American Mutoscope and Biograph Company (USP 722,382 of 19 January 1903, issued 10 March 1903) which was first used by Biograph on its 35 mm apparatus and was apparently shared with Charles Urban in England, becoming a key part of Urban's successful apparatus.

6. Of the more than 200 patents in America, France, Germany, and England issued between 1895 and 1910 suggesting a plethora of solutions to optical intermittent movements, none are discussed in the historical literature and the vast majority not even listed. The example of a 'failed' artifact being used here, the optical projection intermittent, is not an imaginary alternative to mechanically

intermittent film bands: one solution was brilliantly proposed by Emil Mechau in 1912 with his Model I projector using a ring of mirrors to intermittently break the optical path of projection. With Mechau's Model III of 1922 the Leitz photographic firm began manufacturing the projector commercially, building a factory in Rastatt, Germany, for its production. Over 500 examples were made through 1934 (by AEG after 1929), and the apparatus was widely used on the Continent and in England, where it was known as the Arcadia projector. It was a superb machine, very gentle in handling its continuously moving film and providing a bright and steady picture on the screen. After 1945 it had a revival in television studios, as it was particularly suited to originating broadcasts of film with the flying-spot television system. Perhaps the most interesting early cinema optical machine was the Mutagraph of the magician John Nevil Maskelyne, an experienced mechanic and illusionist who constructed much of his own unique magic apparatus. The Mutagraph was a device with continuously moving film and a series of fixed and rotating lenses providing the intermittent, patented in the United Kingdom as early as 28 May 1896 (UK patent 11,639 of 1896), in France on 1 April 1897 (French patent 265,582), and in Germany on 15 April 1897 (DRP 100 559). The machine was in use in Maskelyne's presentations at the Egyptian Hall, London, for several years after its introduction in 1897, and for scientific high-speed cinematography at the Woolwich Arsenal through at least 1903, but despite patenting in three countries, Maskelyne evidently never brought the apparatus to the open market. As readers of his autobiography will be aware, he placed a very high value on the magicians' traditional injunction to 'never give away the trick', and perhaps this habit inhibited him from proselytising a fine apparatus.

7. As Bijker and Pinch state, '... a historical account founded on the retrospective success of the artifact leaves much untold'. In 1898 Auguste and Louis Lumière filed patents in France (No. 278,347 of 31 May; addition of 22 July) and Germany (No. 103 314 of 3 August) for a projection apparatus with a steadily moving film band whose intermittent was provided by a wild system using a flexible liquid-filled prism whose dimensions were mechanically varied. In 1902 the Société Anonyme des Plaques & Papiers Photographiques A. Lumière et ses Fils filed patents in France (No. 323,667 of 12 August) and Germany (No. 157 698 of 19 August) on a projection apparatus with a steadily moving film band whose intermittent was provided by oscillating mirrors in the optical path. There is no discussion of these devices in any of the Lumière studies by Sadoul, Rittaud-Hutinet, Bernard Chardère, or Maurice Bessy and Lo Duca. It is as if they do not exist (Chardère does include the patent number of the first device in a list in *Les Lumières*). Although both devices are illustrated and discussed in Karl Forch (*Der Kinematograph und das sich bewegende Bild*, 1913), there is also no discussion of the apparatus in any of the other technical literature, such as Coissac (1925) or Gosser (1977).
What is most interesting about these patents, however, is perhaps not their technical contents but the questions that they raise, elsewhere ignored, about the intentions and the work of the Lumières at this time. By Summer 1898 they were well on their way out of the film business. Did they think that, by developing a radically new system for the cinema, they would be able to revive the publicity and commercial successes of 1896? That they could recover a prominence in the fast-developing new industry that they had clearly lost? And why was the company still working on cinema apparatus for normal exhibition in 1902? And committed enough to seek protection for the work in at least two countries? Here, the exercise of looking symmetrically at the period of invention uncovers a few intriguing clues to the ongoing life of an important firm and helps us raise previously unforseen questions about its involvement with the cinema.

8. Wiebe E. Bijker and Trevor J. Pinch, 'The Social Construction of Facts and Artifacts: Or How the Sociology of Science and the Sociology of Technology Might Benefit Each Other', in Bijker, Hughes & Pinch (eds), *The Social Construction of Technological Systems*, op. cit., 40–44.

9. The Lumières also defined the future market for cinema as a home consumer market including animated portraits at an early point, patenting their Kinora home flip-card viewer on 10 September 1896 in France (No. 259,515) and also in other countries. It became a popular device manufactured in several designs, and had a flourishing revival after the turn of the century that brought the Lumière and Biograph companies together for collaborative production and marketing of the apparatus. Charles Urban was a proponent of this device in England. For a full account, see Stephen Herbert, 'Kinora Living Pictures', in *Photo Historian* (UK), no. 95, (Winter 1991): 104–113.

10. Henry Langdon Childe produced his dissolving views in London around 1834. Professional

lanternists in the nineteenth century produced at first double, then magnificent triple lanterns as the intricacy of their dissolving apparatus increased. Throughout the century there were many devices as well for automating the changing of slides, both as a way of aiding a lecturer to manipulate his own lantern and as a means of increasing the rate of the projection of images; methods included using slides attached to flexible bands (William Speirs Simpson, French patent 234,734 of 12 December 1893), cassette trays (William Henry Duncan, UK patent 934 of 8 January 1884), chained stacks (Edmund Hudson, German patent 79 062 of 11 April 1894), and bins or hoppers. In 1888 Walter Poynter Adams patented his Roller Slide (UK patent 16,785 of 19 November 1888), a long flexible transparent strip of gelatine or algin with an automated gearing system to advance the band. The most famous of these devices was J.A R. Rudge's automated lantern of 1889, which William Friese-Greene demonstrated and for which he and Mortimer Evans designed their camera of the same year; the rate of operation of both machines was four or five pictures per second.

11.   British film pioneer Robert W. Paul recalled in 1936 that his first cinema projector was intended 'to be capable of attachment to any existing lantern'. Robert W. Paul, 'Kinematographic Experiences', in Raymond Fielding (ed), *A Technological History of Motion Pictures and Television* (Berkeley: University of California Press, 1967), 43. [Reprinted from the *Journal of the Society of Motion Picture Engineers*, 27 (November 1936).]

12.   Wiebe E. Bijker, 'The Social Construction of Bakelite: Toward a Theory of Invention', in Bijker, Hughes & Pinch, *The Social Construction of Technological Systems, op. cit.* p. 168.

13.   *Ibid.*, p. 168.

14.   Particularly through combining dissolving slides and mechanical slides that provided motion by means of pulleys, rackwork gears, ratchets, levers, or sliding elements. Some of these slides could be extremely ingenious and complex, as with double rackwork astronomical slides to show the movements of heavenly bodies, or Beale's Choreutoscope of 1866, which projected a disk of painted figures representing phases of movement and motivated by a near-Maltese Cross spur gear. The effect was startling, and was revived by William Charles Hughes in 1884 with great success in England and by the firm of Molteni on the Continent. Many specialised slides became quite elaborate in their representations of motion. Fantoccini slides, also made by William Cheffins in England (from 1891), fit in a standard lantern slide stage and held jointed metal figures, between two sheets of glass; the tiny puppets could be manipulated by thin rods projecting below the slide-holder and made to jump, run, walk, sit, or engage in a sword-fight or other animated scene, bringing the repertoire of the shadow puppet theatre and the magic lantern wholly together.

15.   To some extent, the present state of research would suggest that this description is more pertinent to the European experience than to the American one. Magic lantern culture seems to have been more dense and more pervasive in Europe than in America; Europe seems to have had more intimate links between lantern culture and the cinema in its first decade than was the case in America. This would seem to be indicated by the limited range of apparatus that appeared in the US in the period 1896–1900; for which patent office policies and the aggressive stance of the Edison organisation also bear an influence. The early dominance of vaudeville theatres in America as a major exhibition circuit, as recorded in the extant literature, would also be an influence; the combined result was a climate of invention, or a technological frame, in which American inventors needed to deal with optical and illumination issues in devising their apparatus which in Europe were provided by a widespread foundation of experience amongst magic lantern manufacturers, inventors, and practitioners. A caveat to this seemingly divergent experience is the extreme scarcity of historical magic lantern research in American. Very little is known about the extent, range, and practise of magic lantern culture in the US, which remains a fertile ground for further investigation.

16.   Again there is a divergent practice in the United States: first with the Kinetoscope and again, briefly, with the Armat/Jenkins Vitascope, the Edison organisation franchised the dissemination of the apparatus, a business practise which Edison modelled on his experience with the gramophone and one that was not widely used in Europe, except by the Lumière company. See Charles Musser, *The Emergence of Cinema: The American Screen to 1907* (New York: Charles Scribners' Sons, 1990), 57–62, 81–89.

17.   Henry V. Hopwood, *Living Pictures: Their History, Photoduplication and Practical Working* (London: The Optician and Photographic Trades Review, 1899), 188. Compare also C. Francis Jenkins, *Animated Pictures* (Washington, D.C.: By the Author, 1898), 100: 'The fact is, the moving picture

machine is simply a modified stereopticon or lantern, i.e. a lantern equipped with a mechanical slide changer'.

18. Tom Gunning, '"Primitive" Cinema: A Frame-Up? Or, The Trick's on Us', in Thomas Elsaesser (ed), *Early Cinema: Space, Frame, Narrative* (London: BFI Publishing, 1990), 95–103.

19. *Ibid.*, p. 98. I have re-read this passage carefully after a long discussion with Tom Gunning in Bradford, and while it is certainly the case that he continues immediately in the article to say 'it would be equally distorting to see Méliès' trick splice as the equivalent of cuts which perform basic spatial and temporal articulations' and then cites André Gaudreault to reinforce this point, his next paragraph, quoted below, about the concern of early filmmakers with 'precise continuity of action over a splice ... *in order to maintain the flow and rhythm of acting which a mere stopping of the camera could not provide*' [my emphasis], situates his argument firmly in a narrative context which is not, as I argue, appropriate for Méliès at this time (if ever), and which is definitively subsidiary to Méliès' dominant concerns as a magician and lanternist, drawn from his high degree of inclusion in a technological frame of magic lantern practise; as I contend, the issue of the 'splice of substitution' does not concern narrative flow but rather the replication, on celluloid film, of a stabilised practice of lantern shows.

20. *Ibid.*, p. 98. If this were true, then the history of the 'splice of substitution' would need to begin with Max Skladanowsky in mid-1895. Skladanowsky's Bioskop projector was a double-lens, double-film-band apparatus whose conception was wholly derived from dissolving magic lantern practice; the machine projected alternate frames from each of the two film bands when in use. Skladanowsky prepared his first film bands by photographing moving subjects on his chronophotographic camera which used paper film with no perforations, and produced inconsistent registration of the images. The original was then developed, the individual images cut up, and painstakingly laid out in alternating order on sheets of cut celluloid 1.5 metres square where they were printed as positives. This produced strips of images 1.5 metres or 48 'frames' long, which themselves were then glued together to make each of the two film bands for the Bioskop double-projector. Clearly, Skladanowsky was working here on a purely technical/inventive process; while he was concerned to create proper registration of his images for projection and create technical or mechanical continuity (a problem that equally faced chronophotographers like Ottomar Anschütz, Georges Demenÿ and others in mounting their individual images on their projection apparatus), he was hardly concerned with the splice in its incarnation as a device for narrative continuity in the usual sense of the word.

21. Charles Musser, *op. cit.*, pp. 15–54. This chapter of Musser's history presents not only a concise, thoughtfully written argument for a history of screen practise across the nineteenth century and into the twentieth, regardless of the technological mechanisms of projection, but also a responsible and often well-researched précis of magic lantern history in America which exists itself as almost the major work on the subject now in print. What is curious about this opening chapter to his book, is that after its end, the magic lantern, and lantern practise, is nowhere mentioned in the succeeding 440+ pages of text. There are no referential integrations of screen practice at all after Musser sets out on his motion picture history, which somewhat undercuts and dilutes his eloquent arguments for a 'history of screen practise', once again relegating magic lantern culture to the role of a 'precursor'.

22. Dai Vaughn, 'Let There Be Lumière', in Thomas Elsaesser (ed), *op. cit.*, 63–67. This film was also frequently singled out for special notice at the time of its first release, for example by an anonymous writer at the *Bremer Courier* (no. 256, 15 September 1896, 2) who thought it 'a picture rich with poetic atmosphere' and specifically noted the deep waves of the sea and the way in which the boat 'sliced through the surging waters, rowed by powerful hands'.

23. *Ibid.*, p. 66.

24. *Ibid.*, p. 65.

25. My comment here somewhat diminishes the compositional quality of many lantern slides; here I wish to emphasise the centrality of the image and its motion as the elements being taken over from lantern slide practise; without the familiarity of this lantern material as a foundation, there is no earthly reason why this film should have been taken or why it should have affected audiences so strongly. We cannot here retrospectively argue a 'home movie' aesthetic.

26. For a few examples, see George C. Pratt, *Spellbound in Darkness. A History of the Silent Film* (Greenwich, CT: New York Graphic Society, 1973), 15–18; '... all the bustle incident to affairs of this kind was shown to perfection ...' (*The New York Dramatic Mirror* on Lumière's *Arrivée d'un*

train en gare (The Arrival of a Train at the Station), 4 July 1896, 17 [Pratt, 16]); '... the pretty background of trees and shrubbery, whose waving branches indicate that a stiff breeze is blowing ...' (The Rochester *Post Express* on Lumière's *Repas de bébé* (Feeding the Baby, (6 February 1897), 14 [Pratt, 18]).

1895

Early Film Theory in Poland: The Work of Karol Irzykowski

Elżbieta Ostrowska

Department of Audiovisual Culture, University of Łódź, Poland

THE FILM THEORY OF Karol Irzykowski (1873–1944) – a famous Polish writer and critic – is the most representative of early Polish reflections on cinema and, at the same time, the greatest achievement in this field. The first Polish texts on cinema were written mostly by novelists and literary critics[1] who were predominantly interested in the social and cultural function of the cinema. On the one hand, they noted the documentary value of films in reproducing reality and, on the other hand, they saw that the cinematograph gave new possibilities for creating fictional spectacles addressed to a wide variety of audiences. Therefore, two basic functions were attributed to the cinema in the earliest Polish writings on film – the scientific and that of entertainment.

In his writing, Karol Irzykowski also adopted this wide cultural perspective but, at the same time, he noticed the necessity of presenting other aspects of the cinema which had previously been left out, or rather not noticed at all. In his article written in 1913 and entitled *Śmierć kinematografu?* (The Death of Cinematograph?) he claims that: 'The cinema asks some aesthetic and philosophical questions. If it is an art, then what kind of art is it? A combination of arts that are already known or a new art?'.[2] The propositions included in the article form the foundation of a later more developed theory of the cinema presented by the author in his book *Dziesiąta Muza: Zagadnienia estetyczne kina* (The Tenth Muse: The Aesthetic Problems of the Cinema) published in 1924.

Irzykowski was given a government grant for the book's preparation, which may appear today quite surprising. Equally surprising is the explanation of why the grant was made. As the author explains in the preface to his book, the Department of the Ministry of Arts and Culture decided to back '... the project about the cinema, which would exert an ennobling and inspiring influence on Polish cinema through the elaboration of film aesthetics' (p. 7). For us, this is likely to seem a peculiar way of attempting to raise the standards of Polish cinema (which in fact, was not highly developed at that time and could not take pride in many achievements). The majority of films exhibited were foreign and these therefore formed the basis of cinema's early popularity. Why was this a problem? We need to consider that the government initiative

1895

came only four years after Poland had regained independence after almost 150 years of being a dependency of neighbouring countries. Until 1918 we can only speak of cinema *in* Poland – not of Polish cinema. Only after the end of the First World War can we speak of Polish cinema, the development of which became, for quite obvious reasons, a concern of the government in its attempt to develop Polish culture. It was this context which lay behind the project of raising the standards of Polish cinema through film theory. [It is worth noting here that the first trace of Irzykowski's interest in the cinema may be found in his earlier literary works – in 1908 he wrote a one-act play, *A Man in Front of the Lens* (Człowiek przed soczewką), whose main character is a 'cinematographic genius', Aron Ithaker.]

To return to Irzykowski's article from 1913 in order to look at his early views on cinema, the article contains a range of fascinating insights, although it is by no means free of contradictions. The author begins by characterising the position of cinema within modern culture. He notices that 'cinematic spectacle' is becoming more and more popular (he speaks of the relation between supply and demand, which leads him to conclude that in some contexts films should be treated as a commodity); on the other hand, however, the cinema was being condemned as a vulgar entertainment which debauches and depraves. 'The modern European uses the cinema but is ashamed of it' (p. 15) he claims, and identifies 'corporate social hypocrisy' in the audience's attitudes towards cinema. But Irzykowski firmly stands out against any attempts at ennobling the cinema because, according to him, such attempts would only cause the cinema to become boring and impede its natural development. However, he does not rule out the possibility of film being 'an ore which contains precious material for art' (p. 16). Considering the possible aesthetic value of 'the cinematic spectacle', he claims that cinema is predominantly the art of movement. 'The cinema opens out the Kingdom of Movement', he wrote, and here the distinct character and peculiarity of the cinema is revealed. It is in the later elaboration of this

apparently obvious idea that the distinctiveness of Irzykowski's theory is to be found.

According to Irzykowski, the viewer experiences reality in an absolutely novel way in the cinema thanks to the analogy he draws between the cinematograph and the human mind. He claims that the cinema, because it is 'as fast as thought' is able to 'adapt itself to the vaults of imagination'. It is as if 'a nameless nature is revealed in the cinema, nature not covered with a net of human concepts' (p. 21). Therefore, for Irzykowski, the cinema is predominantly a new means of cognition and of experiencing reality – extraverbal and extraconceptual. It should not be surprising, then, that he claims that the invention of the cinematograph had caused the same 'cultural change in the human soul' as that caused by the invention of writing. It should be stressed here, however, that he does not identify reality with its cinematic image. Considering the possibility of combining the cinematograph with a phonograph (that is, introducing sound to 'the cinematic spectacle') he speaks of combining 'the *signs* of motion with the *signs* of sound' (p .13). It could be said today that Irzykowski had thus pointed out quite accurately (although obviously rather intuitively) that cinema was both a reproduction of reality and a sign system.

As I have already mentioned, these ideas were amplified in the book *The Tenth Muse*. The basic thesis of the book is that the cinema makes visible human beings' co-existence with the physical world. What does this mean? To understand him, we need to make reference to Irzykowski's aesthetic views as a whole, views which have their origins in German idealism represented by Fichte, Schelling and particularly Hegel, with whom he became acquainted mostly through Hebbel. His understanding of the relationship between human beings and the physical world thus becomes clear if we think of it as the counterpoising of two spheres of reality: the spiritual and non-spiritual. For Irzykowski human beings were the personification of *spirit*, in the sense of *consciousness*, while the physical world, on the other hand, was perceived by him as chaos and expressed by the Latin phrase *dira moles* ('dark mass'). Perhaps it is worth noting that

1895

this dialectical concept of reality was also applied to human beings, who were perceived by the author as psychophysical individuals, and composed, consequently, both of spiritual and material elements. That is, where the concept of treating a human body as a material element comes from, the concept which he elaborates and illustrates with examples from film, especially American slapstick comedy. The most interesting fragments, for Irzykowski, were those where the transfer of the spiritual sphere into the sphere of the physical took place – a kiss is according to him 'the dividing line between the play of spirit and the play of body' (p. 78). Therefore he insisted that love should be presented in the cinema in its physical aspects. He realised, however, that in practice erotic scenes could be identified by viewers as reality rather than representation and this could lead to vulgarisation and, finally, to pornography.

On the basis of this approach to the duality of human beings he developed his views on film acting. Irzykowski was strongly opposed to mime and the overuse of facial expression. According to him, the elementary task of a film actor is expressing his or her own body and demonstrating the material aspect of a human being.

To sum up this part of Irzykowski's argument, it needs to be stressed that, according to him, only cinema can present reality in its physical dimension and the relationship of human beings to it. In other words, only cinema can make this relationship visible, and what makes this possible is *movement*. Adopting such a concept of cinema naturally influenced his views on the artistic potential of cinema. For him, films which make visible human beings' relationship with the physical world were not necessarily *art*; the priority for film was to be *cinematic* – that is, to reveal this relationship, rather than to be 'artistic'.

It is not surprising, therefore, that considering the problems of cinematic form in terms of contemporary cinema, he wondered whether its particular elements were, in fact, 'specifically cinematic', or whether they derived from other arts. In considering montage as the basic means of cinematic narration in contemporary cinema, Irzykowski analyses in detail the methods employed by D.W. Griffith in the

films *Orphans of the Storm* (1920) and *Way Down East* (1921). The characteristic method of story construction he refers to as creating 'a mosaic out of fragments', which, according to him, is a method characteristic of the realist novel. In *Way Down East* he analyses the way the two separate but parallel plots are linked together, plots which he calls 'action and counteraction', noticing that the dramaturgic tension built in that way is nothing other than a form of delay which is a device known to literature, as well. Irzykowski compares the devices used by Griffith with equivalent literary methods, quoting many examples from novels.

It has to be stressed, however, that Irzykowski, noting the literary sources of these kinds of cinematic narration, does not evaluate them negatively: 'I think', he wrote, 'that there is no reason for the cinema to be ashamed or afraid of that similarity. It simply relies on the "poetry" that is common to all arts' (p. 161). He analysed the remaining elements of cinematic form (for instance the close-up) in a similar way, finding their equivalents in painting and literature. The close-up could be categorised as a poetical trope based on the formula *pars pro toto*, that is metonymy, examples of which he found in the films of Max Linder as well as Griffith. He also indicates the possible occurrence of some other poetical tropes, most of all, of metaphor, but also of allegory, hyperbole and synecdoche. However, according to Irzykowski, each of them could be regarded as a particular instance of a broader category of poetical tropes independent of their substance of expression.

He also marked off the types of associational and lyrical montage as well as various types of montage transition. He also noticed the importance of the principle of rhythm in film. He did not treat them, however, as originating from the peculiarity of cinema but as being merely translated from literature.[3] It was this part of the author's argument that was most often criticised. He was reproached for a groundless search for the literary origins of what his critics regarded as specifically cinematic. Today we can say that Irzykowski over-simplified the relationship between film and literature but, on the other hand, it would be hard to deny the validity of his arguments,

1895

especially when he discusses the dominant methods of constructing narrative.

It is worth stressing, however, that when considering the question of the relation of cinema to other arts, Irzykowski does not construct any sort of hierarchy; rather, he suggests their interdependence. He claims that: 'These boundary disputes should be settled in such a way that every art, wanting to enhance its value, has to make use of the elements or material of other arts .... It is not, however, "a necessary evil", which has to be put up with and if possible avoided, but a symbiosis which tangles the roots even more deeply' (p. 115). The thesis about the mutually informing nature of the arts, expressed in this statement, as well as the argument for the necessity of common areas of concern, seems to be particularly interesting and deserves recognition.

The films described and analysed by Irzykowski and which he located on the borderline between cinema and the other arts actually depart from his beliefs about the cinema. This contradiction between his theoretical concept of cinema and contemporary cinematic practice is resolved by introducing a distinction between 'extensive' and 'intensive' films. The criteria for this division were derived from the various kinds of movement characteristic of both types of cinema. The 'intensive' film is based on movement within the shot, an 'extensive' film is based on montage – movement between shots. (It is hard not to recall Bazin's much later formulations here.) Irzykowski did not consider any of the films he had analysed as 'intensive' but he noticed in them some symptoms, which strengthened his opinion that such films would be created in the future. The 'extensive' film, identified by him with popular cinema, would prosper at least for the reason that there would always be a demand for cinema which 'instead of movement gives facts'. Using modern terms, we could say that, through his typology, Irzykowski introduces the categories of popular cinema and cinema which is alternative to it. Popular cinema, for Irzykowski, was characterised by its conventionality – pleasure was derived from variations in form within strong patterns of repeated content.

It was not Irzykowski's intention to create a descriptive poetics of cinema but rather to unveil its essence, which had not yet been revealed in the films known to him. Considering the question of whether or not the cinema could become an art in the future, he saw this possibility only in the case of animated film, which – as he said – 'gives the cinema artistic character'. Animation presents reality transformed by the artist, which was the defining characteristic of art, according to the traditional aesthetic criteria he employed. Consequently, animation, as opposed to the photographic film, did not imitate reality but was able to present a model of reality.

Irzykowski could be reproached for being unable to perceive artistic potential in films photographing reality. However, he did not treat animation as cinema's 'destiny'. He merely saw it as one area that gave cinema the opportunity of reaching the status of art. Of the cinema he had seen it was only the animated film which created 'a film of pure movement'; that embodied the kind of movement which for Irzykowski was the constituent element of cinema. In considering the possibilities of creating 'the cinema of pure movement', he gives examples from modern painting, arguing that, for example, Kandinsky could have developed his ideas much further only in film. He even claimed that 'generally, it is only the cinema that solves the puzzle of modern trends in pictorial art: futurism, cubism, suprematism in painting are too constrained; it is only in the cinema of pure movement, that is one without a literary plot, without people, horses, trees, trains and other divine and humane beings, where modernism's aims could be achieved' (p. 262). Of course Irzykowski saw animation as an area of pure artistic experiment and had no idea that it would develop into a significant strand of popular cinema.

Irzykowski very often relates his views on cinema to German aesthetic theorists and philosophers, finding in their texts inspiration or confirmation of his own observations. Far more rarely does he draw on texts solely about cinema. But he gives some attention to the views of Jean Epstein in *Cinéma* and of Louis Delluc in *Photogénie*, which he considers in detail. The concepts of cinema posed by the two authors, especially the concept of 'photogénie', he evaluated negatively. His main reproach concerns the lack of a precise definition of the term 'photogénie', which they so often used in the hope of reaching the very essence of cinema. Irzykowski argues that this originally technical term was taken over by impressionist writing on film, which made an aesthetic category out of it, identifying it with the essence of cinema. He argues that the term 'photogénie' is a classical example of a situation in which: 'The word outpaces the notion. First, there is a word, and then a meaning for it is searched for .... The word "photogénie" is ... wandering in search of meaning – and the con-men are on the look out for such words. Perhaps in the future someone will write a psychological work on how swindles are born in language, how words that have no meaning exist and are quite successfully used' (p. 142). Irzykowski's sceptical attitude is clear here and when he writes that in approaching 'the problem' of the cinema '... we will find nothing more than what we put into it' – in other words, we are always in danger of merely confirming our presuppositions.

To return to the controversy about 'photogénie', aside from his remarks on language, Irzykowski reproaches Epstein mostly for his attempt to atomise film – his faith in the method of 'chopping-up', as he puts it. After all, Irzykowski was the advocate of a concept of holistic movement in cinema and therefore could not accept the French writers' approach to analysing the film image through fragments. As we might expect, he also argued that the fragmentation of reality postulated by impressionists had its origins in literary devices, and the devices they perceived as specifically cinematic had their equivalents in poetical tropes. If we take into consideration the fact that the greatest value of cinema was for Irzykowski the presentation of the material aspect of reality, it is not surprising that he also did not appreciate their concept of lyrical impressionist cinema.

The comparison of Irzykowski's views with those of the French impressionists can also suggest other comparative remarks. 'Visibility' which is the key notion in Irzykowski's concept of cinema, encourages a comparison with Béla Balázs whose book *Der sichtbare Mensch oder Die Kultur des Films* (The Visible Man, or Film Culture) was published in 1924, the same year as Irzykowski's book. Both authors indicate that cinema is a landmark in culture, both of them use the term 'visibility' but they understand it in a totally different way. Through cinema, says Balázs: 'Humanity is already learning the rich and colourful language of gesture, movement and facial expression ... it is the visual means of communication, without intermediary of souls clothed in flesh. Man has again become visible.'[4] According to the Hungarian theorist 'visibility' is the means by which psychological experiences are expressed through gesture and facial expression. Irzykowski, on the contrary, stresses the possibility of demonstrating the body, the material aspect of a human being. For him the body is not merely a means of conveying psychological messages; it is a separate element, the most interesting manifestation of the physical world, which can be fully revealed by the cinema through making it visible.

Overall, however, situating Irzykowski's views on cinema within early film theory is not altogether easy. This is mainly because of the contradictions that can be found in his theory. It is difficult, for instance, to describe clearly the author's view on the relation between film and reality. On the one hand, he stresses the possibilities of *reproducing* the material aspect of reality in the cinema; on the other hand, he argues that we can consider the film image also as, in some sense, a sign. He is equally contradictory, when he proposes a definition of cinema as the 'visibility of human beings' co-existence with the physical world', but at the same time he believes that only animated film can achieve the status of art. It would definitely be difficult to situate Irzykowski's views within those defined by Dudley Andrew in *Major Film Theories* as making up the formative tradition in early film theory: 'These theorists', Andrew writes, 'struggled to give the cinema the status of art. Cinema, they claimed, was the equal of the other arts ... During this epoch, comparisons were made between the cinema and virtually every other art.'[5] Irzykowski, as I have mentioned, also drew such comparisons. However, it always resulted in finding common areas rather than formulating a conclusion about the artistic autonomy of cinema. He did not examine cinema only as art because, it has to be stressed again, the cinema, according to him, only in some cases could be considered art. The artistic character of the cinema was not a necessary condition for its momentous cultural significance.

Irzykowski's theoretical views cannot be translated into a system of logically linked statements. This lack of cohesion may, of course, be perceived as a drawback. Yet, when we take into account the different aspects of cinema, which were present from its very beginning, the difficulty of developing a coherent theoretical system is quite understandable. Nevertheless, the book *The Tenth Muse* remains as important evidence of thinking about cinema in its early years. While at this time Polish cinema itself could not take pride in original achievements, Irzykowski's views can be valuably compared with more widely known writings on film. Unfortunately, his concepts did not become a focus of discussion beyond Poland. Irzykowski failed to interest foreign publishers in his work, and his pessimistic conclusion that his reflections on cinema would 'be lost like a seed on a rock' was largely to come true.

Notes

1. e.g. Włodzimierz Perzyński, 'Triumf kinematografu', *Świat* 1908, no. 14; Ignacy Chrzanowski, 'W obronie teatru', *Scena i sztuka* 1909, appendix no. 1 to issue no. 37; Zygmunt Wasilewski, 'Powieść kinematograf', *Słowo Polskie* 1909, no. 368.
2. Karol Irzykowski, *Śmierć kinematografu*, In: *Dziesiąta Muza oraz pomniejsze pisma filmowe*, Kraków (1982), 13–22.
3. Jadwiga Bocheńska, *Polska myśl filmowa do roku 1939*,(Wrocław, 1974), 120.
4. Béla Balázs, *Theory of the Film. Character and Growth of a New Art*, trans. E. Bone (Dover Publication, Inc., New York 1970), 41.
5. Dudley Andrew, *The Major Film Theories: An Introduction*(Oxford University Press, New York, 1976).

2

Exhibition and audiences

1895

Guarding the Borders in Early Cinema: The Shifting Ground of French–American Relations

Richard Abel

Department of English, Drake University, Des Moines, Iowa 50311-4505, USA

IN NOVEMBER 1908, the *New York Dramatic Mirror* surveyed the 'film product of the world' on both sides of a border line dividing the 'American' from the 'foreign' (primarily meaning French) and had this to say about Pathé-Frères, 'the largest producer of moving picture films' not only for Europe but for North America as well:

> Pathé pictures are famous for their good photographic quality, superior panto-mime, ingenious trick effects, beautiful coloured results and the clear, lucid manner of telling a picture story.[1]

In December, the *Mirror* even singled out Pathé's *L'Arlésienne* as 'a model object lesson for every American manufacturer':

> The story is novel and compelling, and it is told in a manner that adds instead of detracts from the dramatic interest. To the spectator, it reads from the curtain like a printed book. Every scene, every action has its obvious meaning, following in its natural sequence, to tell a connected and coherent story.[2]

In the 'selective tradition' of American cinema history, this language has come to be associated with the films of Biograph (where D.W. Griffith was now directing) or even Vitagraph. Yet praising French Pathé films in this way was not uncommon in the American trade press at the time, however grudgingly expressed, as one can see in reading *Moving Picture World*.[3] Within five years, of course, that praise had turned to disdain and not only for Pathé but for French film product generally. John Cher's report from France for *Moving Picture World*, in November 1913, puts this quite bluntly:

> The working conditions of the French moving picture industry ... in the opinion of most people ... [are] the poorest in the world.[4]

According to Cher and others, those conditions implicitly condemned the French to a position of abject inferiority vis-à-vis the American cinema, a position that would be exacerbated by the First World War.

I cite this trade press discourse as a quick

1895

means of framing what I want to say in this essay. My objective is not simply to tell a 'boom and bust' story of French cinema during the early years of silent film. Rather, I want to focus on certain historical moments, as well as specific film titles (admittedly, all fiction films), in order to explore several critical areas of interest concerning French–American relations in early cinema. These include questions of representation and narration, audiences and reception (as mediated by the trade press), marketing and promotion, and national identity. The first of those moments is 1908, the year that Pathé's prominence on the American market probably reached its peak, but also the year that its position became highly contested. Here, two Pathé films released at nearly the same time are apt, *Le Petit Béquillard* (The Little Cripple) and *Nuit de Noël* (Christmas Eve Tragedy): only the latter title, I believe, has been shown previously, at the 1992 Domitor conference. The second moment is 1911, a crucial year in the reorientation of French cinema (and particularly Pathé) within the industry worldwide. Here, the film I want to single out is Pathé's *L'Epouvante* (The Fright), a suspense melodrama produced by S.C.A.G.L. and starring Mistinguett (which was to be shown, but for some reason was not, at the June 1995 Domitor pre-screenings in Paris). The third and last moment is 1916, the year the French cinema industry began to recover from the catastrophic conditions imposed by the War, a recovery in which Pathé and other French companies had to renegotiate once again their relation to the American cinema. Here, I want to focus on *Fleur de Paris*, another film starring Mistinguett (in a double role), this one produced by an independent company (and apparently available for viewing only at the Archives du Film, Bois d'Arcy).

The Little Cripple and *Christmas Eve Tragedy* suggest some answers, I think, to the question first raised by *Views and Films Index*, in January 1908: Why were French Pathé films 'so eminently successful' in the American market, why did their very titles hold 'a strange, magnetic fascination'?[5] One reason, as I have argued in *The Ciné Goes to Town*, was the relatively standardised mode of representation and narration the company had

developed over the previous three years so that any one film (even if the story was unfamiliar) could be understood almost anywhere within its worldwide network of distribution agencies.[6] Pathé titles and intertitles, introduced as early as 1903, were unusually concise (just a word or phrase), designed in bold, red block letters, and anchored by a pair of 'trademark' coqs in the frame corners. Story scenes or sequences often were composed of multiple shots, marked by a variety of changes in framing. There were cut-in close shots, as in *Brigandage moderne* (Highway Robbery Modern Style, 1905) or *Pauvre mère* (Poor Mother, 1906). There were POV inserts, as in *Le Concierge bat son tapis* (The Danger of Carpet Beating, 1906). There was reverse-angle cutting which linked interiors and exteriors, as in *Au bagne* (Scenes of Convict Life, 1905), or *Le Détective* (The Detective, 1906). There were matchcut character exits and entrances through three or more adjacent spaces, as in *Un Drame à Venise* (A Venetian Tragedy, 1906) or *Le Diabolo* (1907). There were several forms of alternation: linking two contiguous spaces through sound cues, as in *Le Braconnier* (The Poacher, 1906) or *La Petite Aveugle* (The Little Blind Girl, 1906), crosscutting simultaneous lines of action in disparate spaces, as in *Chiens contrebandiers* (Dog Smugglers, 1906) or *Ecole du malheur* (Distress, 1907), and parallel editing, as in *Medor au téléphone* (Spot at the Phone, 1907) or *Tommy in Society* (1907). Finally, such editing patterns were combined to create consecutive actions through repeated spaces (for either comedy or suspense), as in *Idée d'apache* (A Hooligan's Idea, 1907) or *Ruse de mari* (Artful Husband, 1907). In short, Pathé films tended to construct a sense of narrative continuity in which every action and space, to cite *Views and Films Index* again, was 'connected, obvious, and self-evident'.[7]

Christmas Eve Tragedy and especially *The Little Cripple* illustrate Pathé's 'clear, lucid manner of telling a picture story' just as well as do two other better known Pathé titles from early 1908, *Le Cheval emballé* (The Runaway Horse) and *Physician of the Castle* or *A Narrow Escape*. In the first film, for instance, repeated movements from background to foreground (or vice versa), along with loosely matched exits and entrances, represent a woman's journey through a series of Brittany landscapes, a journey which carries her away from her fisherman husband and, in conjunction with her daily routine, into an affair with the local miller. In *The Little Cripple*, one sequence uses reverse-angle cutting to connect the exterior and interior of a workers' café as two *apaches* case the place. The next sequence adds a third space, an upstairs bedroom, along with slight changes in shots of the café exterior, to narrate three consecutive actions during the night: the murder of the café owner by the *apaches*, their kidnapping of her young son who (on a sound cue) runs upstairs to help her, and the collapse of a drunk customer who belatedly finds her body. These contiguous spaces then are repeated the next morning when the police discover the crime and arrest the drunk by mistake. The film once again traces consecutive actions through repetition in its narrative climax: after the 'little cripple' sees the *apaches* escape from a bayside dock in a rowboat and swims out to rescue his friend (the kidnapped boy has been tossed overboard), the police swim out to capture the *apaches* (who also conveniently abandon the boat so the repetition can work). At crucial moments in the narrative, moreover, each of these films presents one or more tableaux whose composition and framing suggest some kind of emotional resonance for a character. In one, there is the landscape of scattered stone monoliths through which the woman walks as if through a 'land of the dead' (perhaps evoking the threat of her husband's death at sea). In the 'naturalistic' world of the other, there is the tableau of the delapidated dock where the rescued boy helps the 'little cripple' with his crutches, both 'good boys' now in danger (despite the latter's heroic efforts) of becoming homeless orphans.

Another reason why French Pathé films were so successful in the American market (and elsewhere) by early 1908, had to do with the way they exploited colour. This is something historians are just beginning to re-examine now that film archives are restoring and printing more surviving titles in colour.[8] It is becoming increasingly clear, for instance, that there was a crucial distinction between American and French film product, at least up to 1909 or so, in terms of the percentage (and quality) of colour prints in circulation.[9] Whereas American films did not often circulate in colour, French films did; and Pathé led all other companies in their production and promotion.[10] Pathé long has been recognised for its unique stencil-colour process which initially served as a form of spectacle display in trick films such as *Metamorphose du papillon* (A Butterfly's Metamorphosis, 1904), historical films such as *Le Regne de Louis XIV* (Louis XIV, 1904) or *A Venetian Tragedy* (1906), *féerie* plays such as *La Peine du talion* (Tit for Tat, 1906), and 'advertisements' such as *L'Album merveilleux* (The Wonderful Album, 1905). But the company also systematically exploited toning as well as tinting effects, as early as *Miracle de Noël* (Christmas Miracle, 1905), *Le Déserteur* (The Deserter, 1906), and *Les Voleurs incendiaires* (A Case of Arson, 1907).[11] And it often combined these different colour processes, especially in *féerie* plays such as *La Poule aux oeufs d'or* (The Hen with the Golden Eggs, 1905), *La Fée printemps* (Spring Fairy, 1906), and *Le Pêcheur des perles* (The Pearl Fisher, 1907), but also in the 1907 version of its *Passion Play*, probably the most popular film that year in the USA.[12] Throughout 1907 and 1908, toning and tinting tended to be used for *grand guignol* melodramas such as *Vengéance du forgeron* (Blacksmith's Revenge) or *Le Bagne de gosses* (Children's Reformatory). Moreover, in such melodramas colour effects seem to have been used quite selectively, as *Christmas Eve Tragedy* nicely illustrates. Whereas the opening seaside departure is marked by rose tinting, most of the remaining landscapes are toned sepia, with these exceptions: yellow–green tinting marks the wife's meeting with the miller, amber tinting suffuses the church interior for midnight mass (viewed through a silhouetted doorway), and red tinting from a bonfire lights the community ritual of a round dance. By contrast, the 'close shot' of the woman preparing for mass (and the illicit affair) – arranging her cap and hair before a background wall mirror – remains uncoloured, starkly black-and-white. What might be the significance of 'lack' of colour at this emotionally resonant moment in the narrative: is it a sign of 'moral ambigu-

1895

Fig. 1. *Nuit de Noël, 1908 (poster).*

Fig. 1. *Nuit de Noël, 1908 (poster).*

clearly told and of engaging interest'.[16] And just as important, 'justice is finally satisfied', as if in conformity with the American melodrama tradition of 'bright, happy denouements'.[17] By contrast, *Variety* condemned *Christmas Eve Tragedy* as 'suggestive and repulsive' – a response Pathé may have anticipated in delaying the film's release. Up until the end, the reviewer complained, 'it drags along wearily, with no action', but the last scene (where the fisherman pushes the miller, horse, and cart over a cliff, see Fig. 1) was as 'objectionable ... for children as the interior view of a slaughter house'.[18] In short, this kind of story (whose deadly stunt work did end up in a court case)[19] was the very opposite of what the trade press would soon be defining as a desirable 'American subject'.

Yet others like Walter Eaton of the *New York Sun* had no objection to *Christmas Eve Tragedy* at all. For him, it was a 'touching domestic tragedy'; although troubled by what happened to the horse, he found the ending 'irreproachabl[y] moral'.[20] Eaton's comments on this film, however, tell us something else about the experience of 'movie-going' in 1908, something historians also are just beginning to re-examine: the importance of sound or music in early cinema.[21] For his 'review' includes a rare description of the 'touching ballad' (accompanied by slides) which immediately followed the Pathé film, a ballad 'all about a forsaken maiden "in a village by the sea"'. The audience at the 14th Street cinema, Eaton writes, was invited to join in singing the ballad's chorus, which concluded in this couplet:

> *Now the moon don't seem so bright,*
> *For she's all alone to-night.*

ity', for instance, aligned with the intertitle, 'Coquetry', or can it be read differently?

Both of these films were released in France during the first weeks of January 1908; *The Little Cripple* then came on the market in late February in the United States, but *Christmas Eve Tragedy*'s release was delayed until the middle of April.[13] Undoubtedly, there are several reasons for this discrepancy,[14] but I want to focus on one, Pathé's contested position in the American market, especially as that was articulated in the trade press. From at least the spring of 1907, moral reform groups in Chicago, New York, and elsewhere, as well as some industry leaders, had been concerned about the representation of criminal behaviour, immorality, and simple 'bad taste' in films, a concern which increasingly was displaced onto Pathé as a 'foreign' company.[15] These two films illustrate Pathé's 'problem' concisely, for both received notices when they played at the Manhattan and 14th Street cinemas in New York. *Variety*, the first trade weekly to offer 'reviews' that were more than manufacturers' promos, had this to say about *The Little Cripple*: although running 'to an uncommon length [and] divided into many scenes ... throughout its story is connected ...

How often, one can ask, did cinema managers co-ordinate films and illustrated songs on their programmes, especially this closely? And, in this particular case, how might that song have shaped the way spectators (especially women, who probably comprised the major portion of the audience) 'read' and remembered the Pathé film? Or, conversely, how might the experience of film and ballad, one right after the other, have redrawn the boundary line between grim 'foreign' stories and sentimental American ones?[22]

We now know, from the company's own archives, that, in the spring and summer of 1908, Pathé came to realise it no longer could maintain its prominent position on the American market. Given the climate of almost hysterical nationalism in the United States (perhaps most evident in the perceived threat that new immigrants posed to the 'Americanisation' process), French Pathé films were increasingly dismissed as 'foreign', the Pathé representatives seen as unassimilated 'foreigners'.[23] To not only survive but prosper in the global market, Pathé began to shift the focus of its operations to those sectors of the cinema industry that would ensure steady profits and dividends.[24] By 1911, that reorientation was complete. Film production was decentralised among a dozen or more quasi-independent firms, some of which (like those in the United States and Russia) now produced films geared specifically (but not exclusively) to that market. Film distribution remained crucial to the French 'parent' company, but the primary market was shifting from the United States to central and eastern Europe. The manufacture of 'hardware' had grown to the point where Pathé cameras and projectors were now standard in film studios and cinemas around the world. Finally, the company had made good on its commitment to begin producing its own negative film stock and soon would be competitive with Eastman Kodak and AGFA, at least in the European market. The result was that Pathé no longer 'defined' French cinema as it once had in 1908. Other companies had secured a strong position in one or more industry sectors:[25] Film d'Art and Eclipse, for instance, in production; Aubert and AGC in distribution. Eclair, by contrast, was prospering and expanding into several sectors and soon was the only French company other than Pathé with an affiliate producing films in the USA. Gaumont, of course, was Pathé's largest competitor (in nearly every sector of the industry), the chief difference being that its production remained centralised, and the kinds of films it made may well have 'defined' French cinema just as much, if not even more, than did Pathé's.

Although any number of Pathé, Gaumont, or Eclair titles could be useful in exploring French–American relations in 1911, I think S.C.A.G.L.'s *The Fright* is particularly instructive.[26] First of all, it challenges the notion, still often repeated in general film histories, that French cinema was now 'regressive' or 'retarded' vis-à-vis the American cinema. Let me sketch the story briefly for those who have not seen Pierre Decourcelle's 'terrifying cinedrama'.[27] Playing a well-known theatre actress (much like herself), Mistinguett returns to her fifth-floor Paris apartment one evening to surprise a jewel thief (Emile Milo) in her bedroom. She calls the police, but the thief eludes them and ends up hanging precariously from a balcony gutter; after they leave, she has to decide, now that the tables have turned, whether or not to rescue him. The last half of this film includes an extended sequence of alternation as the police pursue the thief from the bedroom to the outside balcony, over a roof, and back to the balcony – as relatively quick cutting and exact timing combine to keep pursuer and pursued proximate yet constantly separate. The thief is often privileged in closer shots (linking the spectator with his predicament); his descent over the balcony is accentuated by a camera tilt; and his desperate position is revealed by means of a LA shot which catches a cop glancing one last time out onto the balcony and failing to see the thief's hands gripping the gutter at the very bottom of the frame. Unlike the consistent pattern of framing and editing in this sequence, the first part of *The Fright* links the spectator to Mistinguett's predicament with a shock. When she prepares for sleep that night, the spectator knows (but she does not) that the thief has had to hide under her bed. A FS of Mistinguett in bed, tossing aside a book and reaching for a cigarette, suddenly shifts, when she looks down at a dropped match, and the camera dollies away from her to LS. This unexpected camera movement literalises the distance between spectator and character, but the next shot closes that gap with an intensity worthy of Hitchcock. An extraordinary overhead shot past her downward-glancing head (in CU) now frames the thief's hand emerging from underneath the bed and snatching up the match.

This remarkable one-reel film, the equal perhaps of any American film produced that year, was released in May 1911, in France, and, following Pathé's general pattern at the time, four months later in the United States.[28] Yet it received little attention and even less promotion in the trade press.[29] There seem to be a number of reasons why this was so, all of which have to do with Pathé's difficulties in maintaining some kind of position within the American cinema industry. First, there was Pathé's decision, taken in the summer of 1910, to privilege its American product, much of that westerns and comedies, at the expense of its French films, on the American market – a strategy of 'assimilation' that Eclair would follow one year later. Second, there was the company's decision, instituted in July 1911, to promote its weekly newsreel (the first ever) on the American market – a decision which proved highly successful.[30] Third, there was Pathé's concern over how to release the multiple-reel films it was beginning to finance and distribute in France. Eventually, the company chose to distribute its American product exclusively through the General Film Service (which actively discouraged multiple-reel films) and to subsidise a new agency, CGPC, to import French films – one of the first of which, the two-reel *Les Victimes de l'alcool* (*In the Grip of Alcohol*), had been released in France about the same time as *The Fright*.[31] Finally, despite her fame as a stage and screen actress in France and in other parts of Europe, Mistinguett was relatively unknown in the United States; in other words, she could not easily be promoted within the star system that the American cinema industry was then developing as a means of attracting and holding audiences.[32] The consequence of Pathé's responses to the changing global cinema market (like those of Eclair and Gaumont) was that *The Fright*, like many other French films from 1911, had a circulation that was highly circumscribed. And that prompts another question (invoking a 'possibilist' history): how would American perceptions of French cinema during this period have been different, had this title and others such as *Zigomar*, *La Tare*, or *Le Courrier de Lyon* been seen all that widely, and been noticed, in the United States?

Five years later, of course, in the middle of the First World War, conditions had changed drastically for the French cinema industry. Cut off from its central and eastern European markets, Pathé, for instance, resumed its reliance on profits from its quasi-independent American affiliate, Pathé-Exchange. Eclair, by contrast, had been forced to abandon the American market and, even within France (by the fall of 1916), was circulating perhaps no more than ten prints of any one title.[33] Whereas French films were nowhere to be seen in the United States, American films now were beginning to dominate the French market.[34] Here, one could point to the first Pearl White serial released by Pathé in December 1915, Chaplin's short comic films, and DeMille's *The Cheat* which played for six months at the Paris Select cinema. The French cinema industry was hard pressed to confront this American challenge, given the wartime restrictions on capital, facilities, and personnel. And in March 1916, *Ciné-Journal* argued that the industry had to do something besides crank out crime serials like Gaumont's *Les Vampires* or one patriotic polemic after another – films it branded as 'crimes against the state'.[35] That 'something else', at least during much of the 1916–17 season, turned out to be familiar melodramas, some of them adaptations of pre-war boulevard plays, and especially women's stories, which exploited the attraction of French female stars. Most of these stars provided the basis for profitable series at the major companies – for instance, Gabrielle Robinne at SCAGL/Pathé, and perhaps the most popular of all, Suzanne Grandais at Eclipse. A few others formed the nucleus for production at newly independent companies, and here the most significant was Mistinguett, who worked exclusively with André Hugon and Films Succès.

Fleur de Paris was the third title in the Mistinguett series that year and was heavily promoted in the trade press.[36] Released in early November, the film followed the exceptional success of *Suzanne* (with Suzanne Grandais), which had run for two months straight in Paris and played at least 100 major cinemas throughout France.[37] And the date happened to coincide with the initial episode of Pathé's new Pearl White serial, *Le Masque aux dents blanches*.[38] Yet *Fleur de Paris* was different from the dozen other French films with female stars released that fall:[39] its story directly addressed the unequal relationship which had developed between the cinemas of France and the United States.[40] In one role, Mistinguett plays a comic music hall actress wooed by a visiting impresario who offers her a lucrative contract to tour the USA. Her acceptance may allude to the decisions taken by some of France's best industry personnel during the War (including Max Linder, Léonce Perret, Maurice Tourneur, and Albert Capellani), and it is represented as a betrayal, although directed primarily at her partner Harry Podge (Emile Milo again). In her second (and principal) role, however, Mistinguett plays Margot Panard, a young dressmaker whose earnings provide the chief income for her family (a mother, small brother, and drunken, unemployed father). Lured to the theatre by a poster of the actress, she imagines taking her place, but this 'extravagance' has dire consequences for the family: bills fall due, Margot runs away, the father dies, and mother and son are reduced to poverty. Through a series of coincidences (first, Harry recognises that Margot looks like his partner, then the mother comes to believe her daughter *is* the actress), the rest of the film lets Margot (who is now selling flowers on the street) realise her dream, and more. Tellingly, the resolution comes not with Margot and Harry performing on stage but with a pair of scenes in Harry's well-furnished apartment: the first establishes Margot and Harry as a romantic couple, and the second reintroduces the mother and brother to neatly reconstitute the family, but at a higher level in the social hierarchy.

The negotiation of ideological conflict in *Fleur de Paris* is quite deft, if disingenuous. Although acknowledging an individual's desire to leave France for the United States, it primarily reaffirms family relations, particularly in a time of war, as central to French society. And, in the process, it accepts a woman's desire for a professional career (epitomised by Mistinguett), yet also directs that desire back into the domestic sphere over which a 'good father' now presides. The film is just as deft in negotiating strategies of representation and narration: the framing and editing some-times make it difficult to tell whether it is 'French' or 'American'.[41] In the opening sequence, for instance, Margot's difference from the rest of the dressmakers, as well as her boss, is established through high-angle long shots, panning and tilting camera movement, cut-in close shots, and a 90° shift in camera position. Much of the film's first reel alternates between the interior space of the family kitchen (very selectively lit) and the contrasting music hall exterior and interior into which Margot is lured (and where reverse-angle editing connects her with the stage performance). A sequence the next morning links three adjacent spaces – Margot's small bedroom, the kitchen, and the street below – and reverse-angle editing forces Margot (now at the kitchen window) to confront her father who asks for money to pay the neighbourhood butcher. The door framing the music hall has multiple functions: in one shot, taken from inside, mother and brother sit in the doorway, their exclusion and despair accentuated by silhouette; later, Mistinguett passes them, puzzled by the mother's attempts to engage her; and later still, at Harry's urging, she presents the mother with a bouquet of flowers, in reverse-angle close shots. Similarly, Mistinguett's recurring poster at the music hall entrance serves as a different dream image for Margot, her mother, and Harry; ironically, it is one she herself fulfils by becoming something else. Finally, in contrast to the rest of the film, each of the final two scenes enacts its resolution in the stereotypical 'French' space of the long-take, long-shot tableau.

There is one further point I want to make about *Fleur de Paris*, and it can serve as a conclusion. In the cultural war that paralleled the war in the trenches, this was one of several films during the autumn of 1916 that, for the French trade press, defined the French cinema as 'French', in defending the nation and its identity against what was seen as an assault by the American cinema. One measure of their importance was the attention lavished on *Suzanne*, *Fleur de Paris*, and other Succès films by *Le Film*, the new weekly which led the defence of a national French cinema.[42] *Le Film* carried an ad, for instance, announcing a special preview screening of *Fleur de Paris* and another that listed the eleven Paris cinemas into which it was booked for its initial week (relatively unusual for an independent production).[43] Yet that preview screening proved controversial, exposing a growing division within the French cinema industry. According to *Le Film*, Aubert had arranged to preview *Fleur de Paris* outside the usual schedule organised by the national association of exhibitors, which, in turn, threatened to boycott Mistinguett's film.[44] Although the reasons given were procedural, it was becoming clear that many exhibitors and distributors were increasingly dependent on a constant supply of American films; it did not necessarily serve their self-interest to support independent French producers or even French films. But *Le Film*'s preview report included something else. The spectators were mostly women, some of them exhibitors' wives, and they challenged the exhibitors not to jeopardise the industry's recovery by unfairly condemning such 'an excellent French film'.

This incident raises one last question, one raised by others before (most recently at this conference) but still not fully addressed. Was it the case, as the trade press sometimes claimed, that French cinema audiences during the War were primarily comprised of women? If so, how does that matter? What was the relation (ideological and otherwise), for instance, between this constituency, however varied, and the kinds of stories and stars characteristic of French films vis-à-vis American films shown in France? More generally, was the presence of large numbers of women spectators an anomaly of the war period, or did women constitute the primary audience before and after the War as well? And was their presence unique to France, or were women (however differently categorised, again) the primary audience in other countries such as the United States, as Kathy Peiss and others have suggested for the nickelodeon period and Gaylyn Studlar has argued for the 1920s?[45] In short, it is imperative that we look much more closely at the role women may have played in early cinema (either as consumers 'spending time' or as 'rapt and entranced' spectators),[46] and not only as we try to map the shifting ground of French–American relations.

Notes

1. 'Earmarks of Makers', *New York Dramatic Mirror* (14 November 1908): 10.

2. 'Reviews of New Films', *New York Dramatic Mirror* (5 December 1908): 8.

3. See, for instance, Lux Graphicus, 'On the Screen', *Moving Picture World* (25 December 1909): 918–919.

4. John Cher, 'Paris Letter', *Moving Picture World* (8 November 1913): 601.

5. W. Livingston Larned, 'The Public and the Film Maker', *Views and Films Index* (25 January 1908): 3.

6. Richard Abel, *The Ciné Goes to Town: French Cinema, 1896–1914* (Berkeley: University of California Press, 1994), 23–24, 121–156.

7. Larned, 'The Public and the Film Maker': 3.

8. See, for instance, Monica Dall'Asta, Guglielmo Pescatore, and Leonard Quaresima (eds), *Il Colore nel cinema muto* (Bologna: Mano Edizioni, 1996), which collects the papers delivered at the 'Color in Silent Cinema' conference held at the University of Udine, 23–25 March 1995. See, also, Daan Hertogs and Nico de Klerk (eds), *'Disorderly Order': Colours in Silent Film*, Amsterdam: Nederlands Filmmuseum, 1996, which collects the proceedings of the 1995 Amsterdam Workshop, sponsored by the Nederlands Filmmuseum, 26–29 July 1995.

9. Paolo Cherchi Usai was one of the first to make this claim in 'The Color of Nitrate', *Image* 34 (Spring-Summer 1991): 38.

10. I develop this analysis more fully in 'Pathé's "Heavenly Billboards"', in *Il Colore nel cinema muto*, 56–76.

11. Pathé first called attention to its toning process, as 'special tinting', for *The Deserter* – see the Pathé ad in *Billboard* (27 January 1906): 42.

12. Let me cite just one example: between August and November 1907, the Theatre Royale in Detroit screened the *Passion Play* for 'nearly 250,000' people – see 'Moving Picture News from Everywhere',

Views and Films Index (9 November 1907): 6; and Sydney Wire, 'The Casino Amusement Co.', *Billboard* (23 November 1907): 20.

13. See 'Cinématographe', *Comoedia* (17 janvier 1908): 3; Henri Bousquet, *Catalogue Pathé des années 1896 à 1914: 1907, 1908, 1909* (Charente: Editions Henri Bousquet, 1993), 65; the Pathé ad in *Views and Films Index* (22 February 1908): 2; and 'Latest Films of All Makers', *Views and Films Index* (18 April 1908): 9–10. Neither film did Pathé promote, however, as the week's 'feature' or 'headliner'.

14. One reason, for instance, might be that black-and-white prints of *The Little Cripple* could be made in Pathé's Bound Brook factory, whereas the toned and tinted prints of *Christmas Eve Tragedy* may have been made in Paris and then shipped to the United States. Another might have had to do with the balance or composition of Pathé's weekly programmes.

15. I develop this analysis in 'The Perils of Pathé: The "Americanization" of Early American Cinema', in Leo Charney and Vanessa Schwartz (eds), *Cinema and the Invention of Modern Life* (Berkeley: University of California Press, 1995), 183–223.

16. 'Moving Picture Reviews', *Variety* (1 March 1908): 12.

17. See, for instance, 'The Melodrama', *New York Dramatic Mirror* (1 June 1907): 14; and 'Public Taste in Pictures as Viewed by M. E. Feckles', *Show World* (7 September 1907): 9.

18. 'Moving Picture News and Reviews', *Variety* (18 April 1908): 13.

19. See, for instance, 'French Thrill Manufacture', *The Bioscope* (13 November 1908): 3; and 'Foreign News: France', *The Bioscope* (21 January 1909): 24.

20. Walter P. Eaton, 'New Theatrical Problem: Age of Mechanical Amusement', *Views and Films Index* (9 May 1908): 5.

21. Sound in early cinema, especially the music which accompanied films or was performed with illustrated slides, will be the principal subject, for instance, of the 1998 Domitor conference. See also Martin Marks, 'The American Film Scores', *Harvard Library Bulletin* 2.4 (1991): 78–100; and Rick Altman, 'Naissance de la réception classique: la campagne pour standardiser le son', *Cinémathèque* 6 (1994): 98–111.

22. Here, Martin Loiperdinger's comment during a conference discussion session is relevant: in Germany, between 1904 and 1907, *tonbilder* films served as a means of asserting national identity on cinema programmes otherwise dominated by French Pathé films.

23. See, for instance, the 'Rapport du Conseil d'Adminstration' (2 June 1908) – Carton 2, Pathé Archive, Saint-Ouen.

24. For a more extensive analysis of this reorientation, see Richard Abel, 'In the Belly of the Beast: The Early Years of Pathé-Frères', *Film History*, 5.4 (December 1993): 363–385.

25. For further information on the development of the French cinema industry between 1907 and 1911, see Abel, *The Ciné Goes to Town*, 25–46.

26. My description and analysis of *L'Epouvante* or *The Fright* is based on a 35 mm nitrate print, 180 metres in length, at the Nederlands Filmmuseum.

27. 'Mlle Mistinguett', *Le Cinéma* (12 April 1912): 1. Decourcelle wrote the scenario for *L'Epouvante*, but the director has yet to be determined, although either Albert Capellani or René Leprince are likely candidates.

28. See, for instance, *Bulletin Hebdomadaire Pathé-Frères* (1911): 4; the Pathé ad in *Ciné-Journal* (13 May 1911): 2; 'Licensed Release Dates', *Moving Picture World* (16 September 1911): 832; and 'Comments on the Films', *Moving Picture World* (30 September 1911): 972. *The Fright* or *Terror-Stricken* was available in England even earlier – see the Pathé ad in *Bioscope* (23 March 1911): 31.

29. Unlike the Pathé ads singling out *A Tragedy at Sea* or *Raffles Caught*, there was none for *The Fright* – see *Moving Picture World* (26 August 1911): 513, and (30 September 1911): 942.

30. See, for instance, the Pathé ad in *Moving Picture World* (15 July 1911): 7; and 'Reviews of Notable Films: *The Pathé Journal*', *Moving Picture World* (12 August 1911): 359–360. During the week of *The Fright*'s release, Pathé's ad was devoted to *Pathé-Weekly* – see *Moving Picture World* (16 September 1911): 803.

31. See, for instance, 'Licensed Film Stories', *Moving Picture World* (28 October 1911): 318; the GGPC ad in *Moving Picture World* (25 November 1911): 651; and 'Reviews of Notable Films: *In the Grip of Alcohol*', *Moving Picture World* (2 December 1911): 706–707.

32. Only older French actresses such as Bernhardt or Réjane, who had toured the United States, could

be successfully promoted as stars (but not until 1912), the one in *Camille* and *Queen Elizabeth*, the other in *Madame Sans-Gêne*. The comic Max Linder, of course, was an important exception.

33. See, for instance, the Union-Eclair ad in *Le Film* (23 September 1916): 11. The three films listed were scheduled to appear in only four Paris cinemas; one or two weeks later they would be released in the western region of France, but nowhere else. See also Charles Dasnier, writing in *Le Conseiller Municipal* (September 1916) – cited in Georges Sadoul, *Histoire générale du cinéma 4: le cinéma devient un art, la première guerre mondiale* (Paris: Denoël, 1974), 44.

34. See, for instance, the weekly volume of French vs. foreign (largely American) film stock presented in France, cited in *Le Cinéma* (5 May 1916): 1.

35. Edmond Benoît-Lévy, 'Les Limites du cinéma', *Ciné-Journal* (25 March 1916): 41–42. Although Gaumont continued to produce and distribute crime serials, Feuillade's next effort, *Judex* (launched in January 1917), was quite different from *Les Vampires*, clearly nostalgic for the traditional family romance of nineteenth-century French historical fiction and much closer in its mode of representation and narration to American films.

36. The earlier Mistinguett films were *Chignon d'or* and *Mistinguett détective*.

37. See the Eclipse ads for *Suzanne* in *Ciné-Journal* (21 October 1916): 50–51, and in *Le Film* (21 October 1916): 2–3.

38. See, for instance, 'Programmes des Editeurs de Films', *Le Cinéma* (20 October 1916): 6: and 'Programmes des Grands Cinémas', *Le Cinéma* (3 November 1916): 6.

39. Others included Réjane in the reprise of Film d'Art's *Alsace* (20 October), Huguette Duflos in Film d'Art's *L'Instinct* (20 October), Gabrielle Robinne in Pathé's *Zyte* (3 November), Fabienne Fabrèges in Gaumont's *Les Mystères de l'ombre* (3 November), and Yvette Andreyor in Gaumont's *Un Mariage de raison* (17 November).

40. The following description and analysis of *Fleur de Paris* is based on a 35 mm print, 800 metres in length, at the Archives du Film, Bois d'Arcy.

41. Because the original release print ran 1100 metres, and the surviving archive print runs only 800 metres, I focus on sections of the film which seem most complete.

42. See, for instance the Films Succès ads for *Mistinguett détective* in *Le Film* (3 June 1916): 14–15, and (10 June 1916): 14–15, as well as the ad for the company's Mistinguett and Marie-Louise Derval films in *Le Film* (12 August 1916): 10–11. Films Succès began advertising *Fleur de Paris* in *Le Film* in early September and offered ads every two weeks for the following two months.

43. See the Aubert ad in *Le Film* (14 October 1916): 8, and the Films Succès ad in *Le Film* (4 November 1916): 22.

44. Danvers, 'La Présentation hebdomadaire', *Le Film* (21 October 1916): 20.

45. See Kathy Peiss, *Cheap Amusements: Working Women and Leisure in Turn-of-the-Century New York* (Philadelphia: Temple University Press, 1986), 139–162; Miriam Hansen, *Babel & Babylon: Spectatorship in American Silent Film* (Cambridge: Harvard University Press, 1991), 2–3, 10–11, 91–92, 103–106, 115, 121–125; Gaylyn Studlar, 'The Perils of Pleasure: Fan Magazine Discourse as Women's Commodified Culture in the 1920s', *Wide Angle* 13.1 (1991) – reprinted in Richard Abel (ed), *Silent Film* (New Brunswick: Rutgers University Press, 1996), 263–297; and Abel, 'The Perils of Pathé'.

46. For an excellent account of 'rapt and entranced' women spectators on New York's Lower East Side, see Mary Heaton Vorse, 'Some Picture Show Audiences', *The Outlook* (24 June 1911): 441–447.

Women Bioscope Proprietors – Before the First World War

Vanessa Toulmin

Assistant Director, National Fairground Archive, University of Sheffield, S10 2TN, UK

ONE OF THE PRINCIPAL ATTRACTIONS on the late Victorian fair was the fairground bioscope. Although mechanised roundabouts first made their appearance in 1861, it was not until the end of the century that they achieved a position of dominance over the fairground shows.[1] Until the emergence of steam powered roundabouts on the fairground, shows, as the term showmen implies, were the dominant feature of the landscape. However, from the 1880s onwards the roundabouts gradually made their appearance on the Victorian fair.[2] The show-women featured here are examples of the two forces prevalent on the fairgrounds by the turn of the century: the roundabout proprietors and the showpeople. The cinematograph arrived on the fairground at a time when the roundabouts were challenging the once dominant position of the fairground shows. They first appeared in 1897 when Randall Williams became the first showman to exhibit moving pictures to the fairgoing public at the annual King's Lynn Mart held on Valentine's Day.[3] His colleagues on the fair soon followed his example, and by the start of the First World War there were approximately 120 bioscope shows showing moving pictures on fairgrounds throughout the United Kingdom. Although film historians such as John Barnes and Geoff Mellor have credited the part played by the showmen in exploiting the infant cinema, it is only recently with the publication of Dave Berry's *Cinema and Wales*, and Colin Harding and Simon Popple's *In the Kingdom of Shadows* that showmen such as Randall Williams, George Green and William Haggar have been fully appreciated.[4] However, the role of showwomen has not been researched, and apart from the biographies of Sophie Hancock and Madame Olinka, a show-woman who presented exhibitions in Berlin, Amsterdam and Hamburg, little has been published.[5] There are accounts of women operators which appeared in the trade press such as Mrs. J.D. Walker, for example, who is credited as being the first woman operator of a cinematograph in the world and then went on to manage the Empire Cinema in Watford. However, others were not so successful.[6] The *British Journal of Photography* records an incident from 1898 when Miss Maud Huet was sold a cinematograph which was found to be unworkable. The transcript from the court case leaves us with no doubt of the esteem in which women

1895

1895

who attempted to operate cinematograph equipment were held, when the witness told the Court that:

> Being a female, she don't know nothing about these machines![7]

However, on the fairground the attitudes towards women being involved in the business side of the industry was very different. Throughout the history of travelling fairs show-women have played an equal role in the innovations occurring on the fairground. The structure of showland society allowed and encouraged women to perform whatever role at which they were accomplished; this would include all the traditional male jobs such as driving and manual work, and was not necessarily limited to the family home.[8] The women who participated in fairground society had to know the business as thoroughly as their husbands, and that often included overseeing the building up, and the travelling of the machinery and equipment on the fairground route.

Many of the families who presented these shows had previously exhibited Ghost Shows, Menageries or Marionette sideshows on the fairground. The direct part that women played in this aspect of the business can be

seen in the fairground exhibitions popular at that time. Women not only paraded on the front of these elaborate shows, but were also the proprietors and sometimes the main performers (Fig. 1).

The show-women discussed here have been selected in order to demonstrate the variety of shows operating at the time, and the evolution not only of the structures in which the films were presented but also the presentation of such films. All the women mentioned in this discussion originally travelled or were involved in fairground shows prior to the introduction of the bioscope, and this was a major factor in their success. They have been chosen, primarily, for three reasons. Firstly, to provide an overall historical development of the social forces prevalent on the fairground at that time. Secondly, by examining the structural evolution of their individual shows, the growing popularity of the medium of film exhibition on the fairground and its eventual transition to permanent-site exhibition will be illustrated. Finally by examining the contribution made by show-women an evaluation can be made of the significance of the fairground bioscope, and we can assess the role the fairground played in developing film as a medium of popular culture.

Pre-cinematograph shows on the fairground

Before the first appearance of the bioscope show at the Agricultural Hall in Islington in December 1896, the features dominating the fairground landscape would have been wax-works booths, ghost shows, and marionette theatres. Madame Tussaud, Madame James,[9] Mrs. Ruth Williams,[10] and Mrs. Emma Fossett[11] are amongst just a few of the women proprietors who managed these elaborate attractions. Mrs. Cohen's Photo Studio was a common sight in the United Kingdom and Ireland from the 1860s onwards, and the reporter for *The World's Fair* in 1908 writes:

> Mrs. Cohen is at present with her Photo Studio in Ireland, and though 74 years of age, travels alone in her living carriage and still builds up her own marquee alone.[12]

Therefore, show-women, like their male contemporaries on the fairground, had not only the experience and business acumen necessary for operating a cinematograph show, but also a ready-made portable booth and audiences to which to show the new attractions.

Combination exhibitions

Although the early pioneers on the fairground were predominantly showmen, by 1914 over ten per cent of the proprietors were women. The firm of W., C. and S. Hancock, under the management of Sophie Hancock, was one of the first travelling firms to present moving pictures in the West of England.[13] Sophie Hancock (Fig. 2) ran the family firm with her brothers; it comprised fairground shows, rides and the cinematograph booth which was one of the most lavish of its time.[14] Although there is no mention of the Hancock family exhibiting pictures in 1897, newspaper accounts from August 1898 mention the unique exhibitions to be found on the fair:

> This year a first class variety of unique exhibition, comprising Edison's Electric-Biographe and Japanese Entertainment.[15]

In Wales, Mrs. Crecraft travelled the family

Fig. 2. *Sophie Hancock c. 1910. [Mervyn Heard.]*

bioscope show, and was still in overall control of it until her death in 1917 at the age of 98.[16] In the year before her death, her sons informed *The World's Fair* reporter that their mother was:

> ... still hale and hearty, she still counts the money every night and has not made a mistake for years.[17]

Perhaps the most lavish of cinematograph booths travelling before the First World War was Annie Holland's *Palace of Light* which reputedly housed up to a thousand people at one time. However, Annie Holland was only one of many women who travelled these exhibitions. Other women bioscope proprietors included Mrs. Weir who travelled Weir's *Electric Chronograph Empire* and Mrs. E. Tiller's *Marionettes and Bioscope*.[18] Their shows ranged from the small wagon-fronted walk-up booths popular around the early 1900s to the larger purpose shows manufactured by Orton and Spooners. Some of the most successful of these exhibition booths were often under the control of a widow left to continue the family business until the children were old enough to gain control. One famous example of this was Mrs. Annie Holland of Nottingham who was a prominent fairground exhibitor of the Victorian period. Her family's entry into the fairground business arose out of necessity. Her mother, Mrs. Payne, had been left to bring up three children when her father died at the age of 40. Mrs. Payne's solution to the problem of a lack of income was to exhibit one of her children (who according to family tradition weighed in excess of 40 stone) to the public. Arthur Holland, her great grandson, recalls how the family first made its start on the British fairground:

> She had two sons this Mrs. Payne and one daughter, my grandmother, the daughter, Annie Holland they called her but she wasn't Holland at all then, she was a Payne and she got this forty stone son and one of these here chorus girls or whatever it was said, you ought to take him around the shows, show him. That was the only thing she could do because her husband died ... and this is what she decided to do. What she did, she used to hire a town hall out for half a crown and she used to take him round all the town halls, wherever she could, you understand and show him. This went on until I think she eventually decided to have a little booth of her own, and she bought one, I don't know what it was like and then she used to go around the fairs, with this fat boy, her other son he had been introduced into the fairground business through the fat boy, through him you know him being forty stone, and he started up then and in the olden days he was called Captain Payne.[19]

The fairground exhibitors first presented films in shows which would have been originally any of the types found on the Victorian fair: menageries, illusion booths, marionette or puppet theatres, or circuses. These early presentations usually took place in converted exhibition shows of the two-wagon fronted type. In the case of exhibitors such as Mrs. Crecraft or Mrs. Harris who exhibited her *Living Pictures and Variety Show* in Scotland around 1899, for example, the films would have been shown between acts of lion taming or illusion type performances.[20] A very early combination presentation was exhibited by

Mrs. Bailey.[21] Mrs. Bailey continued to travel the show after the death of her husband and continued to use her ghost show as a combination presentation until 1907 when she appeared with a combined ghost and bioscope show at the Hoppings Temperance Fair in Newcastle.[22]

By the early 1900s these early combination exhibitions gradually expanded as exhibitors like Sophie Hancock and Mrs. Crecraft began to develop their shows in order to satisfy the tastes of an evermore sophisticated audience. Both Sophie Hancock and Elizabeth Crecraft were experienced presenters. Although Sophie Hancock managed the family firm in partnership with her two brothers, the origins of Hancock's *Palace of Varieties* show is confusing as either Hancock's menagerie or their Orton and Spooner *Bio-Tableau* show may have been adapted to form the *Palace of Varieties and Living Pictures*. However, from 1900 to 1906 the two wagon-fronted show gradually became a large organ-fronted exhibition complete with an elaborate 89-key Gavioli organ which was fitted in the centre of the stage, allowing room for the paraders and dancers.[23] These alterations brought further success to the showpeople, and their achievements on the fairground can be gauged by the rapid conversions made to the shows in order to increase their audience capacity. From the 1880s onwards the Hancocks travelled the West Country with their shows and rides including a menagerie and an early Orton, Sons and Spooner works shot reveals a show called the *Bio Tableau* (Fig. 3). In 1899 when the success of moving pictures as a novelty became apparent, a second show was operated by their brother-in-law, Richard Dooner. By 1900 the second show was exclusively Dooners, and left the West Country to travel South Wales, where the family eventually settled and operated permanent-site cinemas.[24] It is likely that this success encouraged Hancocks to convert their show into a cinematograph, but they retained for a year or more several of the lions and the occasional circus act. This two-wagon fronted show was advertised as Hancock's *Palace of Varieties and Living Pictures*. Between 1900 and 1906 further alterations were carried out and the new Marenghi organ was placed in the centre

of the showfront. When the redesigned show was exhibited at Bridgwater Fair, the local reporter for the *Bridgwater Mercury* wrote:

> The show was a veritable showman's triumph ... the whole of the extensive front was occupied with an intensely elaborate organ and lit by varied coloured electric lamps.[25]

However, Sophie Hancock was not only famous in the West Country for her business skills but also for her ability to hold her own in a fight. Father Greville, the editor of the *Merry-Go-Round* wrote the following tribute in 1955:

> Miss Sophie, the female of the species – what a woman she was! She was the undisputed boss of the fairground, and to prove her right, would enter into a battle with anyone, man or women, policemen or civilian. Her vocabulary of swear words was longer and better than any man's, and it was said, that if crossed, she could go on for half-an-hour without repeating herself.[26]

In 1913 the Hancock family suffered a disaster when the majority of their equipment burnt to the ground. A spark from a fire lit by the suffragettes in a timber yard, protesting at the government's refusal to allow Christabel Pankhurst into Plymouth, spread onto the fairground, and caused major damage to the Hancock's equipment.[27] Although the leading showmen of the day arranged a collection in *The World's Fair*, the family never recovered

from this disaster.[28] However, they continued to travel with the equipment they had salvaged, but the First World War severely restricted the movements of fairs, and the business gradually declined. After the death of her brother Charles on 31 August 1914 and William at the end of the War, Sophie Hancock sold what was left of her once thriving business and retired to a small amusement park in London, where she died on 31 August 1926.[29] However, her impact as a pioneer in the early days of cinema exhibition was recalled by Leslie Wood in *The Miracle of the Movies*:

> Everyone in the Cecil Court know well another fairground show-woman, Sophie Hancock, for her great booming voice could be heard long before she came into sight, while her sunburned and weather-beaten face, was as one film maker put it, 'like a map printed on leather'.[30]

In the period between 1900 and 1907, the bioscope shows throughout the country underwent rapid transformations, and showmen like Pat Collins from the Midlands and George Kemp invested heavily in the latest presentations. Another female proprietor of equal standing and business acumen to Sophie Hancock was Madame Crecraft who travelled the Crecraft show with her two sons. The Crecraft family could rightly claim to be showpeople as their family had been travellers for generations. The family began travelling around the turn of the nineteenth century, and when Elizabeth Crecraft was born in 1818 in a living

waggon at Chelsea, her father had already been in show business for approximately thirty years. Their original exhibition was a two-wagon fronted show which featured wax-works, freaks, and a boxing bear. However, it achieved greater fame as a Menagerie, and by 1898 it was presenting films as part of the performance. Like the Hancocks, the Crecraft family also continued to retain lions as part of the performance until 1906. The Crecrafts travelled throughout North Wales, Cheshire and Lancashire.[31] Their show was adapted at a slower rate than the Hancocks, but by 1910 it too had become an organ-fronted show when the large paper organ which had origi-

nally stood on the showfront was replaced by a 75-key Marenghi model. *The World's Fair* in 1910 published the following tribute:

> Mrs. Crecraft is rightly named the veteran of the van, as she is the oldest show

proprietress in the world. This wonderful old lady is 92 years of age, and is still controlling one of the biggest bioscope shows on the road.[32]

The decorations on this show were highly elaborate, and cream and gold was used on the highly original design of the front and organ with its art nouveau shells. By 1908 the bioscope shows were on the increase, and the showpeople adapted, converted or purchased exhibition shows in order to display the latest attraction for the fairgoing public. At the peak of their popularity there were over one hundred of these shows exhibiting on the fairgrounds throughout the United Kingdom. with at least ten per cent of the cinematograph booths being presented by women. Father Greville writing in 1952 remembers Mrs. Simon who attended Buxton Well Dressing in 1899 with her *Electrograph and Vaudeville Show*,[33] and Mrs. Johnston who attended the fair at Ayr in 1909 in the company of George Green and James Manders.[34] These elaborate exhibition shows dominated the landscapes of the great Charter fairs at Hull, Nottingham (Fig. 4) and Oxford. Not since the days of the theatrical booths at Bartholomew Fair in the 1800s had shows been on the increase. The same structures which would have once presented illusions, lions and marionettes now exhibited moving pictures in a variety of booths ranging in size and capacity depending on their original purpose. Mrs. Paine of Kinross, for example, continued to exhibit moving pictures in her old mari-

Fig. 6. *Mrs Annie Holland with bioscope shows and engines, Nottinghamshire, 1900s. [National Fairground Archive.]*

onette show until she bought a purpose-built booth in 1910. After the death of her husband, Mammie Paine was left to bring up a family of seven girls and one boy (Fig. 5). The show travelled in the north east, attending New-castle Town Moor fair each year. Mrs. Paine was a renowned orator, and told a tale at every performance. In 1911 she replaced the old marionette show with its diminutive trumpet organ with the beautiful art nouveau organ-fronted show which had originally belonged to the Cottrells. This was to be the last Bioscope Show to open on the Town Moor.[35] Mrs. Paine died at the age of 95. One famous incident associated with Mammie Paine occurred at King's Lynn. Whilst presenting a show called *Storm at Sea* a misfired rocket landed in a box of live rockets. Knowing the damage this would cause to her customers and her show, Mammie Paine threw herself onto the box to shield the audience. The consequences of this action resulted in severe burns to her face, and henceforth she apparently always gave her performance wearing a mask.

In the period leading up to the First World War, the showpeople continued to invest in their equipment. The fairground business was proving to be a profitable concern and although no records of the weekly income of a cinematograph booth survive, a comparison with the takings of Mrs. Hannah Waddington, who travelled a Switchback Gondola ride throughout Yorkshire from 1898 to 1910, reveals that her average weekly takings were in the region of £100, a considerable sum at that time.[36]

The great shows

It was at this time of prosperity that the bioscope shows underwent their final meta-morphosis when the Orton and Spooner Great Shows started to make their appearance on the fairgrounds. Unlike their predecessors the ground booths and walkup shows, these cine-matograph booths were custom-built for the exhibiting of films, with later models incorporating a projector box to comply with the Cinematograph Act of 1909. One of the leading types of this show which exhibited films on the fairground was Annie Holland's *Palace of Light*. Mrs. Annie Holland, the sister of the *World's Fattest Schoolboy*, travelled one of the largest cinematograph shows on the road (Fig. 6). The Holland family went on to dominate the fairground landscape until the outbreak of the First World War, with their great shows only equalled or surpassed by the shows that Orton and Spooner constructed for William Taylor, Kemps and the Thurstons.

Arthur Sellman provides us with a description of the interiors of these shows which purportedly measured 63 feet by 45 feet. The great shows built by the firm of Orton and Spooner reputedly seated six hundred people, with standing accommodation for another 400. Purpose-built booths such as the *Theatre Unique* and the *No 2 Wonderland* shows, constructed for President Kemp and Pat Collins, also appear to have the same dimensions as the shows that the Holland family exhibited. An idea of the size and cost of these types of show can be found in the for sale columns in *The World's Fair* from around 1912 onwards. A series of advertisements in *The World's Fair* in June and July 1914 furnish us with a description of President Kemp's *Theatre Unique* shows. The show is described as being fifty feet in length, complete with covered trucks, large Marenghi organ, and traction engine. The *Theatre Unique* could claim to be one of the most lavish shows ever travelled throughout the United Kingdom, and it formed part of the great shows constructed by Orton and Spooner from 1906 onwards. The showfront had been custom built by the firm around one of the new 106-key Marenghi organs from Paris, and supposedly cost in the region of £2,000. The centre truck which was constructed to carry twenty tons was purchased for an additional £300. The organ was lowered onto the truck which then opened out to form a fifty foot parading stage. The two carved and gilded staircases which were surmounted by four tall elegant columns from which arc lamps were suspended, cost a further £300.[37]

The original *Palace of Light* began in less grand circumstances as a two-wagon-fronted show built by Orton and Spooner. Annie Holland travelled two versions of the *Palace of Light*. This was a result of a fire in 1912 which severely damaged the show. After the original show was engulfed in flames, Annie Holland purchased an Orton and Spooner show, which had originally belonged to Edwin Lawrence, at an auction in Sheffield. One of the main features was the new show front which dominated the front stage, and was surrounded by elaborate figures and ornate archways. Edwin Lawrence advertised the show for sale in *The World's Fair* in 1911, but it was not until 1912 that it was sold by Tom Norman the auctioneer. An advertisement in *The World's Fair* from March 1912 appears to suggest that Annie Holland bought Lawrence's show purely for the showfront and organ:

> *For Sale:- Wanted known that Mrs. Holland has purchased the whole of Lawrence's cinematograph show.*

> *For sale:- Marionette stage, fit up with truck for sale, one set of seatings, standing gallery, cinebox, two Gaumont cameras and three trucks to go behind the traction engine. All lots to be sold cheap.*[38]

The shows were then taken to Orton and Spooner's yard, and the front stage and organ of Lawrence's show were fitted to the stage, trucks and interiors of Annie Holland's old exhibition. A description from Arthur Fay, who was originally the doorman for the Holland show, reveals a glimpse of their dimensions and extravagance:

> *In the Palace of Light there was seating accommodation for six hundred people with standing room in the gallery for another four hundred. The seating was upholstered in Italian green figured cloth with backs to match, while the side linings were of heavy blue figured plush trimmed and ornamented with gold tassels as also were the side door curtains. From the inside top lining which was of red and gold, were suspended sixteen Japanese lampshades (eight down either side of the ceiling) in pink and gold.*[39]

Orton and Spooner also built a gilded, carved proscenium to frame the screen. It comprised sixteen pieces and included two winged angels holding ribbons supporting a cartouche. This in itself required a 26-foot packing truck.

Performance

As the exhibition became more sophisticated the type of performance presented by showpeople also improved radically. The early film shows relied on the novelty factor of the event, and an incident recalled in *The World's Fair* illustrates the naivety of the first presentations. Mrs. Weir, an exhibitor from Burton on Trent exhibited moving pictures in her *Elec-*

tric Chronograph Empire. Like her contemporaries, Mrs. Weir always tried to use the latest novelties to attract people into her show which featured the Gaumont Chronophone. *The World's Fair* correspondent in 1929 recalls listening to a Gaumont Chronophone in Mrs. Weir's Touring Chronograph Empire in Rugeley, Staffordshire,[40] and Southdown, one of *The World's Fair* columnists in the 1930s, recalls an incident when the weather conditions resulted in the family opening their exhibition without the canvas tilt which covered the booth. However, they still continued to present films in the show and play to full audiences despite the fact that the smoke from the traction engine blew into the show and obscured the films. Although in the early years the novelty of presenting films was a big enough attraction in itself, by 1906, the reporter for the *Bridgwater Mercury* was critical about the overall quality of films presented in the shows:

> Though it may be unkind to say so, the exterior of these shows are more interesting than the interior, for the proceedings prior to filling the house are more lengthy and attractive than the show itself, which usually consists of three living pictures and the thanks of the showman for the public's patronage.[41]

Such artless acceptance on the part of the public could not last, and as the competition grew, the audiences demanded better facilities, newer attractions and greater novelties. The showpeople competed with their rivals, including some of their own fraternity such as George Green and Pat Collins who were opening permanent cinemas in the places at which the showpeople had previously exhibited. The presentation of these films became more advanced with the introduction of the Gaumont Chronophone and with changes in film exhibition practice. Arthur Fay writing as *Southdown* in *The World's Fair* in the 1930s, provides an interesting account of developments in exhibition. In April 1912 when the news of the sinking of the *Titanic* broke, a Gaumont Film Company newsreel was shown of the disaster. To accompany the film, the Holland family arranged a musical sketch which was played on the show's Gavioli organ. As the footage of the disaster was shown,

the musical accompaniment incorporated such tunes as *Afloat on the Ocean Blue, Ship's Bell Rings, The Sailor's Two Step, Crash, An Iceberg, Excitement on Board, Lowering the Boats, Women and Children First*, and the performance ended with *Nearer my God to Thee* and Chopin's *Funeral March.* Admission to such a performance, according to a handbill reprinted in *The World's Fair* in 1936, ranged from 3d to 6d. However, as the shows expanded and the parades became more elaborate, the costs of presenting such attractions became increasingly difficult to meet, and an article that appeared in *The World's Fair* in 1913 contained the following warning:

> The big show has grown past its strength; it will not pay for the proprietor to show for the popular penny admission; the upkeep of the show is too expensive in many cases, two engines and a staff of artistes for parade that in themselves cost the showmen as much almost as it cost a few years ago to run the entire show.[42]

Transition to permanent-site exhibition

Several of the fairground proprietors had already realised the change in fortunes that would eventually result in the decline of cinematograph presentations on the fairground. The most famous and successful of the showmen exhibitors was George Green of Glasgow who by the time of his death in 1915 had opened a chain of thirteen cinemas throughout Scotland.[43] From 1913 onwards the bioscope shows on the fairground gradually declined, and with the outbreak of the First World War, all the cinematograph shows ceased travelling. Instead, they presented static exhibitions in towns and villages where there was no permanent cinemas. The showwomen exhibitors also made the transition to static presentations. These included Mrs. Studt who, after the death of John Studt in 1912, took over the travelling amusements, and eventually built a permanent cinema in Pontyclun.[44] Mammie Paine presented the last bioscope show at Newcastle Town Moor Fair in 1914, then went on to run the Town Hall Cinema in Kinross.[45] Mrs. Annie Holland's *Palace of Light* was open in Measham throughout the First World War, and was still in use when the permanent cinema was erected around the old bioscope show. Mrs. Crecraft and her sons opened a static cinema in Glynneath which was affectionately known by the local people as 'Mams', but still continued to present travelling film shows until it was advertised for sale in *The World's Fair* in 1915.[46] Other women cinema proprietors included Mrs. Whiteley who with her husband travelled a cinematograph show, and opened up a large circuit of halls around Salford and Manchester.[47] However, despite the initial success of the showpeople who made the transition to permanent cinemas, the majority of the showpeople returned to the fairgrounds. After the restrictions were lifted at the end of the War, families like the Hollands, Simons and Proctors all returned to their former life on the travelling fairs.[48]

In conclusion, it can be seen that the bioscope proprietors were a victim of their own success. In the formative years of the introduction of the moving image they cajoled, enticed, and finally created a fascination for the film medium that would eventually prove their downfall. The reasons for the early success of fairground cinema was, according to E.V. Lucas writing in 1906, that:

> The invented story, comic, tragic, pa-

thetic was the staple, there was no royal processions, no conferments of the freedom of cities, no military manoeuvres. Instead of taking the place of illustrated papers, as the cinematograph first did almost exclusively, and still does at the more pretentious halls, it was taking the place of the theatre.[49]

Although exhibitors like George Green, Mrs. Studt and Mammie Paine became pioneers in both fairground exhibition and permanent-site exhibition, other exhibitors were not so farsighted. Historians of early film such as John Barnes and Geoff Mellor have demonstrated that the fairground exhibitors created an audience for the moving image in its formative years, and bridged the gap between the town hall exhibition events and the advent of the static cinema.[50] Although fairground women, unlike their counterparts in settled society, demanded and attained an equal share in the pioneering and lucrative development of the early cinematograph business, the role and contribution made by fairground women still awaits research.[51]

Acknowledgements: I should like to thank Richard Brown, Mervyn Heard and Dave Berry for their assistance in the preparation of this text.

Notes

1. Further information on the latest research into this subject can be found by consulting Stephen Smith, *History of the Fairground Ride*, on the National Fairground Archive, World Wide Web pages: http://www.shef.ac.uk/~nfa/history/rides.

2. See David Braithwaite, *Fairground Architecture* (London: Hugh Evelyn, 1968), and Geoff Weedon and Richard Ward, *Fairground Art* (London: White Mouse, 1981) for a full history of the fairground ride.

3. Stephen Peart, *The Picture House in East Anglia*, (Lavenhalm: Terence Dalton, 1980), 7.

4. For William Haggar, see Dave Berry, *Cinema and Wales* (Cardiff: University of Wales Press, 1994); for Randall Williams, see Vanessa Toulmin, 'Moving Picture Pioneer', *The Fairground Mercury*, 19, (Winter, 1996): 9–15. For biographies of other fairground showmen, see Vanessa Toulmin, 'Bioscope Biographies' in *In the Kingdom of Shadows: A Companion to Early Cinema*, Colin Harding and Simon Popple (eds) (London: Cygnus Publications, 1996): 249–262.

5. Stephen Herbert and Luke McKernan, *Who's Who of Victorian Cinema* (London: British Film Institute, 1996). For considerations of Sophie Hancock and Madame Olinka, see 62–63, 103.

6. *Kinematograph Weekly* (17 June 1926): 54.

7. *British Journal of Photography* (Supplement) 1 April 1898.

8. Vanessa Toulmin, 'There's No Women Like Show-Women: The Pullen Women of South Yorkshire', *Yorkshire Journal* 9 (Spring 1995): 42–50.

9. *The World's Fair* (28 December 1912): 11.

10. See *The Showmen's Year Book 1919* for the obituary of Thomas Horne which recalls his early life as a doormen for Mrs. Ruth Williams' Waxworks show.

11. See *The World's Fair* (8 June 1912): 1 for obituary of Mrs. Emma Fossett and an account of her life on the circus.
12. *The World's Fair* (15 August 1908:): 1.
13. For full details of the fairground proprietors operating living pictures in 1897, see 'The Showmen's World', a weekly column which appeared in *The Era*.
14. Father P. Greville, 'Hancocks of the West', *TheMerry-Go-Round*, 9, no. 1 (1955): 2–7.
15. *Torquay Directory*, 10 August 1898.
16. *The World's Fair* (5 May 1917): 3.
17. *The World's Fair* (28 August 1916): 12.
18. *The World's Fair* (9 April 1909): 4.
19. Arthur Holland, interviewed 20 August 1994.
20. Mrs. Harris' *Living Pictures and Variety Show* travelled in Scotland. It was reported open at Hamilton Fair in 1899, the Vinegar Hill Fairground at Christmas 1905, and was still travelling in 1906.
21. Little else is known other than an account by Father P. Greville in 'Famous Bioscope Shows', *Merry-Go-Round*, 7 (March 1951): 2, in which films shown at Hull Fair in 1898 were presented by Mr and Mrs. Bailey. see *World's Fair* (27 April 1912): 4.
22. Vanessa Toulmin, 'Temperance and Pleasure at the Hoppings: A History of Newcastle Town Moor Fair', *North East Labour History Bulletin*, 29 (1995): 50–64.
23. Father P. Greville, Famous Bioscope Shows, vol. 7 *Merry-Go-Round* (August 1951): 2–3.
24. Dave Berry (1994), 59–60.
25. *Bridgwater Mercury*, 3 October 1906.
26. Father P. Greville, 'Hancocks of the West', *The Merry-Go-Round*, 9, no. 1 (1955): 2.
27. *The World's Fair* (20 December 1913): 12.
28. For details of the Hancock appeal organised in *The World's Fair*, see from 27 December 1913 to 24 January 1914.
29. *The World's Fair* (4 September 1926): 1.
30. Leslie Woods, *The Miracle of the Movies* (London: Burke Publishing, 1947), 112.
31. Dave Berry (1994), 60.
32. *The World's Fair* (5 November 1910): 1.
33. Father P. Greville, 'Famous Bioscope Shows', *Merry-Go-Round,* vol. 7, no. 5 (February 1952): 5.
34. Little is known of this show but it presumably travelled in Scotland because a *World's Fair* report of Ayr Fair in 1909 mentions that Mrs. Johnson's Circus and Bioscope appeared at Ayr along with George Green's and Manders' shows.
35. Father P. Greville, 'Famous Bioscope Shows', *Merry-Go-Round*, vol. 7, no. 10 (New Year, 1953): 4–5.
36. Cash books of Mrs. Hannah Waddington, National Fairground Archive, University of Sheffield.
37. See *The World's Fair* (4 July 1914): 1, 6 and also *The World's Fair* (11 July 1914): 7.
38. *The World's Fair* (12 March 1912): 3.
39. Arthur Fay, *Bioscope Shows and their Engines*, (Lingfield: Oakwood Press, 1966), 27.
40. *The World's Fair* (11 May 1929): 14.
41. *Bridgwater Mercury*, 3 October 1906.
42. *The World's Fair* (7 June 1913): 11.
43. Charles A. Harkins, *We Want U' In: The Story of a Glasgow Institution* (Erdington: Amber Valley Print Centre, 1995).
44. Dave Berry (1994), 60.
45. Father Greville (1953), 5.
46. See *The World's Fair* (3 July 1915): 7 and Dave Berry (1994), 497.
47. *The World's Fair* (18 November 1911): 10.
48. Vanessa Toulmin, 'Telling the tale: The story of the fairground bioscope shows and the showmen who operated them', *Film History* 6 (Summer 1994): 219–237.
49. Cited in Leslie Woods (1947), 113.
50. John Barnes, *The Rise of the Cinema in Great Britain* (London: Bishopsgate Press, 1983).
51. M. C. B. Arthur, 'The Birth of the Super Cinema', *Merry-Go-Round*, vol. 5 (May 1946): 9.

1895

Swedish 'Quality' Film: The Production Output of Orientaliska Teatern, 1911–1912

Mats Björkin

Department of Cinema Studies, Stockholm University, Sweden

IN AN ARTICLE DATED 12 April 1911, the president of the Cinema Committee of The Pedagogical Society of Stockholm, Walter Fevrell, wrote that the leading cinema owner in Stockholm, N. P. Nilsson had 'introduced many bad Danish films that have flooded the market'.[1] For some years, Fevrell had criticised Nilsson, especially for films that 'showed Copenhagen night-life in unseemly detail', e.g. *Massøsens offer* (The Masseuse's Victim), *Den hvide slavhandels sidste offer* (The White Slave-traders' Last Victim, 1911), *Den farlige alder* (The Price of Beauty, 1911) and *Foran Fængslets port* (Before the Prison Gates, 1911). Fevrell reported Nilsson to the police, and although they sometimes forced Nilsson to cut the films he exhibited, they rarely banned them. When Fevrell learned that Nilsson was to produce a further film, Nilsson was again reported to the police.[2] N.P. Nilsson owned six theatres in Stockholm, of which Orientaliska Teatern (The Oriental Theatre), the largest and finest, showed mostly Danish and French three-reelers. Fevrell's irritation concerned the impact

Nilsson's successful repertoire had on other exhibitors in Stockholm. Fevrell argued that Nilsson's 'sensational pieces had destroyed the entire cinema culture in Stockholm', and that the films he was exhibiting were dangerous for 'teenage boys and girls'.[3] Fevrell also criticised the practice of re-titling films where exhibitors did not use a direct translation of the original foreign-language title, and cited the instance of the Danish film *Foran fængslets port* (Before the Prison Gates, 1911) which Nilsson advertised as *Storstadens frestelser* (The Temptations of the Big City). Banned titles were also used to advertise other films.

The films Fevrell regarded as 'sensational' were advertised by Nilsson as *konstfilm* (art films). But Nilsson's art films were not comparable to French *film d'art* or Vitagraph's 'quality films'. The only feature Nilsson's films had in common with such output was the emphasis given to famous Danish, French and German actors. Nilsson's art films were to a large extent modern melodramas, and the terms, *konstfilm* and *heltimmesskådespel* (i.e. three-reelers)[4] were used to characterise

Nilsson's programme and marketing policy. At the same time, he was criticised for the sensational quality of the Danish films he exhibited in a period when the term, 'Danish' had became synonymous with critical opprobrium. This paper will examine the production and exhibition strategies of the Orientaliska Teatern production company, so named after Nilsson's cinema, Orientaliska Teatern. I will argue that the company's early success and its later demise can be explained in terms of its programme and marketing policies.

As Easter 1911 approached, Orientaliska advertised a programme of 'Biblical pictures' that was intended to be screened on Good Friday and Easter Sunday.[5] Given that after Easter the company reverted to its normal programme policy, we may regard the exhibition of quality films as the combination of a wish to be taken seriously, with the desire to exploit the fact that in Stockholm, Easter was regarded more as a holiday than a religious festival. The film the company next exhibited, the Danish *Två mennisker* (Two People, 1911), was advertised as a film with a 'contemporary city setting', so emphasising, once again, a programme of contemporary melodrama.

The film produced by Nilsson that worried Fevrell most was *Stockholmsfrestelser eller Ett Norrlandsherrsskaps äfventyr i den 'Sköna synderskans' stad* (Stockholm's Temptations, or The Adventures of a Northern Lady and Gentleman in the City of 'the Beautiful and Sinful Woman', 1911). This film was written by the journalist and author, Gustaf Uddgren, and directed by his wife, the well-known theatre director and singer, Anna Hofmann-Uddgren. The film is a story about how a sawmill-owner and his young wife from northern Sweden come to Stockholm on vacation. The young wife goes shopping in some exclusive shops. The husband becomes involved with a dancer, and the wife is seduced by a baron. The film ends after a dramatic chase before the couple are reunited.

The advertisements for the film's premiere designated the film as 'the first Swedish three-reeler (*heltimmesskådespel*), set in Stockholm, written by Gustaf Uddgren, performed by popular actors from Stockholm's thea-

tres'.[6] Famous actors from the popular stage (for example, Gösta Ekman) were probably important to the film's successful reception, but more significant was the fact that the film was largely shot in Stockholm. A critic noted the film's many exterior scenes, for example the final chase, but since the film is lost, we do not know how these scenes may have looked. The critic concluded that the patriotic local atmosphere of the film would be in keeping with the theme of 'Swedish Week'.

'Swedish Week' was a campaign for the sale of Swedish products and involved many shops in Stockholm. The campaign started in Stockholm two days after the opening of *Stockholmsfrestelser*. The cinema where the film was shown, Orientaliska Teatern, was situated in the commercial area of the city, so Nilsson exploited the marketing opportunity by advertisements on the third day of the film's exhibition (the first day of Swedish Week) that announced: 'Swedish Week! Swedish Artfilm';[7] and two days later, 'Swedish Week! Support Swedish Art!'[8] Swedish Week coincided with an intense period of consumer spending in which all kinds of shops were involved. Fashion shops and the process of choosing and buying clothes constituted a major interest in the film. Thus the interests of Swedish Week and those commercial interests represented in the film strongly coincided. In a period when an exhibition run of two weeks was standard, *Stockholmsfrestelser* ran for four weeks and may thus be regarded as a highly successful film, as a number of newspapers noted. When the film was revived in October 1911, Nilsson announced that *Stockholmsfrestelser* was 'The only [film] which has been exhaustively reviewed and praised by the Stockholm press'.[9] Although this was an overstatement, the film certainly attracted more attention than usual, a fact that indicates that media attention was important for Nilsson's marketing strategy. According to the critics, the film's attractions lay in the familiarity of its surroundings (street scenes and well-known restaurants where audiences could recognise themselves or friends), and in its topicality.

The next two films Orientaliska produced, *Blott en dröm* (Only a Dream, written and directed by Anna Hofmann-Uddgren, pre-

1895

miere 9 September 1911) and *Stockholmsda-mernas älskling* (The Stockholm Ladies' Darling, written by Gustaf Uddgren, directed by Anna Hofmann- Uddgren, premiere 13 October 1911), continued this tendency. *Blott en dröm* was a two-reeler about a young girl who dreams of romantic love with a young officer only to wake up to reality with a not so romantic fiancé. This film was exhibited with a more sensational piece, *Badlif vid Mölle* (Beach Life in Mölle, 1911), which showed scenes from a beach where men and women bathed together, a film that probably displayed more attraction than *Blott en dröm*. *Stockholms- damernas älskling*, on the other hand, may have demonstrated a more commercial concern since the ladies' lover was Carl Barcklind, a famous singer and actor from the popular stage whose name was given greater emphasis than the film's title in the advertisements which announced the premiere. The fourth film produced by Orientaliska in 1911, *Systrarna* (The Sisters, written by the young female author, Elin Wägner, directed by Anna Hofmann-Uddgren, premiere 12 January 1912) continued the interest in topical events, on this occasion featuring the visit of William Booth, the founder of the Salvation Army, to Stockholm in the summer of 1911. The film is about two sisters, one good and one bad. Even in this film there is a chase – initially by tram then train – through the streets of Stockholm to a fashionable suburb. The film ends with the two sisters walking together in a Salvation Army procession led by William Booth.

After *Systrarna*, the films produced by Orientaliska changed: *konstfilm*, the term that had been used to advertise the earlier films, was given a new meaning. Gustaf Uddgren was a good friend of August Strindberg, and according to a newspaper article, Strindberg was very interested in cinema.[10] Uddgren received permission to film Strindberg's plays and novels, and they started with one of his most famous plays, *Fröken Julie* (Miss Julie) directed by Anna Hofmann-Uddgren. The film opened on Friday, 19 January 1912, three days before Strindberg's 63rd birthday. Strindberg was, by then, a very famous and celebrated author. Weeks before his birthday, a committee had been established to plan his

birthday celebrations which included plans for a national collection to buy Strindberg a gift from the nation. In the advertisements that accompanied the film's premiere, Orientaliska announced: 'Six screenings today [...] The entire gross goes to the Strindberg collection!'[11]

Fröken Julie was heavily criticised by the press. Some reviewers praised the cinematography, but in the main they were negative. The absence of speech was the aspect that most caught the attention of the reviewers, but a disturbing aspect that was also noted was the alliance the film was perceived to make between established author and cinema, the latter regarded, at best, as 'cheap' amusement. Reviews also criticised the ending of the film since the film portrayed the suicide of Miss Julie, an ending which is only implied in the play.[2] This scene was later removed by the censor,[13] Nilsson's old antagonist, Walter Fevrell. Although *Fröken Julie* used actors from Intima Teatern, the company with which Strindberg had been closely associated, neither the advertisements nor the reviews commented on this association. Nilsson, used to poor critical reception, announced, in an advertisement which appeared on 24 January 1912, that even if the reviewers considered the filming of *Fröken Julie* to be inappropriate, Strindberg himself appreciated the film.[14] After only one week, *Fröken Julie* was removed from the programme.

The next film Orientaliska produced was *Fadren* (The Father, directed by Anna Hofmann-Uddgren, premiere 18 March 1912). This three-reeler is the only surviving production from Orientaliska. Although descriptions of the five earlier films show that they were visually advanced and concentrated on city locations (the script for *Systrarna*, for instance, gives instructions for many street scenes), the combination of non-fictional elements and fictional events had been rare in earlier Swedish film. *Fadren* is quite different since, apart from the sequence when the captain goes for a ride, the film is largely a recorded stage performance. Gustaf Uddgren later explained that the actors (some of whom had taken part in the stage production of *Fröken Julie*) wanted to appear as they had appeared in the stage production.[15] *Fadren* was screened for only one week. Later in the year N.P. Nilsson became seriously ill and died in September 1912. Gustaf Uddgren and Anna Hofmann-Uddgren gave up filming, and Orientaliska stopped producing films. In less than one year, Orientaliska had produced six films, only one of which exists today.

The production activities of Orientaliska give rise to many questions, not least the relation of director to producer given that Anna Hofmann-Uddgren was the first Swedish female director. However, in the context of an exhibition history of Swedish film, the shift in the company's production strategies was particularly significant since the film represented a move from the concerns of Copenhagen 'night-life' to Stockholm 'day-life'. The change of location was not only geographical. When Fevrell wrote about 'Danish' films, he was not referring to national specificity. Rather, he invoked a notion that as long as the films were set in Copenhagen (or, for that matter, Berlin or Paris), they took place 'somewhere else'. However, when the films were set in Stockholm, they did not merely employ Stockholm as a backdrop since the shots of the inner city (street scenes, shops, restaurants) were an integral part of the story. As noted earlier, the films were probably successful due to the fact that audiences had, potentially, the opportunity of seeing themselves on the screen. For Fevrell, this must have given cause for concern since the connotation of 'Danishness' in fictional film production had been transferred to the Swedish capital. This not only gave prospective audiences a new perspective on their city, but inscribed it in a discourse associated with modernity and consumption. The ostensible purpose of Swedish Week, however, was to promote Swedish products even if they achieved only local consumption. This event, as a contemporary newspaper article noted, was more important for Stockholm shops than for the sale of Swedish goods

per se.[16] The shift, then, from 'national' to 'local' was reflected in production at Orientaliska Teatern, just as the process of consumption mediated the national in terms of local enterprise.

In the two Strindberg adaptations, the Stockholm milieu was largely absent, although *Fröken Julie* did contain one shot of a famous restaurant at Mosebacke. In *Fadren*, no identifiable location was used though the stage of Intima Teatern, where *Fadren* was produced, would have been regarded as a cultural landmark albeit different to those familiar to the broad mass of cinema-goers. In short, it was difficult, it would appear, to make artistic capital out of Strindberg's reputation, even when the film received a negative response from the press. This was probably due to the fact that Strindberg was perceived to be the leading Swedish author whose artistic status was inviolable. He had become a national monument, and it was deemed inappropriate to use his work in a medium of popular entertainment.

Maybe the emphasis accorded everyday life in representing contemporary Stockholm marks Orientaliska's films as an exception in the history of early Swedish film. While the designation 'Danish' did not accord with the emerging, non-quotidian concerns of Svenska Biografteatern's film dramas, production at Orientaliska demonstrates how a small production and exhibition concern could use consumerism and topical events to attract a predominantly local audience. The company's production strategy also demonstrates that in 1912, it was difficult – if not impossible – to make capital out of a nation's major cultural asset. In this respect, the production interests of Orientaliska Teatern demonstrate that the nation's public sphere could not be easily reconciled with the development of a popular entertainment medium.

Notes

1.   Walter Fevrell, *Stockholms Dagblad (StD)* (12 April 1911).

2.   *Ibid.*

3.   *Ibid.*

4.   Literal translation, 'one-hour drama'.

1895

5. *Stockholms-Tidningen (StT)* (13 April 1911).
6. *StD* (27 April 1911).
7. *StD* (29 April 1911).
8. *StD* (1 May 1911).
9. *StD* (2 October 1911).
10. *Dagens Nyheter (DN)* (1 December 1911).
11. *StD* (19 January 1912).
12. 'Strindbergs 'Fröken Julie' på biograf', *Social-Demokraten* (16 January 1912); 'Strindberg på biograf', *DN*,16 January 1912; ''Fröken Julie' som biografdrama', *Aftonbladet* (16 January 1912).
13. Censorship card nr. 3.777.
14. *StD* (24 January 1912).
15. Gustaf Uddgren, 'Om Strindberg och filmen', *Filmjournalen*, 6, (1920).
16. Notarius (pseud), 'Butikshandeln under Svenska veckan', *StT* (4 May 1911).

The Emergence of an Alternative Film Culture: Film and the British Consumer Co-operative Movement before 1920

Alan Burton

Lecturer in Media Studies, Department of English, Media and Cultural Studies, De Montfort University, The Gateway, Leicester LE1 9BH, UK

OVER THE LAST TWO DECADES there has developed a substantial body of research on left political film activity. The re-emergence of concerns with radical filmmaking practices and theory in the late 1960s prompted a younger generation of cinema historians, critics and practitioners, to examine earlier attempts at 'cultural intervention' by workers' film groups and progressive organisations. Taking an example from Britain, members of the Independent Film Makers' Association recognised that oppositional film practices during the late 1920s and 1930s had constructed:

> ... an important beginning of a struggle for an independent cinema concerned not simply in economic terms but also in terms of the necessity for seeing it in relation to a broader social struggle; they challenged the static situation in which films were simply part of leisure and consumption in capitalist society by setting up different relationships between audiences and films as well as different production relationships, establishing film activity as part of a struggle in ideology.[1]

The new generation of radical filmmakers, through the analysis of an earlier workers' film movement, sought both inspiration and an awareness of the pitfalls to be avoided. The historiography now embraces studies of many of the leading western democracies where left filmmaking was attempted – Germany, Britain, USA and France. A crucial stimulus to that activity, it has been argued:

> ... was the stunning impact of Soviet filmmaking that mobilised concerted left interest in film in the West ... groups organised around the exhibition of *Battleship Potemkin* (1925) and other Soviet films.[2]

1895

However, as an American film historian has recently asserted, films emerged as class weapons from the start and not, as some have argued, in the late 1920s and 1930s.[3] In only two countries has left political filmmaking been considered for the earlier silent period.[4] The political, educational and cultural use of film by left parties in Weimar Germany has long been acknowledged. An important major study has revealed that the German Social Democratic Party (SDP) had been stimulated into an interest in the film medium through an awareness of the widespread film activity of its political opponents, and on the eve of the First World War was already organising film events.[5] After the War the extensive work of both the German Communist Party and the SDP to build a separate working class culture led to an appreciation and utilisation of film far beyond anything attained by left political organisations in the rest of Europe. Attending to a different geo-political context, studies by Steven Ross have described the tension and conflict between progressive and conservative interests within early American film. His examination of this 'Unknown Hollywood' has revealed:

> ... a time when a wide array of liberal, conservative, and radical organisations made theatrical films – films produced for regular cinemas – aimed at politicising millions of viewers. During the early decades of the twentieth century, when the Progressive movement was in its heyday and the fledging (*sic*) film industry in its infancy, suffragettes, labour unions, socialists, religious groups, business associations, government agencies, and a wide array of reformers used film as a means of challenging or defending ideas about society, authority and political life.[6]

Film as an aid in the battle for reform in the Progressive Era has been well documented,[7] yet given the conventional emphasis of the historiography it is striking to have to confront that:

> As early as 1907 – when a Cleveland union man shot and exhibited films of the strike-ravaged Cripple Creek area to enthusiastic audiences – workers, union members, and radicals began making and using movies as a means of reaching millions of Americans with their political visions of past, present, and future struggles. 'We are going to make the projecting lens a weapon for labor', pledged one working-class filmmaker. These films were used for publicising union battles, raising funds, attracting greater turnouts of meetings and rallies, promoting the candidacy of radical politicians, and educating an undifferentiated mass public about unions as a necessary part of American life.[8]

Thus, there existed a clear recognition of the agitational potential of cinema by left activists well before the establishment of the oligarchic studio system and its attendant representational forms which has traditionally been conceived as marking the characteristic capitalistic formation against which worker and labour cinemas posited an 'alternative'. Left cinema, in that early period, can be conceived of as maintaining an oppositional stance against a dominant political economy. However, in the absence of a dominant mode of film production and cinematic representation, pioneer left filmmaking can hardly be considered an 'alternative' cinema practice (alternative to what?), but should rather be appreciated as a particular response to the potential afforded by a new medium that allowed for a multitude of other forms. Ultimately, as historical forces led to the consolidation of a dominant mode of cinema centred on industrial and stylistic practices that reflected and reinforced the established business and political interests, American left political filmmaking of the silent era, which had achieved remarkable success with theatrically released narrative feature films as well as newsreels and actualities, was thwarted by an inability to meet the rising costs of production, oligarchic business strategies and the intransigence of censorship bodies.[9] A second phase of American radical filmmaking commencing in the early sound era has been well documented.[10]

There remains a forgotten side of Labour Movement film activity during the silent period. In Britain the Co-operative Movement, a democratically organised body of millions of consumers which controlled thousands of stores and hundreds of factories and workshops, enthusiastically embraced film to

1895

further its publicity, propaganda and cultural aspirations.[11] The remainder of this paper will examine the Co-operative Movement's use of film, and by complementing the research of Steven Ross, will stress that the historiography of left political filmmaking requires expansion to include an earlier generation of activists.

Studies of the British Labour Movement and film have accorded the Co-operative Movement a marginal role. With a research impetus stimulated by the concerns of the New Left, the post-1960s generation of film historians have placed emphasis on the more radical elements of Labour film, discerning significance in groups like Kino and the Workers' Film and Photo League either allied to, or inspired by, Communist bodies and Marxist-Leninist ideology.[12] Indeed, as Dutch film historian Bert Hogenkamp recently alluded at a Co-operative history conference, despite ample evidence of Co-operative film production and activity on the Continent, none has found its way into existing studies of European left filmmaking.[13]

Similarly, historians of the British Labour Movement, inspired by the same ideals as their colleagues assessing Labour film, have generated little enthusiasm for an institution perceived as reformist and seeking gradual change within existing economic and political structures; accommodating rather than confronting Capitalism. Socialist historians R. Samuel and G. S. Jones have summarised that disregard of Co-operation and suggest a corrective interpretation:

> It is usually treated as a nineteenth century remnant harking back to the remote days of Robert Owen and the Rochdale Pioneers and this picture is reinforced by its nineteenth century historians who conceived its evolution to be that from community-building to shop-keeping. But, in fact, the greatest period of the growth of Co-operation was the first 30 years of this century, not only as a form of retailing, but also as a social and political movement. The utopia of most Labour Party activists at least until the Second World War was entitled the 'Co-operative Commonwealth'. Nearly all Labour families were convinced co-

operators. Thus Co-ops were represented on the National Executive Committee, not out of deference to the pre-history of the Labour Party, but because they represented a crucial component of Labour inter-war strength. The largest women's organisation in the Labour Party was the Co-operative Women's Guild. Meetings of local Labour Parties often took place in recently built Co-op halls.[14]

The 'passivity school' of Labour historians has begun to be challenged and a notion of 'Co-operative Culture', integrating the activities of trade, politics and education, has emerged.[15] The economic and political attacks conducted by business interests on the Co-operative Movement are cited, and the antithetical relationship between Co-operative and Capitalist ideology is stressed. As a Co-operative textbook argued in 1937, Co-operative business organisation offered:

> … a standing challenge to capitalist business, just as Co-operative ideas form a criticism of capitalist economies.[16]

Cultural and educational activities were crucial in developing an awareness of the Movement's history, aims and ideals. Co-operative values and beliefs were communicated through a wide repertoire of cultural forms: the press, libraries, classes, demonstrations, choirs, tea parties, exhibitions, festivals etc. Co-operative propaganda, whether it be a meeting, demonstration, trade-drive, educational class or poster, was pursued with vigour and with the intent of moving one step closer 'Towards the Co-operative Commonwealth'.

As early as 1898 moving pictures were incorporated into the educational and propaganda work of the Movement. That was among the first instances, anywhere in the world, of a Labour organisation putting to use the new technology. Initially, film complemented the traditional magic lantern lecture, a well-established form of address familiar to educational, political and reform organisations. The central manufacturer and banker of the Movement, the Co-operative Wholesale Society (CWS), arranged programmes of illustrated lectures for Co-operative retail societies, and lecturer-lanternists were em-

1895

ployed to tour the trading districts. The nature and extent of Co-operative business and productive activities was a core subject as evidenced by a promotional article for the CWS lantern lectures which appeared in 1898:

> Our slides include views of the Manchester premises and the various home and foreign branches and depots, complete sets to illustrate the processes and manufactures carried on at Crumpsall Biscuit and Sweets Factory, Irlam Soap and Candle Works, Leicester Boot and Shoe Works, Middleton Jam and Pickle Factory, Batley Woollen Factory, Leeds and Broughton Ready-mades and Tailoring Factories, Broughton Cabinet Works, Dunston Flour Mill, and the Irish Creameries of the CWS.[17]

A supplementary lantern lecture service was provided by another federal organisation, the Co-operative Union. With an education department of national responsibility the approach was broader, as was apparent in an address 'on the aims and immense development of Co-operation' at the Birmingham Industrial Co-operative Society in the winter of 1897:

> The lecturer dwelt upon Rochdale the original, Oldham the most advanced, Leeds the largest. Twenty-five slides illustrated the buildings, works and ships of the Wholesale all over the world. Productive Co-operation was then explained, illustrated by views of the Equity, Sundries, Cutlery, and Hebden Bridge works. The indebtness of Co-operation to the great departed was indicated by views of Messrs. Neale, Hughes, and Mitchell; the great living forces by presentments of Messrs. Gray, Maxwell, B. Jones, and McInnes.[18]

The combined lecture programme offered by the CWS and Co-operative Union undoubtedly made an attractive and useful contribution to the propaganda work of a local society's education committee. Members were being provided with a detailed discourse on 'their business': its productive capabilities; the model conditions enjoyed by employees in its factories; its history, aims, ideals and

achievements; its leaders and thinkers. The magic lantern lecture provided an attractive 'audio-visual' component which supplemented numerous pamphlets, periodicals, newspapers, meetings and classes. Lantern lectures also offered comment on social and political issues, as in the case of a Co-operative Union lecture by Miss Mayo when she addressed Chester-Le-Street Society in 1900:

> The lecturer reviewed the conditions under which work in many of our large industries is carried on, showing the many hardships and dangers to which factory and home workers, male and female, are subjected. She condemned the conditions of industrial life which permitted, and even encouraged, the dark horrors of the sweating system, and the regulation of wages by the poverty of the employed; and quoted verified instances of the abject poverty of the workers under the most favourable circumstances ... The lecture concluded with an earnest appeal to the audience to support the Co-operative factories, which were equipped on the most humane and modern methods, and whose work was carried on under trade union conditions as to hours of labour and rate of pay, and who were thus enabled to turn out products of enhanced value.[19]

Taken together, those submissions articulated a powerful confrontation to competition, and construct what Bert Hogenkamp has called, for a later period, a 'Deadly Parallel': a kind, just and humane system of trading offered by Co-operation, contrasted with a cruel and exploitative system embodied in Capitalism.

The novelty of 'animated photographs' was readily appreciated for attracting audiences to meetings which would then be presented the requisite propaganda through the tried and tested method of lecture – 'illuminated with limelight views'. As early as November 1897 a professional entertainer, MARCROFT, was advertising his services to Co-operative societies offering them 'living pictures' through the magic of a cinematograph.[20] It is not possible to ascertain if, indeed, it was this actual performer who was involved with the initial presentations of animated pictures to gatherings of Co-operative society members. Such shows began to appear early in 1898 with exhibitions at the Carluke Society and the Norwich Society.[21] At the former a cinematographic exhibition provided entertainment following a jubilant meeting wherein the chairman informed members that a local boycott by hostile traders had been defeated. The novelistic 'living pictures' were undoubtedly a popular draw, and were frequently featured to interest children in the proceedings.[22]

Commencing in 1899 the CWS began to commission films of its own productive works which were interspersed with conventional lantern slide presentations. The first films showed views of the soap works at Irlam, the Crumpsall biscuit factory and the tea warehouses of the English and Scottish Joint Co-operative Wholesale Society in London. It is probable that a CWS employee, Mr T.P. Crowther, was responsible for shooting the films, and a suitable commentary was provided by a member of the lecturing staff during projection. One of the earliest reports of a film show featuring a Co-operative subject recorded the procedure thus:

> The lecturer's subject was 'The Co-operative Wholesale Society: Its Origin and Work'. A large number of ordinary lantern slides were shown, illustrating the primitive way in which the Wholesale began, the difficulties with which it had to contend, and the gigantic strides the society had made. He concluded with the cinematograph, showing the operatives at work at the great Wheatsheaf boot factory at Leicester, tea weighing by electricity at the London warehouse, and various other processes.[23]

At the turn of the century a typical film 'programme' might consist of CWS industrials, humourous subjects, scenics, and war films depicting topical events in the Cape.[24] A film show could last as long as one and a half hours.[25] In the winter of 1903–04 the CWS purchased a Gaumont camera and projector which allowed for an increase in the length of an individual film to 150 feet,[26] and was employing two full-time lecturer-projectionists to tour the country (Mr T.P. Crowther and Mr P. Ryan).[27] Screenings would have

typically taken place in Co-operative halls belonging to the society, although shows were also given in churches, chapels and village halls, even some in the open air. Such provision, especially in rural districts, undoubtedly gave many their first encounter with moving pictures:

> It is worth noting that they helped to popularise the cinema as it is understood today by taking films into hundreds of towns and villages, particularly in the North of England, where they had never been seen before.[28]

Film and lantern shows were often used to support specific trade campaigns. A presentation given at Congleton Society in 1913 illustrates the policy, and also shows how slide and moving picture technologies were used in tandem up till the First World War. A lecture on 'The CWS and Its Works', illustrated by lantern slides and cinematograph films:

> ... showed goods manufactured by the CWS from the raw material to the finished article. Mr. H. Redfern (Chairman of the educational committee) impressed upon the members the need for more loyalty to their own society and to the CWS. At the conclusion of the lecture samples of CWS productions were distributed free.[29]

Usually, lecture, films and/or slides, and samples were themed:

> 'The CWS Pelaw Works and Workers' – polish; 'The Orchards and Fruit Farms and Works of the CWS' – fruit; 'The CWS Jam Works at Middleton Junction ' – preserves; 'Factory Land Folk and Crumpsall Biscuit and Sweet Land' – biscuits and confectionary.[30]

A humorous approach was adopted in a promotional campaign for soap produced at the CWS Irlam Soap Works, again supported by films and lantern slides:

> Mr Crowther (CWS) gave a most interesting account of the manufacture of soap and candles at the Irlam works, which was greatly enjoyed by the large audience present. The lecture concluded with a washing competition for men. The competitors were allowed five minutes in which to wash an article of domestic use.

1895

The first and second prize-winners were Messrs. Tranter and Williamson who received parcels of Irlam specialities, kindly presented by the CWS. Great amusement was caused by this competition ... samples of CWS soap & c., were distributed at the close.[31]

A more serious event had been staged at Tonbridge in 1911, where the local cinema, the Star Picture Hall, was hired, and two presentations by a Co-operative Union lecturer, Mr Hainsworth, were given to a combined audience of 1200 on the subject of 'The Principles and Benefits of Co-operation'. He began by:

> ... calling attention to the evils of the 'sweating' system. He urged upon those who were not already members to join the stores and share the benefits, and help to remedy this great evil. Views were also shown of various productive factories at home and abroad. At the close of each performance Co-operative literature was distributed.[32]

In the years leading up to the First World War the Movement's appreciation of film continued to develop. Most of the major factories were filmed, as well as CWS operations abroad. The average length of a film was 1000 ft, which by then were produced with their own intertitles, precluding the need for an accompanying lecturer if desired. It has been claimed that the lecture service drew on a library of nearly 40 films.[33]

In 1914, a perceptive article appeared in the widely read *Co-operative News*. It argued for the Movement to adopt a wider utilisation of the cinema, and further indicated how much more progressive the Co-op was, in comparison with other elements of the British Labour Movement, in its consideration of the new medium. Cinema policy was to conform to the traditional Co-operative ideal of 'universal provision':

> The ultimate object of our activities should be that we should not be dependent upon anybody except ourselves. We should have our own colleges, our own educational institutions of every character. We should provide our own amusements, our own forms of social

enjoyments. And our amusements and social enjoyments should be as pure as should be the food and the clothes we supply for our material needs ... Why then not bring in the cinema? We are extremely well organised for its use; we have our buildings in which it could be utilised. Its purpose would be that of entertainment, education and social contact.[34]

The Movement thus claimed a responsibility for the members' leisure as well as material needs. Moreover, the author recognised the potential of film to expand the membership:

> The cinema would lend itself to a splendid means of propaganda, an attractive means of propaganda, and at the same time it would be a fine educational feature in both Co-operative and general subjects. The great advantage to us would be its spread of a knowledge of Co-operative activities in a way that the rank-and-file of the movement would come to see and learn. We are always talking about the necessity of reaching the masses and bringing the masses together. The cinema would do this for us.[35]

The writer showed an awareness of the ideological significance of leisure and culture warning that:

> If we do not make use of it, it will remain in the hands of other people to detract from our own forms of entertainment.[36]

And finally, a prescription was offered in the recommendation for a national organisation to arrange production, to control distribution, and organise exhibition. In the context of the pre-war British Labour Movement that was a progressive attitude.

Discussion regarding the value of the cinema to Co-operation continued. Only a few days after the appearance of the article, a lecture entitled 'The Camera as an Educator' was delivered at Holyoake House, the headquarters of the Co-operative Union. Once again the educational potential of moving pictures was explored, and in the demonstration the lecturer:

> ... threw on the screen illustrations of the CWS factories, at the same time appealing to his audience to support the productions

of these factories, *and thus aim a decisive blow at the sweated industries.*[37]

Films could thus aid in stressing the 'Co-operative difference', the crucial ideological and economic distinction between Co-operation and Capitalism. Advocates of cinema had not yet begun to grapple with questions of film form. In all cases the simple actuality film, depicting successful Co-operative production, was envisaged, and the potential of narrative film was not explored, somewhat in contrast to developments in America.

Film production and exhibition was also organised at the level of the local society: Co-operative production in the society's bakery, farms and workshops; retailing in its numerous branch stores; and the activities of the guilds, children's groups and educational committee – collective expressions of the 'Co-operative Community' – were all likely subjects of cinematic representation. For example, in 1905 members of the Stratford Society enjoyed:

> A cinematograph display of the procession of the society's horses and waggons during Congress.[38]

The only two surviving Co-operative films of the pre-First World War period depict Co-operative society processions (usually refered to as 'demonstrations'), and would have been screened as reminders of the day's joyous events.[39] At the eastern coastal town of Lowestoft film was used in a more enterprising manner. To help promote custom for the recently opened fifth branch store, the society:

> ... adopted the cinematographic film for advertising purposes. Striking films have been obtained of the central premises showing the movements of members in and out of the buildings, and also being served in the grocery department; the processes of bread-baking and despatching also have been filmed. The scenes are being shown three times daily to crowded audiences at the Picture Palace.[40]

Lowestoft Society's use of the local cinema in its promotional endeavours indicates another facet of the interaction of Co-operation and film, at the level of exhibition. In some regions, and for some societies, the local Co-op hall had proved a convenient site for early film exhibition. For instance, the Finedon Industrial Co-operative Society gave regular cinematograph entertainments, the revenues from which helped cover the financial losses incurred through other activities such as flower shows and garden fetes.[41] In addition, Co-op halls were regularly hired to local showmen. A study of early film production and exhibition in the North of England has revealed multiple occasions whereby a Co-op hall was put to such use: Henry Hibbert held a display at the Co-op Hall, Bingley on 22 February 1900; the Weisker Bros., who by 1914 operated a circuit of twenty-two halls in the North, had begun with shows in the St. Helen's Co-op Hall in 1907; in 1909, A.O. Andrews from Batley utilised the nearby Industrial Hall of the Dewsbury Pioneers Industrial Society for an exhibition of 'Andrew's Pictures'; and before the First World War, the Co-op Hall at Crewe, known locally as 'Hand's Kino', became a regular venue for Arthur Hand and Son.[42] Consequent upon the provisions of the 1909 Cinematograph Act, numerous Co-operative societies licensed their premises for cinema exhibition. The 1914 edition of the *Kine Year Book* lists the following in its directory of Kinemas: Co-operative Hall Cinema, Fleetwood; Co-operative Hall, Crewe; Co-operative Picture Hall, Batley; Co-operative Hall, Leigh; Co-operative Hall, Ashton-in-Makefield; Co-operative Hall, Bacup; Co-operative Hall, Bradford; and the Co-operative Hall, St. Helens, amongst others.[43] Such provision emphasised the local society's central position within the culture of the local community, and would have aided public relations and ultimately membership.

The advent of war precluded further progression by the Movement in its cinema activities. Nationally, the First World War led to many crucial developments in terms of film propaganda and a more general awareness of its uses and potential. Shortly after the ending of the hostilities, innovation was again apparent in the Co-operative Movement's approach to cinema. A further article appeared in the Movement's influential weekly newspaper, which then had a circulation of about 100,000. It was strongly advocated that local societies should take the lead demonstrated

1895

by a few pioneers, and invest in picture houses:

> Co-operation, that great industrial and commercial union of the working people, has, or should have, the strongest possible interest in the cinema world. At present there are very few societies which can boast of their own picture house, and yet, as we hope to point out, every society in Britain should certainly possess its own movie-house for the pleasure, profit, and education of its members.[44]

A scheme was proposed which went considerably beyond the operation of an entertainment palace:

> From the educational standpoint, the cinema can be of great use to us. Let us envisage Co-operative cinema-houses in every decent-sized town or village, with a central film-producing department at the CWS.[45]

The reasoning behind this expansive proposal was unextraordinary: the traditional desire to confront the private capitalist:

> We strongly urge that the Co-operative people of this country take up the cinema movement with enthusiasm. Not alone from a point of pleasure or profit do we urge this upon our readers, for there are more serious issues to consider. The 'movie' trade of this country is at present in the hands of private companies, whose sole aim is personal aggrandisement. These folks must of necessity become linked up with the vested interests that the Co-operative ideals look forward to shattering. The press of this country, as is well known, is largely in the hands of the reactionaries; and the day is not far distant, if it has not already dawned, when these same people will endeavour to mould the public mind to their way of thinking through the picture world.

> On the other hand, if our movement is alive to its opportunities we shall be able, by the aid of our local cinema-houses, to carry out splendid propaganda work for Co-operation. The time to do it all is now. The need was never more urgent than it is at present. We possess both the capital and the people to make our scheme a splendid success. Let us take our courage in both hands and start building our flicker palaces at once.[46]

Unsurprisingly, the full details of the proposal were never acted upon, and those developments which were realised are outside the period of review of this paper. However, their general contours are worth noting. In 1921 a new scheme was announced whereby a series of films would receive national distribution to commercial cinemas. In what was an important advance, the films assumed a narrative approach in their advocation of the benefits of Co-operation, and six titles were produced in the initial series: *Money in the Wrong Place; Manufacturing Goods for Use, not for Making Profit; Marrying Money; Clothing a Statue; The Penny, What Can be Done With It?;* and *Economic Power: the Power of Possession.*[47] Film production was also commenced at the Royal Arsenal Co-operative Society (RACS) in South London. In 1918, a young and energetic Joseph Reeves was appointed as the society's education secretary, and he would prove an outstanding innovator in putting film to use in the cause of Co-operation, and a tireless propagandist for political filmmaking on the left.[48] His first involvement with the medium came in 1920 with a film commission from the Gaumont Company, *The Evolution of Modern Bakery,* which detailed the activities at the RACS bakery at Brixton. A second film followed in 1921, constructed in the popular newsreel format, which, it was reported, included views of the Brixton bakery, the society farm, 'Shornells' the society education centre, and a football match between employee clubs. A further film of 1922 expanded on the range of trading and cultural activities undertaken by the society: the garage, tailoring, housing estate, engineering shops, sports ground and travel club.[49] The RACS, under the stewardship of Joe Reeves, continued to develop its cinema activities throughout the inter-war period.

This paper has sought, in alliance with earlier researches by Steven Ross, to move emphasis away from the inter-war period in discussing political filmmaking on the left. It has demonstrated that such activity was well-established in the early cinema period,

1895

when the British Consumer Co-operative Movement had pursued its commercial, political and cultural aims through investment in the new technology. None of the numerous CWS films produced prior to 1920 have so far been located and, therefore, the construction of a history of Co-operative film has had to rely on evidence available in Co-operative/labour newspapers and periodicals. In introducing his work Steven Ross has recognised that such sources have been under-valued by film historians, just as film and mass communications have not achieved adequate attention from traditional social and Labour historians. The research agenda inaugurated by Steven Ross, and complemented here, will hopefully unite film and Labour historians in the common aim of determining the nature and extent of workers' filmmaking and socialist propaganda in the first three decades of the twentieth century, a period so crucial in the formation of both the cinema-industrial apparatus and the Labour Movement. If that can aid a contemporary generation of radical filmmakers in their challenge to hegemonic elites then it is effort well expended.

Acknowledgements: The author gratefully acknowledges permission from John Libbey to publish this essay in *Celebrating 1895*. This work first appeared in *Film History* 8 (1996): 446–457.

Notes

1. Quoted in Paul Willemen, 'Presentation' in Don MacPherson (ed), *British Cinema: Traditions of Independence* (London: BFI, 1980), 3.

2. Jonathan Buchsbaum, 'Left Political Filmmaking in the West: The Interwar years' in Robert Sklar and Charles Musser (eds), *Resisting Images* (Philadelphia: Temple University Press, 1990), 2. The essay provides a useful summary of the subject and secondary sources.

3. Steven J. Ross, 'Cinema and Class Conflict: Labour, Capital, the State, and American Silent Film' in Sklar and Musser, *op. cit.*

4. It should be noted that for both financial and technical reasons most workers' films were produced on sub-standard film without sound well into the 1930s. However, a conventional periodisation of cinema history has it that the sound film was firmly established in the industrialised democracies by 1930–31, and to all intents and purposes the silent era was over.

5. Bruce Murray, *Film and The German Left in the Weimar Republic* (Austin: University of Texas Press, 1990), 17–18.

6. Steven Ross, 'The Unknown Hollywood', *History Today* (April 1990): 41.

7. In particular, see Kay Sloan, *The Loud Silents – Origins of the Social Problem Film* (Chicago: University of Illinois Press, 1988); Kevin Brownlow, *Behind the Mask of Innocence* (London: Johnathan Cape, 1990).

8. Ross, 'Cinema and Class Conflict' :77.

9. *Ibid.* For an influential thesis on the emergence of an industrial-stylistic basis for a dominant cinema, see David Bordwell, Janet Staiger and Kristin Thompson *The Classical Hollywood Cinema* (London: Routledge, 1985). For a discussion of the early narrative Labour film, *A Martyr to his Cause* (1910), which dealt with the McNamara case, see Philip S. Foner, '*A Martyr to his Cause*: The Scenario of the First Labor Film in the United States', *Labor History* 24 (1983): 103–111.

10. See Russell Campbell, *Cinema Strikes Back: Radical Filmmaking in the US, 1930–1942* (Michigan: UMI, 1982); William Alexander, *Film on the Left*, (Princeton: Princeton University Press, 1981).

11. In 1914 the British Consumer Co-operative Movement comprised 1385 retail societies, a combined membership of 3 million, and an annual turnover of £88million. For a recent popular history of the Movement, see Birchall, J. *The People's Business* (Manchester: Manchester University Press, 1994).

12. In particular, see MacPherson, *op. cit.* Bert Hogenkamp, *Deadly Parallels: Film and the Left in Britain, 1929–39* (London: Lawrence and Wishart, 1986); Trevor Ryan '"The New Road to Progress" The Use and Production of Films by the Labour Movement, 1929–39' in James Curran and Vincent Porter, *British Cinema History* (London: Weidenfeld and Nicholson, 1983).

13. B. Hogenkamp, 'Co-operative Film Production on the Continent', paper delivered at the 'Towards Tomorrow' Co-operative History Conference, Stanford Hall, July 1994. In 1927 the International Co-operative Congress resolved to promote the use of propaganda films among its member societies.

1895

In 1930 the International Co-operative Alliance published its first *Catalogue of National Co-operative Films* which included 135 titles from 17 countries.

14. R. Samuel and G.S. Jones, 'The Labour Party and Social Democracy' in R. Samuel and G. S. Jones, *Culture, Ideology and Politics* (London: Routledge and Kegan Paul, 1982): 327–328.

15. Peter Gurney, 'Heads, Hands and The Co-operative Utopia: An Essay in Historiography' in *North West Labour History* 19 (1994/95).

16. Fred Hall and Will Watkins, *Co-operation* (Manchester: Co-operative Union, 1937): 357. For an examination of the attacks on the Movement, see Paddy Maguire, 'Co-operation and Crisis: Government, Co-operation and Politics, 1917–1922', and Neil Killingback, 'Limits to Mutuality: Economic and Political Attacks on Co-operation During the 1920s and 1930s', in Stephen Yeo (ed) *New Views of Co-operation* (London: Routledge, 1988).

17. *The Wheatsheaf*, vol. 3, (December 1898): 94. An anecdotal account of the work of the CWS lecture staff before the First World War can be found in Harry Holden, 'Magic Lanterns Publicised CWS Productions', *The Producer* (April 1960): 33–34.

18. *Co-operative News* (11 December 1897): 1374. The named persons are an assemblage of Co-operative and Socialist luminaries.

19. *Co-operative News* (20 October 1900): 1187. By the turn of the century female lantern lecturers were becoming increasingly evident in the ranks of the profession, and the 'fair sex' were attracting comment in the trade press for their technical competence, see *The Optical Magic Lantern Journal* (May 1900): 57.

20. *Co-operative News* (6 November 1897): 1244.

21. *Co-operative News* (19 March 1898): 307; *Co-operative News* (23 April 1898): 453.

22. See, for instance, the report of a CWS film show at Lincoln, *Co-operative News* (3 February 1900): 118.

23. *Co-operative News* (15 December 1900): 1440.

24. 'War views' were a part of the entertainment at both Burton-on-Trent and Haywards Heath in the spring of 1900, see *Co-operative News* (17 February 1900): 174; *Co-operative News* (24 February 1900): 191.

25. *Co-operative News* (5 April 1902): 408.

26. Sydney Box, 'Britain's First Advertising Films Were Shown in 1899', *The Commercial Film* (March 1936): 6.

27. 'Sevices provided by the CWS Film Department', *The Co-operative Education Bulletin* (March 1952): 15.

28. Box: 6.

29. *Co-operative News* (25 October 1913): 1421.

30. *Co-operative News* (15 March 1913): 348; *Co-operative News* (21 November 1914): 1418; *Co-operative News* (4 April 1914): 439; *Co-operative News* (11 October 1913): 1364.

31. *Co-operative News* (28 February 1914): 281.

32. *Co-operative News* (4 March 1911): 267.

33. Box: 6.

34. Anon, 'The Cinema. Should It be Used for Co-operative Purposes? How to Reach the Masses', *Co-operative News* (28 February 1914): 268–269.

35. *Ibid.*

36. *Ibid.*

37. Anon, 'Co-operators and the Cinema', *Co-operative News* (21 March 1914): 358, emphasis added.

38. *Co-operative News* (25 February 1905): 231.

39. The film of the Wishaw Co-operative Gala (1909) is preserved at the Scottish Film Archive, and the film of the Wrexham Co-operative Society Procession (1912) is preserved at the Welsh Film Archive.

40. Anon, 'Lowestoft's Enterprise', *Co-operative News* (1 August 1914): 984.

41. William M. Amey, *Jubilee History of the Finedon Industrial Co-operative Society Ltd., 1868–1918* (Manchester: CWS, 1918): 27.

42. G.J. Mellor, *Picture Pioneers* (Newcastle: Frank Graham, 1971).

43. For a history of Co-operative cinemas spanning the period up until the late 1960s, see Alan Burton,

1895

'The People's Cinemas: The Picture Houses of the Co-operative Movement', *North West Labour History Journal* 19 (1994/95).

44. Robert Fyfe, 'Co-operation and the Cinema. Why not our own Picture Houses as a means to Splendid Propaganda Work?', *Co-operative News* (17 January 1920): 4.

45. *Ibid.*

46. *Ibid.*

47. Anon, 'Pictorial Propaganda', *Co-operative News* (9 April 1921): 5. For a brief description of *Money in the Wrong Place* and *Clothing a Statue*, see 'A Silent Teacher', *Co-operative News* (10 September 1921): 9. None of these films has been located.

48. For a history of the Co-operative Movement and film into the sound era, see Alan Burton, *The People's Cinema: Film and The Co-operative Movement* (London: NFT, 1994).

49. *Co-operative News* (5 November 1921): 10. *The Evolution of Modern Bakery* (1920) and the untitled film of 1922 have recently been preserved at the National Film and Television Archive. For further details on these films, see Alan Burton, *The British Co-operative Movement Film Catalogue* (Trowbridge: Flicks Books, 1997).

1895

Corruption, Criminality and the Nickelodeon

William Uricchio and Roberta E. Pearson

University of Utrecht, Kromme Nieuwegracht 29, 3512 HD Utrecht, The Netherlands;
and Centre for Journalism Studies, University of Wales, Cathays Park, Cardiff, UK

WE BEGIN WITH THE SAD STORY of the rise and fall of Gaetano D'amato, a young Italian-American who went from bootblack to the relatively prominent position of deputy chief of New York City's Bureau of Licenses, the government office that issued common show licences to the city's nickelodeons. In October 1908, following an extensive investigation of the Bureau, D'amato was arrested, 'charged with grafting'.[1] Said a government report:

> The facts indicate that in place of allowing these matters to take the regular course, he put himself to considerable trouble in many cases, and interested himself beyond the limits of his usual duties, in order to 'expedite' the issuance of licenses, notwithstanding that in so doing, he was acting contrary to rule and prescribed practice."[2]

In one such instance, D'amato issued a licence contrary to the Fire Department's expressed disapproval of the proposed nickelodeon premises. Despite such 'expediting', often done for his fellow countrymen, the majority of those testifying against D'amato were Italian. Others among his countrymen supported him, as D'amato's plight called forth contra-dictory reactions from the 'Italian colony of New York, with its several hundred thousand members', which *The New York Times* reported was 'split wide open over [his] arrest':

> Little else has been talked of all week among the politicians of the colony. The older men, the ones who have always resented D'amato's rapid rise, shake their heads and declare they had long foretold it. But with the younger element, who accepted D'amato as a sort of leader, they declare it is all a plot.[3]

The story, as was typical for the times, places the nickelodeon within a sordid nexus of political corruption, an alien underclass, and public menace. The new film medium had quickly found itself caught up in the social debate over national values and identity that raged at the time of its widespread proliferation during the first decade of the new century. Between 1880 and 1920, so intense were the pressures exerted upon the social fabric by rapid urbanisation, increasing immigration, labour strife, economic depressions and so forth that some historians have characterised the period as one of hegemonic crisis.[4] During its first decade, the cinema posed no threat to bourgeois culture: short 'actuality' (non-fiction) films served a didactic purpose and were shown in vaude-ville houses which savvy entrepreneurs had transformed into sites of 'family entertain-ment'. But circa 1905, when story films emerged as the major genre and the nickel-odeon emerged as the primary exhibition venue, the formation of a large urban audi-ence, frequently perceived as composed of workers and immigrants, caused the cinema to be associated in the public mind with those 'cheap amusements', such as dance halls, penny arcades and even ice-cream parlours, that were all held to have a demoralising influence upon their patrons.[5] In 1908, the mayor of New York City revoked the licences of some 500 nickelodeons, attesting to a moral panic shared by social/cultural elites around the country who saw the cinema as emblem-atic of the larger social crisis. Industry executives responded by struggling to disas-sociate the medium from the workers and immigrants perceived as threatening the status quo and to establish it as a mainstream, respectable entertainment, while tales of cor-ruption, immorality, fires, collapsing balconies and other outrages circulated pub-licly in the popular press and privately in the official reports of state and civil institutions. Government officials, both corrupt and up-right, clergymen, both moralistic and supportive, civic reformers, both repressive and progressive, and theatrical entrepre-neurs, wanting simply to crush the competition, all pursued their own agendas, in the process contributing to this negative discourse.[6]

During the nickelodeon period, anecdotes about D'amato and his ilk formed part of an interpretive framework constructed in the popular press and private documents and tracing a progression from the disequilibrium of anarchy and corruption associated with the marginalised worker and immigrant classes to a rational equilibrium associated with so-cial/cultural elites imposing control on the new medium. The period's archival record (court cases; fire insurance records; journal-istic reports; police investigations; city ordinances and civic reform groups' investi-gations) fits within this interpretive framework and thus both constituted and was constituted by the discourse of rationality.

The period's interpretive framework posi-tioned Gaetano D'amato as a corrupt individual, an exploiter of the underclass, vanquished by the powers of progressive re-form.

Today's historians might take a similar view of D'amato, for, in the absence of other sources, the archival record established by the period's elites has come to constitute the 'facts' that comprise historical evidence. Film historians relying upon this record have per-force worked within the period's own interpretive framework, perceiving the eco-nomic and moral controls imposed upon the film industry as beneficial, or, at least, inevi-table, and not considering the motivations or responses of those largely excluded from the archival record. One of the first chroniclers of the American film industry, Benjamin Hampton, wrote of the 'utmost confusion' that permeated:

> ... the exhibiting branch of the industry. [There were] a few store-show owners of intelligence, good taste and sound busi-ness sense, who were struggling to elevate the tone of the business. In competition with this handful of progressives were nine or ten thousand other exhibitors who were working their way up from the low-est levels of commercial and industrial experience.

Among this nine or ten thousand were 'immi-grants who had been operating cheap lunch rooms and restaurants, candy and cigar stores ... Few of these foreigners could read or write English ...'[7] But after a few astute men im-proved film quality and cleaned up exhibition sites, 'not only did dimes instead of nickels pour into the better theaters, but more throngs of customers formed the habit of "going to the movies"'.[8] Lewis Jacobs, another early film historian, wrote approvingly of moral con-trols, avowing that the National Board of Censorship was formed 'to insure respect-ablity and good citizenship principles in future films'. He closed his chapter on the beginnings of the nickelodeon period by stat-ing: 'Secure on the moral front, the close of this period saw the business foundations of the motion pictures laid'.[9]

Later generations of scholars, although more

1895

sympathetic than their predecessors to the people at the bottom, nonetheless produced similar models of top-down moral and economic control; this replication resulted, we would argue, from their reliance upon the same evidentiary sources. Robert Sklar, in his admirable and groundbreaking *Movie-Made America*, says:

> The growing notoriety of nickelodeons brought movies to the attention of the middle-class men and women who served the institutions of social control – the churches, reform groups, some segments of the press, and ultimately the police ... Although they wanted to exert their authority over the producers, it was clear that the exhibitors were both a more vulnerable and more acceptable target for attack.[10]

Sklar concludes his chapter on 'Nickle Madness' by stating that 'as power changed hands in the motion picture industry it passed not to middle-class reformers and cultural custodians, but to members of the very immigrant ethnic groups they sought to influence and control'.[11] While aware of the irony of this triumph of what we might now term the 'under-class', Sklar neglects to point out that the 'immigrant ethnic groups' achieved their successes because 'middle-class reformers and cultural custodians', in concert with some elements of the film industry, had established moral and economic controls that transformed the medium from a despised cheap amusement to a respectable mainstream entertainment. Tom Gunning makes precisely this argument:

> The stage was set for struggle and transformation. Production wanted to reassert control over distribution. Individual production companies fought among themselves for pre-eminence within the reorganisation. Along with this economic struggle, an ideological transformation of the image of film had to take place to turn aside the criticisms of reformers and public officials. For both economic and ideological reasons, film had to be raised from the status of a cheap entertainment and take its place among other socially respectable forms of narrative representation.[12]

When we began our investigation of cinema exhibition in New York City between 1907 and 1913, we too found the period's interpretive framework powerfully persuasive and would have told the story from a top-down perspective in the following manner. Faced with the social upheaval engendered by the growing popularity of the new film medium, Mayor George B. McClellan and other city officials at first relied upon the powers granted them by pre-existing state statutes and city ordinances, but this legislation rapidly proved inadequate. Realising the inefficacy of existing control mechanisms, various social elites – McClellan's successor, Mayor William J. Gaynor, civic reformers, fire underwriters and others – joined together to draft a detailed ordinance regulating moving picture exhibition venues, eventually passed by New York City's Board of Aldermen in 1913.

Were one seeking to impose coherence upon these events through the customary historiographic practice of periodisation, one could characterise the 1907–09 period as fairly anarchic, with the state's primary response being outright suppression, and the 1910–13 period as one of containment, regulation and rationalisation. One might even detect in the period's discourse a Foucauldian trajectory from morality and personified authority to rationality and systematisation, in which highly visible means of control, such as suspending licences, were replaced by the disciplinary micro-techniques of the regulation of the architectural space, the employees and the cinema audience. This trajectory would position Gaetano D'amato as a relic of an outmoded and rapidly transforming system.

We at first relegated much of the D'amato incident to the status of 'period colour', along with other fragmentary and anecdotal material that failed to fit comfortably within our narrative. We had concluded that the comparative rarity and random occurrence of such evidence prevented it from fitting the historiographical models of consistency, resonance, etc. that determine what constitutes 'valid' historical evidence. But in one of those radical and fortuituous shifts of perspective that sometimes occurs in historical research, we realised that this lack of 'fit' stemmed from the period's archiving practices – selecting records for preservation generated by institutions of social control – and the present-day acceptance of the period's interpretive framework. Given the source of most archival evidence, data that would permit an alternative and perhaps more favourable positioning of D'amato may never be forthcoming, but re-examining the available data from a slightly different perspective, reading it against the grain, as it were, might cast a more favourable light upon D'amato's behaviour. We examine those few pieces of archival evidence that do not fit readily within either the period's own interpretive framework or the subsequent adoption of that framework by film historians, seeking clues to the perceptions of those at the bottom of the social scale.[13]

The New York Times tells us that 'the younger element [among the Italians], who accepted D'amato as a sort of leader' declared that 'it is all a plot'. Might D'amato have been a hero of sorts to some of his people, even after the discovery of his grafting? Might they have appreciated the fact that he 'expedited' their licence applications? Might they have seen his approval of premises disapproved by a fire department inspector as an appropriate response to a city department reputedly controlled by and run for the benefit of the Irish immigrant population? Might they have perceived yet another in a series of systematic discriminatory actions directed against Italians? These questions must remain unanswered but posing them suggests that adopting the probable/possible perspective of marginalised social formations, most traces of which have been excluded from the historical archive, might result not only in repositioning D'amato but in causing us to question many of our assumptions about 'corrupt' and 'criminal' behaviour during the nickelodeon period as we broaden our scope beyond our initial anecdote.

Does questioning these assumptions entail condoning graft or, worse yet, the truly appalling conditions existing in some New York City nickelodeons before the enactment of the 1913 ordinance? Were we ourselves somehow magically transported back to 1908 New York

City, we must admit that a serious concern for life and limb might outweigh the immediate urge to undertake a personal investigation of some of the less salubrious nickelodeons. Between 1907 and 1909, the popular press and official reports indicate that nickelodeon owners obtained licences illegally, safety inspectors demanded payoffs, projectionists smoked while handling volatile celluloid film, and understandably panicky audiences made conditions even worse. But conditions seem to have been bad enough, with fire exits leading to bricked up walls, balconies collapsing and a general failure to meet even the minumum safety requirements. Consider a few excerpts from the official report to Mayor McClellan that preceded the famous 1908 nickelodeon closings:

> A wooden stairs led up at the left side to the top of the fence at the rear of the yard. Nine steps take one up to a small platform and three higher lead to the top of the fence. On the left is a sheer drop of eighteen or twenty feet into the yard of the adjoining house. There is no stairs leading from the before described stairs to the yard behind that of the yard of the moving picture show.

> The exit on the right hand side of the hall was blocked up by a chair behind the door. The courtyard is bounded by a board fence about 6' 6" and by a four or five storey brick building. There are no doorways through the fence. To get out of the yard one must scale the fence or else go through an iron door leading into an adjoining building. This was not open when I inspected the premises.

> Here one is given his choice of leaping a picket fence, behind which there is a drop of ten feet, or of going up a stoop into the kitchen of the adjoining house.[14]

Do we mean to excuse such flagrant disregard of basic safety standards? Can we even understand it? We could challenge the 'accuracy' of the 'facts' reported in the press and official documents – was the fire exit really bricked in? Did the balcony really collapse, killing three people? We could 'explain' these conditions in terms of the excesses of an early twentieth-century capitalism, concerned

1895

with profit at any price, that gave rise both to robber barons such as Andrew Carnegie and to cockroach capitalist nickelodeon owners with few means and fewer scruples. But, as we did with D'amato, we might once more read the evidence against the grain, attempting to take the perspective of those marginalised social formations largely excluded from the period's archival record and from the period's interpretive framework, who nonetheless played a prominent part within it. How might members of such social formations, from whose ranks came many nickelodeon proprietors, employees and audience members, regard the laws which mandated compliance with safety standards or forbid grafting?

The law, as the discursive realm of definition, regulation, and arbitration, might have seemed the quickest route for the motion picture's incorporation into (or exclusion from) the social order. Yet, as we have said above, the social order was itself in flux, undergoing change so rapid that some historians speak of a hegemonic crisis in the decades between 1880 and 1920, perhaps most apparent on a local level, in the cities that were initially the primary site of both cinema production and exhibition. The medium found itself caught between modes of social organisation that sociologists such as Weber might have characterised as 'pre-modern' and 'modern'. On the one hand, there was the charismatic, *ad hoc* and personalised authority of the clergy and of the political machine: Tammany Hall in New York City. On the other, there was the rationalised, systematic authority of the managerial classes: civic reform groups, professionals such as fire underwriters and engineers, 'progressive' city officials.[15]

Tammany saw the new medium as yet another opportunity for personal gain in a field that had already yielded them a rich harvest. As John Collier, of the People's Institute, a civic reform group concerned with the film industry, noted: 'All the exhortations that can be made and all the laws that can be passed won't break the grip of Tammany as long as Tammany controls the people's amusements'.[16] Some Tammany politicos quickly added nickelodeons to their existing theatrical interests

while the Tammany aldermen (city councilmen), whom the City Charter granted the ultimate authority for the issuance of licences, demanded pay-offs from nickelodeon proprietors. Many of these proprietors, hailing from the 'old country', found nothing surprising about a personalised authority that demanded individual tribute and the aldermen may indeed have been more responsive to their needs than an impersonal government bureaucracy.[17] Even the organ of a progressive reform organisation, *The Civic Journal*, was sympathetic to this perspective, as it answered the question, 'What, in practice, is an alderman?':

> In the congested districts the alderman is the poor man's lawyer (getting people out of trouble by politics not by law). He is an employment agency (representing his political organisation always, whether helping out those on civil service lists or getting the applicant a place with some friendly corporation). He gives stand permits for news dealers, bootblacks, and the like. In some districts he collects toll for these services, and those affected pay the five or ten dollars as if it were a fine imposed by law; it is imposed by custom and tradition.[18]

Some *clergymen* hailed the new medium's potential for 'uplift', but others, like the Tammany politicos, simply extended their previous practices and rhetoric to encompass it. These repressive clergy associated the cinema with all the other 'cheap amusements' that wrecked havoc by distracting the 'lower orders' from their religious obligations and exposing them to texts of dubious morality. Seeking to counteract the deleterious influence of these cheap amusements, the clergy mounted a rigorous defence of 'blue' Sundays, bringing pressure to bear upon civic officials to enforce archaic laws that prohibited various activities on the Sabbath day. Unlike many European countries, but like England, the United States had a strong tradition of Sabbatarianism, and even the entertainment media of a cosmopolitan urban centre such as New York City were occasionally subject to Sunday closing laws, despite the fact that for many working people the Christian Sabbath was the single day of leisure. Many New

York clerics associated the danger to the Sabbath, and by extension to fundamental American values, with the ever-rising influx of 'aliens' from southern and eastern Europe, ill-disposed to conform to dominant, i.e. white Anglo-Saxon, Protestant values, yet constituting a large proportion of the city's population and, according to the clergy, of nickelodeon audiences. Banning the Sunday showing of moving pictures, thought certain clergymen, was a tactic for disciplining these unruly elements who, as Methodist minister John Wesley Hill said, substituted 'the red laws of riot, carnival and immorality' for the blue laws of puritanism.[19]

The *managerial classes* saw the new medium as yet another field for rationalisation through the imposition of their professional expertise. This ethos drew upon an emerging social science paradigm predicated upon the gathering of data that would 'objectively' reveal patterns of human behaviour and thus enable predictions about the ameliorative possibilities of particular regulations. During the first decade of the twentieth century, surveys proliferated on various aspects of the urban condition: demographics; living conditions; the 'social evil' (prostitution) and cheap amusements among others.[20] These surveys rendered individuals as statistical constructs marked only by aggregate variables such as age, gender, ethnicity and occupation. Here, the reformers' stance closely resembled reform rhetoric about tenement conditions, with researchers investigating conditions such as crowding, sanitation and potential fire hazards. Evidence such as this enabled these reformers to make both predictions and recommendations, as they called for better air flow or more frequent fire inspections, hoping that such ameliorations would better the lot of an underprivileged and relatively powerless audience whom the reformers saw as benefiting from the establishment of a modernised bureaucracy.[21]

In the *film industry*, the more successful producers, their opinions represented in such trade journals as *The Film Index* and *The Moving Picture World*, generally allied themselves with the managerial classes and supported the framing of legislation to rationalise and modernise their industry (as well as providing a way to rid the industry of its 'lowest' elements), viewing this as a route to respectability and increased profits. At the same time, they resisted those laws, often framed and/or supported by the repressive clergy, that aimed at the outright suppression of cinema exhibition, seeing them as emanating from the groundless moral panic over the new medium. The more marginal nickelodeon proprietors, the cockroach capitalists, shared their more fortunate brethren's suspicion of repressive legislation, while sometimes suffering on the one hand, from Tammany's use of the law for personal gain and, on the other, from their more powerful rivals' use of the law to drive them out of business.[22]

Caught as they were among these conflicting discourses and practices of corruption, morality and rationality, members of the film industry harboured a certain justifiable suspicion of the law. Articles in the trade press reveal that the successful producers, both the members of the Motion Picture Patents Company and their independent rivals, considered negative discourse about the cinema a weapon employed by those hostile to the industry and wishing to frame repressive legislation. With a certain (justifiable) paranoia, members of the industry may have deemed everything from official reports about bricked-up exits to the popular press's constant refrain about fire as easily discounted 'enemy propaganda'. For example, in 1910, *The Nickelodeon*, a trade journal for the moment allied neither with the MPPC nor the independents, complained of the law's attitude toward motion picture exhibition:

> Municipal authorities seem generally prone, without reason, to assume that the proprietors and managers of motion picture theatres are natural violators of the law, and that special ordinances are requisite to hold them in restraint. This spirit is responsible for much of the peculiar legislation that has harassed the exhibitor since the first picture theatre opened.[23]

Once more reading the available evidence against the grain, we conclude that the 'cockroach capitalists' of the film industry's low end suspected the motivations not only of municipal authorities but of the financially more secure producers, whom they believed were attempting to impose control over the industry through such means as the establishment of the MPPC and an alliance with the managerial classes. Hence, some nickelodeon owners probably appreciated the power of their many enemies – conservative clerics, rival theatre and vaudeville owners, the MPPC – to use the law and the press against them. However 'true' the reports about health and safety dangers, however necessary regulatory statutes, low-end nickelodeon proprietors may have had ample grounds to discount them as yet another attempt to drive them out of business. From their perspective, discrediting both 'disaster reports' and the 'laws' designed to prevent them might have been simply the necessary evasion of their opponents' knavish tricks.

Certainly the more prosperous elements of the film industry, as they strove for a 'middle-class' respectability, constantly fulminated against the more marginal nickelodeons. In December 1908, Francis V.S. Oliver, Chief of the Bureau of Licenses, included the views of a Mr. Rubenstein, editor of Trust-controlled trade journal *The Film Index*, in his report on the Bureau's inspection of moving picture theatres:

> Every man who has the interest of the business at heart is looking forward to the time when every moving picture show in the country will be shown not in a cut-out front store, but in an actual theatre put up for the production of moving pictures as they are put up at the present time for plays ...[24]

Rubenstein's statement is an early example of the Trust's anti-storefront show rhetoric, oft-repeated during the following years' debate over nickelodeon regulation. In 1910, *The Film Index* lauded New York City's efforts to curb the 'moral' and safety hazards of the storefront shows:

> In New York, the authorities are going after the dark houses and the irresponsible machine operators with a vengeance that is wreaking havoc among cheap exhibitors of the East Side. This is as it should be. There is no excuse for a dark house where unmentionable evil may

flourish, and there is no excuse for a ten dollar a week foreigner turning the crank of a picture machine on the ground floor of a tenement containing a hundred other excitable foreigners.[25]

Any 'foreign' entrepreneur, struggling to make a go of his 'dark house', would probably have sensed the anti-immigrant bias here and may have had good grounds to regard regulations concerning theatre lighting and the employment of qualified projectionists as yet more unfair impositions originating from his business rivals. Indeed, during the battle over the framing of the 1913 audience, the smaller proprietors repeatedly claimed that some of the more stringent requirements were specifically designed to drive the 'small fry' out of the business.

Reports of dark houses, irresponsible machine operators and excitable audiences may have circulated primarily to the detriment of the low-end operators, but the industry as a whole resented the exaggerated and often groundless reports of cinema-related fires, distrusted a popular press that sought to boost circulation through attacking the highly visible film industry and believed some of the more stringent regulations proposed by frightened legislators to be unnecessary. The Iriquois theatre fire of 1903 had forged a popular association between fires and theatres, reinforced by the Boyertown fire of 1908, that led to great public concern about the mandating of safety standards to avoid future disasters. Said the National Board of Fire Underwriters in 1909:

> The Iriquois fire in Chicago, 30 December 1903, in which 600 persons lost their lives, was a terrible object lesson in bad construction and equipment, yet this was not sufficient to stop these disasters. The 13 January 1908 fire in an opera house in Boyertown, PA, cost the lives of nearly 200 women and children.[26]

Neither of these famous fires, however, occurred in nickelodeons. And, despite the wide-spread impression to the contrary, while the Boyertown opera house was exhibiting films on the disastrous day, official reports stated that the motion picture equipment did not cause the fire.

1895

Industry representatives continually sought to counter the conviction that motion picture projectors inevitably led to fires. Gustavus Rogers, representing the New York exhibitors at the hearing that preceded the Christmas Eve, 1908 nickelodeon closings, spoke directly to the issue of fires:

> So as far as fires and panics are concerned – and I challenge contradiction of the statement I now make – an examination of the records of the Fire Department of the City of New York will show that there have been more fires in butcher shops and in other places where articles of merchandise are exhibited than in moving picture places.[27]

A year later, *The Nickelodeon* said much the same thing about Chicago:

> There were 7,075 fires in Chicago in 1909 … There is no reference whatever to picture theatres or to motion picture films. It will be noted that they are not represented under 'explosions' – that favourite expression of the theatre fire reporter; neither are they mentioned under 'ignition'. The conclusion grows upon us that there were no film fires in Chicago in 1909.[28]

Given the disparity between public impressions and what seem to have been the actual 'facts' of the matter, members of the film industry might be excused for having a fairly cynical attitude toward fire regulation laws, viewing them not as necessary for the preservation of life but rather as a necessary public relations ploy.

> So much exaggeration has existed in the treatment of picture theatre fire reports that exhibitors have come to detest and avoid the very word, even when used in a protective way. They are inclined to overlook the fact that the danger lies not in the actual liability to fire, but purely in the minds of the people themselves.[29]

A broader public shared the film industry's cynical attitude toward the law, since the period's hegemonic crisis entailed a widespread critique of the legal system as corrupt and inefficient, particularly within the nation's machine-ruled urban centres. New regulations or changes in existing ones were frequently viewed as but another means of extorting graft from the struggling businessman. New rules meant new payments, and thus often functioned more to exclude those who would not pay than to regulate the behaviour of those who would. City inspectors, policemen, firemen, and petty city bureaucrats like Gaetano D'amato found new ways to supplement their incomes through new regulations. The 'law', in practice rather than theory, often came down to a matter of whom to pay, not what regulations to follow. A 1913 article written by New York City's Commissioner of Accounts Raymond Fosdick, head of the department charged with investigating illegalities in city agencies, makes it clear that corruption on all levels had become an accepted business practice. Talking about the city's building trade, he asserted that even the initially honest city inspector came to participate in the corrupt system: 'By and by he comes to expect it [pay-offs], and learns how, by rigorous application of minor features of the law, to make the life of the non-tipping contractor miserable.'[30] In paying city inspectors or bribing Gaetano D'amato or their aldermen to issue them licences, nickelodeon proprietors simply followed the era's standard operating procedures.

Seeing the potential for corruption everywhere, the film industry's trade organs, as well as progressive reform organisations concerned with cinema regulation, often denounced legislators, their proposed legislation and the entire legal system. For example, a 1910 editorial in *The Film Index* suggested that New York state politicians wished to establish a state censorship board not to protect the people but to line their own pockets and continued by extending its critique to the law generally: 'The way not to have a thing properly done is to give someone authority by law to do it.'[31] *The New York Times* reported on a meeting in which members of civic reform organisations denounced the Board of Aldermen for obstructing the ordinance to regulate motion picture theatres:

> Some of the speakers said that the reason the ordinance was being held up was because 'the motion picture show proprietors had "reached" the Tammany Aldermen'. Other speakers said that the

1895

Aldermen had been 'reached' by the vaudeville theatre proprietors who didn't want the rival business of motion pictures to improve and develop. All agreed, however, that the Aldermen had been subjected to some mysterious and malign influences and they were characterised generally as 'grafters'.[32]

But critics went beyond excoriating the most obvious excesses of corrupt politicians, as a ubiquitous lack of respect for the law, its framers and its agents made suspect every aspect of the legal system, from the drafting of legislation to its enforcement, this being particularly the case with regard to the often vague laws regulating entertainments, cheap amusements and the cinema. Highly regarded public figures openly challenged legal decisions and the motivations of those who made them, while the press represented aspects of the legal process, especially the deliberations of the Board of Aldermen, as a cross between a circus and a prize fight. William Sheafe Chase, canon of the Episcopal Church and one of motion pictures' most vociferous opponents, was once charged with contempt of court for having 'viciously and maliciously criticised' a New York judge who made a Sunday closing decision favourable to the film industry.[33] Theodore Bingham, having resigned his position as New York City's Police Commissioner, asserted that Mayor McClellan had closed the nickelodeons merely to appease his political opponents. 'I asked the Mayor why he had taken such a sudden interest in the moving picture question, and he answered: "I am playing a little game to win the ministers"'.[34]

Newspapers delighted in reporting on the more bizarre aspects of legal decision making and the Board of Aldermen proved a ready source of good material, with the Aldermen engaging in name-calling and even the occasional fist-fight. In 1907 *The New York World* reported on the Aldermen's deliberations re the Doull ordinance, a piece of legislation designed to amend Sunday closing requirements:

> The Aldermanic meeting yesterday was a peppery occasion literally and figuratively. Soon after it began a man in a crowded gallery sifted about a pound of cayenne pepper among the throng of spectators standing below. Sneezing and coughing and the wiping away of tears became the occupation of everybody in the rear of the chamber.

Later in the same meeting, an Alderman Peters who refused to be quiet and take his seat had to be restrained by two sergeants at arms and forcibly put back in his place.[35]

The situation did not improve once the laws were on the books, as those charged with their enforcement seemed unclear as to their intent and even questioned their usefulness. After the 1908 closings that also affected vaudeville and other theatres, entertainment executives asked Police Commissioner Bingham to clarify the Sabbath laws. Said Bingham, 'I'd like to know what the law is myself ...'. A little while later, in answer to another question, the Commissioner said: 'Oh, I don't know the law myself. Why don't you go at once to the Corporation Council's office?'[36] The famous Tammany magistrate 'Battery Dan' Flynn dismissed a complaint against a nickelodeon proprietor charged with admitting an underage (under sixteen) patron, saying: 'The law is an outrage. It deprives poor people of going to the theatre, and I believe it was passed in the interest of the big theatres that don't want people to go to the five- and ten-cent shows'. Flynn said that he himself had bought nickelodeon tickets for unescorted children.[37]

Not only were the laws represented as unclear or unjust, they were also represented as unequally enforced. Some interpretations of the statutes held that both nickelodeons and saloons should be closed on Sundays, yet a widespread system of payoffs enabled the latter to continue their operations even on the 'Lord's' day. In 1909 *The Moving Picture World* complained of this inequity, reprinting an article from *The Brooklyn Standard Union* that criticised the police for permitting the saloons to sell liquor on Sunday:

> Few people could be convinced, in view of the evidence on all sides, that the police knew the excise law was placed on the statute books to be enforced ... And perhaps not until hypocrisy is banished from local police affairs and intelligent and

fearless leadership directs police activity will the laws be enforced impartially.[38]

An unlucky but ingenious nickelodeon proprietor, Mr. Cohen, of whom we shall hear again shortly, was arrested numerous times for showing films on Sundays. On the occasion of his fifth arrest, Cohen said that 'he was being harshly treated by Captain Reynolds, who allowed other men to do the same things without arrest. "He says he can't arrest them because they sell soda water," said Cohen. "Well, last week I was selling soda and he arrested me".'[39]

Faced with unjust or unequally enforced legislation, its opponents could simply ignore it and face the consequences of fines or imprisonment, but the more astute used the legal system against itself in an attempt to get the law repealed. Said *The Nickelodeon* re the under-sixteen admission requirement: 'The quickest way to kill an obnoxious law is to enforce it so rigidly that the people grow sick of it and see that it is repealed'.[40] The test case, arresting a violator in the hopes of a judicial decision invalidating the law, was also a useful tactic. *The Tammany Times* asserted that this was Mayor McClellan's motivation for strictly enforcing Sunday closing laws:

> Mayor McClellan wants neither a blue Sunday nor the pleasure of the people unduly curtailed or restricted ... What the Mayor wants is to obtain from the courts a proper definition of the laws now on the statute books. There is only one way of getting this desired information, and that is through the medium of a test case ... To make a test case arrests are necessary.[41]

As we have seen, several factors, ranging from corruption to unequal enforcement, combined to undermine the legal system's authority during the nickelodeon period. The motion picture entrepreneurs, often drawn from the ranks of lower or immigrant classes, had good reason to share the period's general disdain for the law. Not yet fully acculturated within the idealised ethics of the system, nor economically able to stand by and watch their investments destroyed, and perhaps even inspired by the model of robber-baron entrepreneurial capitalism, nickelodeon proprietors seem to have developed a set of unorthodox, innovative responses to legal constraints. Adopting our 'reading against the grain' perspective, it is possible to see the sometimes curious, sometimes outrageous, and sometimes startlingly dangerous actions of nickelodeon proprietors and their personnel as the guerrilla-like activities of those simply struggling to remain afloat in a harshly competitive environment.

Nickelodeon owners adopted several survival strategies. Some worked within the legal system, co-operating with those who sought test cases or seeking court injunctions to prevent city officials like McClellan from suspending their licences. Others evaded the law, violated fire-regulations or Sunday closing statutes and paid off city officials like D'amato. And others responded in a more imaginative fashion, claiming to stay within the letter if not the spirit of the law. The Mr. Cohen who was continually arrested for violating the Sunday closing laws continually contrived ingenious defences. At one of his court appearances, 'Captain Reynolds told Magistrate Hylan that Cohen had been charging admission to his show by a subterfuge. Persons were admitted free of charge, but when seated on the inside everyone had to purchase five cent's worth of candy, or incur the displeasure of the management.'[42] Cohen had earlier claimed that the profits from Sunday exhibitions went to charity or that he charged his patrons for soda water, not the films.[43] Two nickelodeon owners fined twenty-five dollars for admitting under-age minors attempted to make life difficult for the court clerk by paying:

> ... in nickels from three large paper bags they carried under their arms. Court clerk Fuller refused to count the money in court and said it must be taken up to a quieter room ... On their way up one of the bags broke and the contents scattered in all directions. This was too much, and the two prisoners were taken before the justices again while the question of legal tender was considered.

The pair relented when told to pay their fine in paper money or go to jail.[44]

Proprietors also engaged in less veiled ridicule of the law. When the Police Department

1895

finally enforced Sunday shut-downs in 1907, ironic signs appeared on the closed nickel-odeons: 'Little Old New York died to-day. We have gone to the funeral. We will be back to-morrow;' 'We are on the ice temporarily. Will get off to-morrow;' 'We have not gone into the undertaking business. Not yet, but …'; and, most mordant of all, 'We are thinking of moving to Boston'.[45] The next year's closing gave rise to unintentional humour as the proprietors of Hammerstein's Victoria (a vaudeville house) strove to keep within the letter of the law by providing a lecture to render a travel film of northern Europe an 'educational' show suitable for the Sabbath:

> 'A railroad track', said the lecturer, the moving pictures having been taken evidently from the front of a train.
>
> 'Some men', continued the educationalist presently when a group of men on skis were shown. The next scene revealed them speeding downhill.
>
> 'Men skiing', announced the man.
>
> The pictures again switched to the railroad track.
>
> 'Another railroad track.'
>
> The track ran across a low trestle.
>
> 'The Brooklyn Bridge', bellowed the announcer.
>
> Pictures showing reindeers tramping about in the snow were explained as 'animals eating snowballs'.[46]

Sometimes the owners of moving picture venues engaged in a more active resistance aimed at the persons of the lawmakers. At the 'peppery' meeting at which the aldermen debated the Doull Ordinance, a Mr. Moses, owner of an establishment that showed films, first raised the issue of corruption, saying to those who opposed the bill, 'What do you mean by voting against an open Sunday? Is it another hand-out for graft?'[47] This tactic producing no results, Moses resorted to more strongly persuasive means, physically attacking Alderman Cornelius D. Noonan, who had voted against the ordinance.[48]

Survival tactics that entailed flouting the regulatory apparatus constructed by law and civil statute occasionally resulted in violations with disastrous consequences, such as the collapse of a balcony at a Rivington Street nickelodeon that cost several lives. More often, however, the potential danger was subject to strong discursive amplification. But we do not wish to trivialise attempts to 'better' the conditions of film exhibition, but rather to offer a new vantage point on seeing 'transgressions', that is, the many incidents of 'criminal' or 'corrupt' behaviour associated with the emergent nickelodeons. As noted at the outset, the interpretive framework used to understand the period tends to emphasise the sordid nature of these 'violations' and the subsequent triumph of 'progress'. We have suggested an alternate paradigm that might see these 'violations' as perfectly consistent with the period's dominant practice. The laws regarding nickelodeons – from their conception and formation, to their deployment and enforcement – were represented as corrupt and sometimes as specifically designed to subvert the film business. In this context, the various nickelodeon tactics we have outlined seem not so much as 'corrupt' or 'irrational' as motivated and reasonable acts of survival.

In concluding this essay, a return to the kind of anecdotal evidence with which we began may help to reinforce our point concerning reading period evidence against the grain or within the perspective of the period's marginalised social formations. In 1908 *The Moving Picture World* ran a story titled 'Audience Applauds His Shrieks of Agony', relating the horrifying experience of projectionist John Riker:

> Reaching into the sheet-iron cage that covered a moving-picture machine with which he was giving an exhibition, John Riker seized a bare electric wire instead of the switch. He was held fast while a current of 1000 volts went through his body. He shrieked for help. His cries, coming through the narrow aperture of the booth, sounded to the audience like a phonographic accompaniment to the blood and thunder drama that was being portrayed in the moving pictures. The audience, not suspecting the dangerous plight of the man, applauded … [When he was rescued] Riker's hand still gripped

the wire and had to be pried off. His hand was almost roasted by the strength of the current. [When will operators learn? We cannot understand why a bare wire was allowed to be used. Every operator ought to use only properly insulated wires, and if any bare surface shows they should be bound with tape. – ED.]⁴⁹

Why did the journal print this story – to appeal to their readers' rubber-necking propensities, their potential *schadenfreude*? For that matter, why do we reprint it? We do so because we wish to suggest that such anecdotes might have had a powerful communicative function. The top-end of the film industry joined with groups such as the fire underwriters or New York City's Department of Water, Gas and Electricity in promulgating certain 'reasonable' (non-moral, non-judgmental) propositions: 'don't touch bare wires'; 'don't smoke around nitrate film'; 'don't hire inex-perienced projectionists'. But in an environment where authority was so fundamentally subverted, so suspect, where statute, law, or even 'common sense' safety standards were undermined and suspect, where every law could be seen as yet another attack or opportunity for graft, how were 'rules' to be communicated? With the discursive structure of imperatives, of laws and regulations invalidated, cautionary tales, narrativised vignettes of operators with horribly maimed arms and others that we have found, were called into service.

Acknowledgements: The authors gratefully acknowledge permission from the Regents of Duke University Press to publish this essay in *Celebrating 1895*. The paper also appears in Henry Jenkins, Jane Shattuck, Tara MacPherson (eds) *Hop on Pop: the New Cultural Studies* (Durham: Duke University Press, forthcoming).

Notes

1. 'D'amato's Arrest Stirs Italians', *The New York Times* (4 October 1908).

2. The complaintants and prices paid for a $25 initial license and/or $12.50 renewal included M. di Christopero, $185, Roger di Pasca, $100, Joseph Brunelli, $75. Special examination of the accounts and methods of the Bureau of Licenses, Office of the Commissioners of Accounts, 2 November 1908, Accounts, Commissioner of, MGB 44, New York City Municipal Archives.

3. 'D'amato's Arrest Stirs Italians', *The New York Times* (4 October 1908).

4. See, for example, T.J. Jackson Lears, 'The Concept of Cultural Hegemony: Problems and Possibilities', *American Historical Review*, 90, 3 (1985): 567–593.

5. On the subject of cheap amusements, see Lewis Erenberg, *Steppin' Out: New York Night Life and the Transformation of American Culture, 1890–1930* (Westport, CT: Greenwood Press, 1981); John Kasson, *Amusing the Million: Coney Island at the Turn of the Century* (New York: Hill and Wang, 1978); Kathy Peiss, *Cheap Amusements: Working Women and Leisure in Turn-of-the-Century New York* (Philadelphia: Temple University Press, 1986); Roy Rosenzweig, *Eight Hours for What We Will: Workers and Leisure in an Industrial City, 1870–1920* (New York: Cambridge University Press, 1983) and Robert Sklar, *Movie Made America: A Cultural History of American Movies* (New York: Vintage, 1975).

6. For more on the social/cultural position of the early cinema see Eileen Bowser, *The Transformation of Cinema, 1907–1915* (New York: Scribner's Sons, 1990); Richard deCordova, *Picture Personalities: The Emergence of the Star System in America* (Urbana: University of Illinois Press, 1990); Thomas Elsaesser with Adam Barker (eds), *Early Cinema: Space, Frame, Narrative* (London, British Film Institute, 1990); Tom Gunning, *D. W. Griffith and the Origins of American Narrative Film* (Urbana: University of Illinois Press, 1991); Miriam Hansen, *Babel and Babylon: Spectatorship in American Silent Film* (Cambridge: Harvard University Press, 1990); Charles Musser, *The Emergence of Cinema: The American Screen to 1907* (New York: Charles Scribner's Sons, 1990); *High-Class Moving Pictures: Lyman Howe and the Travelling Exhibitor* (Princeton: Princeton University Press, 1991); *Before the Nickelodeon* (Berkeley: University of California Press, 1991) Roberta E. Pearson, *Eloquent Gestures: The Transformation of Performance Style in the Griffith Biograph Films* (Berkeley: University of

California Press, 1992); William Uricchio and Roberta E. Pearson, *Reframing Culture: The Case of the Vitagraph Quality Films* (Princeton: Princeton University Press, 1993).

7. Benjamin B. Hampton, *History of the American Film Industry: From Its Beginnings to 1931* (New York: Dover Publications, 1970), 58.

8. Hampton, p. 61.

9. Lewis Jacobs, *The Rise of the American Film* (New York: Teachers College Press, 1939), 65–66.

10. Robert Sklar, *Movie-Made America: A Cultural History of American Movies* (New York: Vintage Books: 1994), 30.

11. Sklar, 32.

12. Tom Gunning, *D.W. Griffith and the Origins of American Narrative Film: The Early Years at Biograph* (Urbana: University of Illinois Press, 1991), 60.

13. While film historians have tended to accept the period's own interpretive framework two social historians have sought evidence of the perceptions of those at the bottom of the social hierarchy. Kathy Peiss has drawn upon oral histories to analyse the way in which the experience of the nickelodeon fit within the lives of young, immigrant women (*Cheap Amusements: Working Women and Leisure in Turn-of-the-Century New York* (Philadelphia: Temple University Press, 1986)). Roy Rosenzweig has shown how the workers of Worcester, Massachusetts responded to the arrival of the new medium of film in their town (*Eight Hours For What We Will: Workers & Leisure in an Industrial City, 1870–1920* (New York: Cambridge University Press, 1983)).

14. Francis V.S. Oliver, Chief, Bureau of Licenses to George B. McClellan, Mayor, 'Regarding Inspection of Moving Picture Theatres', December 1908, Folder 4, Bureau of Licenses, MGB 51, New York City Municipal Archives. The inspections were carried out under the city's mandate to protect the safety of its citizens, even though specific statutes regarding nickelodeon construction were not approved in New York City until 1913.

15. For a discussion of how these various competing interests perceived the nickelodeon audience, see William Uricchio and Roberta E. Pearson, 'Constructing the Audience: Competing Discourses of Morality and Rationalization During the Nickelodeon Period', *Iris* 17 (Autumn, 1994): 43–54.

16. 'People's Amusements', *New York Daily Tribune* (19 December 1908).

17. Mario Maffi, among others, argues that the organisation of social life particularly in southern Italy was based upon a pattern of social stratification and personified power which was transferred to and quickly adapted by the immigrant community in the US. See *Gateway to the Promised Land: Ethnic Cultures on New York's Lower East Side* (Atlanta-Amsterdam: Rodopi, 1994).

18. 'Worrying about the Aldermen', *The Civic Journal*, v. 1, no. 7: 3, 8.

19. 'Commends the Mayor', *The New York Times* (28 December 1908).

20. For an overview of these surveys, see Alan Havig, 'The Commercial Amusement Audience in Early Twentieth-Century American Cities', in *Journal of American Culture* no. 5 (1982), 1–19. For period surveys see, among many others, Edwin R.A. Seligman, (ed) *The Social Evil: With Special Reference to Conditions Existing in the City of New York* (G.P. Putnam's Sons, New York, 1912), Robert Coit Chapin, *The Standard of Living Among Workingmen's Families in New York City* (Russell Sage Foundation, New York, 1909) and Louise Bollard More, *Wage-Earners' Budgets: A Study of Standards and Cost of Living in New York City* (Henry Holt and Company, New York, 1907).

21. One of the problems faced by the managerial classes in their reform programme was the entrenched corruption of the system upon which they were forced to rely for social change. After he was pushed out of his office by Mayor McClellan, former Police Commissioner Bingham said that the Mayor ordered a hearing about the nickelodeons but the man put in charge was the head of the licence bureau. 'Not only was it [the License Bureau] found to be doing a land office business in graft, by charging double and sometimes treble the legal cost of common-show licences, but it was also trafficking in peddler's licenses in the same outrageous way.' Theodore Bingham, 'Why I Was Removed', *Van Norden's; The World Mirror* (September 1909): 595.

22. For a more detailed account of these conflicting positions, see Uricchio and Pearson, 1994.

23. 'Putting the Picture Theatre Right', *The Nickelodeon*, v. 4, no. 2 (15 July 1910): 27.

24. Francis V.S. Oliver, Chief, Bureau of Licenses to George B. McClellan, Mayor, 'Regarding Inspection of Moving Picture Theatres' (December 1908), Folder 4, Bureau of Licenses, MGB 51, New York City Municipal Archives.

25. 'Answer New York Sun's Editorial', *The Views and Film Index* (31 December 1910): 245.

26. Proceedings of the 43rd Annual Meeting of the National Board of Fire Underwriters (13 May 1909): 70.

27. Francis V S. Oliver, Chief, Bureau of Licenses to George B. McClellan, Mayor, 'Regarding Inspection of Moving Picture Theatres' (December 1908), Folder 4, Bureau of Licenses, MGB 51, New York City Municipal Archives.

28. 'The Causes of Fires', *The Nickelodeon*, v. 4, no. 5 (1910): 120. The list of probable causes curiously includes seventeen fires resulting from 'rats and mice with matches'. Beware of pyromaniac rodents!

29. 'Panics', *The Nickelodeon*, v. 2, no. 5 (November 1909): 136.

30. Raymond B. Fosdick, 'Driven From the City: Another Point of View', *Outlook* (18 January 1913): 134.

31. 'Casual Comment', *The Film Index* (26 November 1910): 2.

32. 'Denounce Fight Law Fight', *The New York Times* (18 June 1912): 6.

33. 'Rector Chase Found Guilty of Contempt', *The Moving Picture World* (18 January 1908).

34. Theodore Bingham, 'Why I Was Removed', *Van Norden's; The World Mirror* (September 1909): 596.

35. *The New York World* (18 December 1907): 2.

36. 'Diluted Vaudeville To-Day's Show Menu', *The New York Times* (27 December 1908): pt. 2, 1.

37. 'Magistrate Flynn doesn't like law', *The Film Index* (13 November 1909): 17.

38. 'Trade Notes', *The Moving Picture World* (October 1909): 521.

39. *The Moving Picture World* (1 June 1907): 201.

40. 'Putting the Picture Theatre Right', *The Nickelodeon*, v. 4, no. 2 (15 July 1910): 27.

41. 'The Mayor No Puritan', *The Tammany Times* (22 May 1909): 8.

42. *The Moving Picture World* (8 June 1907): 217.

43. *The Moving Picture World* (1 June 1907): 201.

44. Nickles to pay their fines, *The Nickelodeon*, v. 5, no. 10 (1911): 282.

45. *New York World* (9 December 1907).

46. *New York World* (28 December 1908).

47. 'Aldermen Fail to Doctor Blue Laws', *The New York American* (11 December 1907): 1.

48. 'One More Silent Sunday Certain; Aldermen Halt', *The New York Herald* (11 December 1907): 1.

49. 'Audience Applauds His Shrieks of Agony', *The Moving Picture World* (22 February 1908): 138. Countless of these cautionary tales appeared in *The Moving Picture World*, usually with an admonitory comment at the end. See also 8 August 1907, 359 and 14 September 1907, 438.

1895

'At the Picture Palace': The British Cinema Audience, 1895–1920

Nicholas Hiley

British Universities Film & Video Council, 77 Wells Street, London W1P 3RE, UK

DESPITE THE ASSUMPTIONS of most film historians, the medium of film does not depend upon a mass audience. Research into the pre-history of moving pictures has clearly demonstrated that much of the technical impetus behind the development of film came not from entertainers, but from scientists eager to record and analyse natural motion. Even without the intervention of showmen or lantern lecturers it is evident that both film cameras and peepshow viewers would have appeared around 1895, as tools by which scientists could record and reconstitute movement in the laboratory. It is also apparent that in time these scientific devices would have been adopted by doctors wishing to demonstrate surgical techniques, by anthropologists trying to record vanishing cultures, and by salesmen needing to demonstrate heavy machinery, all without the intervention of the music hall or shop show. Eventually there would have been both projected moving pictures and even film historians, all without the appearance of either a mass audience or of purpose-built cinemas.

This alternative history of the medium is not entirely fanciful. If celluloid film base had been only a fraction more expensive to produce, or just a little more fragile, it would have rendered it impossible for travelling showmen and entertainers to adopt the new moving pictures. The film camera would have remained a scientific instrument, and there would have been no impulse to develop dramatic narrative or to appeal to a mass audience. There would have been film, but not film history as we understand it, for the study of genres and styles, of actors, directors, and studios, of cinemas and fan magazines, would have had no meaning. The more we contemplate this alternative history of film the more it becomes obvious that what we call film history is nothing of the sort. It is not the history of the medium of film, but rather the story of how that medium was adapted to the needs of a paying audience.

This simple observation creates considerable problems. Following the 1978 FIAF conference in Brighton, the trend of research into early film has been archive-based, and principally concerned with tracing the developing art of film through the surviving prints and negatives.[1] The basis of this history is the individual film, and yet this approach is misleading, for over the first 25 years of projected moving pictures, from 1895 to 1920, the individual film was of little significance. The basic unit of exhibition was not the individual film but the programme, and the commodity that most patrons wished to buy from the exhibitor was not access to an individual film, but time in the auditorium. Paradoxically, film historians now value these early films more highly than the people who originally paid to see them, and certainly more than the companies that originally produced them. Charles Urban, one of the pioneers of British film, frankly admitted that only a small number of negatives from the early period survived for the simple reason that 'very few of the old film firms attached sufficient importance to the value of negatives once they were "published"'.[2]

Early film history thus takes its justification from the mass audience, but has become so fixated upon surviving prints that the characteristics of that audience are generally discovered only be inference. Changes in film style are assumed to be evidence of developing tastes, and a complex film is taken to imply a subtle audience, although it is clear that the link between production and reception was far more complex than this. Film producers do not need to please audiences so much as to satisfy renters and exhibitors, and stylistic changes may reflect the growing ambitions of film purchasers, rather than the changing tastes of film audiences. There is indeed evidence that film audiences were left behind by the development of more complex narrative styles, and were forced to rely upon the running commentary provided by the lecturer standing beside the screen. By 1903 some producers were adding explanatory intertitles to their films, but, as one proprietor of one London shop show recalled, it was still necessary to add a spoken commentary to dramatic films 'which, owing to the almost entire absence of explanatory matter, were not at all easy to follow'.[3]

The question of comprehension is indeed an important one, for it is clear that during the first fifteen years of exhibition, film drama simply could not stand on its own. 'In many a bioscope theatre', noted the *Bioscope* in 1909, 'films that are really dramatic and films that are really interesting are watched without

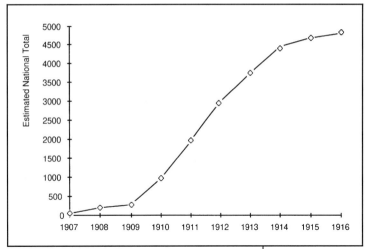

Fig. 1. *The pattern of construction of purpose-built cinemas, 1907–18.*[6]

a glimmer of intelligence and frequently with complete boredom'; 'Anyone with a long experience of picture halls knows that the stories of many dramatic pictures are quite incomprehensible to many of the people who watch the events that transpire on the screen'. Soon after these words were written the task of explaining the action began to pass to the intertitles, but it would be wrong to ascribe this solely to the developing art of film. In 1909 it was already acknowledged that in film lecturing 'the supply of good men is by no means equal to the demand', and in the subsequent boom of British cinema construction the demand quickly outstripped the supply.[4] By the end of 1910 there were some 2900 regular film shows, rising to 3800 by 1912, and to 5000 by 1914. Most of these took place in purpose-built auditoria, but the traditions of showmanship endured. It was noted as late as 1915 that in one northern town 'the people … favoured lectures, nearly every theatre having its guide to the film story', but there simply were not enough lecturers for this to be widespread. With 5400 regular film shows by the end of 1915, the art of explication had to pass to the film itself.[5]

A second mistake arising from the concentration upon film prints comes in the belief that they grew in length to permit detailed characterisation and facilitate the development of complex plots. Such developments were certainly possible with longer films, but the impetus came as much from changes in exhibition as it did from the growing ambitions of film producers. Figure 1 shows how in 1909

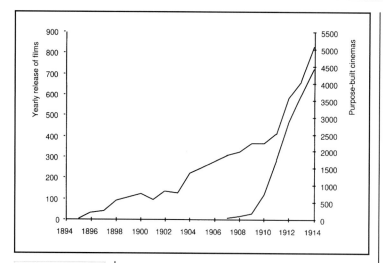

Fig. 2. *The impact of cinema construction on the output of British studios.*[8]

Fig. 3. *The impact of purpose-built cinemas on film length, 1909–14.*[11]

a radical shift of investment in the entertainment industry led to the rapid construction of purpose-built cinemas, in a process that was hastened after 1910 by tighter controls on exhibition introduced under the Cinematograph Act. This transformed the context of film exhibition, but the rapid construction of

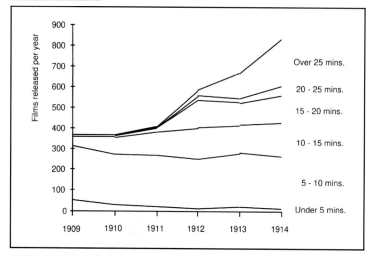

purpose-built cinemas also had an immediate effect on the demand for films – as can be seen from Figure 2, in which the yearly production of British fiction films is plotted against the total number of purpose-built cinemas. The number of fiction films jumped from fewer than 400 releases in 1910 to more than 800 in 1914, as the focus of exhibition shifted from travelling exhibitions to the new purpose-built venues. This occurred because the new cinemas encouraged more regular atten-

dance, and thus obliged exhibitors to change their programmes more frequently. As early as 1910 it was claimed that a typical cinema 'is often visited by the same people several times in a week', and by 1911 it was possible to think in terms of 'the "cinema habit"', forcing exhibitors to change their programmes twice a week.[7]

The construction of cinemas also produced an important change in the pattern of attendance, by encouraging patrons to stay in the auditorium for a whole evening. This new pattern took some time to develop, and in 1910 the cinema was still regarded as a refuge from the street, which offered 'a pleasant and amusing hour' to the patron 'who uses it as an umbrella or a waiting room'.[9] In 1912 the majority of exhibitors were still running a 'continuous show', attracting casual visitors with a mixed programme that ran through the projector eight or nine times every day. Yet a minority of cinema managers had already changed their pattern of exhibition, and were giving just two performances a day, in the afternoon and evening, each lasting for around three hours.[10] By 1914 it was obvious that the new generation of picturegoers was prepared to spend much longer in the auditorium, and would tolerate individual films which lasted for twenty minutes or half an hour, rather than the five or ten minutes of the earlier travelling shows. As Fig. 3 demonstrates, the rapid increase in British film production that was apparent by 1914 had been achieved by overlaying a whole new class of long films on top of the established pattern of short subjects, in order to exploit these new patterns of attendance.

These longer films gave producers the chance to develop their art, but they had an even more important role within the economics of exhibition. The older pattern of short subjects satisfied the needs of the fairground bioscopes and shop shows, which could seat only 200 or 300 patrons, and charged just 1d. or 2d. admission, but survived by showing their half-hour programme as many as 25 times a day. However, when the first purpose-built cinemas appeared in 1909 they had 700 or 800 seats, and charged 3d. or 4d. admission, which enabled them to run a programme of an hour and a half and still make a profit on three or four shows a day. Long films favoured larger venues, and were carefully fostered by the major exhibitors as a weapon against their smaller rivals. By 1920 the big cinemas were offering programmes of two-and-a-half or even three hours, and it was noted that with such long programmes the majority of British cinemas 'are not large enough to hold sufficient money to pay the running costs'.[12] Long films were certainly attractive to film producers, but more importantly they satisfied the industry's major investors by underwriting the new generation of large cinemas. 'The last of the converted shops, misnamed "palaces", are fast disappearing', noted one writer with satisfaction in 1921: 'Bigger kinemas have been opened. Some, seating 3,000 people, represent the very last word in cinema design, comfort and adornment.'[13]

The fact is that the art of film cannot be divorced from its economic context, and, as the case of film length shows, an archival focus will never show the whole picture. A further example comes in the current belief that early films should be projected at the speed of natural action, for there is a great deal of evidence to suggest that British exhibitors projected their films considerably faster than this. Those who did not regularly attend film shows were indeed surprised by the rapid movement of people and objects, one critic complaining in 1907 that 'the exaggerated pace of the cinematograph destroys all sense of proportion as to time'.[14] Yet regular picturegoers accepted the acceleration as part of the medium. The nominal speed of filming was sixteen frames per second, but the London music halls habitually projected much faster than this, one writer noting in 1909 that 'at the *Alhambra* I was informed by the operator that he got the best results with a speed of eighteen to twenty pictures per second, but this may be considerably increased'.[15]

Accelerated motion has no place in the modern conception of film art, but early audiences seem to have enjoyed it, and, as one historian has suggested, they may even have valued the cinema precisely because it offered 'an expanded and concentrated experience of time – more time for their modest outlay'.[16] Rapid movement was certainly tolerated by regular cinemagoers, most of whom were working-class, despite remaining a constant puzzle for those middle-class critics who seldom visited a moving-picture show: 'Pictures are, as a rule, passed too rapidly before the audience', complained one middle-class writer in 1912, adding that in most of the films he had seen 'people appear to run where they should be walking'.[17] This hostility was particularly evident in 1916, when showings of the official documentary *Battle of the Somme* attracted many middle-class patrons for whom moving pictures were still a novelty. The official musical accompaniment assumed a projection speed of around nineteen frames per second, but eager exhibitors forced it through their machines at an even higher rate, causing the poet Henry Newbolt to complain 'that an ordinary march becomes a double quick, and a running pace becomes a Walpurgisnacht revel', while the novelist Rider Haggard observed that 'as usual all the pictures move too fast; even the wounded seem to fly along'.[18]

These high-projection speeds were influenced by the economics of exhibition, for the managers of small cinemas were tempted to accelerate the projection of long films to increase audience turnover. As one insider explained in 1914, 'if there are a number of people waiting for admission, the operator is often ordered to cut out pictures, and rush the others', in a practice known throughout the trade as 'shooting the show'.[19] Regular cinemagoers could apparently tolerate the distortions which this produced, and the limit was only reached in 1917, when exhibitors in Birmingham started to project at more than 32 frames per second in an effort to compress their long programmes into two full performances. Complaints were heard that this was 'such a speed as to make the motions in the picture ridiculous and their patrons' eyes tired', but in 1918 it was admitted that the unscrupulous exhibitor was still 'working his film as a fairground manager works his roundabout; slowing down or speeding up, no longer in the cause of art, but in the unholy pursuit of "making things fit in"'. A maximum speed of eighteen frames per second was suggested, but there is no evidence that it was ever enforced.[20]

The folly of using modern sensibilities to reconstruct exhibition is further indicated by recent efforts to add musical accompaniment to surviving prints. The belief that appropriate music enhances the art of the silent film obscures the fact that over the first fifteen years of exhibition most films were either accompanied by the sound of the projector, or by mechanical music which bore no relation to the pictures on the screen. The music halls had orchestras, but, as the *Kinematograph Weekly* complained in 1907, when the bioscope was shown most of them played 'a meaningless repetition of chords which have apparently been strung together at random'.[21] In the smaller venues the situation was even worse, for in 1908 a report on London's shop shows revealed that fourteen of the 36 venues had no music at all. Another twenty venues had some musical accompaniment for the pictures, but there was little attempt at synchronisation, for in eleven of them the accompaniment came from a pianola or barrel-organ, while in another three it came from a gramophone or phonograph. Only six venues had truly synchronised music, four of them using a piano or harmonium and only two boasting an orchestra.[22]

There was little improvement in the purpose-built cinema. 'A piano is the usual type of music provided', observed one expert in 1911, adding that 'an efficient pianist is easy to get for £1 5s. a week'.[23] Such low rates of pay guaranteed poor work, and another writer observed that most of the hundreds of cinema pianists he had encountered played music which 'had not ... the faintest connection with the pictures they were supposed to be accompanying'.[24] Some full-time accompanists were little better than pianolas, for it was reported that one cinema pianist 'knew about six tunes, which he played over and over again in regular sequence'.[25] The majority of pianists had a wider range, but in 1914 the *Illustrated Films Monthly* still professed itself 'disgusted with the incongruous tinkling of amateurs on cottage pianofortes at the picture shows'.[26] The larger cinemas built up small orchestras, augmenting the piano with a violin, a cello, and a drum, and sometimes replacing it with an harmonium to give an even wider range of sounds. By 1917 the accompaniment had become a significant factor in choosing which cinema to visit, and

there was said to be an average of three musicians per cinema. Yet in 1918 there were still complaints about 'the general absence of any form or system in the fitting of music to pictures'.[27]

Fast projection and incongruous music may contradict the usual depiction of the developing art of film, but it has to be accepted that these early film shows were undeniably crude because their patrons were terribly poor. In 1909 the success of the purpose-built cinema was due less to the pictures that were shown, than to the fact that it was cheap to enter and, unlike the theatre or the music hall, did not impose a minimum standard of dress. 'Best clothes are a *sine qua non* for the music hall', observed one writer in 1910, 'whereas the cinematograph may be visited without this formality': 'It is also rather cheaper. Admission is only 2d., whereas the *Hippodrome* is at least 3d.'[28] The low price of tickets, and the fact that patrons could wear their work clothes, were enormously important in the success of the cinema, but they brought their own problems. Working-class audiences had few opportunities to wash themselves or to change their clothes, and they naturally smelt strongly. In 1914 it was admitted that in many cinemas 'the "great unwashed" are a very real problem', and managers were advised to purchase sprays and deodorisers with which to disinfect their halls, not only after each performance but also 'during the time the pictures are being shown'.[29]

For these patrons the cinema did not only supply entertainment, it also offered a refuge from the cold. As one writer commented in the winter of 1914, 'one wonders what we did without them':

> The opportunities to escape from weather like we are now having, and at the same time to be accommodated with comfort and entertainment were far less in the old days than now.[30]

Warmth has no place in the developing art of film, but in 1917 it was acknowledged as a significant factor in attracting the working classes:

> You must bear in mind that some of these people only live in one room, and perhaps they find it cheaper to take a short time

at the pictures. You see, it means they have not got to light a fire at home, and that would be cheaper for them.[31]

The unemployed were also attracted to the cinema by the warmth. Soon after the end of the war in 1918 the manager of the *Crown Theatre* in Coventry found that his cinema was being used by men 'just above the bread-line':

> When the theatre opened in the afternoon, the portion of the seating priced at 4d. always attracted a fair number of patrons. They were the elderly or the rather untidy individuals without jobs. Three quarters of this number put their heads down automatically and went to sleep.[32]

For other patrons the cinema offered privacy, another commodity that was in short supply at home. In 1915 the newly-appointed manager of the *Scala Theatre* in Liverpool discovered that young couples wanted to buy time in the darkness. The 4d. ticket was indeed known locally as 'four penn'orth o' dark', and he was amazed to find that when the lights were turned out 'hardly any member of the audience seemed to bother to look at the screen'.[33] A similar situation was reported from the East End of London in 1917, where young couples visited their local cinemas to escape the prying eyes of their parents. 'It is a dark place', explained one local resident, 'and if you have a young lady it is very convenient to go there': 'The expression down there is that you take your "bird" to the pictures'.[34] It is important to remember that early audiences did not buy films, but bought time in the cinema, which they used for a variety of purposes. The manager of the *King's Hall* in Birmingham admitted that by 1918 his daytime audience was 'very mixed':

> There were lady shoppers from the Lewis Store who had become tired; overflow from the city picture houses when most of them had filled; dwellers on a rather poor residential estate adjacent to the hall, on the side away from Birmingham; and commercial men waiting for business appointments.[35]

The cinema also appealed to working-class audiences by welcoming the whole family. It was observed at the end of 1909 that in the London suburbs 'fathers, mothers, and children regard a weekly visit to the picture palace as indispensable to a happy life', and by 1911 moving pictures were said to have changed the recreational habits of the working man, for 'the small charges for admission permit him of taking mamma, the baby and the "kids"'. The purpose-built cinema attracted 'whole families of the industrial classes', and it was said that by breaking the masculine dominance of the public house it 'makes for the good of the family'. As one exhibitor noted in 1912, 'it's the "pub" we compete with':

> There are two coal-heavers in there now, each with two children. Where did they formerly spend their Saturday nights? In the public house ... Well, that's where they would have been if they hadn't been here.[36]

The question of where the early audiences found the money to attend is enormously important, although it is seldom asked. By 1917 some 21 million tickets were being sold each week at an average price of 4d., amounting to an outlay of around £350,000.[37] This money must have come from somewhere, and the likelihood is that it came from the public house, for beer consumption was declining and, as the *Kinematograph Weekly* acknowledged in 1918, 'people are more and more forsaking the public-houses for the kinema'.[38]

For those historians committed to the developing art of film these working-class audiences, with their love of comedies and crude melodramas, their indiscriminate passion for movement, their dirty clothes, and their tendency to rowdyism, must seem very unattractive. This is hardly surprising, for contemporary exhibitors also found them unattractive, and struggled both to separate them from the middle-class patrons and to overawe them with uniformed attendants. In order to increase their profits the major investors simply had to move their audience upmarket. 'It is quite true that a very respectable income may be derived from amusing the working classes', admitted the *Bioscope* in 1910:

> ... but he who would extract all the gold from the rich mine which the bioscope business places within his reach must not lose sight of the very considerable extra

profit which may accrue from a judicious admixture of the better class element.[39]

The solution was eventually found in a strategy of building larger cinemas, booking longer features, and sponsoring a style of filmmaking which absorbed the spectator into the illusion and thus broke the power of the working-class audience.

The study of these early audiences reinforces the lesson that the history of film lies in the past, not in cans in the archives, and that it can only be recovered by the careful study of a wide range of sources. The surviving prints have considerable value as evidence of the developing art of film, but historians can learn more about the British film industry between 1895 and 1920 by studying the venues in which these films were exhibited, than by restoring these prints and projecting them according to their own personal tastes. Film history is not the history of a medium, it is the story of how that medium was transformed by the intervention of a mass audience with its own desires and demands. Like the travelling showmen and cinema managers who pioneered film exhibition in Britain between 1895 and 1920, film historians must come to terms with an audience that was awkward, dirty, and unruly, but whose patronage supported the entire industry.

Notes

1. The proceedings of the Brighton conference were published in two volumes as R. Holman (ed), *Cinema 1900–1906: An Analytical Study* (Brussels, 1982).
2. South African National Film Archives, Gutsche Papers, C. Urban to T. Gutsche (7 January 1939).
3. L. Wood, *The Romance of the Movies* (London, 1937), 73–76; B. Salt, *Film Style and Technology: History and Analysis* (2nd edn: London, 1992), 59.
4. *Bioscope* (25 February 1909): 3, 'Explaining the Pictures'.
5. *Kinematograph Weekly* (3 June 1915): 107, 6, 'Northern Notes'. Cinema numbers are derived from returns in the *Bioscope Annual* for 1910–11 and 1913, and the *Kinematograph Year Book* for 1916. The 1915 yearbooks are unreliable, as this was the first year when cinema managers were urged to send returns to both publications, and the result was under-registration. The 1914 figure is thus that accepted by the exhibitors: *Times* (4 March 1914): 8, 'The Cinematograph and Education'.
6. Data concerning the construction of purpose-built cinemas, 1907–18, were determined by taking the known dates of the opening of purpose-built cinemas in Birmingham, Leeds, Bristol, Bradford, Hull, Newcastle and Oxford, and enlarging this sample to national scale. Details of cinema construction in Leeds were kindly supplied by Robert Preedy. Other figures were derived from P.J. Marriott, *Early Oxford Picture Palaces* (Oxford, 1978); C. Anderson, *A City and its Cinemas* (Bristol, 1983); G.J. Mellor, *The Cinemas of Bradford* (Leeds, 1983); V.J. Price, *Birmingham Cinemas: Their films and stars 1900–1960* (Studley, 1986); R.E. Preedy, *Remembering the Old Cinemas of Humberside* (Leeds, 1988); F. Manders, *Cinemas of Newcastle: A comprehensive history of the cinemas of Newcastle upon Tyne* (Newcastle, 1991). These figures were enlarged to national scale on the basis of the 4700 cinemas which the producer Cecil Hepworth had on his mailing list in 1915: H. Bolce 'Crowding Cinemas in War Time', *System* (April 1915): 260.
7. Public Record Office, London, BT 31/19440/109321, Associated Electric Theatres, Limited file, prospectus dated 29 April 1910: C. Calvert, *Historical Review of the Cinematograph* (London, 1911), 3.
8. These statistics of 'entertainment films' released in Britain are taken from Dennis Gifford's *The British Film Catalogue 1895 – 1985: A Reference Guide* (2nd edn: Newton Abbot, 1986). Gifford's definition of an entertainment film excludes 'all newsreels, documentaries, and films of pure actuality, advertisement, education, information, propaganda, and travel'.
9. *Answers* (15 October 1910): 576, 'The Picture Palace Menace'.
10. F.A. Talbot, *Moving Pictures: How They Are Made and Worked* (London, 1912), 325.
11. Calculated from Dennis Gifford's *The British Film Catalogue 1895 – 1985: A Reference Guide* (2nd edn: Newton Abbot, 1986).
12. *Hansard*, House of Commons (18 July 1921), col.1964 [A.E. Newbould].
13. *Daily Mail Year Book 1922* (London, 1921), 42, 'The Kinema in 1921'.

14. *London Argus* (26 January 1907): 334, 'Time and Tide'.

15. G.L. Johnson, *Photographic Optics and Colour Photography* (London, 1909), 31.

16. I. Christie, *The Last Machine: Early Cinema and the Birth of the Modern World* (London, 1994), 12.

17. *Times Educational Supplement* (6 August 1912): 90, 'Pictures in Education'.

18. J.M. Hutcheson 'Music in the Cinema', *Bioscope* (17 August 1916): 627; M. Newbolt (ed), *The Later Life and Letters of Sir Henry Newbolt* (London, 1942), 230; D.S. Higgins (ed), *The Private Diaries of Sir H. Rider Haggard 1914–1925* (London, 1980), 84.

19. W.T. George, *Playing to Pictures: A guide for pianists and conductors of motion picture theatres* (2nd edn: London, 1914), 9.

20. *Cinema* (6 December 1917): 9, 'Birmingham Branch'; *ibid.* (13 December 1917): 88, 'Cinema Notes from Brum and the Midlands'; *Kinematograph Weekly* (13 December 1917): 76, 'The Right Spirit'; *ibid.* (15 August 1918): 74, 'Technical Section'.

21. *Kinematograph Weekly* (12 September 1907): 274.

22. Public Record Office, London, HO 45/10376/161425, file 6, Document no.3, 'Cinematograph Displays (Unlicensed Premises)', (February 1908).

23. G. Edgar (ed), *Careers for Men Women and Children* (London, 1911), vol.I 108, 'How to Become a Bioscope Theatre Proprietor'.

24. L. Trevelyan, 'The Picture Pianist', *Bioscope* (15 June 1911): 565.

25. *The Stage Year Book 1915* (London, 1915), 172, 'Non-Flam Films and Music'.

26. E. Strong, 'On the Screen', *Illustrated Films Monthly* (January 1914): 251.

27. W.R. Titterton, *From Theatre to Music Hall* (London, 1912), 68: *Cinema* (1 March 1917): 28, 'National Service and the Entertainment Tax'; W. Beeson, 'The Modern Picture House and Its Music', *Music Student* (June 1918): 392; A.E. Davison, 'Picture Music', *Musical News* (7 December 1918): 163; A.L. Salmon, 'Music at the Cinema', *Musical Times* (1 December 1920): 804.

28. C.B. Hawkins, *Norwich: A Social Study* (London, 1910), 310–311.

29. *How to Run a Picture Theatre: A Handbook for Proprietors, Managers, and Exhibitors* (2nd ed: London, 1914), 24.

30. *Leicester Daily Post* (22 December 1914), quoted in D.R. Williams, *Cinema in Leicester 1896–1931* (Loughborough, 1993), 105.

31. [National Council of Public Morals] *The Cinema: Its Present Position and Future Possibilities* (London, 1917), 17–18.

32. R.H. Dewes, 'Cinemagoing in Silent Days: A Midland Tale', *Picture House*, no.3 (Spring 1983): 18.

33. V. Van Damm, *Tonight and Every Night* (London, 1952), 30.

34. [National Council of Public Morals] *The Cinema: Its Present Position and Future Possibilities* (London, 1917), 239–240.

35. R.H. Dewes, 'Cinemagoing in Silent Days: A Midland Tale', *Picture House*, no.3 (Spring 1983): 19.

36. [London] *Evening News* (16 November 1909): 1, 'London's Picture Palaces'; C. Calvert, *Historical Review of the Cinematograph* (London, 1911), 4, 6; D. Crane, 'The Picture Palace: How are we to regard it?', *Quiver* (March 1912): 455.

37. [National Council of Public Morals] *The Cinema: Its Present Position and Future Possibilities* (London, 1917), 3.

38. *Kinematograph Weekly* (2 May 1918): 77, 'Southport Notes'.

39. E.F. Spence, *Our Stage and Its Critics* (London, 1910), 242–243; *Bioscope* (5 May 1910): 3, 'Best Seats at the Back'.

1895

3

Popular culture

1895

The Depiction of Hispanics and Other Races and Ethnicities in United States Film, 1895–1920

Gary D. Keller and Estela Keller

Hispanic Research Centre. Arizona State University, Tempe, AZ 85287-2702, USA

UNITED STATES FILM has often been called a 'dream factory' partly because of its catering to wish fulfilment ('the dream') and its production according to assembly-line models (the 'factory'). This paper suggests that the 'dream factory' that has been a conventional metaphor for the film industry had a precursor in what by the 1870s were often known as 'fiction factories'.[1] These factories, beginning about 35 years before the invention of cinema, were known for their mass fabrication of cheap, popular, widely distributed fiction in accordance with conventions later adopted by the US film industry. Most notably, the Western and the detective story genres were produced in considerable numbers first by the American fiction factories and subsequently by the US film industry.[2] While the US film industry was a vast enterprise that was based on numerous sources including comic strips, minstrel shows, vaudeville, melodrama, cheap popular fiction (story-papers, dime and nickel novels, 'libraries', pulp magazines), genteel (slick) fiction and serious (highbrow) fiction, and the legitimate theatre, especially with respect to Westerns and the detective story, the conventions of cheap popular fiction were dominant.

Let us focus solely on Westerns. We are directing our attention to two intertwined entertainment industries, one distributed via story-papers as early as 1800 and via dime and nickel novels and cheap 'libraries' by 1860,[3] the other, film, emerging around 1894 and 1895. Both of these industries had much in common, and once film was invented, also influenced, borrowed from, and reinforced each other. By the 1870s the 'fiction factories', foreshadowing the film factories, already were known for formulaic plots, characters, and genres that were manufactured assembly-line style,[4] mass distributed by means of creative new methods,[5] and readily consumed by an audience totalling millions of readers.

Both cheap, popular fiction and, subsequently, film were the result of technological advances; both took society by storm and both were characterised by enormous unit production. The number of cheap, popular fiction titles that were produced greatly surpassed all serious and genteel fiction combined. One alone of the five major fiction factories, Beadle, produced 3158 separate titles in the space of 50 years. By comparison, Lyle Wright's bibliographies of American fiction for 1850–1900, which omit all dime and nickel novels and serialised fiction, have a total of 9003 entries.[6] Both the fiction factories and later the film factories were characterised by explosive sales. In 1864, William Everett, writing in the *North American Review,* noted that Beadle had sold five million units in a mere five years from 1860–1864 and judged that such sales were 'almost unprecedented in the annals of booksellers' and that the cheap fictions had 'undoubtedly obtained greater popularity than any other series of works of fiction published in America'.

In the cases of both factory fiction and film, works were produced and marketed by easily identifiable genres providing variations on familiar plots that made participation an easy experience on the part of consumers. By the late nineteenth century the fiction factories had shifted from selling authors to selling characters and series. Thus a major marketing device of cheap fiction was the creation of series of Buffalo Bill, Deadwood Dick, Wild Bill, Joaquín Murrieta, Texas Jack, Kit Carson, Daniel Boone, Davy Crockett, Calamity Jane, Leonie Locke, Old Sleuth, Young Sleuth, Young Badger, Nick Carter, Frank Merriwell, Diamond Dick, Old King Brady, and Young Wild West books. Authors were de-emphasised so that often hosts of anonymous hack writers manufactured the books in question. However, sometimes the authors of the 1860s and 1870s were used for marketing books much later. Long after they had died, hack writers anonymously produced scores of Ned Buntline and Bertha M. Clay novels.

Capital investment in both the fiction and film industries centred not on production but on distribution. Steady turnover was necessary in order to ensure revenues that depended on regular consumption of the merchandise on a continual basis as the priority rather than on high consumption of any one particular product. Both industries went national soon after their establishment. Beginning in New York or Philadephia, by the 1870s factory fictions were distributed everywhere through the creative use of railroads, the US postal system (which had a crucial influence over their fortunes), and newsboys. In addition, both the film and the fiction factories produced what might generously be called a form of pollution: damaging stereotypes of minorities and out-groups. Two fundamental components of the formulas in both cheap fiction and story films were wish-fulfilment and Americanism. Often the novels and the films combined both nationalism and hedonism at the expense of out-groups, including Hispanics, Native Americans, and Asians.

As a result of an extensive analysis of hundreds of popular Western fictions of the nineteenth and early twentieth centuries and as many as 2,000 United States' films produced between 1895 and 1920 in which Hispanic or other out-group characters appeared (hundreds of these Westerns), this paper concludes that the conventions of the cheap, popular Western fictions, established in the second half of the nineteenth century, were essentially adopted into film Westerns during the early silent period.

The basic fictional stereotypes of both Anglo and Mexican appeared in the cheap, popular Western and in the more ambitious, genteel or slick works set in the West during the time and place in which the characters and incidents first appeared; that is, in works written in the heat of emotion generated by the Texas Revolution, the war with Mexico, and the invasion of the far Southwest. Nevertheless, the image of the Hispanic that was generated in American literature was strongly influenced by earlier, negative depictions that originated in the period of the Reformation and the Counter-Reformation giving rise in that period to what Hispanic historians have called the 'Black Legend'.[7] By the time of the Texas Revolution, the conventional image of the Mexican was that he was a degenerated offspring of cruel, intolerant, overbred, and morally loose Spaniards who had coupled with even more inferior native peoples. The Mexican, a product of racial miscegenation, was dark, yellow, or greasy,[8] lazy and cowardly, instinctual and lustful, avaricious and dishonourable. But he also was opportunistic and had a degree of cunning, and he could be pretty good with a knife.

The fixed, strongly negative images of Hispanics in American literature, both popular and genteel, perpetuated themselves forward in time as well. Distance from the subject did not lend detachment. The stereotypes about Mexicans had become firmly established in Western novels by 1870 and few authors or, subsequently, filmmakers attempted to refute or avoid following these images in the next 50 years. One element explaining the static perpetuation of stereotypes is to be found in the use of local colour and history by the Westerns. The need for veracity in popular fiction with an historical setting is less important than the use of background information to merely create an air of plausibility. Kingsley Amis aptly calls this process the Fleming effect, after the creator of James Bond.

Such a process cannot be dismissed as a mere manifestation of racism, although it was that, too. To some extent the Mexican was simply another element of local colour of the Southwest. For example, part of the formula for both cheap, popular novels or silent films of certain genres was to depict forbidden female temptresses to offset virtuous heroines. Such works with a southwestern setting tended to feature a loose-principled brown woman as counterpoint to a chaste white heroine and as a test of the hero's degree of moral commitment. In both novels and films, the white hero often was good–bad, failing in the middle of the work and ultimately rising at the end, overcoming base, interracial lust, and returning to lily white morality.

One prolific group of popular fictions were penned under the name of Ned Buntline (an actual writer and later the pseudonym for ghost writers).[9] Catering to his readers' craving for immoral stimulation followed by moral instruction, the Buntline novel placed the male characters in compromising situations with Mexican women from which they extricated themselves only after a series of close calls which enabled the novel to have it both ways: sex first, sermon afterward.[10]

Another part of the explanation for the perpetuation of stereotypes reflects the craft and conventions of popular fiction writing with respect to character and conflict. Writers of popular fiction quickly perceived the acceptability of a given series of stereotypes, and they began both to copy each other and to use those conventions as a shorthand, a quick form to set up characters, plots, or conflicts that were immediately recognisable to the avid, experienced reader of popular fiction.

One popular fiction writer, Ryerson Johnson, well known in the guild in his time, now obscure, working in the 1920s and 1930s described his modus operandi in a fashion that would be equally descriptive for the popular Westerns of 60 or 70 years earlier. He states:

> There was a cliché among pulp writers that if you wanted to establish a good guy, you showed him petting a dog. A bad guy? He kicks the dog. In a western story you could do it with a horse. Pat him or cruelly spur him.[11]

With respect to characterisation, this writer tells us:

> We didn't do much probing into personality or motivation. We generally used 'character tags' to establish our characters. A line or two, sometimes a word or two, was enough to 'tag' the minor characters ... Whatever the 'character tag' you decided upon, you'd return to it at intervals throughout the story to keep the reader reminded. Redhead, lantern-jawed, gentle giant, dead eyes, scar-faced, etc. – quick identification devices to keep a fast-reading reader from getting his characters mixed up.[12]

The reliance on routinised behaviours such as kicking the horse versus patting it was made to order for film, which in fact made ample use for character identifications of these routines as well as props such as black hats versus white hats.

Both in fiction and subsequently in film and fiction the tried and tested American projections of themselves were juxtaposed against negative projections of the Mexican. All that was needed to establish most of the characterisation and some of the action was to expose certain elements of American character on one side of the fictional or filmic ledger and to offset them with traits attributed to the Mexican. Thus, the Mexican tended to be defined negatively, in terms of qualities diametrically opposed to an Anglo hero. Moreover, with respect to film, the *mise-en-scène* centred the Anglo heroes, heroines and Anglo culture, with Hispanic elements occupying the periphery. The *mise-en-scène* was strongly Anglo-centric even in those films that depicted contemporaneous events taking place in the Hispanic world such as the Mexican Revolution of 1910. The films of the Mexican Revolution often revolved around Anglo heroes who entered benighted Mexico to right wrongs.

Just as the cheap, popular Westerns evoked Hispanic characters with a handful of stereotypes, the depiction of Hispanics in US film from 1895–1920, despite the vast number of films in which Hispanics appeared, was characterised by a range and typology of roles (mostly played by non-Hispanic actors) that was extraordinarily limited. The content analysis that has been conducted[13] identified only three primary female and eight primary male roles, and even these eleven roles were closely interconnected.[14]

The primary female roles were the cantina girl; the faithful or self-sacrificing señorita; and the vamp. The cantina girl was a passive sex object, dancing or otherwise behaving in an alluring fashion, primarily for an Anglo love interest whom she sometimes favoured over a Latin suitor.[15] Often she performed a seductive dance that was a peak scene in the film. The vamp, on the other hand, was a Hispanic variant on a type that was very common in silent film, featuring white female roles or personages appearing in period pieces, spectacle films, and epics. With respect to Hispanic vamps, Carmen or a character very much like her predominated.[16] The Hispanic vamp was a psychological menace usually to white males ill-equipped to defend themselves. She tended to differ somewhat in degree from her white counterparts in that passionate sex more than psychological manipulation was her trademark, and, accordingly, she often displayed a willingness to commit physical violence rather than merely manipulate men. These traits reflected the frequent projection by the more puritanical Anglo culture of easy sex onto both Hispanic females and males.

The faithful señorita displayed fidelity to Anglos from ethnocentric, Anglo expectations: fealty to the Anglo ethnicity, the United States and its symbols such as the flag, sheriff, or the cavalry, or to American culture or mores.[17] The faithful señorita was most often a 'good–bad' character in that she went wrong in the middle of the film and at the end, realising her 'poor' behaviour, placed her body in front of the knife or bullet intended for her Anglo love interest. Because of her fidelity to Anglo-Saxonism, the faithful señorita often appeared as a turncoat, a traitor to her culture and her family which she put above her Anglo love interest and Anglo culture. The faithful señorita is the analogue to the faithful Mexican male. However, where typically the male displayed respect or gratitude to an Anglo patriarch (a rancher, a sheriff), the faithful señorita followed her Anglo love interest.

Outside of the parameters of romance or sex, most typically interracial, there were virtually no Hispanic female roles from 1895–1920; older female characters rarely appeared. In fact, as in films such as *Martyrs of the Alamo* (1915, Triangle), *The Spirit of the Flag* (1913, Bison), *Under the Yoke* (1918, Fox), or *The Woman God Forgot* (1917, Artcraft Pictures Corp.), history, including the conquest of Mexico by Cortez or the birth of Texas, appeared driven by interracial, heterosexual behaviour.

Hispanic males were primarily bandits or otherwise bad men, 'good bad' men, faithful Mexicans, 'greasers', Latin Lovers, and two more aggressively positive types, both closely connected, the Hispanic avenger and the 'gay caballero', a variety of Latino Robin Hood.[18] Whereas the Hispanic female functioned primarily in relation to an Anglo lover, the Hispanic male was typically a foil to an Anglo hero. He was almost always either the physical antagonist of that Anglo or his loyal and subordinate partner. When the Hispanic and the Anglo were antagonists, they struggled over power, money or property, or a woman, usually a Latina. As collaborator, the Hispanic was usually either the loyal, often inept side-

1895

kick, a 'good bad' man who came to appreciate Anglo values, or a faithful Mexican or other Hispanic, repaying a debt of gratitude. The relationship between Hispanic males and Anglo women tended almost always to revolve around either sex or romance. The Hispanic either lusted for the Anglo women or he worshipped her abjectly.

In contrast to the circumstances of the Hispanic female, various Hispanic males did appear in other, albeit negative roles that cast them as covetous, greedy, lusting for power, property, and the like, rather than driven exclusively by sexual passion or romance. Also, in contrast to the situation obtaining for Hispanic females, older Hispanic male characters sometimes did appear, but almost never in appealing roles. They were among the most evil Hispanics, typically bent on selling into marriage or otherwise realising financial or property gains by proffering their daughters.

The most unusual Hispanic male roles were the greaser[19] and the gay caballero. The greaser had an innate status derived from his birth; greaserhood was a condition of life, primarily of the lower social status Mexican, although examples appeared among the higher classes of Mexicans and Spaniards when they engaged in behaviours odious to Anglos. This phenomenon of assigning innate greaserhood by American popular fiction, film, and American society permitted the production of films where greasers appeared in various roles ranging from bandits to bullfighters to generals to tramps to peons to landowners. Similarly, because the status of greaserhood was innate, there appeared in American film both evil greasers, the most common variety, and what on the surface would appear to be an oxymoron, 'good' greasers, those who were faithful to Anglo morality. The 'good' greaser appeared in director D.W. Griffith's *The Greaser's Gauntlet* (1908, Biograph) and in *Tony the Greaser* (1911, Méliès, remade 1914, Vitagraph). The unenviable good greaser wanders between the longed-for world of the Anglo, and the stigmatised world of the Mexican, doomed permanently in a middle position between Anglo heroes and greaser villains.

The role of the gay caballero was a variant of the noble outlaw, one of the most ubiquitous in literature, and of course one of the most famous of these is Robin Hood who is supposed to have inhabited a part of England not far from where we are convening. The noble outlaw made his debut in the cheap, popular Western on 15 October 1877, when the House of Beadle and Adams released *Deadwood Dick, the Prince of the Road; or, The Black Rider of the Black Hills* by Edward L. Wheeler, 'Sensational Novelist', one of the more prolific writers of the period. Deadwood Dick was enormously popular and soon became the hero of an extensive series of cheap Westerns. The character of Deadwood Dick strongly attracted the beautiful women who peopled the novels. Usually he resisted their advances, but he did marry three times and father two children. Each time, however, his wife's unfaithfulness or death banished him once again to a rootless, roaming life with his two valiant sidekicks, Calamity Jane and Old Avalanche, the Indian fighter.[20]

The gay caballero was essentially a Latino Robin Hood; or a pseudo-Latino one in that occasionally the plot has the masked man turn out to be an Anglo in Latino disguise.[21] The specific allusion to the Hispanic Robin Hood was common in trade advertising or the reviews of the films. The most famous gay caballeros were Zorro and the Cisco Kid. Gay caballero films primarily were set in colonial California under Spanish rule and featured conflicts between the corrupt peninsular Spanish administrator on the one hand, and on the other, the oppressed, who ranged from rich Creole hacendados to the peasant class. The gay caballero was similar to the good badman, but generally the essential difference is skin colour and/or social class. The good badman was more often than not, a bandit. The gay caballero was, of course, an aristocrat. He also tended to be white, European (i.e. a Castilian criollo) while his arch enemy was a peninsular Spaniard.

We conclude in a somewhat different chord. This paper has examined the continuity, primarily in the Western, of negative stereotypes that preceded both cheap popular fictions and film Westerns, but were perpetuated by both. There are also important discontinuities. For one, both the fiction factories and the filmic ones were technologically revolutionary, and

1895

like any revolution, they brought new and liberating elements. The popular novel both reflected and reinforced the emancipation of women by contributing to the decline of the domestic novel and its ideology, and introducing in its stead, fictions depicting female detectives, Western figures such as Calamity Jane, and working women, in mills, factories, and other settings.[22] If the popular novel could be characterised as corrosive, a hydrochloric acid, then film was Aqua Regia. Its well-known powers of illusionism, immediate accessibility, and its market extension to both the literate and illiterate alike, intensified everything. Thus, while on the one hand many more people were 'treated' to negative racial and ethnic stereotypes by film, the medium also greatly expanded the emancipation of women, and even, to a certain extent, of out-groups. On the one hand, the film theatre, and, later, palace itself became an occasion for the liberation of women, who now had access to a new entertainment venue outside of the home. There was a link between the box-office support by women of film and film content itself. Films began to portray women in uncharacteristic roles, as detectives such as in *The Fatal Hour* (1908, Biograph) and as physically strong, often beating up on ethnics such as in *The Arizona Cat Claw* (1919,

World Film Corp.), but occasionally collaborating with members of other races and ethnicities as in *The Red Girl* (1908, Biograph) and *Unprotected* (1916, Lasky). In addition, feminists and suffragettes financially backed and produced films.

There are also discontinuities, of course, between cheap fiction and film. There emerged no Black equivalent of dime novels, and there appears to have been little Black readership of them.[23] However, in the case of film, which had even more impact on mass taste, the segregation of audiences led to the establishment of black movie theatres which in turn encouraged a black film movement.

Finally, even as United States film eventually became world dominant, from the very beginning in the then US territories of Puerto Rico and the Philippines, there emerged film production of a nationalistic, non-Anglocentric nature. Moreover, in Mexico there emerged a film industry that counted on the export of its product – vastly different in its depiction of races and ethnicities – to the Hispanic populations of the south-west of the United States. Mexican film in Spanish was able to cross the border and was exhibited in several hundred United States theatres.

Notes

1.   See Michael Denning, *Mechanic Accents: Dime Novels and Working-Class Culture in America* (London: Verso, 1987), 17, in which he reproduces an interesting description of the fiction factories by a commentator, Edward Bok in 1892: 'Of course we all know that all kinds of factories exist in New York, but until last week I never knew that the great metropolis boasted of such a thing as a real and fully equipped literary factory ... It employs over thirty people, mostly girls and women. For the most part these girls are intelligent. It is their duty to read all the daily and weekly periodicals in the land ... Any unusual story of city life – mostly the misdoings of city people – is marked by these girls and turned over to one of three managers. These managers, who are men, select the best of the marked articles, and turn them over to one of a corps of five women, who digest the happening given to them and transform it to a skeleton or outline for a story. This shell, if it may be so called, is then returned to the chief manager, who turns to a large address-book and adapts the skeleton to some one of the hundred or more writers entered on his book ... [The stories are then sold] to the cheaper sensational weeklies, to boiler-plate factories and to publishers of hair-curling libraries of adventure ... This business is of the most profitable character to its owners. The "factory" does not care where its authors get their material from, so long as the story, when finished, is calculated to please the miscellaneous audience for which it is intended. "Situations", and of the most dramatic and startling character, must be frequent, and two or three murders and a rescue or two in one chapter are not a bit too many.'

2.   It should be noted that American literature did not break out of the traditional moulds of European literature until after the war of 1812. There were a few earlier attempts to write genuine native literature, but for the most part, the authors have been forgotten. One of the earliest was Royall

1895

Tyler who published an early book of adventure, *The Algerine Captive* (1797). An early sea and adventure story, *Fortune's Football,* by James Butler appeared that same year. Soon after, George Brockden Brown, although his novels were crude in construction, wrote about frontier life in *Edgar Huntley* (1799), one of the earliest stories where a fair maiden was rescued from the Indians. After 1812, two of the most significant writers to break with the traditional European models of American literature were James Fenimore Cooper, known for his Leatherstocking tales, bold, imaginative frontier stories of flight and pursuit heavily populated with American Indians and Edgar Allan Poe, famous for, among other works, his creation of the modern detective story. Cooper published five Leatherstocking novels, the first in 1823, *The Pioneers,* and the most famous, *The Last of the Mohicans,* in 1826. Poe was publishing supernatural tales in the 1830s and in April 1841 he published the first detective story in *Graham's Magazine,* a Philadelphia journal, 'The Murders in the Rue Morgue'. It is interesting to note that Poe's first stories were initially published in dime novel form, the size being about five by eight inches, with paper covers, and thus relegated to being considered second-class literature not worthy of a clothbound book.

3. By the 1830s the new American generation eagerly sought Westerns; the West had been opened to the extent that the mysteries of the new land were of intense interest. The December 1833 issue of *The Western Monthly Magazine* carried an essay, by Isaac Appleton Jewett, addressed to the writers of America that was a plea for the new and distinctly national literature based on the richness of the wilderness and the West. Among the literature that was produced during the period were the *Border Romances* in several volumes published from 1834 to 1840. The first crude story-paper appeared in 1839, the *Brother Jonathan Weekly,* a mammoth-sized news and story paper measuring 22 x 32 inches, aimed at the mass audience. The popularity of the story-papers encouraged Erastus and Irwin Beadle in 1860 to publish the first dime novel, *Maleska: The Indian Wife of the White Hunter,* written by Ann S. Stephens. Within a few months more than 65,000 copies had been sold. Publishing a tale of stirring action, all in one 'book' for a dime or a nickel immediately attracted other publishers (as well as many would-be authors) and the flood of dime novels was upon the American public. Stories galore were produced of pirates, detectives, soldiers, highway men, sea adventurers, outlaws, bootblacks and villains. With tales of history, crime, adventure, love, war, urban and rural life, and above all, the West, the acceptance was phenomenal. In less than five years, by April 1964 Beadle's Dime Books alone had sold more than 5 million copies. For approximately 60 years the dime novel represented the low-cost fiction that the public demanded, but competition arose in the attempt to give the reader more for a dime and the pulp magazine was born. As early as 1888 the thick *Argosy* appeared, an outgrowth of the juvenile story-paper *The Golden Argosy,* and in 1903 appeared *The Popular Magazine. Blue Book* commenced in 1904 under the title *The Monthly Story Magazine,* and *All-Story* in 1905. The 32-page dime novel soon passed into history, but it was replaced by a plethora of pulp magazines, with Westerns and crime pulp at the forefront.

The cheap novels were also clearly connected to popular melodramas. Beginning in the mid-nineteenth century not only are dime novels 'dramatised for the stage' but they are 'narrativised for the story paper'(W.H. Bishop, 'Story-Paper Literature', *Atlantic* 44 (September 1879): 387). Grimstead (David Grimstead, *Melodrama Unveiled: American Theater and Culture, 1800–1850* (Chicago: University of Chicago Press, 1968), 73) suggests that the Astor Place Riots of 1849 (led in part by dime novelist Ned Buntline) was a sign of the end of a theatre that united different classes in boxes, pits and galleries: 'one theater was no longer large enough to appeal to all classes'. After 1850, the melodrama and the dime novel increasingly found a predominantly working-class audience. Moreover, with the narrativisation of melodramas by dime novels and story-papers, the latter appeared to become a way of preserving and recapturing a public moment or a favourite performance. This relationship between the popular theatre and the popular novel prefigures an analogical one between popular fiction and film.

4. With a population of nearly twenty million by mid-century, most of whom were literate, the United States was a ready-made audience that could now be satisfied with reading material produced at low cost. With the introduction of the steam rotary press, the emergence of stereotyping and the erosion of jobs for skilled compositors, the printing industry experienced radical transformations. Larger amounts of capital were required for printing plants. One way that a few successful entrepreneurs dealt with both the transformations of and shakeout in the printing business as well

as the opportunities provided by technological advancement was to turn failing newspapers into highly-advertised story-papers and to sell pamphlet novels for a nickel or a dime. The nickel and dime novels themselves succumbed to pulp magazines around the turn of the century due to further technological advancements that permitted reductions in unit costs that in turn permitted the magazines to sell more and varied material in one issue for a dime than could be provided by a 30,000 dime novel.

5.   Distribution was greatly aided by utilising the railroads and the capabilities of the US postal service to establish the nickel and dime novels as national industries. Market penetration was also greatly aided by the fact that the new generation of Americans were mostly literate (partly the result of the movement of public school reform so ardently and effectively spearheaded by Horace Mann), but the majority of readers were denied access to popular literature by the relatively high cost of the hardbound books and the limited number of and access to libraries. The marketing technique of selling series of novels based on characters was a successful innovation.

6.   Lyle Wright, *American Fiction, 1774–1850: A Contribution Towards a Bibliography* (San Marino, California: The Huntingdon Library, 1969); Lyle Wright, *American Fiction, 1851–1875: A Contribution Towards a Bibliography* (San Marino, California: The Huntingdon Library, 1978); Lyle Wright, *American Fiction, 1876–1900: A Contribution Towards a Bibliography* (San Marino, California: The Huntingdon Library, 1978).

7.   The term, *leyenda negra* (black legend) was popularised by Julián Juderías, in his 1914 book, *La leyenda negra*. For good relatively recent overviews of the development of Anglo attitudes toward Hispanics (and other minorities), see Arnoldo de León, *They Called Them Greasers: Anglo Attitudes Towards Mexicans in Texas, 1821–1900* (Austin: University of Texas Press, 1983), Ronald T. Takaki, *Iron Cages: Race and Culture in Nineteenth-Century America* (New York: Knopf, 1979); Reginald Horsman, *Race and Manifest Destiny: The Origins of American Racial Anglo-Saxonism* (Cambridge: Harvard University Press, 1981); and Arthur G. Pettit, *Images of the Mexican American in Fiction and Film* (College Station, Texas: Texas A an M University Press, 1980). See also Norman D. Smith, 'Mexican Stereotypes on Fictional Battlefields: or Dime Novel Romances of the Mexican War', *Journal of Popular Culture*, 13 (1980): 526–540; and Michael K. Simmons, 'Nationalism and the Dime Novel', *Studies in the Humanities* 9 (1981): 39–44.

8.   Already by the early 1860s, vicious and virulent novels had been produced that evoked without any scruples or self-consciousness at all the Catholic tyranny, half-breed degeneracy, Mexican sexuality, and unfitness of the mass of 'greasers' to run their own country. For example, one prominent jingoist was A.J.H. Duganne, a founder of the Native American or 'Know-Nothing' Party and a prolific author of novels, poems, and patriotic writings. Two novels written by Duganne set in central Mexico just before and during the Mexican War (1846–48) were *The Peon Prince; or, The Yankee Knight-Errant: A Tale of Modern Mexico* (1861) and *Putnam Pomfret's Ward; or, A Vermonter's Adventures in Mexico on the Breaking Out of the Last War* (1861). The hero of both novels is a Yankee from Vermont who does not think well of 'greasers and yaller-jackets', 'yaller chaps', and 'yaller-skins'. He states that a 'pack o' greasers' is no match for one Green Mountain Boy; he ridicules the Mexicans' inability to talk English, 'like Christians', and their lack of technology ('as for 'lectric telegraphs or locomotives, I guess they'd as soon believe in harnessing 'chain-lightnin' to their old go-carts.') In this and other novels of the period, American invincibility contrasts sharply with Mexican vulnerability. Victims of centuries of political chaos, priestly corruption, and racial miscegenation, the mixed-blood and poverty-stricken Mexicans have long been fated to extinction. The theme is sounded repeatedly that the Spaniards and their 'polluted' descendents have committed racial and national self-genocide by mixing voluntarily with inferior dark-skinned races.

9.   Ned Buntline (Edward Zane Carroll Judson, 1821–1886), adventurer, bigamist, and general confidence man who launched Buffalo Bill in show business in the 1880s was a prolific writer in his own right with the house of Beadle. Beginning in 1905, long after his death, his name was used as author by numerous ghost writers employed by the publishing house of Street and Smith which also produced the Buffalo Bill Stories. Over six hundred novels of the Buffalo Bill imprint were published, at least one-third of which depicted a Mexican somewhere in their pages.

10.   For example, Buntline's *The Ice King* introduces Doña Elementa, a 'handsome, dark-eyed woman, whose brunette cheek, jetty hair, long eyelashes and delicately voluptuous form, talk of a southern clime for her birthplace [and] an ardent temperament for her heritage'. Elementa is as elemental in

her passions as her name implies. She declares to Lord Edward Wimsett, a neurasthenic 'Limey' who is traveling with her by ship '... if I cannot be your wife, let – let me be – your – mistress!' Wimsett, who lacks the moral fibre of his American cousins, hems and haws, but finally summons sufficient courage to tell Elementa that they can only be friends. Elementa promptly puts a match to the powder magazine on the ship and blows the novel's entire cast of characters to kingdom come.

11. Quoted in Nick Carr, *The Western Pulp Hero* (San Bernardino, California: The Borgo Press, 1990),10.

12. *Ibid.*, 10.

13. See Gary D Keller, *Hispanics and United States Film: An Overview and Handbook* (Temple, Arizona: Bilingual Press, 1994).

14. In succeeding notes appear a few of the earliest film examples of each of these eleven roles. Strong documentation of a bridge between cheap popular Westerns and film Westerns would be established if it could be documented that the writers of the former also worked as scenarioists (to use the term of the early film period) for the latter. Similarly, a bridge between cheap popular fiction and film would be established if the films listed the works of popular fiction writers as the source for their films. However, the relationship between cheap fictions and films based on the appearance of the same writers or titles is a complex matter. A few Western writers such as Max Brand, and Theodosia Harris are listed as either the source for films (the latter's *Martyr's of the Alamo,* for example) or as scenarioists. However, this is uncommon, the overlap is small, almost insignificant. Yet, this should not be surprising for the following reasons: (1) While there were some very well-known formula fiction writers, beginning in the 1880s, writers were de-emphasised in favour of characters such as Buffalo Bill and Deadwood Dick; (2) Most of the cheap fiction writers were either obscure or anonymous; (3) Perhaps, most important, because the cheap fiction writers used established formulas, conventions, and stereotypes in the first place, the film industry could simply arrogate those without acknowledging authors. In this regard, perhaps Ryerson Johnson's lament is instructive. Johnson tells us: 'When I later tried my luck in Hollywood (I wrangled one lone credit, a segment of *Death Valley Days* titled "Dangerous Crossing"), I discovered that there, too, western pulps were stacked against the walls. But for a different reason. Hollywood writers drew from our stories in working up situations, characters, backgrounds, and premises for their scripts ... the same with us in New York. When we got stuck for a new story plot, we could go to a western movie. Somewhere along in the storyline there was bound to be a decision scene. The hero could choose to take this course of action or that one. Whichever way he went, we could go home, start with a similar opening situation and angle our story the "other way". We came out with a fresh new story. I guess we kind of swallowed up each other, New York and Hollywood ... One time I went up to the New York Paramount office with a tear-sheet of a slick magazine story I'd sold. I hoped they'd read it as a possibility for a movie vehicle. Somebody told me, "Wait a minute". She opened a file cabinet and flipped – to Ryerson Johnson. The Paramount office had synopsised this story and every other slick-paper story I ever sold. And they'd done the same with every other slick-paper writer,' quoted in Nick Carr, *The Western Pulp Hero* (San Bernadino, California: The Borgo Press, 1990), 11–12.

15. The very first examples of this character are evoked in purely Hispanic settings with all Hispanic characters (played by Anglos): *Her Sacrifice* (1911, Biograph), *The Dove and the Serpent* (1912, IMP), and *A Mexican Romance* (1912, Lubin). Beginning with the 1913 *On the Border* (American), the inter-racial formula is established as in *The Masked Dancer* (1914, Vitagraph).

16. One of the first vamp films, approximately three-minutes long, is *Mexican Sweethearts* (1909, Vitagraph) where a pretty señorita pretends to love an American soldier, which almost gets him killed. Also: *The Spanish Girl* (1909, Essanay) and *Broncho Billy's Mexican Wife* (1912, Essanay, reissued in 1915). Regarding Carmen films: *A Love Tragedy in Spain* (1908, Méliès) which was billed as 'a thrilling episode in the style of Bizet's *Carmen*', *Love in Madrid* (1911, Pathé), *The Test of Love* (1911, Yankee), and *The Last Dance* (1914, Picture Playhouse Film Co.).

17. One of the first films is *The Mexican's Jealousy* (1910, New York Motion Picture Co.) featuring a dark-skinned señorita, Rita, who saves and escapes with the Anglo and his half-breed friend. Also: *Bonita of El Cajón* (1911, American), *Carmenita the Faithful* (1911, Essanay), *Saved by the Flag* (1911, Pathé), and *Chiquita, the Dancer* (1912, American).

18. Early examples are as follows – *Bandits: A Cup of Cold Water* (1911, Selig), *A Fair Exchange* (1911, Selig), *The Long Arm of the Law* (1911, Kalem), *Betty's Bandit* (1912, Nestor), and *The Outlaw's Sacrifice* (1912, Essanay). *Bad Mexican: A Mexican's Crime* (1909, New York Motion Picture Co.),

A Tale of Texas (1909, Centaur), *A Cowboy's Generosity* (1910, Bison), *Western Justice* (1910, Lubin), and *What Great Bear Learned* (1910, Méliès). *Good or Faithful Mexican: A Mexican's Gratitude* (1909, Essanay), featuring G.M. Anderson before he assumed the role of the famous Broncho Billy, *The Mexican's Faith* (1910, Essanay), and *The Two Sides* (1911, Biograph, director, D.W. Griffith). *The Good Badman: The Half Breed* (1916, Triangle), *The Bad Man* (1923, First National), and *That Devil Quemado* (1925, FBO). It should be noted that Douglas Fairbanks starred in *The Good Bad Man* (1916, Triangle) but this film does not have any Hispanic roles. On the other hand, Fairbanks starred in *The Half Breed* in the same year. *The Hispanic Avenger: The Thread of Destiny* (1910, Biograph), *The Mexican* (1911, American), and *The Ranchman's Vengeance* (1911, American). *The Latin Lover: In the Land of the Cactus* (1913, Lubin), with Romaine Fielding in the role of the Mexican, and *House of Hate* (1918, Pathé), a twenty-episode serial with Antonio Moreno opposite Pearl White.

19. The film *Lost Mine* (Kalem, 1907) appears to be the first film in which the term greaser was specifically used, in this case in the title cards. Other early films depicting greasers were *The Pony Express* (Kalem, 1907,) *Mexican's Crime* (1909, New York Motion Picture Co.) and *Across the Mexican Line* (1911, Solax). Most greaser films used the epithet in the actual title including, *The Greaser's Gauntlet* (1908, Biograph), *Ah Sing and the Greasers* (1910, Lubin),*Tony the Greaser* (1911, Méliès, remade in 1914, Vitagraph), *The Greaser and the Weakling* (1912, American), *The Girl and the Greaser* (1913, American), *The Greaser's Revenge* (1914, Frontier), *The Greaser* (1915, Majestic), and *Broncho Billy's Greaser Deputy* (1915, Essanay).

20. The character is prototypical of many filmic characters as well, such as Broncho Billy. The first Broncho Billy film (the name was later changed to Bronco), according to Katz (see entry in Ephraim Katz, *The Film Encyclopedia* (New York: Thomas Y. Crowell, 1979) starring Gilbert M. Anderson, was *The Bandit Made Good* (1907, Essanay). The Broncho Billy character often interacted with Hispanics and Indians in accordance with the conventions of the cheap, popular novel.

21. One of the first examples of the type was *The White Vaquero* (1913, Bison). *Moving Picture World* (29 November 1913, p. 1009) described the hero: 'The White Vaquero, a very romantic Mexican bandit is a character who will win many friends'. *The Mark of Zorro* (1920, Fairbanks/United Atists) featuring Fairbanks in the first Zorro film, was produced almost immediately after publication of the 1919 short story, by Johnson McCully, 'The Curse of Capistrano', which created the character.

22. Denning suggests that the Civil War contributed to the decline of the sentimental, domestic novel, (see Michael Denning, *Mechanic Accents: Dime Novels and Working-Class Culture in America* (London: Verso), 187) although some post-war novels such as the very popular Elizabeth Stuart Phelps, *The Gates Ajar* (1868), attempted to reconstruct the vision of a benign God and a domestic heaven in the face of the war dead. For that matter, Griffith's *The Birth of a Nation* (1915) partakes of that same, anxious reconstruction.

23. The Black Periodical Fiction Project, headed by Henry Louis Gates, has not found a Black equivalent of dime novels, although considerable fiction was published in Black newspapers and journals. For a discussion of the relationship between dime novel conventions and early African-American fiction, and of the Black reading public in the nineteenth century, see Hazel V. Carby, *Reconstructing Womanhood: The Emergence of the Afro-American Woman Novelist* (New York: Oxford University Press, 1987). Dobkin searched through 8000 nickel library serials of 1879–1910 and found 'no black hero figure', (J.B. Dobkin, 'Treatment of Blacks in Dime Novels', *Dime Novel Round-Up* no. 580 (August 1986): 50–56), about fifty Black characters important to the story line, and the virtual disappearance of Black characters after 1906–07. The Black characters that did appear were almost invariably negatively stereotyped. One significant exception, Black Tom, The Negro Detective, turns out to be a White in disguise.

1895

Bad Boy: Notes on a Popular Figure in American Cinema, Culture and Society, 1895–1905

Peter Krämer

Department of American Studies, Keele University, Keele ST5 5BG, UK

THE VERY FIRST FILMS made by Auguste and Louis Lumière in the spring of 1895 with their recently patented Cinématographe included a carefully staged sketch about a mischievous boy. The film was originally entitled *Le Jardinier et le petit espiègle* (A Little Trick on the Gardener), but it is better known today as *L'Arroseur arrosé*, which is usually translated as, 'The Sprinkler Sprinkled'.[1] It belongs to a series of early Lumière films focusing on children – a baby being fed, boys diving into the sea, quarreling babies, children at play.[2] While some of these films, such as *Repas de bébé*, feature members of the Lumière family, *L'Arroseur arrosé* is a family affair in a different sense: the basic 'scenario' (with the boy stepping on the gardener's hose to then release the water into the man's face) was apparently suggested by the youngest Lumière brother, ten-year-old Edouard.[3] It would seem, then, that one of the earliest Lumière productions was inspired by the mischievous imagination of a boy, who, while he didn't actually play the part in front of the camera, surely identi-

fied strongly with the screen character's actions. Edouard's imagination in turn had probably been fuelled by French comic strips, which had depicted very similar pranks since the late 1880s, as for example in Christophe's 'Histoire sans paroles – Un Arroseur public', which had been published in the children's magazine *Le Petit Français Illustré* on 3 August 1889.[4] Intriguingly, this and other strips ended with the boy's triumph, and not as the film version with his punishment. While the older Lumières obviously felt the need to punish the boy for his prankish behaviour on screen, off screen they must have been very grateful for Edouard's mischievous idea, which gave them the basis for what next to *Arrivée d'un train en gare* (Arrival of a Train at the Station) became their most famous and influential film.

When *L'Arroseur arrosé* was included in the programme of the American premiere of the Lumière brothers' Cinématographe at Keith's Union Square Theatre in New York on 29 June 1896, it was titled *The Gardener and the Bad Boy*, and the *New York Dramatic Mirror*, one

1895

of the leading entertainment trade papers, singled it out for comment:

> The second picture showed a lawn with a gardener using a hose to sprinkle it. A bad boy steps on the hose, causing the water to squirt into the gardener's face. He drops the hose, runs after the boy, and gives him a sound thrashing.[5]

While this reviewer emphasised, perhaps even relished, the harsh punishment of the boy, other American reviewers praised the film's comedy, presumably cherishing the daring and the ingenuity of the boy's attack on his elder (who, after all, gets what he deserves for not paying attention to what is happening around him), and they declared it to be 'the funniest view yet given in any series of this sort'.[6]

As Charles Musser, Tom Gunning and others have argued, the success of *The Gardener and the Bad Boy* gave rise to one of the most important genres in early American filmmaking, the so-called bad-boy film.[7] This, typically, was a one-shot sketch showing the boy playing a trick on an unsuspecting adult, most often ending with the prankster visibly enjoying the success of his actions, rather than with his punishment. Bad-boy films and closely related subjects such as prank films featuring girls or adults as well as films displaying the antics of very young children, were produced in large quantities. In fact it could be said that of all genres, the bad-boy film came closest to dominating the overall output of story films during the first decade of projected motion pictures in the United States. During this time vaudeville houses such as Keith's Union Square Theatre provided film manufacturing companies with their primary exhibition outlet catering for a broadly based middle-class audience. For vaudeville's 'respectable' family audience, the bad boy was a lovable rascal; in particular he offered men a nostalgic evocation of a much less restricted and in some ways more 'manly' younger self, rebellious, physical, ingenious. However, with the rise of extended narrative films of a more serious nature in the early 1900s (most notably after the success of Edwin S. Porter's *The Great Train Robbery* in 1903) and with the subsequent nickelodeon boom (from 1905), the genre became increasingly marginal. It has been argued that boyish pranks did not lend themselves easily to narrative elaboration, and that the social implications of the bad boy's unpunished transgressions for the new nickelodeon audience made up to a large extent of immigrants and unsupervised children were considered dangerous.

Building on this by now familiar historical analysis, in this essay I should like to explore the rise and fall of the bad-boy film in the United States in more detail, taking my cue from the circumstances of the genre's inception. The crucial importance, for the production of *L'Arroseur arrosé*, of Edouard Lumière's mischievous imagination and of the comic strips he is likely to have read, indicates that the bad-boy figure had considerable cultural currency *prior* to its cinematic representation, both in terms of the self-image and lived experience of actual boys and in terms of popular representations. As I will show, this was the case in the United States as much as it was in France. In the first section of this essay, I will outline the popular literary tradition of bad-boy fiction in late nineteenth-century America, which provided the film genre with its name and its largely middle-class protagonist, and informed the response of its primary audience in vaudeville. Here, I will also look at the everyday culture of boyhood, which these novels claimed to represent in a realistic fashion. The second section will examine the prevalence and range of American bad-boy films from the period 1897 to 1903, and link them to some of the major themes in bad-boy literature by treating them as a connected series of sketches portraying typical scenes from the lives of middle-class boys. The third section will then be concerned with newspaper comic strips which evolved in a striking parallel to cinematic developments. Comic strips became a regular feature of mass-circulation newspapers in the United States from 1895 onwards, heavily featuring mischievous boys, who soon became the object of severe criticism and were subsequently marginalised. This discussion will allow me to shed new light on the decline of the bad-boy film after 1905.

Bad-boy books and boy culture in late nineteenth-century America

Whoever decided to present *L'Arroseur arrosé* to the American public as *The Gardener and the Bad Boy* must have been aware of the link this title established between the Lumière film and a rich tradition in American popular literature reaching back to Thomas Bailey Aldrich's semi-autobiographical bestseller *The Story of a Bad Boy* (1869). Among the many works included in this tradition were Mark Twain's *The Adventures of Tom Sawyer* (1876), perhaps the most popular of all literary classics, and his *The Adventures of Huckleberry Finn* (1885), arguably the most highly regarded popular American novel, as well as George Wilbur Peck's widely read sketches featuring 'Peck's Bad Boy', which had been published in newspapers and in books throughout the 1880s (the first collection of these sketches in book form was *Peck's Bad Boy and His Pa*, 1883).[8] To gauge the popularity of bad-boy books, it is worth noting that Frank Luther Mott lists all of the above amongst the top ten bestselling books of their respective years in the United States, with *Huckleberry Finn* making it into the top two of 1885, and *Tom Sawyer* residing in 'best seller heaven' as one of the twenty all-time bestselling books in the US.[9]

This popular literary tradition was initially shaped by the authors' desire to get away from the then dominant prescriptive approach to literary representations of children which self-consciously projected model characters (little saints) rather than aiming at realistic depictions. Aldrich, for example, took his own experiences as a 12-year-old as the starting point for his novel and opened the book as follows:

> This is the story of a bad boy. Well, not such a very bad, but a pretty bad boy; and I ought to know, for I am, or rather I was, that boy myself ... I call my story the story of a bad boy, partly to distinguish myself from those faultless young gentlemen who generally figure in narratives of this kind, and partly because I really was *not* a cherub. I may truthfully say I was an amiable, impulsive lad, blessed with fine digestive powers, and no hypocrite. I didn't want to be an angel ... In short, I

was a real human boy, such as you may meet anywhere in New England, and no more like the impossible boy in a storybook than a sound orange is like one that has been sucked dry.[10]

Bad-boy fiction, then, sought to address the richness and ambiguities of boys' lives, including all their 'faults' and 'badness'; that is their transgressions of adult norms. Rather than condemning what strict moralists would have considered to be serious flaws in the child's character, Aldrich and his followers celebrated boyish mischief as the expression of a lively and energetic personality. An avid reader of adventure books, a fan of private theatricals and a member of a secret society, Tom Bailey, the protagonist of *The Story of a Bad Boy*, spices up his life in a small Eastern town with imagined and real exploits, including dangerous boat trips, violent fist fights and harmless pranks. The novel is equally concerned with the boy's maturation, signalled by his first love and then abruptly brought about by his father's death. At the end, he leaves his childhood world behind to go to New York where he joins his uncle's counting house, destined to become a merchant (and a successful writer).

In *The Adventures of Tom Sawyer*, Mark Twain followed Aldrich's model quite closely, making, for example, a strong claim for the book's authenticity in an opening statement, in which he also attempted to identify his readership and to outline the ways in which he wanted to engage them:

> Most of the adventures recorded in this book really occurred; one or two were experiences of my own, the rest of those boys were schoolmates of mine. Huck Finn is drawn from life; Tom Sawyer also, but not from an individual ... Although my book is intended mainly for the entertainment of boys and girls, I hope it will not be shunned by men and women on that account, for part of my plan has been to try pleasantly to remind adults of what they once were themselves, and of how they felt and thought and talked, and what queer enterprises they sometimes engaged in.[11]

The author, then, invited children to identify

1895

with Tom's adventures as an extension of their own everyday exploits, and he invited adults to relive their past, to recover a different, perhaps more creative and satisfying outlook on life.

Tom Sawyer shares many character traits and experiences with Aldrich's Tom Bailey, and, like Aldrich, Twain makes it clear right from the start that his protagonist's mischief is endearing and admirable. In the first chapter, Aunt Polly, having just been fooled by Tom, muses:

> Hang the boy, can't I ever learn anything? Ain't he played me tricks enough like that for me to be looking out for him by this time? ... But, my goodness, he never plays them alike two days, and how is a body to know what's coming? He 'pears to know just how long he can torment me before I get my dander up, and he knows if he can make out to put me off for a minute, or make me laugh, it's all down again, and I can't hit him a lick.[12]

When he does get punished, by having to paint the fence on a Saturday morning, he demonstrates that his manipulativeness is a good preparation for leadership as an adult: he gets his friends to do the work for him, and to pay him for the privilege, too. When he strikes it rich by finding a treasure towards the end of the novel, it is perhaps Twain's way of saying that, just as with Aldrich's hero, Tom Sawyer's vivid imagination and daring pranks do pay off, preparing him for success in his later years. Unlike Tom Bailey, however, Twain's Tom is never shown to grow up.

The relationship between boyish pranks and later professional success is highlighted in George Wilbur Peck's stories. Although there is no development across the dozens of bad-boy sketches Peck published in newspapers and then collected in books, the author makes it clear that eventually this small-town boy will make it big. In one of the earliest published stories, Peck declares categorically:

> Of course, all boys are not full of tricks, but the best of them are. That is, those who are the readiest to play innocent jokes, and who are continually looking for chances to make Rome howl, are the most apt to turn out to be first-class business men.[13]

In the obligatory opening statement of the first collection of his stories, Peck assures the reader of the stories' authenticity:

> The 'Bad Boy' is not a 'myth' ... The counterpart of this boy is located in every city, village and country hamlet throughout the land. He is wide awake, full of vinegar ... He gets in his work everywhere there is a fair prospect of fun, and his heart is easily touched by an appeal in the right way, though his coat-tail is oftener touched with a boot than his heart is by kindness. But he shuffles through life until the time comes for him to make his mark in the world, and then he buckles on the harness and goes to the front, and becomes successful ... This book is respectfully dedicated to boys, to the men who have been boys themselves, to the girls who like the boys, and to the mothers, bless them, who like both the boys and the girls.[14]

Unlike Twain who refers to children and adults in his introduction, Peck makes it clear that first and foremost his writing addresses boys and men, offering his bad boy as an object of direct or nostalgic identification for them, whereas the females are expected merely to observe and appreciate the boy's antics from a distance (as does Aunt Polly).

Peck's bad boy is much less likeable than the two Toms, in that all he is ever shown to do (in the exploits that he mostly relates himself in conversations shortly after the event) is to cheat and lie, to physically attack and publicly humiliate his elders, especially his father. For this he often receives severe beatings which, however, never have any lasting effect. The violent, relentless and at the same time static quality of Peck's series of sketches could be seen as a direct inspiration for the peculiar feel of the physical and social world that the filmic bad-boys inhabit: this world hardly exists in its own right, but serves primarily as a stage for the boys' carefully planned and executed pranks, and staging such pranks is all the boys ever do. The following advertisement for *Peck's Bad Boy and His Pa* spells out

1895

the anarchic implications of Peck's stories, which apply equally to its filmic successors:

> Peck's Bad Boy is a 'holy terror'! He is full from top to toe of pure unadulterated cussedness. He hungers and thirsts after mischief. No day passes but he invents and puts in practice some new form of deviltry. One such boy in every community would retard the march of civilization. One such boy in every family would drive the whole world mad.[15]

Thus, in bad-boy fiction, as in later bad-boy films, the secure knowledge of the boy's inevitable maturation and adult success is balanced with a shockingly apocalyptic and at the same time highly pleasurable vision of total social disorder.

Literary and social historians have attempted to determine the cultural function of these representations of bad boys in late nineteenth-century American society. Anne Trensky, for example, writes about the character and social role of the bad boy within the novels' fictional community:

> He is typically rough and tough, quick to play and quick to fight. It is the boy's prerogative, if not his duty, to prove his full-blooded maleness. Most of all, he is disobedient, but his badness is endearing rather than unpleasant; it is humored and enjoyed, for it is the declaration of his free spirits. He is adored by parents, aunts, and grandparents, who pretend anger but are secretly grateful to him for enlivening their otherwise dull, placid lives, or for saying and doing what they themselves would like to but cannot because of social codes.

The boy's misbehaviour and practical jokes, his deliberate breaking of adult rules, his stealing, lying, cheating, playing hookey, walking barefoot, express his desire for 'a natural enjoyment free from stifling social rules', and also often serve to reveal 'an adult's dishonesty, unkindness, selfishness, and hypocrisy'.[16]

In this way, the 'bad boy' functioned as another ideal image for the mostly rural or small-town community he inhabited and, we may assume, for the novels' readers. This new ideal was both more realistic and more masculine than the previous ideal of the saintly child. The boy's transgressions allowed him to assert his freedom and his manliness playfully and aggressively, to follow his instincts, challenge authorities and invigorate community life. The bad-boy novels implied that the boy's transgressiveness was not only highly functional for the community but also constituted a precondition for his future integration into the world of adults. His challenge to authority prefigured the authority he would later assume himself; his pranks and adventures rehearsed the qualities needed for subsequent success in the working world. Indeed, as Trensky notes, with the exception of Huckleberry Finn, all bad boys 'belong to respectable middle-class families' and 'will grow up to be respectable and successful lawyers, doctors, businessmen, and maybe even senators and governors'.[17]

This conception of middle-class boyhood was not confined to bad-boy books but had much wider cultural currency in late nineteenth-century America. It served to define the actual experiences of boys between the age of about six and sixteen as a separate and fundamentally masculine stage of life, contrasting sharply with early childhood and the sphere of feminine domesticity. E. Anthony Rotundo has reconstructed this middle-class 'boy culture':

> Boys ... were drawn to activities that offered excitement and physical exercise. Dirt and noise were often by-products of such pastimes ... Above all, the pastimes favoured by Northern boys set their world in sharp contrast to the domestic, female world – the world from which they emerged as little boys and to which they returned every evening. Where women's sphere offered kindness, morality, nurture, and a gentle spirit, the boys' world countered with energy, self-assertion, noise, and a frequent resort to violence. The physical explosiveness and the willingness to inflict pain contrasted so sharply with the values of the home that they suggest a dialogue in actions between the values of the two spheres – as if a boy's aggressive impulses, so relentlessly opposed at home, sought extreme forms of release outside it; then, with stricken con-

1895

sciences, the boys came home for further lessons in self-restraint.[18]

A crucial reference point for bad-boy scenarios, then, is the absent mother and the set of values she represents and is able to impose on the younger children. This is made explicit in the iconography of childhood used in advertising and in decorations of accessories such as napkin rings, porcelain, and trivets, which became popular in middle-class households in the second half of the nineteenth century. Mary Lynn Stevens Heininger notes the 'intense and ubiquitous characterisations of the young as gems and treasures, pets and plants', imbuing them with 'the redemptive qualities of innocence and simplicity'. Boys of school age, however, disappeared from these sentimental representations, and figured instead in mini-scenarios of transgression and/or punishment that were heavily encoded in terms of gender:

> The most commonly depicted naughty acts – smoking cigars, shaving, gazing up women's legs while shining their shoes – all carried obvious associations with masculinity.

Mild forms of corporal punishment by mother figures tested the boy's capacity to take it 'like a man', and established his resistance to feminine power and influence:

> The common image of a woman spanking or scrubbing a boy is as much a mockery of her as it is a real reprimand of the boy ... She is often portrayed as obese, unattractive, or simple-minded.

Heininger interprets this comic iconography in relation to cultural contradictions. Similar to bad-boy books, the iconography of boyhood projected qualities seen as essential for a man's success in life: aggressiveness, risk-taking, manipulativeness, rule-bending, competitiveness. However, '(t)he very attributes that would make a man occupationally successful were unwelcome in the domestic environment of his own creation'. Here, women ruled, largely excluded from the working world and cherished as guardians of morality. By literalising and exaggerating this cultural conflict, the image of the bad boy, forever harmlessly breaking the rules, and the caricature of the mother reprimanding him,

helped temporarily to dissolve the tension between the real demands of masculinity and the ideal values of femininity, a tension which both boys and men constantly had to negotiate in their everyday movements between the public sphere and the domestic arena.[19]

Thus, the boyish prank culminating in outright triumph or in ineffective punishment emerges as an imaginary scenario central to late nineteenth-century American culture, and widely circulated in the form of snapshot-like iconography, literary sketches and extended novelistic narratives. In all of these manifestations, the prank scenario was used comically, its recipients being invited to acknowledge, and identify with, the boy's transgressions, yet also to play down its seriousness, to reject its challenge to the social and domestic order with a smile or a laugh. Pranks were seen as a necessary assertion of masculinity on the part of boys, a playful rehearsal of crucial aspects of their later adult roles. Rotundo's comments on the function of real-life pranks also apply to the interpretation of their fictional representations:

> (Pranks) ... reversed men's and boy's roles, giving younger males the power to disrupt the lives of older males and forcing the elders to do their boyish bidding ... Pranks resembled petty theft, trespassing, and other forms of vandalism in that they served as skirmishes in a kind of guerilla warfare that boys waged against the adult world. These youthful raids on adult dignity and property gave boys a chance to assert their own needs and values and lay their claim to the out-of-doors as a world for them to use as they saw fit.[20]

American bad-boy films, 1897–1903

In the light of its centrality for late nineteenth-century American culture, it is no surprise that the bad boy, who was first introduced to the cinema by the Lumière brothers, became a popular choice for American film manufacturing companies in the years following the Cinématographe's US debut at Keith's, and that vaudeville audiences, who were highly familiar with earlier bad-boy representations, responded positively to this film genre. In order to estimate the numerical importance of bad-boy films during this period, it is useful to examine the findings of Richard Sanderson's statistical analysis of film content in American films from the period 1897–1903, based on a representative sample of films copyrighted in the United States during this period (Anderson examined 681 films, about a third of the total).[21] His analysis shows that narrative films were a minority in the overall output.[22] He lists the majority of films under categories such as 'Documentary', 'News' and 'Travelogue'. Only two of his categories contain narrative films (but not exclusively), and here 'Entertainment', comprising comic sketches as well as dances and vaudeville acts, greatly outnumbered 'Melodrama' (96 to 7). A separate analysis of subject matter (in both narrative and non-narrative films), gives an indication of what the content of the comic sketches in the 'Entertainment' category is likely to have been: 49 films are listed under the heading 'Pranks, Jokes, and Slapstick' and 33 under 'Children' as opposed to only 19 under 'Love and Romance' (all other headings would seem to apply mainly to documentary films). This indicates that pranks, in particular those executed by boys, were crucial to early narrative filmmaking in the United States.[23]

These general findings are supported by a look at the film listings and descriptions contained in the published Biograph bulletins.[24] The Biograph catalogue of Spring 1902, for example, lists 65 items under the category 'Comedy Views'.[25] Surpassing the number of trick films, recordings of vaudeville acts, tramp films and films about faithless husbands being beaten up by their wives, about a quarter of these 'Comedy Views' feature bad boys or closely related figures (such as the occasional bad girl or the merely inept and stupid boy), making bad-boy films Biograph's leading comic genre. Since 'Comedy Views' is the only category in the catalogue that mainly covers narrative films, while the other (much larger) categories are predominantly concerned with descriptive genres such as 'Scenic Views' and 'Views of Notable Personages', it also follows that, while they are all extremely short (25 or 50 feet), in numerical terms bad-boy films dominated Biograph's overall output of story films in the late 1890s and early 1900s.

While Sanderson's analysis suggests that the vast majority of prank films were made from 1901 onwards (and especially in 1903) with hardly any earlier examples, my own analysis of the Biograph bulletins and of filmographic information obtained from Gunning and Musser's writings, indicates that there also was a modest but regular output of bad-boy films between 1897 and 1900 (at least three or four per year).[26] Due to the regularity of this output and the familiarity of audiences with episodic depictions of the lives of pre-cinematic pranksters, I think it is justified to treat bad-boy films not as isolated sketches but as loosely connected scenes from the lives of archetypal boys. Indeed, by stringing together the descriptions of some of the bad-boy films in the 1902 Biograph catalogue, we arrive at a series of sketches which is very similar to the collected stories of *Peck's Bad Boy and His Pa*:

– 'Two bad boys fill lamp chimney with flour, and schoolmaster is fooled.' (*The Schoolmaster's Surprise*, 1897);

– 'Moving day. Putting up stove. Bad boy pours soot over father.' (*A 'Moving' Picture*, 1898);

– 'Father asleep. Bad boy ties cord to chair and wash-tub. Father is tipped over, and wash-tub upset.' (*A (W)ringing Good Joke*, 1898);

– 'Barn scene. Bad boy pours bag of meal over father.' (*Farmer Oatcake Has His Troubles*, 1899);

– 'Bad boy puts firecrackers in pan of flour, and policeman is covered with white.' (*How Hora Entertained Officer Duffy/Nora's Fourth of July*, 1901);

– 'Bad boys shave off man's whiskers. Man goes to hit them with pail, but strikes barber instead.' (*A Close Shave*, 1901).

How closely these films were seen to be related to each other (and to the literary tradition) is indicated by the persistent reference to the term 'bad boy'. As early as 1899, Biograph even considered making such connections between the films more explicit by creating a series around a particular character:

– 'Bad boy paints comic face on dad's bald

head, and rumpus follows.' (*Little Willie Puts Head on His Pa*);

– 'Willie puts water in potato pan; cook tries to get pan, and is drenched with water.' (*Little Willie in Mischief Again*).

The picture of the bad boy's life which emerges from these sketches is quite close to that depicted in Peck's stories and to Rotundo's descriptions of boy culture. Working on his own or with a friend, the boy is always on the look-out for a chance to attack an older man, preferably an authority figure (father, teacher, policeman). He shows great ingenuity in turning household tools and equipment into weapons and traps, and his pranks result in pain, injury and humiliation for his chosen target. While (unlike the regular beatings in Peck's stories) there is rarely any intentional punishment of the boy, occasionally a prank backfires. In *A Joke on Whom?* (1901), for example, '(b)oy sticks pin in man in hammock; hammock falls on boy'. In general, before a boy graduates to the rank of fully certified and highly accomplished bad boy, he is likely to do harm to himself rather than to others. In *Little Algy's Glorious Fourth of July*(1902) the fireworks explode in the little boy's face, and in *Ding, Dong, Dell, Johnny's in the Well* (1899) the small boy has to be fished out by his mother, which is the kind of situation that the older bad boy would most try to avoid. Occasionally, instead of boys, the exploits of girls are depicted, blowing themselves up (*How Bridget Made the Fire*) or attacking a man (*The Poster Girls*, 1899). Women are rarely targeted (in *A Good Shot*, 1902, children hit a woman during 'target practice' only by accident).[27]

It is not clear from the catalogue descriptions what the social background of these children is. Judging by their dress (often rather fancy costumes) in the few films I have been able to view from the period 1898 to 1907, they mostly would seem to be middle-class kids. There are certainly only a few examples of boys being clearly identified, through stereotypical costumes, as the off-spring of immigrants, as homeless and/or criminal street kids, or as working children (an example would be *The Sandwich Man* (1899) in which a newsboy beats a man in the fight for

a cigar butt). In fact, one of the few appearances of a lower-class boy is used precisely to demonstrate the manliness of the well-dressed, socially more elevated boy: in *The Tough Kid's Waterloo* (1900), a '(s)treet urchin teases a little Lord Fauntleroy, and is soundly thrashed by the boy'.[28] Thus, the bad-boy film followed the tradition of the bad-boy book and focused on middle-class children, staging their pranks for the benefit primarily of middle-class males in the vaudeville audience.

American newspaper comic strips and more bad-boy films, 1895–1905

It is in terms of the social class of its protagonist that bad-boy films are most clearly distinguished from the earliest newspaper comic strips with which they otherwise have so much in common. Mischievous boys and closely related figures such as tramps, disruptive babies and boy-adventurers dominated American comic strips in the decade after they first became a regular feature of mass circulation newspapers in 1895, in the same way that bad boys dominated American story films in the first years after motion pictures became a regular feature on the programme of American vaudeville theatres. Yet, while the film genre began with the perfectly respectable social setting of *L'Arroseur arrosé* (the boy must have belonged to a rather well-off family who could afford employing someone to tend to their large garden, much like the Lumière family itself perhaps), the American comic strip started in an immigrant ghetto.

On 5 May 1895, Richard F. Outcault's regular single panel cartoon *Hogan's Alley* in the Sunday colour supplement of Joseph Pulitzer's *New York World* introduced, among a variety of other characters, an immigrant street urchin, 'a large-headed, jug-eared boy of about six or seven, clad in a plain dress or nightshirt smudged with dirty handprints'.[29] This character made regular appearances in the cartoon from then on, and became increasingly important within it. The drawing of the boy underwent various changes, in the process of which he acquired his characteristic baldness and toothless grin, and the highly noticeable yellow colouring of his shirt. Although the boy's name was Mickey Dugan, he soon came to be known as 'The Yellow Kid'

1895

(and since the strip was seen to symbolise the approach of Hearst and Pulitzer's sensationalist journalism, mass-circulation newspapers came to be known as the 'yellow press'). When in May 1896, in the course of the big newspaper circulation war of the mid-1890s, Outcault was poached by William Randolph Hearst's *New York Journal* to develop a comic strip dedicated exclusively to 'The Yellow Kid', this cartoon figure turned into a cultural phenomenon, with numerous manifestations beyond the newspaper pages: buttons, statuettes, toys, games, puzzles, a joke magazine, a play and books consisting of reprints of the strip, as well as billboard and magazine advertising using the kid's likeness.

Outcault's *The Yellow Kid* was neither the first American newspaper comic strip to feature the exploits of regular characters in weekly installments, nor was it even, strictly speaking, a strip (a sequence of panels depicting a causally linked series of events) in its initial form; Outcault only gradually replaced his single-panel cartoon with strips made up of four or six panels during his two years at the *New York Journal*. Yet, the enormous success of this cartoon character signalled the arrival of a new popular art form, and heavily influenced subsequent cartoonists. When, for example, Outcault's colleague at the *New York Journal*, Rudolph Dirks, was given the task to adapt the popular German comic book *Max und Moritz* into a multi-panel strip for the paper, he retained *The Yellow Kid*'s immigrant theme, by featuring two lower-class German kids who spoke an odd mixture of English and German, and by setting the action in an imaginary English-speaking African island colony (which stood in for the United States). However, unlike their predecessor, who often was merely an observer and commentator of events in the ghetto, Dirks' *The Katzenjammer Kids* (who debuted in the *New York Journal* on 12 December 1897, making weekly appearances from then on) were in active and open revolt against their mostly middle-class surroundings, in particular against any form of authority such as their parents or teachers. They were constantly engaged in the highly calculated and ingenious staging of often very violent pranks, much like 'Peck's Bad Boy' and their filmic contemporaries. Although

virtually every installment ended with their ritualistic spanking, they never changed their ways.[30]

Subsequent comic strips developed the themes and characters introduced so successfully by *The Yellow Kid* and *The Katzenjammer Kids* in different ways. The idea of the strip protagonist as social outsider, for example, was picked up in Frederick Burr Opper's *Happy Hooligan* (starting in 1900), which featured a tramp. Childish mischief characterised the animal protagonist of James Swinnerton's *The Little Tiger* (1897) and the human protagonist of his *Little Jimmy* (1905), whereas inadvertently disruptive children were at the centre of Winsor McKay's *Little Sammy Sneeze* (1904), featuring a young boy given to devastating sneezes, and George McManus' *The Newlyweds* (1904), centring on a baby prone to tantrums and the parents' efforts to appease and entertain the child. Boys were featured as dreamers and adventurers in McKay's *Little Nemo in Slumberland* (1905), McManus' *Nibsy the Newsboy in Funny Fairlyland* (1905) and Lyonel Feininger's *The Kin-der-Kids* (1906), while Charles Schultze's *Foxy Grandpa* (1900) focused on an older man turning the tables on two bad boys forever trying to play tricks on him.

Yet, arguably the most successful strip during this period was the one that stayed closest to the original models. Outcault's *Buster Brown* was launched in 1902 as a development of his earlier success *The Yellow Kid* and of Dirks' *The Katzenjammer Kids*. Its protagonist was the ten-year-old son of a well-to-do suburban family who despite his fancy dress and angelic face was forever playing tricks on everyone around him, often causing serious damage to property and people. Although episodes ended with the boy's plans being thwarted or with severe punishment, followed by a 'Resolution', in which Buster showed remorse and insight, and reflected on the lesson he had been taught, in the next installment he would invariably be back to his old ways. The strip gave rise to a wealth of spin-offs and a merchandising craze which rivalled the one for *The Yellow Kid*.[31] With *Buster Brown* (and the equally respectable *Foxy Grandpa*), the bad-boy comic strip reverted from its immigrant beginnings to the literary tradition of middle-class bad-boys. In the introduction to the first collection of his strips, Outcault even replicated the rationale of the obligatory opening statements in the bad-boy books:

> Buster is not a bad or naughty boy as thousands of parents of Buster know. He is an industrious person, full of energy and ingenuity. If all the energy of the vast army of Busters around us could be directed into some useful channel and brought to bear upon some practical work it would accomplish wonders ... (Buster) is not an invention; these pictures of his pranks are simply records of the usual happenings in any healthy household.[32]

With their middle-class protagonists, *Buster Brown* and *Foxy Grandpa* also tied in nicely with the predominant concerns of bad-boy films, and it is therefore no surprise that these strips were adapted into film series.[33] Biograph's *Foxy Grandpa* series was based on the successful stage musical derived from Charles 'Bunny' Schultze's strip. A Biograph announcement on 20 August 1902 emphasised its popular origins:

> Foxy Grandpa! The great scenes arranged by 'Bunny' and enacted by Jos. J. Hart and his original company. Positively the only moving picture production of the most attractive comic character of modern times.[34]

The series consisted of eight self-contained one-shot scenes, which could be shown separately or in combination.[35] When shown together, the 500-foot Foxy Grandpa series constituted one of the longest multi-shot narrative films of the time (although there was no narrative development from shot to shot). When in 1904 Edwin S. Porter adapted Buster Brown for the Edison company as a 710-foot, seven-shot film entitled *Buster Brown and His Dog Tige* (which included an appearance of Richard F. Outcault making a charcoal sketch of his characters, and again had no overarching narrative development), it was meant to be sold 'in one length only' to be used as a 'headline' or 'feature' attraction on the vaudeville bill.[36]

In addition to its quantitative importance for narrative filmmaking, then, the bad-boy film also seems to have been quite crucial for the development of longer narrative films. This impression is supported by the fact that one of Biograph's most complex and most carefully integrated multi-shot story films during this period, the 288-feet long *The Story the Biograph Told* (1903), is a combination of a bad-boy prank (the office boy secretly filming the extramarital affair of his boss with the secretary, the film later to be shown in a theatre) and the faithless-husband-getting-caught-and-beaten-by-his-wife formula.[37] Furthermore, in 1905 Porter 'remade' what was arguably the most successful and influential American story film up to this point, *The Great Train Robbery* (1903), as a 730-feet film featuring bad boys and a bad girl as a gang of outlaws: *The Little Train Robbery*.[38] It would seem, then, that formally nothing stood in the way of the bad-boy film retaining its pre-eminence after 1905. Through parody and formula hybridisation (combining pranks with love triangles and chases, for example) the bad-boy genre could easily be extended into one-reel 'feature' films, which began to become the focus of film production and exhibition in the United States during this period.

Yet in fact, after 1905 the bad boy no longer was the preferred protagonist of narrative films in the United States. Charles Musser argues that bad-boy films came under attack when they reached new audiences in the nickelodeons which rapidly replaced vaudeville as the primary outlet for film exhibition from 1905 onwards:

> Bad-boy films were directed at adult, middle-class males who were expected to recall the carefree days of childhood. Yet, when shown to children and working-class immigrants, they became potentially subversive.[39]

They acquired a reputation as 'schools of crime for American youth', seemingly posing a threat to the social order 'when appropriated by those who had previously been all but excluded from theatrical-style entertainment'.[40] As a consequence of such unwelcome social meanings, the bad-boy film was replaced around 1906/7 by the Western genre with its cow*boys* which provided models of transgressive manly action outside the framework of the contemporary urban world: 'The personal nostalgia of the male filmmakers and spectators was replaced by the more mythic conception of the recent but still-fading past'.[41]

While Musser does not document the contemporary concern about bad-boy films, his analysis is supported by Elsa A. Nystrom's investigation of the parallel campaign against newspaper comic strips and their bad-boy protagonists.[42] Around 1906 earlier criticisms of comic strips developed into 'a highly focused movement supported by popular and respected civic leaders, social workers, ministers and educators' who feared that comic strips 'might corrupt (their) children and even break down the very fabric of society. They hoped, through boycott and protest, to force the newspapers to eliminate the comics.'[43] One critic, for example, wrote in the August 1906 issue of *Atlantic* about the effect of the strips:

> Respect for property, respect for parents, for law, for decency, for truth, for beauty, for kindliness, for dignity, or for honor, are killed without mercy.[44]

An article that appeared in *Good Housekeeping* in May 1910 singled out the comics' glorification of the 'self-sufficient kid', who was smart and disrespectful, as a particularly negative influence on children looking for role models.[45] Other critics, according to Nystrom, were most concerned about the fact that 'it was the *children of the poor* who most needed to be protected from the dangers of the comic supplement' since they confronted the strips 'without the advantages and guidance as well as the reading material of the middle class'.[46] *Survey* went as far as to argue that a reformed comic supplement 'should provide these children with the healthy intellectual food now missing from their homes'.[47]

Since this campaign was powerful enough to convince a number of important newspapers to drop their comic strips between 1908 and 1912, it is reasonable to assume that a general awareness of the concerted campaign against strips and their mischievous protagonists after 1905 might well have negatively influenced filmmakers and exhibitors in their perception of the closely related bad-boy films. Thus, the bad boy, after having served for close to 40 years as a key figure in popular literature, childhood iconography, newspaper comic strips and films, offering imaginary scenarios of rebellion and masculine self-assertion to their middle-class audiences, had to step aside from centre stage (although he never stepped down). In the eyes of middle-class observers, the rapidly increasing working-class audiences for newspapers and nickelodeons, in particular the presence of large numbers of immigrant children amongst them, gave the boyish prank a threatening social dimension.

Auguste and Louis Lumière had felt secure enough to indulge their younger brother's mischievous inclination when they made *L'Arroseur arrosé* (albeit with a punishing twist which returned the gardener exactly to where he was before the bad boy's interruption). Yet, after 1905 filmmakers and critics were not so sure about the value of boyish imagination. When Biograph's one-reel 'feature' *Terrible Ted* (1907) depicted a boy shooting police, holding up a stagecoach and killing Indians, critics were worried about the message sent to the audience, especially in those screenings where the ending, in which the action was revealed as a dream, had mysteriously gone missing. The *Moving Picture World* commented:

> *Terrible Ted* was the star film but unfortunately the moral was cut out either by design of the renter, or because he could not afford to buy the worn out piece; anyhow it is bad policy to leave the story finishing with only Ted displaying the scalps and not let the people know it was only a dream.[48]

It was precisely this anxiety that the new working-class audiences would not understand, or would not want to understand, that the bad boy was in fact 'good' and that his exploits were 'only a dream', which seems to have precipitated his decline as a popular figure.

1895

Notes

1. Alan Williams, *Republic of Images: A History of French Filmmaking* (Cambridge, MA: Harvard University Press, 1992), 27, 408. According to Williams, *L'Arroseur arrosé* is in fact a 1896 remake of *Le Jardinier*, and it was originally titled *Arroseur et Arrosé* ('The Sprinkler and the Sprinkled'). For a detailed formal analysis of this and other early Lumière films, see Marshall Deutelbaum, 'Structural Patterning in the Lumière Films', *Film Before Griffith* John L. Fell (ed) (Berkeley: University of California Press, 1983), 299–310. For background information on the business operations of the Lumière family, see, for example, Alan Williams, 'The Lumière Organization and "Documentary Realism"', *Film Before Griffith*, 153–161, and Williams, *Republic of Images*, 21–31.

2. Cf. Charles Musser, *The Emergence of Cinema: The American Screen to 1907* (New York: Scribners, 1990), 138, 141.

3. Donald Crafton, *Before Mickey: The Animated Film 1898–1928* (Cambridge, MA: MIT Press, 1982), 354. Crafton gives Georges Sadoul's interview with the man who played the gardener in the film as the source for this anecdote, referencing Sadoul's *Histoire générale du cinéma*, vol. 1 (Paris: Denoel, 1973), 198.

4. See Crafton, *Before Mickey*, 37–38, and Donald Crafton, *Emile Cohl, Caricature, and Film* (Princeton: Princeton University Press, 1990), 252–253. Crafton also refers to two earlier examples appearing in print in 1887.

5. 'The Cinématographe at Keith's', *New York Dramatic Mirror* (4 July 1896): 17, reprinted in *Spellbound in Darkness: A History of the Silent Film*, George C. Pratt (ed) (Greenwich: New York Graphic Society, 1973), 16–17. See Musser, *The Emergence of Cinema*, 137–141.

6. See Musser's summary of reviews of early Lumière programmes in *ibid.*, 141.

7. See Tom Gunning, 'Crazy Machines in the Garden of Forking Paths: Mischief Gags and the Origins of American Film Comedy', *Classical Hollywood Comedy*, Kristine Brunovska Karnick and Henry Jenkins (eds) (New York: Routledge, 1995), 87–105. There are numerous references to the bad-boy genre in Charles Musser, *The Emergence of Cinema*, and *Before the Nickelodeon: Edwin S. Porter and the Edison Manufacturing Company* (Berkeley: University of California Press, 1991). Cf. John L. Fell, 'Cellulose Nitrate Roots: Popular Entertainments and the Birth of Film Narrative', *Before Hollywood: Turn-of-the-Century American Film*, John L. Fell *et al.* (eds) (New York: Hudson Hills, 1987), 39–44, which discusses, among other things, bad boys and the closely-related figure of the tramp. An extensive discussion of the tramp figure can be found in Charles Musser, 'Work, Ideology and Chaplin's Tramp', *Radical History Review*, vol. 41 (April 1988): 36–66. For a discussion of similar themes in early British cinema, see Thomas Sobchak, 'Gypsies, Children, and Criminals: Anti-authority Themes in Early British Silent Film', *Journal of Popular Film and Television*, vol. 17, no. 1 (Spring 1989): 15–19.

   After the completion of this essay in May 1995, I also came across Davide Turconi's authoritative study of early American film comedy, ' "Hic sunt leones": The First Decade of American Film Comedy, 1894–1903', *Griffithiana*, nos. 55/56 (September 1996): 151–215. In addition to using some of the sources that I have based my analysis on, Turconi also systematically examines two comprehensive film catalogues: Kemp R. Niver, *Early Motion Pictures: The Paper Print Collection in the Library of Congress* (Washington: Library of Congress, 1985) and Elias Savada (ed.), *The American Film Institute Catalog of Motion Pictures Produced in the United States, vol. A: Film Beginnings, 1893–1910* (Metuchen, NJ: Scarecrow, 1995). The results of Turconi's analysis are broadly in line with my conclusions about the importance of comedies in general and bad-boy films in particular during the period in question. However, his work is much more detailed and comprehensive, and deserves extensive discussion, which is beyond the scope of this essay.

8. The secondary literature on bad-boy books is substantial. See, for example, Anne Trensky, 'The Bad Boy in Nineteenth-Century American Fiction', *Georgia Review*, vol. 27 (1973): 503–517; cf. her 'The Saintly Child in Nineteenth-Century American Fiction', *Prospects*, vol.1 (1975): 389–413 for earlier representations of children in American literature against which bad-boy books reacted. For further discussions of the bad-boy genre, mostly concentrating on Mark Twain's *The Adventures of Tom Sawyer* and *The Adventures of Huckleberry Finn*, see John Hinz, 'Huck and Pluck: "Bad" Boys in American Fiction', *South Atlantic Quarterly*, vol. 51 (1952): 120–129; Jim Hunter, 'Mark Twain and

the Boy-Book in Nineteenth-Century America', *College English*, vol. 24 (March 1963): 430–438; Judith Fetterley, 'The Sanctioned Rebel', *Studies in the Novel*, vol.3 (Fall 1971): 293–304; Robert L. Coard, 'Tom Sawyer, Sturdy Centenarian', *The Midwest Quarterly*, vol.17 (July 1976): 329–349; Evelyn Geller, 'Tom Sawyer, Tom Bailey, and the Bad-Boy Genre', *Wilson Library Bulletin* (November 1976): 245–250; Alan Gribben, ' "I Do Wish Tom Sawer Was There": Boy-Book Elements in *Tom Sawyer* and *Huckleberry Finn*', *One Hundred Years of Huckleberry Finn: The Boy, His Book and American Culture*, Robert Sattelmeyer and J. Donald Crowley (eds) (Columbia: University of Missouri Press, 1985), 149–170; Michael Orchard, *Sporting with the Gods: The Rhetoric of Play and Game in American Culture* (Cambridge: Cambridge University Press, 1991), 399–406; Glenn Hendler, 'Tom Sawyer's Masculinity', *Arizona Quarterly*, vol. 49, no. 4 (Winter 1993): 33–50; Marcia Jacobson, *Being a Boy Again: Autobiography and the American Boy Book* (Tuscaloosa: University of Alabama Press, 1994); Ellen Butler Donovan, 'Reading for Profit *and* Pleasure: *Little Women* and *The Story of a Bad Boy*', *The Lion and the Unicorn*, vol.18, no.2 (1994): 143–153. A closely related literary tradition is outlined in Richard Wohl, 'The "Country Boy" Myth', *Perspectives in American History*, vol. 3 (1969): 82–156.

9.   Frank Luther Mott, *Golden Multitudes: The Story of Best Sellers in the United States* (New York: R.R. Bowker, 1947), 8, and Appendices A and B.

10. Thomas Bailey Aldrich, *The Story of a Bad Boy* (Cambridge, MA: Houghton Mifflin, 1942), 1–2. Emphasis in the original.

11. Mark Twain, *The Adventures of Tom Sawyer* (London: Scholastic Book Services, 1983), original 1876 'Preface'.

12. *Ibid.*, 2.

13. George Wilbur Peck, 'The Bad Boy at Work Again', Ch. 2 of *Peck's Bad Boy and His Pa* (Chicago: Belford, Clarke & Co., 1883), 12.

14. *Ibid.*, unpaginated foreword 'A Card from the Author'.

15. Unpaginated advertisement in George Wilbur Peck, *The Grocery Man and Peck's Bad Boy. Being a Continuation of Peck's Bad Boy and His Pa* (Chicago: Bedford, Clarke & Co., 1883).

16. Trensky, 'The Bad Boy': 508–509.

17. *Ibid.*, 510–511.

18. E. Anthony Rotundo, *American Manhood: Transformations in Masculinity from the Revolution to the Modern Era* (New York: Basic Books, 1993), 37.

19. Mary Lynn Stevens Heininger, 'Children, Childhood, and Change in America, 1820–1920", *A Century of Childhood, 1820–1920*, Heininger *et al.* (eds) (Rochester, NY: The Margaret Woodbury Strong Museum, 1984), 23–27.

20. Rotundo, *op. cit.*, 47–48.

21. Richard Arlo Sanderson, *A Historical Study of the Development of American Motion Picture Content and Techniques Prior to 1904*, PhD dissertation (University of Southern California, Los Angeles, 1961). Anderson's 681 films constitute 36 per cent of all films copyrighted in the US between 1897 and 1903, and 66 per cent of all copyrighted films which had by then been restored (see pp. 34–36). Turconi estimates that only about a third of all films produced in the United States during this period were copyrighted, *op. cit.*: 209.

22. Throughout this discussion I would like to maintain one key distinction: between narrative films (depicting a structured sequence of causally linked events) and non-narrative films. The latter might depict a sequence of events, yet do so without establishing any causal connection between them or any overarching structure; in most cases we could also call such films 'descriptive'.

23. The dominance of prank scenarios is even more striking when an additional 346 restored films, which Sanderson was not able to view but which he categorised on the basis of written information, are taken into account: 65, that is almost 25 per cent, come under the heading 'Pranks, Jokes, and Slapstick', see Sanderson *op. cit.*, 61–66, 111, 125, 193.

24. Kemp Niver (ed.), *Biograph Bulletins, 1896–1908* (Los Angeles: Locan Research Group, 1971). These findings are also confirmed by Turconi's comprehensive analysis of the output of the major American production companies, *op. cit.*: passim.

25. Sanderson, *A Historical Study*, 59–73.

26. Cf. Gunning, *op. cit.*, Musser, *The Emergence of Cinema* and *Before the Nickelodeon*. Again, these findings are confirmed by Turconi, *op. cit.*

1895

27. All of these descriptions are taken from the 1902 Biograph catalogue reprinted in Niver, *Biograph Bulletins*, 59–63.

28. *Ibid.*, 62.

29. Maurice Horn (ed.), *The World Encyclopedia of Comics* (London: New English Library, 1976), 711. For more information on Outcault's work, see Richard Marshall, *America's Great Comic-Strip Artists* (New York: Abbeville, 1989), 19–39. On the figure of the Yellow Kid and its cultural impact, see Mark D. Winchester, 'The Yellow Kid and the Origins of Comic Book Theatricals: 1895– 1898', *Theatre Studies*, vol.37 (1992): 32–55. For background information on American newspapers and early comic strips, see, for example, Frank Luther Mott, *American Journalism: A History of Newspapers in the United States Through 250 Years: 1690–1940* (New York: Macmillan, 1942), 524–526, 584–587; M. Thomas Inge, *Comics as Culture* (Jackson: University Press of Mississippi, 1990), ch. 11; Horn, *op. cit.*, 10–20. Numerous early strips are reprinted in George Perry and Alan Aldridge, *The Penguin Book of Comics* (Harmondsworth: Penguin, 1971).

30. For a comparative discussion of *The Yellow Kid* and *The Katzenjammer Kids*, see Lisa Yaszek, '"Them Damn Pictures": Americanization and the Comic Strip in the Progressive Era', *Journal of American Studies*, vol. 28, no. 1 (1994): 23–38.

31. See Marshall, *op. cit.*, 19–39.

32. Richard F. Outcault, *Buster Brown and His Resolutions* (New York: Frederick A. Stokes Co., 1903), introduction quoted in Denis Gifford, *The American Comic Book Catalogue: The Evolutionary Era, 1884–1939* (London: Mansell, 1990), 9.

33. For an overview of early film adaptations of comic strips in the United States, see Robert A. Armour, 'Comic Strips, Theatre, and Early Narrative Films, 1895– 1904', *Studies in Popular Culture*, vol. 10, no. 1 (1987): 14–26.

34. Niver, *Biograph Bulletins*, 75.

35. Musser, *The Emergence of Cinema*, 308.

36. *Ibid.*, 357, and Musser, *Before the Nickelodeon*, 267–272.

37. See Musser, *The Emergence of Cinema*, 355–357, and Niver, *Biograph Bulletins*, 112 (here the film is listed as *Caught by Moving Pictures*).

38. See Musser, *Before the Nickelodeon*, 320–321. Further films to consider in this context are, for example, the slightly later *The Terrible Kids* (600 feet) and *How the Office Boy Saw the Ball Game* (both Edison, 1906), *Terrible Ted* (792 feet, Edison, 1907), *Peck's Bad Boy and His Pa* , a programme of five films and 52 slides offered by the Amusement Supply Company (1907); for all these films, cf. Musser, *ibid.*, 342–347. Also *Tom, Tom, the Piper's Son* (508 feet, Biograph, 1905) and *The Boy, the Bust and the Bath* (410 feet, Vitagraph, 1907).

39. Musser, *The Emergence of Cinema*, 10.

40. *Ibid.*, 494. Along similar lines, Thomas Sobchack writes, with respect to the address of *working-class* audiences in early British cinema, about the appeal of bad-boy films (together with those featuring tramps and criminals) as scenarios of social resistance: 'It is true that the child protagonists who embarass their elders and get away with it are often of the same class, but as children getting back at the adult world – the powerless against the powerful – one can imagine the enjoyment the lower-class audience must have had in identifying with them, aware in some way that the relationship between the classes was similar to that between parents and children', Sobchak, *op. cit.*, 17.

41. Musser, *The Emergence of Cinema*, 478; cf. Musser, *Before the Nickelodeon*, 363.

42. Elsa A. Nystrom, *A Rejection of Order: The Development of the Newpaper Comic Strip in America, 1830–1920*, unpublished PhD dissertation (Chicago: Loyola University of Chicago, 1989), chs. 4 and 5.

43. *Ibid.*, 167.

44. Ralph Bergengreen, 'Humor of the Color Supplement', *Atlantic* (August 1906), quoted in *ibid.*, 163.

45. Summarised in *ibid.*, 175.

46. *Ibid.*, 177. Emphasis in the original.

47. William Wald, 'Make Comics Educational', *Survey* (26 February 1910), quoted in *ibid.*, 177.

48. *Moving Picture World* (11 January 1908): 26, quoted in Charles Musser's entry on *Terrible Ted* in Fell, *Before Hollywood*, 129.

Translating the Tom Show: The Legacy of a Popular Tradition in Edwin S. Porter's 1903 Film of *Uncle Tom's Cabin*

Stephen Johnson

School of Art, Drama & Music, McMaster University, Hamilton, Ont. L8S 4M2, Canada

IN THE SPRING OF 1903 Edwin S. Porter hired a touring production of *Uncle Tom's Cabin* to perform before the cameras of his Manhattan rooftop studio. The resulting film is a potentially valuable document for the theatre historian, especially one interested in the under-documented Tom Show tradition. It is also – potentially – an important early effort to translate live performance into something cinematic.[1] This potential importance is frustrated in two ways. First of all, like so much of early film, it is difficult to read. It relies so heavily on familiarity with the performance tradition that an audience today simply cannot understand the film without the theatre-historical context. Second, like all documentation to a theatre historian, the film is suspect. Consider the circumstances: a group of actors is requested to perform their usual fare, but on a very small stage, without sound or special lighting, in less than twenty minutes, and (perhaps most important) without an audience. 'Tom Show' actors took pride in their adaptability; but this must have taxed even their resources. To assess the accuracy of this document, again we need the theatre-historical context.

This is not a revelation; but the context is not so easy to come by. For one thing, we have no identification, and no other specific documentation, for the troupe of performers filmed by Porter.[2] This is unfortunate; and nothing can replace that resource. But such documentation is only a part of the context. Much can be learned from a comparison with other kinds of documents: the source narrative, Harriet Beecher Stowe's 1852 novel; published dramatic adaptations that have some relationship with the film, in this case George Aiken's 1852 standard text (still available from Samuel French); and documents detailing other productions bearing the name *Uncle Tom's Cabin*. In this paper, I will treat the last of these possibilities, by briefly comparing

1895

Fig. 1. *Eliza escaping across the ice to Ohio. From the William Brady production of Uncle Tom's Cabin, 1901. [Author's Collection.]*

Porter's film with a near-contemporary (1901) Broadway stage production. It begs for comparison, for pragmatic and circumstantial reasons: it is well-documented, by a typescript and a series of photographs; and it was produced only two years before Porter's film, in the same area of Manhattan.[3]

Both productions tap into the 50-year-old tradition of the Tom Show, which raises an additional problem requiring comment. In a world of enforced copyright, authorial control, memorised dialogue, and the intended repetition of performance – that is, in the world of the legitimate theatrical touring industry – two productions with the same title have a strong relationship. There can be great differences, of course; but there is an alleged common source in the script. The theatrical history of *Uncle Tom's Cabin* is not part of that world. There was no copyright on Stowe's novel. Show-business entrepreneurs could use the title, the characters, and the narrative elements in any way they wished; and they did. Between the end of the Civil War and Porter's film, so-called Tom Shows proliferated – probably numbering in the hundreds of productions, three or four per season in a typical small town. They tapped into the moral cachet of the title to attract a broad audience that did not normally go to the theatre. They varied in size, from casts of five to fifty, and appeared in venues ranging from living rooms to circus tents.[4]

It is important to understand that there was no central control over what went into these productions. Not that they had nothing in common; but what they had in common is poorly documented, and an open question. The information is contradictory. Audience expectation seems to have enforced some consistency of narrative, costume, prop, gesture and comic business. On the other hand, the legendary Tom Show actors disdained the script in favour of a commedia-like improvisational skill; and the extreme competition certainly led to a curtailment of narrative in favour of interpolated variety – anything from topical songs to boxing matches.

With that in mind, we should approach these two productions with caution, as adaptations – or translations – of a tradition that was primarily oral, and difficult to characterise. Porter's film records what was probably an authentic and, I believe, rather old-fashioned example of the Tom Show, compressed and pantomimed for the camera. William Brady's stage production was not even, strictly speaking, a part of the tradition. It was instead a conscious effort on this producer's part to gentrify what was – for his middle class, theatrically sophisticated audience – an archaic, laughably naive form. This audience disdained the Tom Show; in the parlance of the day, it was only for 'kids and rubes'.[5] But it was part of their childhood and their cultural past, and Brady tapped into a nostagia for that past through imitation, while avoiding derisive laughter through selective revision. What we are comparing, then, are two translations of a poorly documented original. Their similarities can help to explain obscurities, and suggest a picture of the source tradition. Their differences can suggest the difficulties of translation.

Despite the cautions I have raised, and the expectations I have lowered, the two productions have striking similarities, embedded in the obvious differences. This is best illustrated visually. Brady had the full size of the Academy of Music stage; Porter's stage was tiny by comparison. Brady had access to a spectacular, illusionistic set design; Porter's was stripped-down, in some scenes just a suggestion of a location. If we discount the resources of size and opulence, however, we find considerable visual parallel, including: three-dimensional objects painted on backdrops, which was rather old-fashioned on Broadway; corresponding practical windows and doors, indicating similar blocking patterns; corresponding tableaux, both within and to end scenes; and a similarity in the location of special effects. Eliza escapes through the window of the tavern a few yards away from the slave traders, instead of a few feet. She is chased across the ice floes of the Ohio River by five dogs and four horses (Fig. 1), instead of Porter's one dog (who runs across the camera four times, Fig. 2). When Uncle Tom dies, Brady's 'heaven' physically envelopes him in a spectacular tableau; while Porter's 'heaven' appears as the ghostly double exposure of an angel beckoning to Tom. Differences in size and number are important, of course; but the relative similarity between the two suggests either a direct relationship, or a set of consistent visual patterns in the Tom Show tradition. Actors may indeed have disdained the script; but it is possible that they improvised within a fairly strict set of pictorial requirements.[6] As one manager said, when asked by his new director which script they were using, 'What's the difference, as long as it leads up to the pictures in our advertising ...'.[7]

There are two striking exceptions to this physical similarity. According to Tom tradition, the death of Eva is followed by her ascension into heaven. This was once accomplished by physically hoisting her up with wire or rope; by the turn of the century this effect seems to have been replaced by her appearance behind a scrim.[8] Porter recreates the traditional effect. Indeed, he elaborates upon it with a double exposure (Fig. 3): a ghostly angel descends, appears to lift Eva's spirit from the bed, and then ascends again to heaven (in fact with a doll). Brady, however, uncharacteristically eliminates the ascension completely. He gives the audience a spectacle, a stage full of black singers arrayed around Eva's bed (Fig. 4). And he follows the scene with an extraordinary curtain call, in which Tom carries Eva's body down toward the audience – the theatrical equivalent of a close-up.

Several tentative suggestions can be made

Fig. 2. *Eliza escaping across the ice. Still from the film Uncle Tom's Cabin, by Edwin S. Porter, 1903. [Museum of Modern Art/Film Stills Archive.]*

here. First of all, Brady's suppression of the 'hoisting' of Eva is an understandable translation; it appears to have been one of the old-fashioned, much-parodied traditions of the Tom Show he would wish to keep from the disdainful eyes of his audience. But Brady goes further, suppressing all religious allegory in this scene, in favour of secular pathos. This makes Porter's effect all the more interesting. He may simply have hired an old-fashioned Tom troupe; but he may have been indulging in his own act of nostalgia, by finding the cinematic means to breathe new life into an old trick. In either case, Porter preserves and respects an explicit moral and religious centerpiece of this drama that Brady did not believe his audience wanted to see any more.

A second, less obvious difference occurs in the otherwise consistent physical appearance of character: top hat, spats and umbrella for the comic villain Marks; buckskin with fringe for Phineas Fletcher, the backwoodsman-turned-Quaker who saves Eliza; the traditional blackfaced old man for Uncle Tom; corkscrew curls for Aunt Ophelia; and a black body-stocking and sack dress for Topsy. The exception is Brady's Simon Legree, played by Theodore Roberts (Fig. 5).[9] Instead of shoulder-length hair, mustache and goatee, as documented in the film, Roberts' Legree was red-haired and balding, full-bearded, and

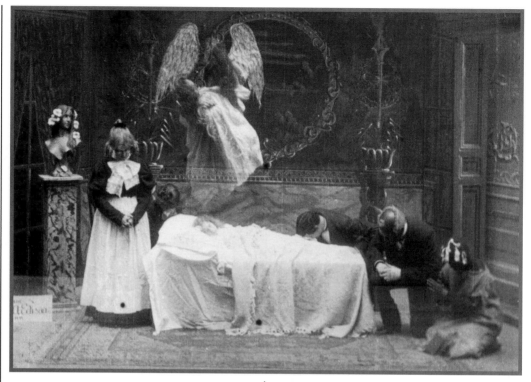

Fig. 3. *The Death of Little Eva. Still from the film by Edwin S. Porter, 1903. Museum of Modern Art/Film Stills Archive. An Angel takes Eva's soul (a doll) up to heaven in a double exposure. The Angel is lowered and raised on a rope.*

sported a prominent (putty) broken nose. The physical change was complemented by changes in the text to give Legree some rudimentary psychological motivation (that is, a mother), and by the addition of more realistic physical business – in particular, a breakaway bottle full of stage-blood in his attack on Uncle Tom.

As with the ascension of Eva, the change to Brady's Legree is understandable as a nod toward prevailing Broadway taste in acting style. The question is more why this character was altered, when so many others were not. Topsy's appearance had not altered in fifty years; it was archaic, not to say grotesque, and the actress was displeased with it. But it did not change. The film suggests an answer to this inconsistency. Porter's Legree struts and poses with extraordinary vigour, far in excess of the other 'serious' characters. The extremes of movement are frankly impressive, as well as laughable – he leaps up into the air to beat Tom on the head, poses facing the audience/camera whenever he is not wanted in the scene, and is physically thrown back when anyone disagrees with him. I do not know if this kind of acting would have been

laughable to the Broadway audience of the day; but that would explain the change in this character. To Brady, laughter at the villain would have been unacceptable; so Legree was remade with more violence and, for the time, greater realism. Porter's film, on the other hand, respects and documents the tradition. How his intended audience would react is debatable. I suspect they would both laugh and hiss; and I further suspect that Legree would talk back to them. That last attribute, if true, could not be translated onto film; just as it was suppressed when translated onto the Broadway stage.[10]

When we turn from a visual to a narrative comparison of these two productions, we should not be surprised to find a substantial difference. Brady had a full evening to tell his story; Porter had twenty minutes, and cut accordingly.[11] The film has none of Brady's dialogue-dependent scenes. Important characters are relegated to walk-ons. And yet there are strong similarities. I will treat just two.

First of all, Porter preserves, at great narrative cost, one interpolated feature also present in Brady's production, the black performer. We know that black singers and dancers were a common feature of the Tom show from the 1870s. Just as we find in our two examples, small Tom shows employed a quartette, large ones a band. Brady advertised two hundred such performers, who supplied on- and off-stage choral music, dance, and a kind of living scenery. Porter only had room on stage for about ten performers. Technically, he emphasised the only element of their work he could record, dance. The repeated presence of these performers in the film, and their baroque use by Brady, suggest that they were more essential to the Tom Show than much of the plot.

Second (and finally), Porter's film includes comic business that we can match with Brady's script. Some of this is broad, and clearly depicted. Marks the lawyer, for example, dominates the Slave Auction scene. He bids for and buys a slave, is chased off stage when he cannot pay, and then disrupts the bidding for the rest of the scene. The same business is recorded in Brady's script. Other examples are much less obvious in the film, lost in the corner of a busy frame, or so brief as to be nearly invisible (without contemporary technology). Phineas Fletcher offers young Harry Harris a 'chaw' of tobacco. St. Clair shows his wife a photograph. These moments are indecipherable today without reference to the script. And in a film that has cut so much character, such small, essentially character-building business seems out of place.

Several points can be made about this 'business'. First, it shows just how useful Brady's script can be in making Porter's film readable. As the smaller moments become comprehensible to the viewer, the scenes take on a greater complexity. After the hundredth viewing, one might almost imagine Porter's film to be a full-length play. Second, one result of this increased readability is to comprehend the importance of the comic characters in these productions and, I believe, in the Tom tradition generally. Depending on the audience, Marks's prominence at the slave auction may have undercut the moral lesson, or emphasised the *reductio ad absurdam* of putting a price on a human being. Certainly it complicates the tone of what was originally a pathetic, harrowing, but simple scene.[12]

Fig. 4. *The Death of Little Eva. From the William Brady production, 1901. Eva is surrounded by a large chorus of black singers. [Author's Collection.]*

Fig.5. *Simon Legree from the Brady Production, 1901, a portrayal touted as a 'new' realism. [Author's Collection.]*

Third, there is the question of inclusion. We can understand the presence in the film of lengthy comic business, as accepted and expected parts of the Tom tradition. The less visible moments, however, are possibly more revealing. Either Porter believed his audience could read them, assuming they had seen these particular moments on stage as many times as I (for example) have seen them on video; or else, these moments were such an intrinsic part of what the actors did in those scenes that, despite all the cutting, they had to perform them. Either reason suggests that the Tom tradition was far more consistent in its 'business' than we might have expected.

Considering the changeable picture of the Tom tradition painted at the beginning of this paper, the extent of the similarities between these two productions is surprising. This raises the possibility that Porter's film is in some way directly based on Brady's production. I believe this is unlikely, as a one-to-one imitation. I have emphasised the similarities; but there are too many differences to make a direct relationship defensible. It is possible that Porter or his actors borrowed something from the Broadway production, just as they might have from any other. Borrowing was a part of the tradition. I note, however, that none of Brady's more obvious 'improvements' found their way into the film. Simon Legree struts and chews the scenery; and Eva goes to heaven.

I have tried to show in this paper how selective comparison can improve our skill at reading early film, and our understanding of its source traditions. I would not want to suggest that this is somehow sufficient. It is a necessary first step for an examination of *Uncle Tom's Cabin* in its turn-of-the-century contexts, including: the theatrical conventions of audience participation, blackface, and parody; the fiftieth anniversary of the Civil War; the proliferation of state segregation laws; and this title's continued capacity to stimulate outraged response from all sides, including Thomas Dixon's play of *The Clansman*.

Notes

1. For the context of Porter's filming of *Uncle Tom's Cabin*, see Charles Musser, *The Emergence of Cinema: The American Screen to 1907* (New York: Scribner's, 1990), 349–352; his *Before the Nickelodeon: Edwin S. Porter and the Edison Manufacturing Company* (Berkeley and Los Angeles: University of California Press, 1991), 242–245; and Noel Burch, 'Porter, or Ambivalence', *Screen* 19/4 (Winter 1978–79): 91–105. Both Burch and Musser have argued against a past tendency to dismiss this film as a kind of cinematic equivalent to the Protestant sin of backsliding, coming as it does between the achievements of *Life of an American Fireman* and *The Great Train Robbery*. Both writers emphasise that this film is difficult to read precisely because it is looking backward, to traditions of popular live performance, and grappling with problems inherent in bringing the effect of that performance to the screen. My impetus for writing about this film comes from these works.

2. To the best of my knowledge, this riddle has not been solved. The difficulty in identifying this troupe is not surprising. The Tom Show, like early film, did not favour the star system, or the advertisement of actors. More generally, this branch of show business is sparsely documented. I should also add, for the record, that I know of no contemporary documentary evidence proving that Porter hired an already formed and touring production to appear on his stage. It seems to be a part of the accepted historical narrative, and it is the most reasonable; but such was the oral-formulaic structure of the Tom Show, that Porter might have hired his performers directly from the pool of unemployed actors in New York. Again, I would be very pleased to hear otherwise.

3. William Brady's production opened at the Academy of Music, New York, 4 March 1901. It is documented in a typescript with pencilled annotations that suggest a rehearsal copy preparatory to the stage manager's book, in the Museum of the City of New York. That script is clearly based on George Aiken's 1852 adaptation, but is heavily cut, rearranged and rewritten. Information on the production has been supplemented by reviews and programmes from the William Brady scrapbooks in the Billy Rose Theatre Collection, Lincoln Centre Library and Museum of the Performing Arts, New York Public Library, New York City.

4. For a history of the Tom tradition as chaotic and undocumented as the tradition itself, see Harry Birdoff, *The World's Greatest Hit: 'Uncle Tom's Cabin'* (New York: S. F. Vanni, 1947). Thomas F. Gassett, *'Uncle Tom's Cabin' and American Culture* (Dallas: Southern Methodist University Press, 1985) makes generous use of Birdoff, with supplementary materials. A number of useful reminiscences can be found in Gossett's bibliography. In my opinion, the very best is J. Frank Davis, 'Tom Shows', *Scribner's* 77 (April 1925): 350–360. A number of excellent discussions of the early stage

adaptations of Stowe's novel have been published, most recently: Bruce A. McConachie, 'Out of the Kitchen and into the Marketplace: Normalizing *Uncle Tom's Cabin* for the Antebellum Stage', *Journal of American Theatre and Drama* 3 (1991): 5–28; and Eric Lott, *Love and Theft: Blackface Minstrelsy and the American Working Class* (Oxford: Oxford University Press, 1993), 211–233.

5. J. Frank Davis, 'Tom Shows', 359.

6. The importance of pictorial tableau (and visual elements in general) in the structure of melodrama has been emphasised in Martin Meisel, *Realizations: Narrative, Pictorial, and Theatrical Arts in Nineteenth Century England* (Princeton: Princeton University Press, 1983). See also his 'Scattered Chiaroscuro: Melodrama as a Matter of Seeing', in *Melodrama: Stage, Picture, Screen*, edited by Jacky Bratton *et al.* (London: British Film Institute, 1994) 65–81.

7. Leon Washburn to George Lowery, quoted in Birdoff 280. Washburn ran 'Stetson's Big Double Uncle Tom's Cabin Company' for many years, including the period covered in this paper.

8. For evidence that the 'hoisting' of Eva was laughable even to the Tom Show audience by the turn of the century, see 'XXth Century "Uncle Tom's Cabin", According to Brady, in Town', *The World* 5 March 1901; and Blaine Quarnstrom, 'Early Twentieth Century Staging of 'Uncle Tom's Cabin'', *Ohio Stage University Theatre Collection Bulletin* 15 (1968): 38–39.

9. For anecdotal evidence about acting inBrady's version, see Birdoff 359–364. For a useful, suggestive account of audience reaction (real or imagined), see *The World* (5 March 1901).

10. As a matter of whimsical analogical conjecture, Porter's Legree reminds me of two characters: King Herod in the medieval mystery plays; and any professional wrestler.

11. Musser, *Before the Nickelodeon*, 242, notes that Porter's film is 'condensed rather than excerpted'. For the record, scenes in Brady's script but missing in the film elaborate on the characters of St. Clair, George Harris, and Aunt Ophelia. Topsy's role, normally prominent in the Tom Show, is drastically reduced in the film, perhaps because so much of her humour and interpolated variety is vocal. On the other hand, there are three scenes in the film that are not in Brady: a model race between two steamships, an interpolated special effect then touring with two of the larger Tom Shows; Uncle Tom saving Eva from drowning in the Mississippi; and the bar-room murder of St. Clair by Simon Legree. The last two scenes are reported by dialogue in Brady's script.

12. Jacky Bratton, 'The Contending Discourses of Melodrama', in *Melodrama: Stage, Picture, Screen* (London: BFI, 1994): 38–49, discusses the neglected importance of the comic character in the history of melodrama, and especially the use of comedy to create a more open, complex, and 'heteroglot' performance than we generally read in the published scripts. The evidence from Brady and Porter, and the whole history of the Tom show, supports this argument.

1895

Saturday Night at the X-Rays – The Moving Picture and 'The New Photography' in Britain, 1896

Richard Crangle

Bill Douglas Centre for the History of Cinema and Popular Culture, University of Exeter, Exeter EX4 4QH, UK

ONE OF THE FAVOURITE TRICKS of the late nineteenth-century British journalist was to attach the adjective 'new' to nouns to indicate an issue worthy of consideration or, perhaps, alarm. The two most obvious examples of this practice were 'The New Journalism' to indicate the various strains of more-popular, more-illustrated or more-radical newspaper and magazine publishing hovering around W.T. Stead, Alfred Harmsworth, George Newnes and others from the 1880s onwards, and 'The New Woman' to indicate people disinclined to bow to gender conventions regarding dress, employment, leisure activities or political status. Numerous other related usages can be found in 1890s newspapers, magazines and novels.[1] In this context it is hardly surprising that there was a 'New Photography' for discussion in 1896; what can be surprising, looking back across a century saturated by moving picture culture, was that the 'New Photography' was not the motion picture but the Röntgen Ray or X-ray.

Konrad Wilhelm Röntgen's discovery of the phenomenon of X-ray photography was announced in a German scientific paper late in 1895, and attracted widespread publicity in Britain when picked up by the newspaper and magazine press in January 1896. As *Windsor Magazine* put it in April of that year:

> In three or four days Professor Röntgen's name was immortal, and in as many weeks the few Englishmen who had succeeded in repeating his results were overwhelmed with queries, with requests for lectures, demonstrations, and assistance generally, and with all the other worries that come to the man who is suddenly popular.[2]

In the first half of 1896, most British popular illustrated monthlies ran copiously-illustrated features on the New Photography. Daily newspapers and illustrated weeklies gave further coverage, and some sections of the photographic trade press went into a kind of ecstasy – the art-photography journal *The Photogram* went as far as to rush out a special

1895

'New Light' issue in February 1896, and ran a monthly 'Radiography' column from April until August, after which its concern retracted into occasional paragraphs in the general news pages. As well as semi-factual discussion of the new effect's capabilities, it appeared as the subject of cartoons, advertisements and other asides. *Punch*, the barometer of self-important middle-class Englishness, carried at least six X-ray references in cartoons and comic verses in the first half of 1896.[3] By mid-year, however, non-trade press interest had more or less evaporated, and few if any peripheral references to the X-ray effect were made in the same sources for the remainder of the year.

The interest surrounding the New Photography in early 1896 seems, a century later, to have eclipsed the almost parallel launch in Britain of an optical sensation which became far more influential: the projected moving picture. Coverage of the moving picture in the general press in 1896 tended to move in the opposite direction from that of the X-ray. From a relatively unreported launch in February, when the press shows and openings of the Lumière and Paul machines were scarcely noticed by *The Times*, *Black and White* and the *Illustrated London News* and completely unmentioned by *Punch* and *The Graphic*, references to the moving picture appeared more frequently through the remainder of 1896 and into subsequent years. Whereas the X-ray was celebrated as a novelty attraction before fading from attention to become a scientific tool, the moving picture took some months to be covered with any significance outside the trade press but was then noted more and more with the passage of time. *The Strand Magazine* was the first British periodical to carry a feature of significant length[4] on the moving picture (in August 1896, a month after its piece[5] on the New Photography), and after that references to the new medium can be found with some regularity in the general press, in both factual descriptions and fictional contexts. It was, though, still to be a few years before *Punch* could bring itself to refer to the upstart.

From the first, uses of the X-ray were clearly envisaged as basically scientific and diagnostic in character: the photographs published in *Strand* and *Windsor* magazines in 1896 were mainly of broken bones, bullets embedded in animal limbs, human and animal skeletons, and so on. Indeed the principal attraction of the effect was 'the fact ... that the skeleton can be photographed through the living flesh',[6] as H. Snowden Ward, editor of *The Photogram*, put it in his *Windsor Magazine* article. In its hint of a Frankensteinian obsession with use of technology to overcome or bypass death, Ward's observation reveals an aspect of the nineteenth-century relationship with scientific progress which on the whole did not survive the shock of technologised warfare in 1914, if it lasted that long. In the 1890s, one of any new visual technology's first functions was investigation and revelation of the human world and the human being, and these were on the whole perceived by contemporary commentators as beneficial pursuits.

But the X-ray photograph has also to be seen in a context in which new technologies were celebrated continuously in popular published and entertainment media, especially when, as in this case, they produced visually spectacular results. Where a new development produced something which could be shown or viewed there was a clear opportunity for commercial gain in selling to the public opportunities to partake, at least visually, in the experience of the latest scientific or technological marvel. Technological developments were regularly exhibited at sites of public spectacle, including not only the regular large-scale international expositions but also the permanent variety 'pleasure palaces' like London's Crystal Palace or Olympia. Amongst other attractions in early 1896 Olympia exhibited bicycling, military hardware, the Paul Theatrograph, and the X-ray, while Crystal Palace hosted a large exhibition of 'horseless carriages' between May and July.[7] In a few cases, new technologies allowed demonstration as music-hall acts, greatly increasing their scope for public exhibition and exploitation, and this is what happened to the moving picture in Britain. In the case of X-rays, however, this was less than easy: by its nature the equipment was delicate and required skilled manufacture and operation, and its results were slow to appear and diffi-

1895

Fig. 1. *Comic cartoon. E.R. [?], 'The New Photographic Discovery. Thanks to the discovery of Professor Röntgen, the German Emperor will now be able to obtain an exact photograph of a "backbone" of unsuspected size and strength!'.* Punch *(25 January 1896): 45.*

THE NEW PHOTOGRAPHIC DISCOVERY.

Thanks to the discovery of Professor Röntgen, the German Emperor will now be able to obtain an exact Photograph of a "Backbone" of unsuspected size and strength !

Fig. 2. *Comic cartoon. E.H., 'The March of Science. Interesting result attained, with aid of Röntgen Rays, by a first-floor lodger when photographing his sitting-room door.'* Punch *(7 March 1896): 117.*

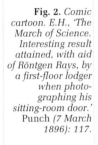

THE MARCH OF SCIENCE.

Interesting Result attained, with Aid of Röntgen Rays, by a First-Floor Lodger when Photographing his Sitting-room Door.

jection. The London slide dealers Newton and Co. advertised new X-ray lantern slides for sale or hire at regular intervals throughout 1896, eventually offering a total of 60 slides[8] illustrating the typical early subjects of damaged bones, animal skeletons, and embedded bullets, with prices dropping from two shillings and sixpence per slide in February to one shilling per slide in September. The extent to which these slides were taken up by the lantern exhibition trade is now impossible to judge accurately, but a paragraph in the *Optical Magic Lantern Journal* [*OMLJ*] of May 1896 recommended that:

> ... one or two included in a lantern entertainment would, no doubt, be interesting, but the well-known hand shadowgraph should be avoided. Snakes, mice, and birds are a little more uncommon.[9]

Other uses of the X-ray were varied, but instructive as to some of the more fanciful perceptions of the possible functions of a new visual technology. *The Photogram* reported in June 1896 that 'Radiographic studios appear to be opening everywhere',[10] with the suggestion that much of their business was surgical. In April 1896 the *OMLJ* noted the use of an X-ray photograph of a broken limb as evidence in a court case and quoted the judge as remarking that 'nowadays a man might be sent to an asylum by having his head photographed'.[11] There was also some lurid speculation about the possibilities of photographing thought,[12] or connecting the new discovery to the 'astral light' alleged to exist by spirit-photography enthusiasts such as Mrs. Besant and Madame Blavatsky.[13]

More popular perceptions of the New Photography's capabilities are also interesting. Most of the accounts in the monthly and weekly press attempted a lay-person's scientific explanation of the effect and process, and in a social environment generally more scientifically impressionable and inquisitive than that of today this must have found a certain amount of understanding in its intended audiences. Equally, though, cartoonists and others employed free imaginative impressions of the equipment, its effects, and its potential uses, as a few examples (Figs.1–4) from the first half of 1896 demonstrate.

cult to realise successfully. In contrast the majority of the moving picture equipment which hit the market in 1896 and 1897 was relatively simple to make and use, readily portable, and adapted to existing projection methods. On the other hand the *results* of the X-ray process, once achieved as photographic negatives, were easily converted to commercial goods in the form of half-tone printing blocks for publication or glass slides for pro-

The essential misunderstanding of the technology inherent in some of its contemporary representations gives an indication of the perceived function and (more to the point) the attraction of the effect. The policeman's Röntgen 'camera' in Figure 4, for example, emits a visible ray like that of a magic lantern or projector, which makes *only* the tramp's bag transparent to reveal the tea inside. The suggestion is that the New Photography was expected to make external coverings transparent, and so to make invisible contents visually available for recording and detailed inspection in the same way that Fox Talbot and Daguerre's inventions nearly 60 years before had made the visible world recordable. The New Photography, like the 'old' photography, was imagined to change the *nature* of things: it made available the hidden or secret information below the visible surface which, like John Bull's backbone in Figure 1, or the tramp's tea, was necessary for a fuller understanding of 'the whole picture'.

At the same time, though, these implied or imagined uses indicate a fundamental limitation of the novelty-attraction attempt to capitalise on a new medium or technology. By making it an investigative tool the possible responses to the new technology were limited, and once they had been explored its novelty-value was used up,[14] particularly in an environment where competing novelty experiences were occurring regularly and often. Rather than broadening its popular or commercial appeal by representation of an increasing number of subjects, the scope of X-ray technology rapidly became limited to a small range of specific purposes, namely scientific, investigative, and medical diagnoses. With hindsight, of course, it is difficult to see how use of the X-ray could have developed in any other way – from a modern perspective it is hard to imagine, for instance, how it could have depicted fictional narrative, although some of its advocates in *The Photogram* certainly saw an artistic side to its potential uses. Perhaps the more interesting question, therefore, is not why the X-ray did not develop as a popular entertainment, but why the moving picture did.

It is easy enough to see how the moving picture might, in other circumstances, have

Fig. 3. *Comic cartoon. C. Harrison, 'A Falstaffian Tree in The Haymarket, as seen by Röntgen Rays'*, Punch *(20 June 1896): 289.*

A FALSTAFFIAN TREE IN THE HAYMARKET,
AS SEEN BY RÖNTGEN RAYS

A SUSPICIOUS CASE — The New Photography and Mazawattee.

Fig. 4. *Advertising cartoon. Phil May, 'A Suspicious Case – The New Photography and Mazawattee,'* Black and White *(4 April 1896): 442.*

followed the same developmental path as the X-ray. Both had their origins in 'pure' scientific experimentation, although the later stages of moving picture development occurred more through the 'applied' science of the photographic and electrical equipment trades. Both essentially offered refinements of existing standards of photographic realism: the X-ray extended the domain of the static photograph into the realm of what was not normally visible, the moving picture extended it across the passage of time. Both were perceived to have functions in *revelation of the invisible* – the X-ray could probe beneath the visible surface, while the moving picture could bring a viewer lifelike representations of events previously unavailable because of their temporal and physical location, as indicated by the numerous early fictional references to the moving picture in which it inadvertently revealed a crime or indiscretion in progress. Why, then, did one of the two technologies develop beyond the novelty-spectacle into a general standard of narrative representation, while the other remained a specialist technical tool?

There was, of course, an important difference between the ways in which the two media were marketed. As Snowden Ward commented haughtily in *Photograms of '96* at the end of the year, early British moving picture producers 'were fortunate in inducing the variety theatres to take up the idea'.[15] Although it also appeared as a spectacle at the pleasure palaces, it was in the variety theatre that the moving picture found its first great commercial success, and its appearance there aligned it with a long and continuing tradition of entertainment. The nineteenth-century music hall operated through continuity rather than novelty, with acts of the same generic types circulating for entire working lives rather than coming and going overnight; it also operated through traditions of itinerance rather than ephemerality – that is, an act would physically move to find a new audience once its novelty with one audience was exhausted. The introduction of the moving picture to the variety circuit also meant that a ready-made publicity system and established mass audience were available instantaneously. None of these aspects were the same for a technological novelty such as the X-ray, which did not make a transition onto the variety bill but remained static at the pleasure palaces and on the pages of the illustrated magazines and newspapers.

The cost and availability of equipment must also have been a significant factor in the two technologies' relative successes. A few photographic dealers did offer X-ray equipment for the photographic studio or the home mar-

ket – it was possible to buy a complete outfit from Newton & Co. for between £19 and £33 (depending on its electrical power) in March 1896[16] – but it remained a luxury item for all but the most established professional photographers. In contrast many dealers quickly offered moving picture projectors for sale – including a lantern light source, one could be had for £36[17] in mid-year, with prices dropping as low as £18 (or £10 for the projector mechanism only)[18] by the end of 1896. Equally importantly, an ever-increasing number of films were available for purchase or hire, if the exhibitor did not make his or her own. Although X-ray and moving picture equipment costs were initially comparable, the essential economic difference was that the moving picture could show a commercial return almost immediately, paying for the equipment within a very short time by a music-hall engagement or by taking pennies at the door, while the X-ray practitioner had no prospect of similar financial gain. Maybe, if he or she was lucky, some slides or the rights to a few images might be sold, but there was no chance of ongoing income arising from ownership of an X-ray outfit except perhaps hospital or other diagnostic work, and the market for that in any given location would be strictly limited. In addition, X-ray equipment was not portable, while the average moving picture camera was: this had an important effect on the potential subjects of the two processes which was, in the end crucial to the development of the moving picture.

Crudely put, the difference was that the subject of an X-ray picture had to be brought to the camera, while most moving picture cameras could go to the subject. This meant that one of the two was always limited in what it could show, while the other was potentially limitless. X-ray subjects had to be relatively small, static, and predetermined; moving picture subjects could be any visible action, anywhere in the world, and were not necessarily predictable. The results of both processes were initially marketed as 'attractions', but the X-ray photograph depended for its attraction on a single visual effect, while the moving picture depended on an ongoing process of representation.

Moving pictures have an inherent narrative

quality which was always present in early film subjects – an action was shown to proceed sequentially from beginning to end, or at least to a subsequent stage, and events could be shown to arise as consequences of one another. The overwhelming majority of early film subjects, though, were what we would now term 'documentary' in content. They showed events of real life, either as specific news items or as generic views of everyday life proceeding as though the camera were not present. The dominant subject of early film was specifically *contemporary life*, both as it was lived in cities, streets and workplaces familiar to the audience, and as it was lived in remote exotic locations. This was a fundamental difference between X-rays and moving pictures, as far as their popular perception was concerned. X-rays generated a spectacular effect which was, by definition, not visually verifiable by any other means. Moving pictures generated a spectacular effect which (however crudely) emulated natural ocular vision, and which took as its subject views similar to those perceptible by natural ocular vision in the course of day-to-day life. As such, the 'attraction' of the early moving picture lay in more than its spectacular nature and its novelty.

If moving pictures had been used to illustrate subjects similar to those of X-ray photographs – a direct extension, perhaps, of Muybridge's and Marey's scientific approaches to movement in animals or humans – they would have had limited popular appeal which would have been less likely to survive the initial novelty of the effect. But instead they were used to show street scenes, people at work, short acted narrative or comic scenes, means of transport, news events and celebrities, and other realities of the surrounding world. The effect of this on their popularity was threefold: first, much of their subject matter related directly to the visual experiences of the audience, whose everyday perceptions were thus transformed into spectacular entertainment; second, they became part of the celebratory reporting of immediately contemporary life; and third, their range of possible subjects was enormous, always capable of showing something new. The documentary nature of early film's content, in a period in which the technological progress of modern life was in itself a subject of wonder and entertainment, was far from the limitation as which it has since been perceived and closer to being a commercial advantage. In the 1890s it was common to launch technological novelties as entertainment commodities, but for one of them to last longer in a public perception than that initial period in which it 'must be seen' it needed something additional to offer. This is what the moving picture could do, and the X-ray photograph could not: once one had seen the transparent hands, animal skeletons, coins inside purses, and so on, and grasped at some level the technical possibilities of the effect, there was nothing new to be had from the experience. It ceased to be the New Photography and became 'radiography'. In contrast, the moving picture, expanding and changing like the real life it claimed to represent, was *always* capable of being 'new' photography.

Notes

1. For discussion of this usage, including 'The New Fiction' (1895) and 'The New Art Criticism' (1893), see John Stokes, *In the Nineties* (Chicago: University of Chicago Press, 1989), 22–23 and 34–35. Other minor examples include: 'The New Cricket', *Punch* (18 July 1896): 27; 'The New Stagecraft', *Punch* 26 September 1896: 154; 'The New Verb', *Punch* (31 October 1896): 213; and 'The New Ars Poetica', *Punch* (12 December 1896): 279.

2. H. Snowden Ward, 'Marvels of the New Light: Notes on the Röntgen Rays', *Windsor Magazine* 16 (April 1896): 372.

3. In addition to the three cartoons reproduced as Fig. 1 to Fig. 3, the *Punch* references were: 'The New Photography' (verse), (25 January 1896): 45; 'The Progressive Photograph' (prose), (15 February 1896): 78; 'Light in the Egyptian Darkness' (verse), (18 April 1896): 183; and 'Policeman X Junior on Science in the Force' (verse), (25 April 1896): 198. A further advertising reference is found in *Black and White*, (18 April 1896): 509–510, in which a drawing of a loaf of bread reveals the words 'Hovis/Cure for Indigestion' inside (printed on the opposite side of the page) when held to the light.

1895

4.   'The Prince's Derby: Shown by Lightning Photography', *Strand Magazine* 68 (August 1896): 134–140.

5.   Alfred W. Porter, 'The New Photography', *Strand Magazine* 67 (July 1896): 107–117.

6.   H. Snowden Ward, 'Marvels of the New Light: Notes on the Röntgen Rays', *Windsor Magazine* 16 (April 1896): 372. See also 'People Photographed as Skeletons: A Startling Discovery in Connection with Photography', *Optical Magic Lantern Journal and Photographic Enlarger* 81 (February 1896): 19–20.

7.   *Black and White* 11 (January–June 1896), advertising pages, *passim*.

8.   *Optical Magic Lantern Journal and Photographic Enlarger*, 1896, *passim*. Newton's advertisements usually appeared on the outside back cover.

9.   'Topical Notes', *Optical Magic Lantern Journal and Photographic Enlarger*, 84 (May 1896): 87.

10. 'Radiography', *The Photogram* 30 (June 1896): 156.

11. 'Notes', *Optical Magic Lantern Journal and Photographic Enlarger* 83 (April 1896): 57–58.

12. 'Correspondence', *Optical Magic Lantern Journal and Photographic Enlarger* 86 (July 1896): 119–120.

13. 'Notes', *Optical Magic Lantern Journal and Photographic Enlarger* 85 (June 1896): 92.

14. By late 1896 *Punch*, for one, was more concerned with the shortcomings of the 'Autocar' or 'Auto-motor' than with any optical novelties.

15. [H. Snowden Ward], 'Technical Progress in '96', *Photograms of '96*, supplement to *The Photogram* (London: Dawbarn & Ward, 1896), 10. The same article opens with the confident assertion that 'By far the most important announcement of the year was Röntgen's discovery'; the moving picture is described as having 'had a great boom this year ,' with the implication of being a passing craze.

16. Newton & Co. advertisement, *Optical Magic Lantern Journal and Photographic Enlarger* 82 (March 1896): xxiv.

17. J. Wrench & Son advertisement, *Optical Magic Lantern Journal and Photographic Enlarger* 87 (August 1896): xv.

18. Riley Brothers advertisement, *Optical Magic Lantern Journal and Photographic Enlarger* 91 (December 1896): xv.

1895

Stunt-Stories: The Sensation Film Genre in Denmark

Casper Tybjerg

Department of Film & Media Studies, Copenhagen University, Njalsgade 80, 2300 Copenhagen S, Denmark

'RAILWAYS, AUTOMOBILES, AIRPLANES – and the film – have made the world so tiny that the everyday and the astounding have been levelled.'[1] So claimed a Danish intellectual in 1908 or thereabouts. In recent years, this pessimistic viewpoint has made a comeback. Inspired by Wolfgang Schivelbusch's 1977 book, *Geschichte der Eisenbahnreise*, a number of film scholars have argued that there is a close correspondence between the experiences of the train passenger and the movie viewer.[2] Both are comfortably seated, looking at a frame (window or screen) through which can be seen a separate, curiously distant, busily moving world. This metaphorical connection is strengthened by the obvious fascination trains had for early filmmakers, and the early film presentations which took place in mock-up railway carriages, showing films shot from actual trains travelling along picturesque routes.

There is a sinister side to this new mode of experience, however. The separation between viewer and world is thought to produce a profound alienation of one from the other. The railway traveller inhabits a stunted universe consisting only of points of departure and arrival; the space in between is, in Schivelbusch's ominous phrasing, annihi-lated (*vernichtet*).[3] This disturbing rush exposed the nineteenth-century traveller to 'shock', an experience held by many commentators to be the very essence of modernity.

Some film scholars have found that many early films also provide 'shocks', allowing audiences to adapt themselves to the intensity of modern life. Through this 'succession of shocks', the films, according to Tom Gunning, 'explicitly acknowledge their spectator'.[4] Gunning further asserts that this 'unique spectatorial address defines the cinema of attractions and its difference from the classically constructed spectatorial address of later narrative cinema'.[5] Thus, 'the scenography of the cinema of attractions is an exhibitionist one, opposed to the cinema of the unacknowledged voyeur that later narrative cinema ushers in'.[6]

Making these definitions in terms of spectatorial address and using this psycho-analytic vocabulary is not, in my view, a very good idea. It produces exactly the sort of inflexible binary opposition Gunning claims he does not wish to create.[7] In the following, I should like to speak about some aspects of film history that this theoretical schema seems unable to accommodate. And rather than trains,

1895

planes and automobiles (especially the former) will provide the theme.

The Danish sensation film genre emerged in 1911; Nordisk Films Kompagni, the biggest production company, made a number of sensation films, and the genre became a staple of several smaller companies. Sensation films were feature-length story films where the characters were placed in thrilling, life-threatening predicaments. In his 1919 book on filmmaking, Urban Gad, director of most of Asta Nielsen's early films, lists four basic types:

> The actor must either expose himself to wild animals, or he must make leaps and climbs where he may fall from great heights, or he must leap on or off vehicles moving at full speed ... or he must run the risk of drowning.[8]

Gad further writes that movie companies will always be interested in clever variations on these. Gad defines sensations in this way: 'What is known as a "sensation" consists in placing a character in as unlikely a situation as possible, and then to save this person through some means of vehicular technology'.[9]

One example of this was *Dødsflugten* (The Fatal Escape, 1912), made by Skandinavisk-Russisk Handelshus, a movie company where sensations were the mainstay. In this film, the hero, a gentleman thief, shakes off his pursuers by flying away in a balloon. The shooting of this scene attracted considerable attention. When the film was about to come out, the newspaper *Ekstra Bladet* had just hired a 22-year-old reporter who was a certified balloonist himself. His job was mainly covering aviation news, but he was sent to talk to the heads of Skandinavisk-Russisk about their new movie. He asked one of them what the story of this sensational film was, and received the following reply:

> The story ... is without importance in the modern film drama ... The views are all that matters, and they are as striking as is altogether conceivable.[10]

The interview, entitled 'The Sensational Film', appeared on 9 July 1912, and it was the earliest contact that we know of between the film industry and the young journalist, Carl

Theodor Dreyer. A month later, Skandinavisk-Russisk were filming Dreyer's first screenplay.

Dreyer had, for a couple of years, been working for various newspapers and illustrated magazines, mainly doing motoring and aviation news. A biographical sketch, written by a colleague in 1911, attests that Dreyer's youthful fervour had made him the butt of quite a few jests:

> Flying machines, automobiles, rubber tyres, gasoline, lubricating oil, automatic ignition, propellers – all this was sacred to Dreyer. He tolerated no jokes about it. Contemptuously, he rejected any attempts on our part at irony directed at his idols. His earnestness and enthusiasm were unshakable when something merely smelled of gasoline.[11]

One of the motor-lovers whose exploits Dreyer had covered was another newspaperman, ten years older than himself, whose name was Alfred Nervø.

Nervø explained his devotion to motoring in his autobiography, *Ten Years Behind the Wheel*:

> There are some people who have a special feeling for music, people whom music affects in an especially violent, completely physical fashion. With motoring it is the same. For the 'true' motorist, speeding along in his beloved vehicle is one of the highest forms of living.[12]

Nervø became an incurable automobile fanatic in 1905 when he covered a nation-crossing road trip, arranged by the Danish Automobile Club. Along the way, he met the inventor Jacob Christian Ellehammer, who rode a motorcycle of his own design.

Ellehammer was a man of extraordinary ingenuity who would eventually have more than four hundred patents to his credit. Among the many contraptions he designed were a cigarette-making machine, an automatic soft-drink dispenser, and even a kinetoscope. Ellehammer decided to let Nervø break the story on his most ambitious project, giving the young newspaperman his first scoop.

'Ellehammer's Airship' ran the front-page headline on 2 November 1905. An illustration

1895

depicted an aircraft soaring over the roofs of Copenhagen with the caption: 'A dream which seems about to become reality'.[31] The Wright brothers had of course flown two years before, but they had kept their accomplishment secret, and it was still largely unknown in Europe. It seemed Ellehammer might become the first man to achieve heavier-than-air flight, and he did become the first European to do so: on 12 September 1906, Ellehammer flew a distance of 42 metres, soaring one-and-a-half metres above the ground. In the next few days, a number of similar flights were made, witnessed, among a few others, by Nervø.

Practical aviation still seemed a distant possibility, however, until Wilbur Wright came to France in the fall of 1908 and demonstrated his flyer. Nervø had gone to France and planned to settle there, but when he saw Wright fly, he was so impressed that he went back to Denmark the very next day:

> I had the fever in my blood, now I had to get home and shake them up and get us going.
> I had to get home to become an airman myself![14]

Back in Denmark, he talked some wealthy motor enthusiasts into investing the money needed to buy an aeroplane; but difficulties arose, and the investors decided to wait. In the meantime, Nervø went on a lecture tour to promote the 'cause of flight'. He was accompanied by his closest friend, Robert Storm Petersen. Storm P. was a man who possessed an astonishingly wide range of talents. He is still renowned as one of the greatest of Danish humorists, but he was also a painter, an actor, a cabaret artist, and a film pioneer. In 1919, he made the first Danish animation films, and years before, in 1907, he acted in many of the earliest Danish fiction films, made by Nordisk Films Kompagni. On the lecture tour, Storm would operate the cinematograph he and Nervø had brought along to show four moving pictures of flying machines.

In August 1909, Nervø went back to France, to the Grande Semaine de l'Aviation at Rheims, a spectacular week-long affair. 'No one who attended this event would ever forget it', writes Robert Wohl in his superb book *A*

Passion for Wings: Aviation and the Western Imagination.[15] Nervø was accompanied by a wealthy businessman and motor enthusiast who put up the money to buy a flying machine as well as training for both Nervø and Robert Svendsen, the businessman's driver. A few weeks later, Nervø was a pilot; at the time, fewer than a hundred people in the world could lay claim to that title.

On the evening of 3 June 1910, Nervø became the first man to fly over Copenhagen: he himself made the dream depicted in the front-page drawing five years before a reality. At the time, few other cities had been flown over by aeroplanes; that same day, Graham White became the first to fly over London.[16] Nervø flew past the city hall spire, and thereby won a prize which had been offered some time before to the first man to accomplish this daring exploit. The money had been put up by none other than Ole Olsen, president of Nordisk Films Kompagni and the first and greatest of Danish movie tycoons.

Like Nervø, Olsen was a keen automobile enthusiast; he had acquired his first horseless carriage as early as the year 1900. At that time, he was the manager of a large fairground in Sweden, the Malmö Tivoli. And the motorcar became one of the attractions; for a modest sum, people could ride in this marvellous contraption. They could also watch balloon ascents and look at their bones in an X-ray apparatus.[17] Olsen had also tried showing films, but without much success. In 1905, however, he opened a cinema in Copenhagen. Encouraged by its success, he moved into production in January 1906. Soon, his company was a major player in the international motion picture business.

In the weeks after Nervø's flight, aviation fever gripped the nation; the newspapers had daily columns called 'From the Airfield'. Journalists, including Dreyer, helped drum up interest in the next challenge confronting Danish aviators: crossing Øresund, the narrow band of water separating Denmark and Sweden. Nationalistic ambition played a prominent role, because one of the men thought most likely to make the crossing was the Swedish aviator, Baron Cederström.

In the early hours of morning on 17 July 1910,

1895

Robert Svendsen, the driver who had learnt to fly together with Nervø, took off from the airfield and turned his machine out over the water. Half an hour later, he landed in Sweden. Dreyer, who followed the doings of the aviators very closely, had sensed that Svendsen was about to try the crossing. The night before, sick with excitement, he went across on the ferry. He was the only Danish newspaperman present at the landing – quite a scoop.

Nor was Dreyer content to stay on the ground and watch. He went up in a balloon on several occasions and in October 1910 flew as far as Norway in one. He took numerous photographs of skyscapes which were published in the illustrated weekly for which he also worked. The next year, 1911, he became the first international aeroplane passenger in history when he flew across the Sound in a chair strapped to the undercarriage of the French aviator Poulain's flying machine. Later that year, he qualified for his balloonist's certificate in Germany.

The previous autumn, a private flying school had been organised in Copenhagen, with Svendsen as instructor, and Dreyer had promptly enrolled, but apparently never completed the course.[18] Among the students who did was the young actor Einar Zangenberg who had already appeared in some films at Nordisk.

In 1911 or 1912, Nordisk set out a brief set of guidelines for aspiring screenwriters. One of the points was this: 'In any film, there must be some sort of effective – and above all, novel – gimmick, which will provide the highlight of the film'.[19] Flying machines could obviously do this. The flimsy and unreliable craft of the time made going up in one a rather daring feat in itself. Few escaped crashes. In 1910, thirty-two aviators were killed; in the first six months of 1911, thirty more.[20]

The sensational appeal of aviation was unmistakable. In the USA, J. Stuart Blackton of Vitagraph learnt to fly himself in order to make several aviation one-reelers in 1911.[21] Thanks to the intrepid Zangenberg, Ole Olsen did not have to take to the air himself. In the summer of 1911, Nordisk made three features with Zangenberg in which he used Robert Svendsen's Danish-built aeroplane, the Kite. *En*

Lektion, eller Aviatikeren og Journalistens Hustru ('A Lesson'; English release title *The Aviator and the Journalist's Wife*), directed by August Blom, opened as early as 19 July 1911. *Den Store Flyver, eller, Ædel Daad* ('The Great Aviator, or, A Noble Deed'; English title *The Aviator's Generosity*), directed by Urban Gad, followed in December. In May 1912 came *Opfinderens Skæbne, et Drama fra Aviatikens Aarhundrede* (English title, *The Aeroplane Inventor*), also directed by Blom.[22] The inventor-hero, like Ellehammer and the Wright brothers, runs a bicycle workshop.

In none of these films can the story be said to be 'without importance'. Rather, they fit well with the recommendations of the earliest Danish screenwriters' manual, *Hvorledes skriver man en Film?* ('How Do You Write a Film?') by Jens Locher, published in 1916. It reproduces Nordisk's brief guidelines, but supplements them:

> A surprising and novel idea that (for instance) saves the hero from a difficult situation, a dangerous and original way to perform a feat, will always be desirable, though the whole film should not be built on this one thing, but this idea or 'gimmick', as it is called in the film industry, should be logically joined with what went before and not merely put in without plan or coherence to create artificial excitement in an otherwise static and trivial screenplay.[23]

All three films have well-constructed stories about love or money-problems or both. Established actors appear; Zangenberg was trained at the Royal Theatre School of Drama, and two of his classmates, Poul Reumert and Clara Wieth Pontoppidan, appear in *The Aviator's Generosity* and *The Aeroplane Inventor* respectively. The former film also boasts a race between two flying machines, the latter a fatal crash (which occurs off-screen, though).

In 1912, Zangenberg started a movie company of his own, Kinografen, which specialised in sensation films, most with Zangenberg himself as director and star. Judging from the few extant pictures of his, he was at best a competent filmmaker. Still, something like *Adrianopels Hemmelighed* (The Secret of Adrianople, 1913) – of which only individual

1895

copyright frames from the Library of Congress survive – shows Zangenberg's commitment to thrilling action. It had a topical subject – the war raging in the Balkans at the time – an escape from a dungeon, a speedboat chase, an aeroplane shot down by an automobile-mounted gun, and much else. Such films made Zangenberg rich and enabled him to buy one of the biggest automobiles in Copenhagen.[24]

Bankability was also the chief concern of the people at Skandinavisk-Russisk. When Dreyer's first script went into production, he did an interview with the director, Kay van der Aa Kühle, for his paper. It appeared under the headline 'The Break-Neck Film'. The unscrupulous Dreyer made no mention of his own contribution to the film. Dreyer asked Kühle: 'Is it really necessary to weave these break-neck sensations into the modern photoplay[?]' Kühle replied:

> Films can only be made in two ways: either as *good* plays – *art*, if you will – or as sensation plays. If you want a good play with a prospect of making money, you must be able to afford hiring world-famous actors and a film-primadonna at 100,000 crowns a year. If you can't afford that – and I freely admit that *we* can't – you have to settle for making sensation films. When they are done properly, you don't run any risks with them.[25]

This cynical attitude produced a great deal of annoyance among those who strove to have film recognised as an art in its own right, because it played into the hands of the many people within the cultural establishment who considered film to be a tawdry sideshow amusement.

In March 1913, a heated debate on the status of the film medium appeared in the pages of the powerful left-liberal newspaper *Politiken*. It was sparked by Nordisk's unsuccessful attempt to buy the movie rights for Ibsen's plays, and by an essay in defense of film art by Urban Gad's mother, the formidable Emma Gad, playwright, socialite, and feminist. Other contributions to the debate came from the sons of Ibsen and Bjørnson (the latter a film director himself), the Swedish poet Verner von

Heidenstam (subsequently a Nobel laureate), and from Alfred Nervø.

Nervø dismisses 'the sensation drama, regarded as harmless idiocy by censors everywhere, with its runaway balloons, flying machines, and constrictor snakes'.[26] But not the film medium:

> ... it is a peculiarity of all great modern inventions that their perfection in material terms happens so swiftly that we only learn to take full advantage of them later on. This is very much the case with the artistic use of the film medium. Film authors are still far from discovering all the 'laws of the film medium' which are completely different from the 'laws of the stage'. But of course the film will have or is already getting its poets, who understand these laws and will create works based on them, which will be as fine as the fine works of the other arts.[27]

That summer, a man set to work who was determined to be a true artist of the cinema. Benjamin Christensen was born in 1879, like Nervø. He was originally trained as an opera singer and actor, and he too was in Zangenberg's class at the Royal Theatre School. His voice failed him, however, and he retired from the stage to become the agent of a champagne company. He was a friend of Robert Storm Petersen, and Christensen supplied the champagne for the celebration of Nervø's flight over Copenhagen.[28] Storm encouraged Christensen to go into the movies, and after a few films as an actor, he made *Det hemmelighedsfulde X* ('The Mysterious X', 1914; distributed in Britain as *Sealed Orders*).

Christensen spent months on shooting the film at a time when a week or two was the norm. But when *The Mysterious X* opened in March 1914, he was amply vindicated; it was immediately hailed as one of the most accomplished films yet made. It was presented as a 'Danish Sensation Drama', and a contemporary reviewer wrote:

> Within the framework of a suspected act of espionage have generously been placed as many effects as are otherwise usually distributed across 5 or 6 films. Beautiful landscapes, burning windmills, ravenous

1895

rats, condemned men, dreadnoughts and subterranean dungeons.[29]

The ads for the premiere boasted:

> While the ingredients of most films only escalate through the first acts and then diminish in intensity, in this work of cinema the story grows from act to act, and from first to last grips the spectator in breathless excitement, which only after the end of the final act is released in a liberating sense of amazement at the masterful direction and excellent subject-matter of this film.[30]

The Mysterious X merges sensational attractions with a powerful narrative drive and a commitment to creating cinematic art. This commitment to an art of the cinema based on coherent and absorbing stories is shared by aviation pioneers like Nervø and Dreyer – the very people who would have decisively experienced the separation of viewer and world held to be so typical of modernity.

And neither they nor Ole Olsen nor Zangenberg nor Christensen seem to have been much troubled by feelings of alienation. 'I was always up for the newest things', said the actress Else Frölich many years later when asked about her aeroplane ride in *The Aviator and the Journalist's Wife*.[31] And an optimistic and enthusiastic view about both the new vehicles and the new art form seems to have been shared by all these people. This comes out clearly in Benjamin Christensen's masterpiece *Häxan* (Witchcraft Through the Ages, 1922). Towards the end of the film, there is a series of comparisons between the demon-haunted superstitious darkness of the middle ages and enlightened modernity, where hysterics are sent to sanatoria instead of the torture chamber, and weird-looking old ladies are given care in nursing-homes rather than being burnt at the stake. These comparisons conclude with an intertitle stating: 'The witch no longer flies on her broomstick over the roofs of the town', followed by shots of an aeroplane taking off, watched by a exuberant young aviatrix in flight leathers. The airplane and the female flyer thus comes to symbolise the triumph of reason over superstition.

Notes

1. Quoted in Arnold Hending, *Filmens Vovehalse* (Copenhagen: Urania, 1948), 7.
2. See Lynne Kirby, *Parallel Tracks: The Railroad and Silent Cinema* (Exeter: University of Exeter Press, 1997), and additionally, Joachim Paech, 'Unbewegt bewegt: Das Kino, die Eisenbahn und die Geschichte des filmischen Sehens', in *Kino-Express: Die Eisenbahn in der Welt des Films*, Ulfilas Meyer (ed)(München: C.J. Bucher, 1985), 40–49; *idem.*, 'Das Sehen von Filmen und filmische Sehen: Zur Geschichte der filmischen Wahrnehmung im 20. Jahrhundert', in *Filmgeschichte schreiben: Ansätze, Entwurfe und Methoden*, ed. Knut Hickethier (Berlin: Edition Sigma, 1989), 68–77; Laurence Kardish (ed), *Junction and Journey: Trains and Film* (New York: Museum of Modern Art, 1991).
3. Wolfgang Schivelbusch, *Geschichte der Eisenbahnreise: Zur Industrialisierung von Raum und Zeit in 19. Jahrhundert* (München: Carl Hanser, 1977; reprint, Frankfurt am Main: Fischer, 1989), 39 (reprint edition cited).
4. Tom Gunning, 'An Aesthetic of Astonishment: Early Film and the (In)Credulous Spectator', *Art & Text* no. 34 (spring 1989): 38. The article is reprinted in Linda Williams (ed), *Viewing Positions: Ways of Seeing Film* (New Brunswick, N.J.: Rutgers University Press, 1995).
5. Tom Gunning, '"Now You See It, Now You Don't": The Temporality of the Cinema of Attractions', *The Velvet Light Trap* no. 32 (fall 1993): 5. The article is reprinted in Richard Abel (ed), *Silent Film* (New Brunswick, N.J.: Rutgers University Press, 1996).
6. Gunning, 'Aesthetic', 38.
7. Gunning, 'Now You See It', 4.
8. Urban Gad, *Filmen: Dens Midler og Maal* (Copenhagen: Gyldendal, 1919), 164.
9. Gad, 23.
10. *Ekstra Bladet* 9 July 1912; quoted in Peter Schepelern, *Tommen: Carl Th. Dreyers filmjournalistiske virksomhed* (Copenhagen: C.A. Reitzel, 1982), 13.
11. *Riget* (5 June 1911). Also quoted in Maurice Drouzy, *Carl Th. Dreyer, né Nilsson* (Paris: CERF, 1982).
12. Alfred Nervø, *Ti Aar bag Rattet*, vol. 1, *Fra Automobilernes og Motorcyklernes Barndomsaar* (Copenhagen: V. Pio, 1917), 11.

13. *Politiken* (2 November 1905).
14. Nervø, *Ti Aar*, vol. 1, 301.
15. Robert Wohl, *A Passion for Wings: Aviation and the Western Imagination, 1908–1918* (New Haven: Yale University Press, 1994), 100.
16. Alfred Nervø, *Ti Aar bag Rattet*, vol. 2, *Fra Flyvemaskinernes Barndomsaar* (Copenhagen: V. Pio, 1918), 196.
17. An interesting discussion of the early history of the X-ray machine may be found in Nancy Knight, '"The New Light": X Rays and Medical Futurism', in *Imagining Tomorrow: History, Technology and the American Future*, Joseph J. Corn (ed) (Cambridge, Mass.: MIT Press, 1986), 10–34.
18. Det Kongelige Danske Aeronautiske Selskab, *Dansk Flyvnings Historie* (Copenhagen: Fh. August Bangs Forlag, 1936), 72.
19. Jens Locher, *Hvorledes skriver man en Film?* (Copenhagen: V. Pio, 1916), 13.
20. Charles Harvard Gibbs-Smith, *Aviation: An Historical Survey from Its Origins to the End of World War II* (London: Her Majesty's Stationery Office, 1970), 158; Wohl, 133.
21. Jim and Maxine Greenwood, *Stunt Flying in the Movies* (Blue Ridge Summit, Pa.: TAB Books, 1982), 92. The Vitagraph filmography of Davide Turconi and Paolo Cherchi Usai lists three 1911 aviation-related titles: *The Sky Pilot, An Aeroplane Elopement, The Military Air Scout*; there are none in 1910 (see 'Filmografia: La produzione Vitagraph dal 1905 al 1916', in *Vitagraph Co. of American: Il cinema prima di Hollywood*, Cherchi Usai (ed) (Pordenone: Studio Tesi, 1987)).
22. The full Danish title may be translated as, 'The Inventor's Fate: A Drama from the Century of Aviation'.
23. Locher, 10–11.
24. *Dagens Nyheder* (2 November 1918).
25. *Ekstra Bladet* (7 August 1912) (emphasis in the original); quoted in Schepelern, 18.
26. Alfred Nervø, 'Film', *Politiken* (14 April 1913).
27. Alfred Nervø, 'Film', *Politiken* (31 March 1913).
28. Nervø, *Ti Aar*, vol. 2, 191.
29. *København* (24 March 1914).
30. *Politiken* (23 March 1914).
31. Arnold Hending, 'Dansk films første luftgaaende dame: Else Frølich Sandberg i *Aviatikeren og Journalistens Frue*', Århus Stiftstidende (21 December 1953).

1895

4

Cultural representation

1895

The Nationalisation of the Mass Spectator in Early German Film

Karen J. Kenkel

Department of German Studies, Stanford University, Stanford, CA 94305-2030, USA

WHEN THE POPULARITY OF FILM could no longer be denied or ignored in Germany, the self-designated guardians of German culture, the pedagogues, professors, the pastors and public servants, entered into an extended debate in which they struggled both to understand the novelty of film's appeal and to contain or channel it. The so-called *Kino-Debatte*, the film debate, began in Germany around 1907 with the establishment of influential film trade journals such as *Der Kinematograph* and *Lichtbild-Bühne* and with the first published attacks on film by members of the *Kinoreformbewegung* (the film reform movement). The film reformers launched the film debate by denouncing the majority of films on the market, which, they complained, exerted a morally corrupting influence on the German people – above all, on women and children. Because most of the so-called *Schundfilme* (trash films) they attacked were foreign films on the German market, their protest merged an assault on the film industry's commodification of culture with German nationalist sentiment. The recurring strains of romantic anti-capitalism, anti-modernism, and pre-war chauvinism shaped the film re-formers' calls for 'healthy' and educational German films. The reformers solicited government regulation of film production and consumption, regulation that did not exist before 1907, in order to foster film production which they hoped would preserve Germany's cultural autonomy and particularity in the face of international processes of capitalisation. Their goal was not only to promote domestic film production under governmental supervision, but also to nurture a national film style saturated with German qualities and values.

The film reformers' concern about film's corrupting effect on the German public successfully concentrated attention on the film spectator in the early battle over film. The reformers were absorbed in a project of observing and defining a film audience with whom they did not identify themselves, and by whom they clearly felt threatened. Entirely typical, for example, in the reformers' discussion of film's negative effect, is the narrative of the male bourgeois reformer who zealously goes to the movie theatre to know the enemy, and to document the danger. While the film reformer typically reports the types of films shown, much of his narrative focuses on the composition of the audience, emphasising the presence of children and women. These narratives assume that by observing the audience and its viewing experience one can ascertain the specific moral, social, and political effects of film on the spectator. For this reason one sees again and again in the film reform writings the phrase 'One has only to observe' a certain expression in the audience's collective face, or its rapid pulse beat, to conclude this or that dangerous effect of film. For example, Germany's leading pre-war authority on cinema law, Albert Hellwig, claimed in his 1914 work *Kind und Kino* (Child and Film) that to be convinced of the sexual dangers of the cinema '*One needs only to observe* the vast numbers of adolescent boys and girls as they stream out of the corrupting abyss of the theatre into the asphalt- and arc-lamp atmosphere of the street with shining eyes and heated blood'.[1] Hellwig worries about film's power to release the latent sexual impulses of youth into the receptive atmosphere of the city. His emphasis on the adolescence of the audience voices a concern shared by many film reformers that the need for sexual excitation evoked by film may form an addictive pattern in impressionable youth. Much of the early theorising about the film audience relies on personal observations like Hellwig's of the effects of film on the cinematic audience. Rare, however, is the confession of such an effect on oneself; the distance as an individual from the audience seen as a group and from the cinema experience as collective experience marks off for the observer the space of rational critique and moral judgement.

The film reformers' questionable assumption that observation of the spectator provided knowledge about film was facilitated by their definition of the film spectator as a mass, and of film as the first artform of truly collective – or mass – reception. The early discussion of the audience's reception of film drew heavily on mass psychology, as a comment by Alfred Döblin in 1913, in an essay on film titled 'Das Theater der kleinen Leute' ('The Theatre of the Small Man'), illustrates: 'Inside, in the pitch-dark, low room, a square screen of a man's height glitters over a monster of an audience, over a mass, whom this white eye, with its fixed gaze, spellbinds [*zusammen-*

bannt]'.[2] The idea of the film audience that Döblin expresses here, of a frighteningly de-individuated group bound together by the seductive and hypnotic power of the screen, is one that the film reformers relied upon in their attempt to control the new medium. Perhaps the most important single source for discussions of the mass psychological audience in this period is Gustave Le Bon's *Psychology of the Crowd*, written in 1894 and published in Paris in 1895.[3] In the preface to *Psychology of the Crowd*, Le Bon states that 'knowledge of the psychology of crowds is today the last resource of the statesman who wishes not to govern them – that is becoming a very difficult matter – but at any rate not to be too much governed by them'.[4] Le Bon intends his investigation of mass psychology to function as a modern machiavellian handbook, a politically useful study to facilitate domination of the increasingly autonomous mass through the use of psychological manipulation. Common to most of the film-reform writings is precisely this premise that the observed masses must be controlled and are subject to influence. Defining the audience as a mass assures the possibility of such control because the mass is, as film reformer Adolf Sellman claimed in 1913, 'neither good nor evil, but rather exactly so constituted, as it is influenced'.[5] The malleability of the mass can result in either the preservation or decline of cultural value.

At the heart of Le Bon's mass psychology is the conviction that individuals gathered into a crowd think and feel differently than they would separately, and they behave as one. The qualitative change effected by the dominance of the unconscious in crowds, he argues, results in the suppression of individual personality. Consciousness as the site of intelligence, the critical faculty of reason, and of rational discrimination and judgement, is also lost in the crowd. Related to its unique position 'on the borderland of unconsciousness', and to its openness to suggestion, Le Bon argues, is the crowd's affinity for images over language: 'A crowd thinks in images, and the image itself immediately calls up a series of other images, having no logical connection with the first'.[6] Participants in the film debate identified the film audience's mode of reception with that of the psychological mass: uncritical, emotional, unconscious, and uncontrolled (or unpatrolled) by a strong ego. Mass suggestion and hypnosis became key elements in early theories of how cinema functioned, whether these theories championed the necessary escape into the unconscious for the deadened masses or criticised the moral dangers of mass suggestibility. Indeed, the film reformers projected the character of mass reception onto the concept of film itself. If the mass receives through suggestion, film is a suggestive medium; if the mass is influenced by images, then film's images are influential. Further, film itself was conceived of as an essentially suggestive, and therefore inherently manipulative, medium.[7]

Perhaps the clearest illustration of the nexus of mass psychology, the film reform movement, and conservative nationalist politics is to be found in an article of 1912 by film reformer H. Duenschmann entitled 'Kinematograph und Psychologie der Volksmenge' (Cinema and the Psychology of the Crowd),[8] published in the *Konservative Monatsschrift für Politik, Literatur und Kunst* (Conservative Monthly for Politics, Literature and Art). The article attacks the predominance of foreign films (above all French films) in the German film market, a state of affairs which, according to the author, is endangering German culture and the health of the German folk. To address this problem adequately, Duenschmann claims, one must first understand the attraction of the cinema for the masses, and in order to do so, he argues, one must turn to mass psychology. Following Le Bon closely, Duenschmann emphasises the submersion of conscious individuality in the collective soul of the film crowd.[9] He assumes a close connection between the psychology of the masses and the particular qualities of film reception, commenting that in this stage of unconscious, almost hypnotic collectivity, feelings and actions are highly contagious, and that each member of the crowd manifests:

> ... an extraordinarily high degree of suggestibility ... which one observes in the individual only in a state of hypnosis. Just as consciousness is paralysed by hypnosis, such that the hypnotised becomes in all his actions the slave of the hypnotist,

so can the single member of the crowd entirely lose control over his actions under certain conditions.[10]

What characterises the mass spectator for Duenschmann is the loss of distance in which the critical faculty subsists, although the author assumes that the educated viewer can maintain such distance, that is, can hold himself outside of the crowd. Because of the importance of strong images in influencing the mass, pantomime and film act, according to the author, much more powerfully and efficiently on the masses than theatre:

> Pantomime as well as the cinema could possibly be superior to the theatre in their suggestive power, precisely because the image of an action excites the imaginative powers of a crowd much more quickly and vividly than the spoken word. Thus we see that the cinema in its suggestive influencing of the imaginative powers of the crowd is qualitatively not only theatre's equal, but its superior. At the same time, cinema is quantitatively infinitely superior to the theatre, because the cinema allows a numerically almost unlimited increase in mass effect through the possibility of mechanical reproduction.[11]

Because Duenschmann is interested in the mobilisation of mass culture for nationalist politics, he is able to draw political possibilities from the uniquely broad access that film's mechanical reproduction affords. The affinity between film image and mass susceptibility to visual suggestion produces a powerful new means of political influence, Duenschmann argues. For him, the issue is not whether political manipulation through mass culture exists – for he sees the film spectator as a mass spectator and, as such, only subject to manipulation – but rather an issue of world politics. Who will control the means of cinematic influence, the democratic French, or the monarchical Germans? He cautions that if the German government continues to ignore cinema, there can be no doubt 'who will take possession of this most sovereign means to influence the masses through suggestion: namely those who have chosen demagogy as their life calling and work to dissolve the German family and to destroy our national customs'.[12]

Duenschmann calls for the use of film to preserve German cultural unity, to create a 'national German film' which will realise a 'German national taste'.[13] The point, then, for Duenschmann, is to reconstitute the German folk from the anonymous mass audience, to fuse the mass's suggestibility and the mechanical reproduction of the image, in order to generate cultural values and a harmonious national audience.

The trade journals of the film industry agitated against the reformers' efforts to impose regulations on film through government censorship and taxation. The trade journals' investment in film's increased profitability clearly encouraged an ideological flexibility that the film reformers did not enjoy. The trade journals did not wish to resolve the tension between a mass psychological audience and a potential German-national audience that the film reformers thematise. In an article of 1911 titled 'Die ganze Richtung passt uns nicht!' ('The Entire Direction Doesn't Suit Us!'), for example, the editor of the trade journal *Lichtbild-Bühne*, Arthur Mellini, takes a stand against the film reformers' attempts to contain the growth of cinema. Mellini insists in the article that the government and the film reformers want to regulate film because they fear its emancipatory potential, its ability to teach the masses to think for themselves. The education that cinema provides, Mellini argues, will eliminate the need for the bourgeois cultural guardian, a role which the condescending and controlling film reformers hope to preserve. Mellini places cinema in a tradition of German Enlightenment culture, arguing that film brings knowledge to the masses and thereby opens the door to a cultural public sphere previously controlled by the educated bourgeoisie:

> By virtue of the honest power that cinema holds within itself, it will clear the way and bring light and knowledge everywhere where superstition and bestial submission have prevailed ... We ourselves know what we need, and we don't need tutelage [*Bevormundung*], because the German *Volk* has come of age, come of age through the enlightening effect of the cinema.[14]

Whereas a century earlier Schiller had de-

fined theatre as the means for overcoming class division in Germany and constituting an enlightened and unified German folk, Mellini argues that it is first film which is truly able and best suited to realise both the national goal of German idealism and the Enlightenment's egalitarian potential. The medium for the masses, in other words, helps to transform them into participants in a democratic national project of cultural expression.

Mellini rightly interprets the film reform movement as an exercise in repressive tutelage over an ideologically defined mass spectator, but he himself easily assumes the position of privileged spokesperson for 'the people'. Clearly worried that his defence of cinema as a means of enlightened mass education will not prove compelling, Mellini develops a second line of attack in the article which directly contradicts the first. He threatens those who oppose cinema with a vision of the mass's destructive power, which is mobilised through film's sublime power of manipulation.

> One senses ... the forces that slumber in the cinema: one isn't yet aware, however, of the gigantic power that it possesses ... We have learned to use film to force thousands of people into certain directions of thought. We can compel people to laugh and to cry; we can excite compassion and lead people to believe in paradisical happiness. We can kindle people's fantasy and bend them to our will. If we wanted to, we could produce a boundless rage, a frenzied hatred, which, appearing to thousands at the same time, would cause the earth to quake.[15]

Mellini abandons his enlightened *Volk* here and describes a volatile mass audience which film can compel to perform the capitalist's will. We see that Mellini will embrace a progressive, enlightenment position if he thinks it will protect the film industry from government interference; he will embrace the opposite position – film as mass manipulation – if it will increase the film industry's freedom to exploit the market.

Despite many articles emphasising the emancipation of the film audience that appear in trade journals from 1911–14, the journals echo the film reformers' mass psychological language of hysteria, suggestion, and hypnosis to describe the film spectator. The journals repeatedly use phrases such as *Kinematographen-Epidemie* (cinema-epidemic) and *Kinofieber* (cinema-fever) to describe film's attraction and to market its appeal. *Lichtbild-Bühne*'s promotion of the mass 'film epidemic' spreading outside the theatres recurs in its descriptions of the most dangerous form of mass behaviour in front of the screen: the outbreak of panics. Spectators often wildly rushed over one other to save themselves when fire threatened in the movie theatres, a particular danger in the early days of film, when film stock was made of highly flammable celluloid. The problem of panics was a very important issue for the trade journals, as panics were seen to manifest the uncontrollable mass hysteria of the cinematic crowd and therefore provided grounds for the authorities to close movie theatres. In December 1911, when two children were trampled to death as people attempted to escape a small fire in a Berlin movie theatre, *Lichtbild-Bühne* condemned the panicky crowd in the following terms:

> Into the midst of the innocent and humble Christmas joy fell the weighty drama of senseless human fear. Two blossoming young lives, delicate children's bodies, were mercilessly trampled down and crushed to death by the wild mass trying to save itself.[16]

The article focuses on panic as the problem; the moviegoers, not the cinema theatres, nor even fire in the theatres, are at fault. The article concludes that governmental regulation of movie theatres is not the answer, however, but rather 'the self-disciplining of the audience. Fire drills with personnel and as a product trained people, who will oppose the fanatic mob through hypnotic force with the power of their imperious personality.'[17] The charismatic personality who could compel the film mob was not only required for the mechanics of crowd control, but was also understood to be one of the functions of film itself, particularly of its stars on the screen. Film reform critics of Asta Nielson, for example, shifted from condemning her films as morally corrupting to viewing her positively

as a 'personality' who could compel the crowd.[18] Interestingly, one important advertising gimmick of the immediate pre-war years was to describe particular female stars as 'box office magnets' [*Kassenmagneten*] who, by the force of their irresistible personality, pulled the mass against its will into the movie theatres.

The tension in the trade journals between conceiving of the film audience as manipulable mass or enlightened *Volk* was one that the film reformers struggled unsuccessfully to resolve both through criticism and state intervention. The inherently conservative impetus shaping Le Bon's concept of the mass was invoked by the film reformers to attack the openness of the cinematic public sphere while attempting to annex for anti-modernist and chauvinistic purposes its purported power of suggestion. The film reformers set a moral agenda for cinema that was tied to a broader conception of German national culture threatened by the international market in the pre-war period. When criticising the international character of film in Germany, the film reformers not only attacked the products of foreign film companies such as Pathé or Gaumont, but also German productions which fed off prurient 'mass instincts' and participated in the capitalist exploitation of culture and its audience. It was not merely France or America that stood in the way of Germany's cultural self-realisation within modernity, but also greedy German capitalists wedded to a technological artform. Both foreign films and the products of the German film industry were often viewed as equally, if differently, 'foreign'; both diverted film from its calling in Germany to generate traditional values and a coherent national identity.[19]

It was not until the opening shots of the First World War that the film reformers saw the possibility of realising their goals, and they welcomed the First World War as a radical extension of their efforts since 1908 to improve the moral quality of film. While the trade journals initially fought the politically motivated closing of economic borders, the film reformers welcomed the walls which would keep foreign films out of Germany. They believed that the War would create space for a domestic film industry devoted to

German cultural values to prosper, in a soil cleared of international competition. Only thus could Hermann Häfker, a prominent force in the cinema reform movement, cry with enthusiasm late in 1914: 'The War is to date the greatest cinema reformer of all'.[20] Like most of the German intelligentsia, Häfker and other film reformers viewed the First World War as a physical battle transfigured by cultural desiderata. In the reform journal *Bild und Film* (Image and Film), Häfker implored the unleashed 'monster' of war to redeem and free German culture, 'to purify our culture of the filth that oppresses us'.[21]

By investing the War with the power to execute the reform they had failed to achieve, the cinema reformers acknowledged the futility of their attempts to fully reshape public demand and the mechanisms of the capitalist market through criticism and regulation. Häfker laments the feebleness of the individual voice in the pre-War period, pitted as it was against the combined strength of the 'uneducated mass' and a modern international capitalism interested in producing and reproducing this mass:

> The trash cinema rested upon a business organisation that spanned the world and whose power was so anchored in private capitalism that it seemed impossible to destroy this organisation or even to shift public opinion against it ... Then the War came, and its first 42-centimetre missiles destroyed this international business organisation. Nothing of it remains, at least not for Germany. No more films, no audience; theatres, distribution companies, film firms – all have been deserted.[22]

The War represents for Häfker a magical storm which has cleared the Wilhelmine cultural horizon. He equates the eradication of foreign film and the closure of the international market with the extermination of all of the structures previously associated with the *Schundkino*, including the domestic audience which enjoyed these films. This public 'is no longer', the first welcome casualty of the War. In other words, the War had transformed the 'foreign' mass and its destructive desires into a unified German body exhibiting a healthy, strong national taste:

To a large extent the taste of the crowd has been refined as if by a flash of lightening: everything false, everything merely mimed and costumed, everything ridiculous, sentimental, difficult and dirty, bores and repels in the face of the sublime reality whose wing-beats we all feel.[23]

Like the thunderbolt that brings Hans Castorp down from the Magic Mountain to the possible redemption of the battlefield, the War holds the reformers' hope of establishing an anti-materialistic Germanic film in the face of civilisation's imperialism. The War will be constructive in its destruction, purifying the folk by excising its foreign (mass) elements, as reformer Will Scheller proclaimed early in 1915: 'It [the War] reaches with powerful force into all the relations of cultural existence and, as a ruthless but effective doctor, tears much that is bad and inferior out of the body of the folk'.[24]

The film reform journal *Bild und Film* finds the most compelling evidence for the War's realisation of true German folk culture in, interestingly enough, the 1914 Italian film *Cajus Julius Caesar* produced by Cines in Rome. Reviews of the film in *Bild und Film* continually draw parallels between wartime Germany and imperial Rome, between the emperor Julius Caesar and the emperor Kaiser Wilhelm II. Critics laud the fact that *Cajus Julius Caesar* focuses the attention and desire of the mass audience, reflected in and guided by the on-screen masses, onto a strong personality, onto a leader par excellence. They believe that the powerful figure of Caesar turns the mass audience's fascination with on-screen masses into a vehicle for *Volk* consolidation.[25]

Most *Bild und Film* critics place particular emphasis on the subordinate relation of the scenic masses to the leader in *Cajus Julius Caesar*. Hilda Blaschitz, one of the few women critics of the film reform movement, highlights Caesar's imperial personality in just such a manner: 'A crushing, mass-dominating, regally noble movement of his hand alone raises him above all others'.[26] The editor of *Bild und Film*, Lorenz Pieper, asserts that *Cajus Julius Caesar* is the aesthetically most successful film in the short history of cinema, precisely because its single protagonist

1895

merges governance with monumentality through the control of the masses. Caesar is a 'colossal personality', the 'autocrat, the *emperor*'.[27] *Bild und Film* critic Malwine Rennert argues that *Cajus Julius Caesar* presents the German audience with two instructive images of a national people: a negative portrayal of the foreign, self-indulgent, fickle crowd (defined in mass psychological terms); and a positive image of the militarised and self-sacrificing (German) folk which functions as a unified body under the force of the political personality:

> One sees in this film the senate sessions, folk rebellions, addresses to the crowd, intervention of the crowd ... The crowd knows nothing, understands nothing, is captivated, shoved here and there by words, now against Julius Caesar, now against the murderers – but it activates itself, becomes intoxicated, decides without sense or reason, without foresight of the consequences, but it decides. The state will be destroyed thereby, but nonetheless: it [the crowd] feels itself to be the ruler, it *is* the ruler ... They are also the enemy, who surge against Germany's borders: those few who understand how to carry away the crowd, masses who become intoxicated and want to make decisions, those who lack a sense for the future, a heart for coming generations ... In front of the film that silently rolls, we become aware of the difference between them and us: there – noisy spectacles, delusion of the folk, living for the moment; here – calm, steady work, untiring effort to raise all classes, to secure the future of the nation.[28]

Viewing the film, Rennert believes, will help consolidate the Germans' perception of their role in the War as one of a unified *Volk* engaged in a defensive battle against the intrigues of hostile countries, who are governed by mass irrationality. While fissures had already begun to appear in Kaiser Wilhelm's proclaimed 'Burgfrieden' in wartime Germany, film critics for *Bild und Film* find in *Cajus Julius Caesar* the exemplary tool for German wartime consolidation, a film which subordinates the fractious cinematic mass and shapes it into a

Volk through the sheer force of its charismatic personality.

The film reformers' belief that the War would solve the problems of social fragmentation and the advancing commodification of German culture quickly faded, exposing how false and desperate their attempts had been to extricate film from the capitalist market and to legislate norms of reception. Already in early 1915, film reformers began to complain about the lack of quality German films, finding the domestic products uninteresting and trivially melodramatic: 'they are almost without exception the most evil sham and a distressing documentation that the artistic development of the cinema has not experienced even the least impetus from the War; on the contrary, it has been thrown back even further than before'.[29]

Reformers held German capitalists and their 'business patriotism' [*Geschäftspatriotismus*] responsible for creating war films that were 'an assassination of the aesthetic, artistic taste of the public'.[30] However, criticism also focused on the domestic audience to explain the continued success of 'trashy' foreign films. Rennert admits in 1915 that the division of the *Volk* and the masses has reemerged within German boundaries, that 'even in war the [film] drama draws the crowd ... for people with a strong, healthy national sense, this mental state is incomprehensible'.[31] Rennert sees audience divisions maintained during the War which continue to prevent the distillation of the folk from the mass.

Rennert and other film reformers developed an idea of the mass which associated the forces fighting against Germany in the First World War with German film consumers. The film reformers thereby attempted to exclude the mass film audience from the terrain of German culture and politics by defining it not only as non-German, but as anti-German, as aggressively destructive of German cultural autonomy. One of the lasting effects of the film reformers' mass ideology was that it made German national identity exceptionally difficult to reconcile with the modern, mass cultural landscape of the Weimar Republic. Equally important, the ideology of the film reform movement helped undermine the political legitimacy of the Weimar Republic by

1895

facilitating the conservative 'stab-in-the-back' explanation for Germany's loss of the War. Brutus sacrificed his friend Caesar, revolutionary German soldiers and workers betrayed their conservative leaders, and the mass spectator destroyed any chance for achieving a unified German *Volk*.

Notes

1. Albert Hellwig, *Kind und Kino* (Langensalza: Beyer, 1914), 33. All translations from the German in this essay are mine. Emphasis mine.
2. Alfred Döblin, 'Das Theater der kleinen Leute', *Das Theater* 1.8 (December 1909); reprinted in Fritz Güttinger (ed), *Kein Tag ohne Kino* (Frankfurt: Deutsches Film Museum), 39–41, here 40–41.
3. The book was quite familiar to German thinkers long before it appeared in German translation in 1908 as *Psychologie der Massen*.
4. Gustave Le Bon, *The Crowd* (New York: Viking, 1960), xxi.
5. Adolf Sellman, *Der Kinematograph als Volkserzieher?* (Langensalza: Beyer, 1912), 26.
6. Le Bon, 23–24.
7. Dieter Prokop discusses this point in the section of his book *Soziologie des Films* (Frankfurt am Main: Fischer, 1982) on 'Film Sociology in Relation to the Participation of the "Masses"', pp. 35–41.
8. H. Duenschmann, 'Kinematograph und Psychologie der Volksmenge', *Konservative Monatsschrift für Politik, Literatur und Kunst* 9 (June 1912).
9. Duenschmann, 923.
10. Duenschmann, 924.
11. Duenschmann, 924.
12. Duenschmann, 926.
13. Duenschmann, 921.
14. Arthur Mellini, 'Die ganze Richtung passt uns nicht!', *Lichtbild-Bühne* 5 (4 February 1911): 3–4
15. Mellini, 3.
16. 'Die Brandpanik im Berliner Kino', *Lichtbild-Bühne* 52 (30 December 1911): 8.
17. 'Die Brandpanik', 8.
18. For this point I am indebted to Heide Schlüpmann, *Unheimlichkeit des Blicks* (Basel: Stroemfeld/Roter Stern, 1990).
19. Fritz K. Ringer points out in his *Decline of the German Mandarins* that the focus of aggression against internal 'foreigners' characterised the attitude of German intellectuals in general in 1914: 'The most important point to be made about the German intellectuals' attack upon the West is that it was produced for domestic consumption. It was directed against a devil who lived in Germany, chiefly in the factories, political assemblies, and big urban centers.' *The Decline of the German Mandarins. The German Academic Community, 1890–1933* (Hanover: University Press of New England, 1990), 187.
20. Hermann Häfker, 'Kinematographie und Krieg', *Bild und Film* IV.1 (1914/15): 1.
21. Hermann Häfker, 'Literatur', *Bild und Film* IV.1 (1914/15): 21.
22. Häfker, 'Literatur', 21.
23. Häfker, 'Kinematographie und Krieg', 2.
24. Will Scheller, 'Über den Einfluss des Krieges auf die Filmkunst in Deutschland', *Bild und Film* IV.10 (1914/15): 197.
25. See Hilda Blaschitz, 'Cajus Julius Caesar', *Bild und Film* IV. 4/5 (1914/15): 82. The rise in popularity of Italian historical epics like *Quo vadis?* and *Cleopatra* from 1911 into the early months of the War contributed to and fed off a fascination with masses portrayed on screen.
26. Blaschitz, 79.
27. Lorenz Pieper, 'Der grösste Römer', *Bild und Film* IV.4/5 (1914/15): 82–83. Pieper was so taken with the film that he insisted all upper-level school children be required to see it (84).
28. Malwine Rennert, 'Der Film Julius Caesar: Die ewige Wiederkehr aller Geschehnisse', *Bild und Film* IV.4/5 (1914/15): 86.
29. L. Hamburger, 'Kriegsdramen', *Bild und Film* IV.6 (1914/15): 119.
30. Hamburger, 119.
31. Malwine Rennert, 'Kriegslichtspiele', *Bild und Film* IV.7/8 (1914/15): 139–140.

Character as Economics: Fordism, The Consuming Housewife, and *The Cheat*

Constance Balides

Department of Communication, Newcomb Hall 219, Tulane University, New Orleans, LA 70118, USA

A MARK OF THE REACH of modern consumer culture is the extent to which conceptions of identity are mediated through consumption. Different meanings of the term 'interest' point to the way modern identities exist across a continuum that begins with the economy and financial transactions and ends with constructions of the self expressed through commodities. As a form of investment associated both with money and with personal proclivities, interest links commercial transactions to individuals. But if the term points to one's imbrication in economic structures, how can it also express the particularity of personality associated with desire or fantasy or cultural self-fashioning?

One way to think about the fate of interest in modern consumer culture is to pose the question along different lines. What is the relationship between economic structures and cultural uses? This question remains central to debates in film studies, and it has fuelled work stressing the fact that cultural agents negotiate the meanings of cultural forms. That is, identities can be fashioned through consumption for purposes other than those of dominant economic and/or textual systems. This emerging agenda for inquiry usefully moves discussion away from economistic notions of culture and deterministic notions of the effects of texts on spectators. Feminist work on early US film, for example, has significantly expanded an understanding of the complexities of film reception.[1]

To return, however, to the starting point of this paper, speculations on the implicated nature of the term interest suggest a somewhat different trajectory. An argument that runs through *Keywords* by Raymond Williams is that certain words bear the historical trace of their relationship to a capitalist economy. The shift from customer with its connotation of a 'regular and continuing relationship to a supplier' to consumer, a 'more abstract figure in a more abstract market'[2] illustrates this relationship. The meaning of interest for Williams has developed along similar lines. He comments:

> It remains significant that our most general words for attraction or involvement should have developed from a formal objective term in property and finance ... It

1895

Jesse L. Lasky Feature Play Co., (Inc.)

Jesse L. Lasky Presents
Fannie Ward in
"The Cheat"
TCll by Hector Turnbull   Produced by Cecil B. De Mille.

"Your extravagance is ruining me."

1895

seems probable that this now central word for attention, attraction and concern is saturated with the experience of a society based on money relationships.[3]

This assessment goes part of the way in explaining the relationship between interest as financial and interest as an expression of individual or group identity. It also suggests another way of asking the question concerning the relationship between structures and uses. Rather than, how are individuals shaped by economic structures or how do individuals negotiate dominant interpellations, one can ask, without assuming a kind of determinism, how are individuals discursively implicated in the economy? Clearly, Williams sees the naturalness of the meanings of certain words, which he sets out to disentangle in *Keywords*, as part of this process. While it should be said that in certain entries in the book he is less sanguine about consumer culture and mass society than more recent cultural studies approaches stressing consumption as negotia-

tion, Williams' analysis of economic issues as they are represented in the words a culture takes to be transparent is enormously suggestive. With regard to filmic representations, one can similarly ask how economic structures and developments find expression in them. How do films represent the economy?

The early decades of the twentieth century in the United States are associated with the emergence of modern consumer culture, and women, especially middle-class women, were addressed by advertisers, by theorists of advertising, and by household management manuals as primary consumers for themselves, for their husbands, and for the family unit.[4] In this context, films that construe consumer culture as the terrain upon which the married relationship is negotiated offer a pertinent place from which to investigate representations of the economy. Consumption treated as a dilemma within modern marriage characterises a number of Cecil B. DeMille's films from the 1910s and 1920s. Unlike *His*

Lesson (Griffith, 1912) or *Way Down East* (Griffith, 1920), for example, in which consumption figures in relation to a moral framework of traditional values associated with rural life, DeMille's films are more thoroughly modern in their celebration of contemporary social mores and consumer culture. Plot lines deal with potential and actual infidelity in marriage, and in the films from the 1920s, with divorce as a legitimate alternative to unhappy marriage.[5] Contemporary reviews of DeMille's films in *Photoplay*, *Variety*, and *The New York Times*, frequently commented on their modern qualities pointing, often disparagingly, both to the 'homiletic' matrimonial stories and to the 'magnificent artificiality' of the settings.[6]

The Cheat, directed by DeMille in 1915, was characterised as a 'modern society' film in reviews, noteworthy for its display of commodities.[7] In France, where the film was applauded for its artistic merit, the novelist Colette praised the representation of consumer culture and gave equal weight to the characters' acting, the Lasky lighting, and the tasteful displays, noting that 'there is a beautiful luxuriating in lace, silk, furs ...'. French films, she argues, could take a lesson from this attention to detail.[8] More recently, Charles Eckert in 'The Carole Lombard in Macy's Window' argues that DeMille's films contained the 'latest styles in fashions and furnishings and created hallmarks of their own', thereby effecting a turn to the modern in film.[9]

While *The Cheat* certainly finds its modernity in the representation of consumer culture and marital sexual dilemmas, its interest for this discussion lies in the way consumer extravagance and matrimonial lessons converge in the representation of the housewife. *The Cheat* formulates the issue of female character in a modern manner. It presents the dilemma of the modern woman as a housewife as a problem of character defined in economic terms.[10]

To begin, the economic nature of relationships between women and men are stressed in the film. A review by Stephen Bush writing in *The Moving Picture World* foregrounds this aspect in a description of the plot:

Like all really strong stories, that of *The Cheat* can be told in a few words. A young, extravagant wife, a social butterfly, is playing with fire. In her craze for fine clothes she gambles with money entrusted to her by a Red Cross society. She loses the money. Her husband knows nothing of the desperate plight of his wife. Even if he knew, however, he would not have been able to help her. His investments had stripped him of ready cash ... A rich Japanese ... says he will give her the money and ward off the impending exposure 'upon condition' ... Here fate intervenes. The troubled wife learns from her husband that he had been successful in his operations and that he is now rich.

'Does that mean I can have ten thousand dollars right now?' asks the agonised wife in a frenzy of joy mixed with fear. She gets the money and then goes to the Jap's home to return his treacherous gift.[11]

Narrative developments revolve around money, which forms the basis of relations between Edith Hardy and her husband, Richard, and between Edith and a Japanese businessman, Hishuru Tori, whose nationality is changed to Burmese in the 1918 re-release of the film when the character's name is also changed to Haka Arakau.[12] Like the plot description in *The Moving Picture World*, a publicity still for the film with the caption, 'Your extravagance is ruining me' (Fig. 1), echoes the issue of the problem of Edith's spending by positioning characters in a tug-of-war over a new gown. In the film, this confrontation is preceded by Richard's discovery that Edith has not paid the maid's wages, and is followed by Edith's decision to keep the dress. She ignores Richard's request, which is noted in an intertitle that reads 'wait till my investment pays, and you'll have plenty'. In its stress on economic exchanges, *The Cheat* moves away from the common indices of romantic love that characterise the heterosexual couple in film.

On this point, *The Cheat* refers to feminist positions on marriage during the period foregrounding the economic aspect of the love relationship in marriage. In *Women and Eco-*

nomics (originally published in 1898), Charlotte Perkins Gilman argues:

> We justify and approve the economic dependence of women upon the sex-relation in marriage. We condemn it unsparingly out of marriage. We follow it with our blame and scorn up to the very doors of marriage, – the mercenary bride, – but think no harm of the mercenary wife, filching her husband's pockets in the night. Love sanctifies it, we say: love must go with it.[13]

While *The Cheat* does not critique marriage as Gilman does, the film illustrates the underlying economic logic in the 'sex relation' in marriage that led Gilman to argue for women's financial independence. In the film, Edith's economic dependence is given narrative expression through various forms of illicit borrowing, including the misappropriation of the maid's wages to purchase her new gown and the loss of money from the Red Cross fund in the stock market. In the final exchange between Edith and Tori/Arakau, he conflates a sexual debt with a financial one and brands Edith with a seal used to identify his property. The racist and Orientalist implications of this scene are discussed by Sumiko Higashi, who stresses the association between consumer culture and Orientalism during this period and argues that anxieties about the 'new woman' are displaced onto a racial 'Other'.[14] In the context of my argument here, the significance of the scene is that it gives dramatic expression to the economic nature of the 'sex-relation' that finds more acceptable representation in the relationship between Richard and Edith.

Bearing in mind the imbrication of the economy and culture discussed by Williams, in the rest of this paper, I will look at emerging definitions of the housewife and the home in early consumer culture during the 1910s as a way of historically locating the problem of domestic economy raised in *The Cheat*. Broadly, this involves an assessment of the relationship between production and consumption, and especially of the implications of Fordism, a phase of capitalist production associated with mass production and mass consumption. Henry Ford introduced moving assembly lines into the manufacture of the

Model T automobile at the Highland Park factory in Michigan during 1913 and in January 1914, he offered high wages to workers in the plant, notably the five dollar day, which was to be an incentive for accepting the new regime.[15] In recent analyses, Fordism is characterised as the period of mass production until the 1970s, especially in Western nations, constituting a phase or regime of capitalism that for some involves a break with the current mode of post-Fordism. In addition to the moving assembly line, Fordism is associated with the production of standardised products, the mechanisation of tasks, scientific management or Taylorism, intensive accumulation, economies of scale, hierarchical organisation, massification, collective bargaining, productivity deals, and a Keynesian view of the state.[16]

Fordism and consumption

Mass consumption tailored to the requirements of standardised production and supported by higher wages and the extension of credit, which would provide a buffer against falls in demand, was central to the logic of Fordism in the United States. As Stuart Ewen delineates in *Captains of Consciousness*, psychological advertising strategies aimed at stimulating demand would secure the fit between commodities and identities.[17] In his analysis, consumption has a structural relation to production mediated through advertising, which constructs the terms through which consumption as a practice of discriminations and preferences expressing individuality is experienced.

Ewen's account of Fordism is interesting because it points to the way consumer culture emerges along the lines of the dual nature of interest as Williams describes it, namely, as an investment that is both economic and personal. A problem with Ewen's assessment is its presumption that the terms of consumption are a consequence of their relationship to production, which implies an orderly fit between the requirements of production and consumption. By contrast, *The Cheat* points to consumption in a disordered state, which is hyperbolically expressed in the branding scene in the film, but is also present in the tensions between Edith and Richard over domestic economy that motivate narrative events.

Disorderly consumption was also construed as a public problem in discourses outside the film. The 'cost of living debate', which included discussion of housewives' proper relationship to consumption, was conducted in various publications during the 1910s including *The Cosmopolitan*, a popular illustrated monthly magazine, *The Annals of the American Academy of Political and Social Science*, a social scientific journal, and *The Independent*, a general religious weekly with a broad readership.[18] Various causal factors were invoked as explanations for high costs including tariffs, free trade, the trusts, the exhaustion of natural resources, Alaskan gold, and the profits of middlemen. One additional cause in this list was the consumer behaviour of housewives.

Suggested solutions, as far as the housewife was concerned, involved explicit calls for regulating housewives' behaviour and assertions of the importance of efficiency through the adoption of scientific management principles in the home. A particularly polemical article in *Cosmopolitan Magazine* from 1910 entitled 'Is the Housewife Guilty?: To What Extent Is the American Woman Responsible for the Present High Cost of Living?' begins with an invocation of Biblical characters: 'Let's blame it on to Eve! Adam did. And he was one of our most illustrious ancestors'.[19] The author, Sloane Gordon, speculates on 'a strange something, an indefinable quality in the feminine make-up, which makes the housewife the easy prey of the smooth tradesman of pliable conscience'.[20] He chronicles women's false sense of economy and concludes with the following advice to husbands: 'Make your wife use scales and a yardstick'.[21] While Gordon's article is largely concerned with detailing the scurrilous practices of tradesman as well as the regulatory efforts of national and municipal bodies, its neuralgic point is women's responsibility for high costs due to their lack of vigilance.

In the case of the cost of living debate, a discussion of the economy and issues such as graft or rising expectations about the standard of living are displaced onto a discussion of women's character in the context of their role as family spenders. In the case of *The Cheat*, Edith's character failing is a refusal to live within the means provided by her husband. This is reinforced in the final courtroom scene in the film in which Edith's admission of guilt for the shooting of Tori/Arakau paves the way for the restitution of the white couple but also links a moral and legal resolution to an economic one. Edith exonerates herself legally by displaying the brand on her shoulder and by pleading extenuating circumstances for the crime. She exonerates herself morally by not allowing Richard to be convicted of her crime. And further, the implication of the last scene is that Edith has moved beyond profligacy toward curbing expenditure.[22] This is visually marked by the last shot in which Edith and Richard walk down an aisle formed by the parting crowd of courtroom spectators, a visual reference to a 'remarriage' on new terms.

Housewives as workers

Antonio Gramsci discusses Fordism in a way that moves beyond the functional or structural understanding of the relationship between production and consumption in Ewen's account. In the article 'Americanism and Fordism', Gramsci makes a link between the rationalisation of production associated with Fordism, and the necessity of developing particular character traits in workers that would support this shift in the productive sphere.[23] Gramsci notes: 'In America rationalisation has determined the need to elaborate a new type of man suited to the new type of work and productive process'. This new man is a result of a 'psycho-physical adaptation to specific conditions of work' which, more specifically, involves a disciplined mentality, including the regulation of sexuality in monogamous marriage. Gramsci argues for the positive potential of internalising such adaptations in the context of a new kind of society in Italy.[24]

Gramsci's link between the economy and types of subjects is a useful way of thinking about the implications of Fordism for women workers in the home and in the factory. While feminists offered radical plans for collectivising household labour, a conservative variant of scientific management in the home

1895

in the United States had a significant impact on emerging notions of the housewife as modern, especially through the influential writings of Christine Frederick.[25] Frederick's version of Taylorism redefined the middle-class housewife as the economic third term in the relationship between producers and distributors and reformulated the terms according to which the home was a sphere of production.[26]

While scientific management as practiced in the home by middle-class housewives in the 1910s has an oblique relationship to Edith as an upper class socialite entertainer in *The Cheat*, the stress on Edith's need to economise by regulating consumption practices is in line with 'a new type of woman' whose character traits would be appropriate for a Fordist production regime. Both the middle-class housewife and Edith require an internalisation of a disciplined relationship to spending and the visibility of their good character is expressed as an efficient allocation of the household budget. Frederick, for example, argues for the importance of self-regulation in consumption. If the housewife does not 'teach herself to become a wise, trained consumer, equipped with knowledge', domestic disorder will ensue.[27] Frederick also describes a new mental orientation for the housewife that involves a regulation of desires. In *The New Housekeeping*, she argues that 'the mind must be taken in hand, *managed and organised*, in order to be efficient'. Furthermore, 'one dare not let the mind doze and dream too much without coming to conclusions; the mind must be *commanded and manipulated* ...'.[28] Frederick continues with an injunction against allowing minds to 'dream', 'dwell', and 'imagine themselves in ideal surroundings', which is an indirect critique of the values of consumer culture and its dreamworld representation in films of the period, especially those directed by DeMille. The version of consumer culture that is expressed in manuals of scientific management for the home requires a mind that is 'managed and organised' and not given to the free reign of fantasy. Finally, this mental attitude binds the housewife to the space of the home, which is expressed in Frederick's timetable for organising the housewife's activity.[29] The narrative resolution in *The Cheat* points to this kind of ordering at the level of domestic economy. Frederick's version of domestic economy also has implications for the space of the household and the housewife's identification with it, which has a bearing on the following final point about Fordism in this paper and on another film directed by DeMille during this period.

Fordism and domestic space

In an article entitled 'The Lustre of Capital' by Eric Alliez and Michel Feher, production is discussed in relation to shifts in conceptions of space and time. For Alliez and Feher, the massification associated with Fordism requires a clear delineation of social spaces, which is the case in the 'factory fortress' associated with heavy industry.[30] The construction of spatial order and a stress on boundaries effected through temporal compartmentalisation, for example, in the distinction between work and leisure, are also central features of Fordism. In post-Fordism, by contrast, there is a blurring of boundaries, which is exemplified by the 'diffusion' of the workplace across formerly distinct spaces. While Alliez and Feher's analysis is problematic for its elision of domestic labour, it offers a framework for assessing the emergence of scientific management in the home that both segregated the home from the factory and authorised the home in terms of production. *Forbidden Fruit* (DeMille, 1921) illustrates the importance of a gendered spatial segregation in keeping with Alliez and Feher's analysis of Fordism. The binary of sexual difference as an issue of spatial segregation is foregrounded in the opening sequence of shots that introduce characters in the film. Mrs. James Harrington Mallory is identified with the space of the home through close up shots of a miniature table with paper figurines that are place settings for a formal dinner party. Rhyming shots of a map with numbered plots and markers of miniature oil derricks introduce Mr. James Harrington Mallory identifying him with his work outside the home.

Approaches to assessing Fordism are useful in understanding consumption during the 1910s, especially the importance of regulating the housewife's consumer behaviour and construing the ordered household in terms of a proper equilibrium between income and expenditure. Both issues are explicit in *The Cheat* in which good character is formulated as an issue of good economics. While consumption within cultural studies is perhaps more frequently understood in terms of identity formation, self-interest and, sometimes, resistance, I have been interested in locating notions of character, agency, and space in a particular historical period. While *The Cheat* has been associated with celebrating consumption, the broad framework outlined here suggests that the film can also be understood as re-articulating a Fordist agenda in the sphere of consumer culture, especially as Fordism involved notions of the modern woman as a modern housewife.

Notes

1. In terms of early US cinema, see for example, Miriam Hansen, *Babel and Babylon: Spectatorship in American Silent Film* (Cambridge, Massachusetts: Harvard University Press, 1991); and Lauren Rabinovitz, 'Temptations of Pleasure: Nickelodeons, Amusement Parks, and the Sights of Female Sexuality', *Camera Obscura* 23 (1990): 71–89.

2. Raymond Williams, *Keywords: A Vocabulary of Culture and Society*, revised edition (New York: Oxford University Press, 1985), 78–79.

3. Williams, 173.

4. One instance of this view is discussed by Benjamin R. Andrews who notes, 'The world in which the typical family lives is the world built for it by the woman who spends'. See Benjamin R. Andrews, 'The Home Woman as Buyer and Controller of Consumption', *The Annals* CXLIII (May 1929): 41. Also see, Benjamin R. Andrews, *Economies of the Household* (New York: Macmillan, 1923).

5. Charles Musser discusses DeMille's comedies of remarriage in Charles Musser, 'DeMille, Divorce, and the Comedy of Remarriage', in Paolo Cherchi Usai and Lorenzo Codelli (eds), *The DeMille Legacy* (Pordenone: Le Giornate del Cinema Muto, 1991), 262–283.

6. In *The New York Times*, *Why Change Your Wife?* is critiqued for its homiletic storyline as is *The Affairs of Anatol*. See reviews on 26 April 1920, 18:1 and on 10 December 1921, 11: 4. The *Times* review of *Forbidden Fruit* comments that the excellent acting is surrounded by 'too much magnificent artificiality' and DeMille is characterised as a 'workman of the utmost skill' who produces fiction that is 'undisguised but ornamented'. The review notes, 'It's all very splendid if spurious ...' . See 24 January 1921, 16:2. All references are from *The New York Times Film Reviews: 1913–1968*, volume 1: 1913–1931 (New York: The New York Times and Arno Press, 1970).

7. Although, once again, it is also 'sensational trash'. See 'Fannie Ward As a Movie Tragedienne', *The New York Times* 13 December 1915: 13.1 in *The New York Times Film Reviews*, vol. 1.

8. Colette, 'Cinema: *The Cheat*', in Richard Abel (ed), *French Film Theory and Criticism: A History/ Anthology*, vol. 1: 1907–1929 (Princeton: Princeton University Press, 1988), 128. Louis Delluc notes that *The Cheat* was greeted with 'violent admiration' in France and that it was 'an event of the tenth order in the ranks of their [the Americans'] artistic production', see Louis Delluc on *The Cheat* in Stanley Hochman (ed), *A Library of Film Criticism: American Film Directors* (New York: Frederick Ungar Publishing Co., 1974), 81. In the American press, *The Cheat* was praised for inaugurating a 'new era in lighting', see 'Lasky Praises "The Cheat"', *Motography* 14.24 (11 December 1915): 1223. For a useful discussion of DeMille's films from 1915–16 and the implications of their lighting arrangements, see Lea Jacobs, 'Lasky Lighting', in Paolo Cherchi Usai and Lorenzo Codelli (eds), *The DeMille Legacy* (Pordenone: Le Giornate del Cinema Muto, 1991), 250–260.

9. Charles Eckert, 'The Carole Lombard in Macy's Window', *Quarterly Review of Film Studies* 3:1 (Winter 1978): 1–21. His remarks are echoed by a contemporary reviewer of *Forbidden Fruit* who comments, 'Maybe Mr. De Mille is setting a new style for parvenu circles', see 24 January 1921, 16:2, *The New York Times* in *The New York Times Film Reviews: 1913– 1968*, volume 1: 1913–1931 (New York: The New York Times and Arno Press, 1970).

10. In focusing on the economic definition of character in the film, I am drawing on an argument by Annie L. Cot, 'Neoconservative Economics, Utopia and Crisis' in *Zone* 1.2 (n.d.): 293–311. Cot assesses the terms according to which contemporary neoconservative economics has extended its boundaries to become an appropriate discourse for describing various aspects of life, including personal life. The negotiation of the married relationship in *The Cheat* as I discuss it here is an

earlier instance of the phenomenon Cot describes. Warren I. Susman also notes a shift in values associated with consumer culture. In the nineteenth century, there is focus on character, associated with a production orientation and Protestant ethics of salvation. In the early twentieth century, this changes to a focus on personality, see Warren I. Susman, *Culture As History: The Transformation of American Society in the Twentieth Century* (New York: Pantheon Books, 1984). Susman's distinction is developed by T.J. Jackson Lears in 'From Salvation to Self-Realization: Advertising and the Therapeutic Roots of the Consumer Culture, 1880–1930', in Richard Wightman Fox and T.J. Jackson Lears (eds), *The Culture of Consumption: Critical Essays in American History, 1880–1980* (New York: Pantheon Books, 1983), 3–38. Lears assesses a shift from a production oriented society to a consumption oriented society invested in a therapeutic logic. My argument, by contrast, stresses the imbrication of consumption with production.

11. Stephen Bush in *The Moving Picture World* 26.14 (25 December 1915): 2384.

12. Lea Jacobs notes that Tori's altered nationality was due to protests from the Japanese Association of Southern California, see Lea Jacobs, 'Lasky Lighting'. In *Cecil B. DeMille*, Sumiko Higashi attributes this change to the fact that Japan fought with the Allies during the First World War. Higashi also details alterations to the script pencilled in by DeMille relating to the credit sequence when Tori is introduced. Originally he is dressed in American flannels reading a magazine or newspaper. DeMille changes this to a shot in which Tori takes an iron from a brazier of coals. In the film, the character is dressed in a Japanese robe and is dramatically shown in low-key lighting. Higashi points out that this change emphasises the 'racial "Otherness"' of the character played by Sessue Hayakawa (101), see Sumiko Higashi, *Cecil B. DeMille and American Culture: The Silent Era* (Berkeley: University of California Press, 1994).

13. Charlotte Perkins Gilman, *Women and Economics: A Study of the Economic Relation Between Men and Women As a Factor in Social Evolution*, Carl N. Degler(ed) (New York: Harper Torchbooks, 1966), 97.

14. See Higashi's *Cecil B. DeMille* and Sumiko Higashi, 'Ethnicity, Class, and Gender in Film: DeMille's *The Cheat*", in Lester D. Friedman (ed), *Unspeakable Images: Ethnicity and the American Cinema* (Chicago: University of Illinois Press, 1991), 112–139.

15. For a detailed discussion of developments at Highland Park, see David A. Hounshell, *From the American System to Mass Production, 1800–1932: The Development of Manufacturing in the United States* (Baltimore: Johns Hopkins University Press, 1984).

16. See Robin Murray, 'Life After Henry (Ford)', *Marxism Today* (October 1988): 8–13; David Harvey, *The Condition of Postmodernity* (Cambridge, Massachusetts: Blackwell, 1990); and Eric Alliez and Michel Feher, 'The Luster of Capital', *Zone* 1/2 (n.d.), which I discuss below.

17. Stuart Ewen, *Captains of Consciousness: Advertising and the Social Roots of Consumer Culture* (New York: McGraw-Hill Book Company, 1976).

18. Other popular discussions of this issue include Ida Hamilton, 'The Cost of a Woman's Wardrobe', *Harper's Bazar* XLII.2 (February 1908): 164; and Frank Ward O'Malley, 'The High Cost of Women', *The Cosmopolitan* n.v. (July 1921): 82. The *Independent* published a series on the cost of living in 1910, which included a range of issues from protectionism and free trade to diet. Also see the Progressive reformer Frederic C. Howe's *The High Cost of Living* (New York: Charles Scribner's Sons, 1917). For a more recent analysis of scientific management during this period, see Samuel Haber, *Efficiency and Uplift: Scientific Management in the Progressive Era 1890–1920* (Chicago: The University of Chicago Press, 1964).

19. Sloane Gordon, 'Is the Housewife Guilty? To What Extent Is the American Woman Responsible for the Present High Cost of Living?', *Cosmopolitan Magazine* L.1 (December 1910): 73. Also see Ida M. Tarbell, 'The Cost of Living and Household Management', *The Annals* XLVIII (July 1913): 127–130. Other articles in this edition of *The Annals*, which was devoted to the high cost of living, include ones by Mrs. Frank A. Pattison, 'Scientific Management in Home-Making', *The Annals* XLVIII (July 1913): 96–103; and Martha Van Rensselaer, 'The Housekeeper and the Cost of Living', *The Annals* XLVIII (July 1913): 256–258. Tarbell was a muckraking reporter of the progressive period who wrote a critique of John D. Rockefeller entitled the *History of the Standard Oil Company* (1904). Although Gordon's article is quite blatant in its rhetoric of blame, there is a similarity between his discussions and academically reputable ones that also point to the housewife's responsibility for high costs.

20. Gordon, 75.

21.   Gordon, 82.

22.   My focus on consumption practices as a central dilemma in the film is informed by a discussion with Patricia Mellencamp. In her work on the film, she argues that Edith's volunteer work for charities, which Mellencamp discusses in the context of an interesting analysis of the women's club movement, is marginalised in the film, see Patricia Mellencamp, 'Female Bodies and Women's Past-times, 1890–1920', *East-West Film Journal* 6.1 (January 1992): 17–70. For other useful feminist work on the film, see Judith Mayne in *The Woman at the Keyhole: Feminist and Women's Cinema* (Bloomington: Indiana University Press, 1990); and Janet Staiger's *Bad Women: Regulating Sexuality in Early American Cinema* (Minneapolis: University of Minnesota Press, 1995). Mayne stresses the fact that Edith's objectification in spectacle constitutes a restitution of order and that her status as an object of exchange between the two men establishes an equivalence between them. Staiger assesses the dilemma of consumption in the larger context of 'talk' about sexuality by the middle classes during this period. While I discovered Staiger's book after having delivered this paper, Staiger describes Edith's dilemma in similar terms to the ones I discuss, noting that the confession in the courtroom scene, which leads to internalising an ethos of balanced spending, is an incitement to speak that is also a form of self-regulation.

23.   Antonio Gramsci, 'Americanism and Fordism', in Quintin Hoare and Geoffrey Nowell-Smith (trans and eds), *Selections From the Prison Notebooks* (London: Lawrence and Wishart, 1976), 277–331.

24.   Gramsci, 286, 303.

25.   See Dolores Hayden, *The Grand Domestic Revolution: A History of Feminist Designs for American Homes, Neighborhoods, and Cities* (Cambridge, Mass.: The MIT Press, 1982).

26.   See Christine Frederick, *The New Housekeeping: Efficiency Studies in Home Management* (Garden City, New York: Doubleday, Page and Company, 1914); Mrs. Christine Frederick, *Household Engineering: Scientific Management in the Home* (Chicago: American School of Home Economics, 1920); and Christine Frederick, *Selling Mrs. Consumer* (New York: The Business Bourse, 1929).

27.   Frederick, *Household Engineering*, 317.

28.   Frederick, *The New Housekeeping*, 187–188.

29.   Frederick, *The New Housekeeping*, 87.

30.   Alliez and Feher, 'The Lustre of Capital'.

1895

'She's just like my granny! Where's her crown?' Monarchs and Movies, 1896–1916

Stephen Bottomore

Film Writer/Historian, London, UK

You all know those biograph pictures,
Celebrities shown on a screen,
The photos of notable people,
Displayed as they daily are seen.

From song, *At the Top of the Tree;
or Biograph Pictures*
by Harry B. Norris (1900)[1]

Introduction

SOME TIME AROUND THE TURN of the century a film show was being given in an English village, and among the films to be exhibited was one of Queen Victoria. As the flickering image of the monarch appeared on the screen, the voice of a little girl in the audience piped up in disappointed tones: 'Why, she's just like my Granny! Where's her crown?'[2] The reporter added that it took the villagers 'some time to recover from the knowledge that their Queen was apparently like any other old lady'.

This story nicely encapsulates one aspect of the impact of early moving pictures on public attitudes to monarchy and on the hereditary rulers themselves. Though monarchs were among the greatest early enthusiasts for the movies, in a sense they were playing with fire, and when their private plaything increasingly became a public mass medium they inevitably exposed themselves to 'comment on the platform', as Lady Bracknell put it. Some royal families, notably the British, managed to attune their image to the new medium. But for other monarchies the adjustment was more difficult; often the cinema was seen as a threat, and in some cases may even have played some part in the decline of royalty. Stephen Kern has suggested that new media and transport technologies of the late nineteenth century were partly responsible for a general process of democratisation and of the levelling down of elites, and the cinema may have contributed to this process.[3]

Film history has rarely examined the relationship between the early cinema and the world's royal families, while more often addressing the opposite end of the social spectrum: the working classes and cinema, though in recent times the theme has been covered in studies of the German and Russian royal families' passions for the movies, and in Nicholas Hiley's work on the relationship between British public figures and the news media. Miriam Hansen's work on the public sphere is also relevant here.[4] In this paper I shall be taking up some of Hiley's themes, but focusing on a slightly different target: the international monarchy of the period. It is an appropriate theme for this British cinema centenary conference, for, while most other countries have lost their monarchies (perhaps partly as a result of media exposure), Britain's still remains in place.

Private movies

The period leading up to the First World War was both the heyday and the last hurrah of monarchy. At this time most European countries had this form of government, including Britain, Germany, Spain and Italy; as did a large number of countries further afield: Persia, China, Korea, Afghanistan and Siam, amongst others.

The mid-nineteenth to early twentieth century was also a period of startling technological change, and in many cases monarchs welcomed such changes, and often introduced the new technologies into their countries. Motor cars are one example of this. Photography is another, which found important royal sponsors in countries as far apart as Britain, India and Ethiopia. The royal example sometimes led to a speedier introduction of the technology into the country than it would otherwise have enjoyed.

The cinema in its early years also attracted great interest from royal families. By the end of 1896 around a dozen of the world's ruling/royal families had seen moving pictures, usually at specially arranged screenings, and many more crowned heads saw films in the years immediately following. Royals also *appeared* in moving pictures themselves: by 1898, members of at least ten of the world's royal families had been filmed. Altogether, I have found that the royalty of about 30 countries showed some interest in the cinema up to 1914.[5]

This enthusiasm for cinema went further: a dozen of the world's royal families in the period appointed contract or permanent royal cinematographers, sometimes simply to project films, but usually to film the activities of the family or court and then project the results to them afterwards. The Kaiser, for example, had many of his official and other activities filmed by a staff of three cameramen, and viewed these and other films at least once a week.[6] The Spanish royal family regularly viewed films in their Madrid palace, and when the King of Spain embarked on a French tour in 1913, he had films of his activities sent back for the Queen to view.[7] The Sultan of Morocco imported four western cinematographers, including Charles Rosher and Gabriel Veyre, though the Shah of Persia, rather than viewing his own activities, preferred French soft porn films to be screened.[8]

Some royals became so keen that they actually fitted out special rooms as private 'cinemas' in their palaces. The Rumanian royal palace was equipped in this way probably sometime in 1911, an ironic development given that the Queen was going blind at the time (and was advised that her condition was made worse by viewing films). The example was followed by the royal families in Germany, Spain and Siam all in 1912, and the following year installation of a private cinema was planned for Buckingham Palace.[9]

For their own private edification, Royal families even became involved in dramatic film production. George V's daughter Mary wrote a humorous script which was privately filmed in 1913, and the following year the Kaiser's brother, Prince Henry of Prussia, helped film a comedy entitled 'Faithful unto the Swimming Bath'.[10]

The crucial point about most of these royal film activities is that they were *private*. As with the royal penchant for family photography which developed in the nineteenth century, these moving pictures were for showing mainly or exclusively to the royal families themselves and their courts.[11]

A good reason why such films were kept private is indicated in a cartoon which satirised Prince Henry's 'Swimming Bath' film, imagining it being screened in a public cinema, with the result that a young soldier stands up and salutes as the royal comedy is

1895

projected.[12] The joke is in the contrast between the hierarchy of royalty and the democracy of the film theatre. The point is that, while there was no problem in royalty making films of themselves and viewing them in *private*, once moving pictures of royal personnages reached the *public* there was likely to be some confusion between the traditional image of remoteness, and the informal reception in an amusement venue. As more and more news films and newsreels showed royalty to the public on cinema screens, such a contrast soon became a real issue.

Lèse-majesté

According to medieval doctrine, the monarch was a special type of being in which two bodies co-existed: the physical body of a person, and the spiritual body of the monarchy itself. Part of the danger in being recorded by the supremely naturalistic medium of film was that it emphasised the physical body at the expense of the spiritual. The royal personnage would appear as a mere human being instead of a demi-God; perhaps seeming rather humdrum, rather like everyone else, with all the usual human foibles. When shown to an audience of the royals themselves within the confines of the palace this image presented no problem; but screened in a public place the consequence might well be *lèse-majesté* writ large.

This possibility received an early confirmation on the very first occasion that a British royal person was filmed. In 1896 Birt Acres recorded the future Edward VII on film, and caught him apparently scratching his head. When the film was shown to the royal family they were amused at this detail, but when it was shown in public, *The Globe* newspaper attacked Acres for having lowered the dignity of royalty:

> At a certain London music-hall at the present time there is on view a cinematoscope which displays the Prince of Wales as, all unwitting, he was caught by the photographic fiend. He smiles and bows and gazes round, and then the house is brought down by a life-like representation of the Heir to the Throne taking off his hat and scratching his head ... It is

appalling to think of such publicity as this ... The old camera filled us with pity for royalty, but the cinematoscope positively brings scalding tears of sympathy to our eyes.[13]

Here the journalist was making a specific comparison with snap-shot detective cameras, which, as used to photograph royals and VIPs in unguarded moments, were raising a storm of protest in this period.[14] The objection was that, photographed without warning, one's expression and demeanour and therefore one's public image, would not be under control. And this problem was even worse in a film than in a still photograph, partly because a whole *series* of unguarded moments were recorded, and partly because the film, shown on a screen, effectively turned the personage into a *performer* open to public comment. As *The Globe* put it:

> A transitory expression may be ludicrous enough, but it cannot absolutely give its possessor away as a whole series can. Think, for example, of the Archbishop of Canterbury sneezing. How could his dignity survive a public exhibition of slides depicting the act?[15]

The monarchs themselves soon realised their vulnerability, and started to raise objections to being filmed without permission. For example, in 1908 King Edward VII was so annoyed to find that he had been filmed without his knowledge during his morning walk at Marienbad, that determined efforts had to be made by the police and his staff to retrieve the film.[16] And in 1902 the Kaiser was reported as being 'very much displeased' to discover that his meeting with the Czar (including his 'grandiloquent speech, accompanied by elaborate gestures') had been cinematographed, without his being warned.[17]

The Kaiser was likely to be especially annoyed by such unauthorised photography, as he liked to maintain a firm control over his own photographed image, an image which was the very antithesis of informal. His photographer revealed in 1914 that in all pictures of Wilhelm taken for publication, he:

> ... assumes a stern, forbidding, martial expression – any showing him laughing,

in his opinion, would lessen his dignity and the sense of his authority.[18]

The Russian imperial family were similarly determined to maintain a stern, distant image to their people, who regarded the Czar as little short of a God. Any film showing a more human side to the Czar threatened to diminish this image, as an incident in 1903 demonstrated. The Czar and Czarina were being filmed, and, as he proved to be rather shy in front of the cinematograph, the Czarina '... entering into the fun, gave him a push and a tug to get him to move, instead of standing awkwardly'. The film was intended for public screening, but certain high officials:

> ... thought their Imperial master was not represented quite so imperial-like as he should be, and so the exhibition of the series of moving pictures was prohibited in Russia.[19]

Photo-opportunities

Russia and Germany, however, were the most autocratic of the European monarchies, and not all royal families were quite so horrified at being depicted informally. In particular, British royalty had long experience of being represented in images in a 'domestic' manner. From as early as the eighteenth century, British monarchs were having themselves painted 'as devoted fathers and doting wives, rather than mounted warriors or imperial judges', though they also presented a ceremonial image at public events. It has been suggested that this 'calculated combination of the ritual and the prosaic, of high ceremony and bourgeois demystification' is part of the reason for the survival into the late twentieth century of those monarchies, especially the British, which have adopted it.[20] This public relations effort may have been aided by the multiplication of the royal image through photography, which began in Britain from 1860 when Queen Victoria gave permission for carefully selected photographs of herself to be sold to the general public.[21]

The sympathetic attitude of Britain's royals toward photography seems to have been maintained when the cinema arrived, and in 1898 *The Phonoscope* commented on a surprisingly informal film showing the Prince of Wales' family at breakfast:

> The fact is that photography is to-day one of the strongest of the ties that bind the people of Great Britain to the throne and the royal family. Scarcely a month passes without a new picture of her majesty or the Prince of Wales finding its way into the shop window, and the prince, who is essentially an up to date man of the most progressive ideas, probably realises that the moving pictures of the kind exhibited in public places of amusement are destined to take the place of the old-fashioned photographs in depicting important events.[22]

But, as Nicholas Hiley has shown, this apparently informal photography was informality of a very special type. Not the through-the-wall shot of the Prince scratching his head, not the illicitly obtained morning promenade, but the 'photo-opportunity', an event at which the subject has 'renegotiated' the terms of the photography so that *he* controls when, where and how the photograph will be taken. 'Controlled informality', one might say.

On this basis, even the King of Italy, known for his dislike of photographers, was prepared to be shown in the domestic manner, when, in 1912 he had films taken of his family to raise funds for charity. A trade paper remarked:

> These differ materially from the ordinary still photographs of the King in military uniform, or the Queen in her ceremonial robes. The new films will show the King and Queen and Royal family in their ordinary everyday life, when, like their subjects, they are at work and moving about.[23]

The same control which could be exercised at such domestic photo-opportunities was also possible at state events, such as processions. Here the royals were presenting themselves as *they* wished to be seen. They expected to be filmed, and therefore might view news cameramen with some sympathy. For example, Cecil Hepworth filming the funeral procession of Queen Victoria in 1901 was embarrassed at the loud noise his camera made as it was cranked, which attracted the

1895

attention of King Edward as he rode by. But the monarch, far from seeming annoyed:

> ... halted the whole procession in front of my camera so that I got almost a close-up of himself with the Duke of Connaught on one side and the German Emperor on the other, stationary on their horses. Perhaps it was a good augury for British films for, ever since, the reigning house in England has always shown a kindly and most encouraging interest in them.[24]

Similarly, four years later, when a bumptious policeman threatened to stop Frank Mottershaw from filming King Edward, the King actually intervened to let the filming continue.[25] And in 1911 when an official tried to protect Franz Josef from the indignities of a cameraman's attentions, the aged Emperor declared: 'Let the man do his work, it doesn't bother me!' and even gave a friendly wave to the camera as he passed.[26]

Control

However, this royal approval for being filmed was strictly qualified, and a number of controls were imposed. Nowhere did these go further than in Russia. Here, the main danger was thought to be in the mixing up of royal images with profane, for, in the proliferating cinemas, films of the Czar were being shown amongst the workaday comedies and dramas in the rest of the cinema programme. By 1911 an edict was passed that not only were all films of the Czar for public exhibition to be cleared by a censor, but when exhibited in public they had to be presented as a special part of the programme, with the curtain lowered and then raised before they came on, to ensure that other elements of the exhibition could not sully the royal dignity. It was also stipulated that films of the royal family had to be projected at the correct speed and without music.[27]

In other countries the controls were less draconian and usually applied at the point of filming rather than at the exhibition site. Royal strictures on filming began in Britain as early as 1899, when Queen Victoria made it clear that she 'did not desire' a cinematograph camera to film her at a review of the Life Guards, though the *British Journal of*

Photography noted that someone had managed to film there anyway.[28] In subsequent years the numbers of cameramen covering public royal events were regulated, as well as the positions from which they filmed, through the issuing of official passes. For some reason British officials were especially concerned that the film cameras should be kept out of sight.[29]

A number of principles in filming royalty were tacitly understood by the cameramen themselves by this time, and usually observed: firstly that royal personnages should only be filmed when, how and where they wanted to be, and not without their knowledge. Another unwritten rule among the press was that royals should not be photographed from too close a position. As Yuri Tsivian has shown, the principles of 'proxemics' or social distance were very relevant in the early cinema, and getting too near to one's betters violated established codes of conduct. A prohibition based on this principle became formalised in Holland in 1913 when Amsterdam's Chief of Police instructed the media to keep their distance from the royal family on pain of having their accreditation taken away, and when a cameraman transgressed, action was swift:

> Already, an operator who filmed the royal family's visit to the zoological gardens has been informed that his film can't be projected, the distance from which it was taken being judged too close.[30]

Some cameramen broke the rules, including Tracy Mathewson when filming the Prince of Wales at the races in 1919, as Matthewson later recalled:

> I worked my way up to within about ten feet of the Prince, cursing my luck because I couldn't get near enough for a good old-fashioned American Close-up. As I began to grind away, the Prince spied me. He smiled and bowed, then summoned me. 'You're an American, aren't you?' he said, shaking my hand and asking me my name. 'I thought so, because in England the cinematographers never make 'close-ups'.

The stills photographer Ernest Brooks then explained to Mathewson that close-ups were one of the taboos in photographing royalty, but the American decided to carry on filming the Prince in this manner regardless. The rules for filming the Kaiser were even stricter, and during a Kaiser Review the officials wouldn't even permit smoking in the Imperial presence let alone close filming. At such an event in 1916, one American cameraman was so overcome with frustration that he raced across the parade ground ('To the frozen horror of the whole German army') and cranked away close to the Kaiser, who fortunately seemed to regard the incident with a similar bemusement at American foibles as did the Prince of Wales.[31]

Democratisation

It was scarcely a coincidence that it was *Americans* who had broken these rules. Coming from a very different kind of society, many Americans would have had little personal experience of royalty or the deference and regard that was expected to go with it. When, in 1908, an American showman was sent a film of Princess Beatrice instead of the Queen of England, *Views and Film Index* remarked that in America 'we wouldn't recognise Princess B. if she sat next to us in the subway'.[32]

Such sceptical American attitudes to inherited privilege and royalty are scarcely surprising; what is more intriguing is that these attitudes may have had a political influence within the more repressive monarchical states, through the very medium of film. The influence came from the avalanche of American movies which were invading the world's screens just before the First World War. These – westerns, modern dramas, comedies, chases – represented a very different way of life than that experienced by ordinary people in many of the monarchies in Europe and elsewhere. In 1913 Stephen Bush in the *Moving Picture World* suggested that through example, American motion pictures were helping to undermine these hierarchical societies of the old world. In an article entitled, 'The Triumph of the Gallery', he noted that:

> ... no single factor in our modern civilization has done more to emphasize the brotherhood of man than the motion picture ... Much of the hostility against the

motion picture abroad is due to its enlightening and leveling influence.[33]

In an article a few months earlier, Bush had claimed that:

> ... the motion picture acts like a solvent – it brings a new and much-needed light. It is today the greatest missionary of Americanism where Americanism would do an incalculable lot of good. From frequent views of American life the people of Germany and Austria learn with growing pleasure that there is a big country far to the west of them where manhood counts for more than rank or even money ... where the policeman is not the final arbiter of things and where men know how to think and how to dare. They begin to feel how cramped their own position is. They begin to feel how restraining and choking are the influences of caste and tradition, and their desire to see American pictures grows apace.[34]

Perhaps we shouldn't take Bush's view too literally. After all America had its own established elites in the form of the 'robber barons', indulging in conspicuous consumption. Nevertheless, Bush's point that American society, lacking much of the hereditary principle, was very different from that in parts of the old world is surely well taken, and the all-conquering American film was clearly more sympathetic to the former than to the latter.

Monarchs too learnt this lesson. In this new cinema age they would have to conform to the new mass media or face the consequences. The First World War saw the collapse of monarchical government in several countries, including the most autocratic European regimes in Germany, Austro-Hungary and Russia. While it would be rash to relate this extinction to the advent of the mass media and film, it would surely not be presumptuous in the case of those monarchies which *did* survive, to place some of the credit on their understanding of this new age of mass society and media.

Perhaps the best example of this was Britain's royal family who, as we have seen, had been media and image aware since the days of Queen Victoria and before. The repositioning of the monarchy vis-à-vis the public

1895

continued during the Edwardian period, but perhaps the turning point came in 1912 and 1913 when King George and Queen Mary went on a series of tours of the working-class and industrial areas of Britain. Royalty was for the first time coming into contact with ordinary people, and even visiting their cottages. This was the beginning of the modern 'walkabout', and was at this time described as 'an entirely novel idea', and a 'revelation' to the public. Probably much of the impact came from the media coverage, which must have been phenomenal. Just one film company, Hibberts Pictures of Bradford, covering the royal tour of Lancashire in July 1913 mainly for local screenings the same day, had a staff of six cameramen in three cars, and claimed to have shot 228,000 feet of film – some 50 hours duration.[35]

Here was the dawn of a new image for British royalty, an image which was increasingly cultivated during the First World War, with King George appearing on cinema screens as a monarch of and among the troops and ordinary citizens, rather than remote from them. It was an appropriate guise for a new and democratic 'cinema age', in which hierarchy was less acceptable, and audiences had lost some of their awe for monarchs.

There were echoes of this new, 'humdrum' royal image elsewhere in the world in the immediate pre-War period, and the cinema was often implicated in this change. Bizarre tales abound at this time of royal and noble persons slumming it in the new cinema professions. In 1912 the son of the King of Dahomey was discovered as a doorman at the Gaumont Palace in Paris, and had a day job as a film 'super' or extra.[36] The following year the Queen of Rumania made an arrangement with Nordisk to film all her novels (written under her pen-name of Carmen Sylva),[37] but perhaps ex-King Manoel of Portugal is the most poignant symbol of the experience of monarchy in the cinema age. Deposed in the revolution of 1910, he came to live in West London and became a regular visitor at his local picture palace. The press reported that:

> No ceremony of any sort is observed when the King visits the theatre. His secretary buys seats at the box-office in the ordinary way, and the two visitors walk to their places almost unnoticed.[38]

The ambivalent attitude to status in the period is exemplified by a West-End cinema manager hauled over the coals when his policy of appealing to better-class patrons was found to be losing money. His boss, after examining the books, yelled at the wretched manager: 'Cut out your perishin' princesses and them no smoking signs! Put some hot posters on the pavement, and hurry! This is a picture palace, not Bal-bloomin'-moral!'.[39]

Conclusion: the 'cinema age'

At the start of this article I quoted the little girl who saw a film showing Queen Victoria and wondered why the monarch wasn't wearing her crown. We are now in a position to answer this question. The Queen simply didn't *need* to wear her crown, at least she needed to only on rare occasions. At the end of the Victorian age monarchy was changing, and in the 'cinema age' of the early twentieth century elaborate rituals and display were no longer the only or the most appropriate means to indicate one's status. Monarchs, on the surface at least, might seem much more like their subjects than they had before. In the language of medieval kingship, the spiritual body of the monarch had been frittered away, leaving more of the physical body on display. Clearly the cinema had assisted in this process through opening up the world's rulers to visual examination by a mass public. During this period, in a very real sense, modern society had seen a fundamental shift of emphasis from the royal palace to the picture palace.

1895

Statistical appendix

N.B. The information presented here pertains to absolute rulers. Democratic rulers, notably in France and America, are excluded.

Likely dates of Royal and ruling families first seeing films:

Mexican:	Jan 1895 (Kinetoscope. Projected: Aug 1896)	Rumanian:	1896?
Belgian:	Nov 1895	Egyptian:	Dec 1896
Monaco:	Feb? 1896	Monaco:	1898?
Austrian:	April 1896	Indian princes:	1898
Danish:	June 1896	Turkish:	1899
Spanish:	June 1896	Chinese:	1900?
Serbian:	June 1896	Persian:	1900
British:	July 1896	Moroccan:	1900?
Russian:	July 1896	Afghan:	1905
Swedish:	1896	Omani:	1910
Italy:	Nov 1896	Siamese:	1910?
Japanese:	Nov 1896 (Mikado: 1911)	Cambodian:	1913

Likely dates of Royal and ruling families first being filmed:

German:	1895	Ethiopian:	1903
British:	1896	Serbian:	1904
Italian:	1896	Greek:	1905
Mexican:	1896	Norwegian:	1905
Rumanian:	1896	Spanish:	1905
Russian:	1896	Danish:	1906
Swedish:	1897	Turkish:	1908
Egyptian:	1897	Austrian:	1909?
Siamese:	1897	Portuguese:	1909
Tunisian:	1897	Tibetan:	1910
Dutch:	1898	Ugandan:	1913
Moroccan:	1901	Bulgarian:	1914

Likely dates of Royal families first employing contract/permanent court cinematographers:

Denmark:	1896 (Elfelt)	Persia:	1900
Italy:	1896 (Calcina)	Turkey:	1906
Monaco:	1896?	Germany:	1909 (3 operators incl. Jurgensen)
Sweden:	1896 (Florman)		
Britain:	1896 (Downey, Walker)	Siam:	1911
Russia:	1898 (5 names known)	Spain:	1912
Morocco:	1900 (Veyre, Noble, Avery, Rosher)	Rumania:	1913 (an Englishman)

1895

Notes

1. Published by Frank Dean and Co, 31 Castle St, Oxford St, W1.

2. *Kinematograph and Lantern Weekly* (4 July 1907), 128.

3. Stephen Kern, *The Culture of Time and Space* (London: Weidenfeld and Nicolson, 1983), 315–318; but Kern's suggestion that elites and royal families were opposed to the new technologies is clearly incorrect. Indeed the telephone – the technology mainly through which he chooses to exemplify this process – was actually concentrated in the homes of the rich, rather than filtering down to ordinary people (the latter happened much more with the cinema). David Cannadine has suggested that aristocratic zeal for new technologies can partially be explained as a means for an anachronistic class to try and demonstrate its modernity.

4. On the Czar: Rashit Yangirov's paper at the Domitor 1994 conference and Yuri Tsivian, 'Some historical notes to the Kuleshov experiment', in T. Elsaesser (ed) *Early cinema: space, frame, narrative* (BFI, 1990), 248–249. On the Kaiser: Martin Loiperdinger, 'Das frühe Kino der Kaiserzeit', in U. Jung, *Der deutsche Film* (Trier: Wissenschaftlicher Verlag, 1993). On British royalty: Nicholas Hiley, 'The candid camera of the Edwardian tabloids', *History Today* (August 1993), and his essay in *Researchers Guide to British Newsreels* vol. 3 (BUFVC, 1993), 47. See also, Miriam Hansen, 'Early silent cinema: whose public sphere?' *New German Critique*, vol. 29 (Winter 1983).

5. The Dutch royal family is the only one for which I have not found any evidence of interest in cinema, though I suspect such evidence will turn up eventually.

6. See for example *The Cinema* (April 1912): 4–5.

7. *The Film Censor* (4 June 1913): 2. Hunting was an especially popular royal activity, and at least six European monarchs were filmed at the 'noble sport' in this period: the Kaiser, Edward VII, George V, Victor Emmanuel III, Franz Josef, Alfonso XIII.

8. The Sultan's imports of gadgets and inventions from the West, including the cinema, were taken by his people as evidence of creeping Westernisation and Christian influence, and he was deposed in 1908. See Veyre's little-known book, *Maroc, dans l'intimité du Sultan* (Paris, 1905); S.L. Bensusan, *Morocco* (London, 1904), 146; WTC catalogue 1901, p. 263; etc.

9. On Rumania see: *Kinematograph and Lantern Weekly* (25 September 1913): 2276; Elizabeth Burgoyne, *Carmen Sylva: Queen and Woman* (London: Eyre and Spottiswoode, 1941), 254–263.

10. *Freie Liebe bis zum Schwimmbassin; The Cinema* (23 July 1913): 15; *The Cinema* (21 May 1914): 17.

11. For example, films of the British royal family's 1913 tour of Lancashire were screened to the Royals, and then promptly destroyed to ensure that no one else should see them. *The Cinema* (16 July 1913): 33.

12. *Ulk* (29 May 1914), courtesy M. Wedel.

13. *The Globe* (28 August 1896): 1. To keep his activities discrete, Acres had been forced to film through a hole in a wall, so it is possible the Prince did not realise he was being filmed. See *ibid.* (31 August) where Acres denies the Prince was actually scratching his head.

14. See Hiley, 'The candid camera.' For the rather different American situation, see '"Kodakers lying in wait": amateur photography and the right of privacy in New York, 1885–1915', *American Quarterly*, 43/1 (March 1991): 24–45.

15. *The Globe* (28 August), *op. cit.*

16. *Kinematograph and Lantern Weekly* (3 September 1908): 365, quoting *Daily Express* of 31 August. The film was eventually surrendered by the cameraman concerned.

17. *Photographic News* (29 August 1902): 560.

18. 'Royalty before the camera', *Strand Magazine* (June 1914): 628, written by famed photographer of royalty, Adolf Baumann. Alice knew how monarchs should present themselves: 'Queens have to be dignified, you know!' (Lewis Carroll, *Through the Looking Glass*, Chapter 9.

19. *Photographic News* (11 December 1903): 797. The film was shown in the West.

20. S. Schama, 'The domestication of majesty: Royal family portraiture, 1500–1850', *Journal of Interdisciplinary History*, 17/1 (1986): 155–183. David Cannadine has attributed most of the British royal family's public relations success to the invention of ritual – see his essay in Eric Hobsbawm (ed), *The Invention of Tradition* (Cambridge University Press, 1992).

21. F. Dimond and R. Taylor, *Crown and Camera* (Penguin, 1987), 7, 20. This conflicts with the suggestion

of a German writer in 1910 that there was some incompatibility between the idea of a unique sovereign, and the almost infinite replication of his image in film and photography, see Miriam Hansen, *op. cit.*, especially 171–172. The writer suggested that the monarch might lose some of his uniqueness in this way, rather in the manner of Walter Benjamin's work of art losing its 'aura' by mechanical reproduction. But in fact the issue was not one of the mechanical reproduction of the monarch as such, but *how* he/she was presented in such replicated images.

22. *The Phonoscope* (April 1898): 9. The film showed the Prince of Wales playing with his grandchild, and his family at the breakfast table.

23. *Kinematograph and Lantern Weekly* (28 March 1912): 1225.

24. 'Before 1910', *Proceedings of the BKS*, no. 38 (1936): 10. See also Cecil Hepworth, *Came the Dawn* (London: Garden City Press, 1951), 56.

25. G Nown, *When the world was young* (London: Ward Lock, 1986), 150.

26. Quoted in Walter Fritz, *Kino in Österreich, 1896–1930* (Wien: Österreichischer Bundesverlag, 1981), 44.

27. See Tsivian and Yangirov, *op. cit.*

28. *British Journal of Photography* (17 November 1899): 722.

29. For example, see documents in the Public Record Office regarding the filming of Edward VII's funeral in 1910: *WORK* 21–6/13: 243, 246, 249. A writer in *The Optical Lantern and Cinematograph Journal* (July 1905): 193, had suggested that the ideal in filming royalty would only be achieved 'when the camera works without a sound, and also from a position least suspected by the subject of special interest'.

30. *Cinema-Revue* (Paris) (November 1913): 369.

31. The Prince and the Pictures', *Photoplay* (March 1920): 56. 'Capturing the Kaiser', *Photoplay* (March 1916): 112.

32. *Views and Film Index* (8 August 1908): 3.

33. *Moving Picture World* (13 December 1913): 1256. Because of this, he added, in autocratic countries like Russia, Prussia and Austria motion picture theatres faced stringent controls.

34. *Moving Picture World* (7 June 1913): 1005. The Chinese Revolution was partly sparked by the population seeing films from the West, claimed one writer, quoted in *The Pictures* (9 March 1912): 16.

35. J. Pope-Hennessy, *Queen Mary, 1867–1953* (London: Allen and Unwin, 1959), 470; *The Bioscope* (24 July 1913): 246.

36. *Kinematograph and Lantern Weekly* (13 June 1912): 456c.

37. *The Cinema* (10 September 1913): 15.

38. *The Pictures* (2 December 1911): 21.

39. *London Mail* (11 May 1912): 18.

1895

Heritage Discourses and British Cinema Before 1920

Andrew Higson

Senior Lecturer in Film Studies, School of English & American Studies, University of East Anglia, Norwich, NR4 7TJ, UK

EIGHTEEN NINETY-FIVE was the year of the first public film screenings. It was also the date of the founding in Britain of the National Trust, known at the time as the National Trust for Places of Historic Interest and Natural Beauty. Then, as now, this body presented certain longstanding private property of the aristocracy as worthy of conservation in the national interest.[1] The late nineteenth century was thus a period in which modernity and tradition went hand in hand: on one side the modernity of cinema, on the other the 'traditional' England of the aristocratic conservation project. What I want to do here is to look at some of the ways in which modernity and tradition are brought together in the first two decades of British filmmaking.

Elsewhere I have described some of the characteristics of what I call the British heritage film. More recent manifestations of these would include the Merchant-Ivory adaptations of E.M. Forster's novels, from *A Room with a View* (1986) to *Howards End* (1992).[2] Films such as these – heritage films – use cinema in part to construct a particular vision of the national past. In so doing, they effectively combine the discourses of modernity and tradition – or rather they absorb the modern within discourses of the traditional. The

modern thereby becomes simply the contemporary, arising out of a long tradition. It is not the revolutionary modernism or the celebration of modernity of a 1920s Eisenstein, breaking radically with the past. It is instead the celebration of continuous history, embodying a vision of the present with more splendid and desirable antecedents.

Central to my argument about heritage films is that they typically combine the aesthetics of attractionism with the drive of narrativity. That is to say that while the narratives of such films have their own engaging pleasures, they also operate as showcases for the display of a whole array of heritage attractions. This obviously provides an important link between contemporary films and those films from the turn of the century defined by Tom Gunning as the cinema of attractions.[3]

In the pages that follow, I will look at some of the ways in which British films from this early period themselves engage with heritage discourses. I will thus examine the way films from the first two decades of cinema history present particular versions of 'national' landscape, culture and tradition, particular versions of the national past. The motivation for such representations was, I would argue, twofold. On the one hand, filmmakers were simply drawing on well-established representational procedures and discursive practices. On the other hand, there was a more self-conscious bid to define a distinctive national cinema by engaging with these indigenous cultural traditions.

Costume dramas, patriotic displays, adaptations of novels, plays, and other familiar stories: the heritage film is at one time or another all of these. Such features also characterise British filmmaking throughout the first two decades of cinema history. Costume dramas and period adaptations of literary classics, for instance, played a vital role in the renewal of British filmmaking from 1911. As on so many other occasions since, British cinema looked back in order to move forward. Of course the revival was relative: Italian, American and French producers remained the world leaders, while there was a worrying increase in American film production in Britain, only temporarily stalled by the First World War.

By the end of the War, the heritage film was more or less fully in place – that is, if we accept that such a genre exists at all. (It is after all a critical rather than an industrial construction.)[4] Films like Maurice Elvey's *Nelson* (1918/19), and Cecil Hepworth's *Comin' Thro' the Rye* (1923/24), are already more or less fully fledged precursors to the more familiar heritage films of the 1980s and 1990s, with many of their characteristics already in place. They are both tasteful feature-length paeans to particular versions of the national past: *Nelson* commemorates the life of a national hero; *Comin' Thro' the Rye* is an adaptation of a nineteenth-century novel. They both also celebrate a very specific vision of landscape, property, class and culture, a vision of 'England, Home and Beauty'. While they are both more or less fully narrativised, they also bear many of the marks of the cinema of attractions. Thus they combine romantic narrative with pictorial display, so producing highly episodic but visually splendid texts. As such, they are as dependent on the aesthetics of the tableau as on the analytical dissection of film space and time pioneered elsewhere.[5]

What are the cinematic practices of the previous two decades that form the conditions of existence of such films? *Nelson*, in particular, is in many ways a virtual compendium of moments from earlier films. Some scenes recall interest films showing old England. Others recall the many fragmentary representations of the exemplary lives of the Great Men (and sometimes Women) of national history that are a feature of the early period. There was nothing new either in equally fragmentary representations of highly familiar stories, whether the known biography or the adaptation of literary classics.

I want to expand on these points by picking out four key representational practices from the previous two decades of British filmmaking. First, I will look at the aesthetic of attractionism; secondly, discourses of patriotism in topicals, actualities and interest films; thirdly, the cult of the national hero; and finally, the adaptation of 'national literature'. Together, these representational practices establish a cultural repertoire with which later heritage films work.

The aesthetic of attractionism

The aesthetic of attractionism dominates early cinema. British films are no exception, with their many theatrical tableaux, their sense of display, the stress on presentation rather than representation, and the dependence on the familiar, on known narratives, and on extra-diegetic knowledge. Such features of course distinguish the cinema of attractions from the more coherent, continuous and internally comprehensible narratives of later years.

There are numerous examples of this mode of cinematic presentation in the early years of British filmmaking. Some of the more obvious include actualities such as Birt Acres' *Rough Sea at Dover* (1895) and gag films like G. A. Smith's *Grandma's Reading Glass* (1900) and Williamson's *The Big Swallow* (probably 1901). Other films present scenes from current stage productions. In the Mutoscope and Biograph 1898 film *Fencing Contest from 'The Three Musketeers'*, for instance, there is no attempt to tell the Alexandre Dumas story. Instead, the film presents a fencing scene from a current London stage production.

From the 1890s on, we can also find numerous early British 'adaptations' of Shakespeare and

1895

Dickens. Most of them present tiny fragments from the source text. Those are often in the form of visually splendid theatrical tableaux, and often depend upon knowledge of the source text, or upon an extra-diegetic lecture to make them meaningful. Among the more interesting examples are the fragmentary scenes from Herbert Beerbohm Tree's 1899 theatrical production of *King John*, again filmed by the Mutoscope and Biograph Company. There is little effort to tell a self-contained story here: the tableau itself, the performance, and the topicality of the production, seem to have been sufficient motivation for the period.[6] In due course filmmakers created longer films by combining such narrative fragments, still as episodes from a known story rather than continuous and self-sufficient narration, still using the aesthetic of display of the tableau. I would argue that such attractionism lingers still as an important feature of the heritage film.

Topicals, patriotism and pageantry

Topicals, actualities and interest films produced in the early period constitute the second representational practice I want to examine. Such films purport to present the real – that is, the extra-diegetic, something beyond the cinema. What interests me about these types of films is the extent to which discourses of patriotism colour pictorial and informational values and thereby enable the films to conjure up images of nationhood.

A central theme for topicals was the Royal appearance. Ritualistic displays such as coronations and funerals produced thoroughly formalised appearances. Other films afforded more informal views of members of the Royal family going to church or visiting one of their estates. Some of the more formal occasions were vital to the development of cinema in Great Britain, notably Queen Victoria's Diamond Jubilee celebrations in 1897. The main royal procession afforded views that attracted large national – even international – audiences and numerous companies and individuals sought to secure appropriate images for display around the country. John Barnes lists nineteen companies as having made their own versions of the Diamond Jubilee procession, and suggests that collec-

tively they invested vast resources in the filming of this event. As he observes, 'the Queen's procession ... provided a marvellous spectacle for the cinematograph cameras ... . So keen was the interest shown in the event, that by the end of the year there could hardly have been a person in England who had not seen this historic scene on the screen.'[7]

Clearly, such events were spectacular. The spectacle was of a very specific nature: images of monarchic ritual and pageantry, processions of famous people, and splendid displays of heritage properties (buildings, coaches, costumes). Here was a very tangible sense of national history in the making. There were inevitably numerous occasions for such films of pageantry. To the specifically Royal occasions, we can of course add naval and military reviews. Such films were instrumental in establishing a particular mode of representation, with the camera at a distance, observing and presenting the pro-filmic spectacle. As one contemporary commentator observed of the Diamond Jubilee procession, 'as carriage after carriage rolls by one becomes almost dazzled by the ever-moving spectacle'.[8]

The function of the cinematographer was not simply to observe, however, but to emphasise the spectacle. Thus film companies competed for the best positions from which to film the Diamond Jubilee procession. Barnes suggests that as a result the Jubilee films played an integral part in freeing the camera from a fixed position on the ground. To secure a reasonable view of the procession almost demanded securing an elevated position, producing the high-angle shot, spectacular in itself.[9] Warwick Trading Company's catalogue of available films, for instance, noted of their 1899 subject, *HM The Queen and Royal Family Entering Their Carriages at Buckingham Palace*: 'As this photograph was taken from a slight elevation a splendid view of the proceedings is shown'.[10]

The historian David Cannadine has shown that most of the monarchic rituals of the late nineteenth and early twentieth centuries, and especially the pomp and ceremony surrounding the Diamond Jubilee, were actually invented traditions. Their purpose was to invest the monarchy with symbolic power as its political power waned.[11] Such ceremony was rare in the mid-nineteenth century and earlier, when royal appearances in public were often ineptly managed and invested with little sense of national significance. Two systems of display, two modes of representation – royal pageantry and cinema – were thus developing alongside and feeding off one another. Indeed, developments in the mass media were undoubtedly vital to the promotion of the novel image of the monarch as head of the nation. Both the events of occasions like the Diamond Jubilee and the films that represented them offered images of a rich, powerful, successful and self-confident nation.

Topicals and related films tend to establish, or, more likely in the very early period, to consolidate the status of certain events as of national significance. Clearly, films of Royalty, the navy, and the military – with their obvious patriotic function – fall into this category. So, of course, do films of various sporting events, including the Henley Regatta, the Oxford and Cambridge Boat Race, and the Derby. A contemporary account of R.W. Paul's filming of the 1896 Derby talks of Paul cranking the camera 'for the benefit of the public who weren't there'. Paul thereby produced a film 'which should show to countless multitudes one of the most popular events of the Victorian age'.[12]

By making views of such events publicly available and deeming them to be of public interest, their significance as national events is underlined. The number of occasions on which such events were filmed certainly gives a good indication of their appeal. As another contemporary commentator noted, '[R.W.] Paul cinematographed the Derby on no less than six consecutive occasions, and there is probably no established British annual event which he has not recorded'.[13] The sense of reproducing a national tradition shines through in such statements.

Actualities and interest films also invoked heritage discourses. The Hepworth company provides good examples, with several of their films imagining England as pictorially splendid and steeped in tradition. Contemporary descriptions of films such as the *Thames River Scenery* series of 1899 stress the pictorial beauty of the image. They also present England as picturesque, semi-rural and of historic interest. In films such as *Wooden Walls of Old England* and *Frigates in Harbour* (both 1899), Hepworth captured the heritage of old naval vessels. His catalogue describes the ships in the latter film as 'thoroughly typical of the ancient warships which have done so much for England's supremacy on the seas'.[14] The same catalogue describes another film of 1899, *HMS Ocean Preparing for Final Trips*, as 'bound to be of interest to all loyal Englishmen'.[15] Later, there are various travelogues favouring historical locations, such as Kineto's *Shakespeare Land* (1910), and a 1914 film, *Old London*.

Topicals and related films thus played a vital role from the outset in establishing a sense of nationhood through cinema. They treated appearances of Royalty, selected sporting events, and various military and naval activities as newsworthy – that is, they deemed them worthy of public celebration. Large numbers of people were thus able to participate through cinema in a limited series of events that helped to create a sense of a nation with shared interests. However recently invented, this was a nation with a heritage, now celebrated in moving pictures. It is important to note too that contemporary discourse acknowledged the heritage qualities of such films. An article about Jubilee films in *The Era* of 1897 thus states:

> By the invention of the cinematographe a means has been discovered for the preservation of what is to all intents and purposes living representations of memorable events. Our descendants will be able to learn how the completion of the sixtieth year of Queen Victoria's reign was celebrated in the capital of the country.[16]

Other commentators discussed the possibility of some sort of national film archive that might preserve for posterity these films of 'memorable events'.[17] It was, of course, some years before such an archive was established. Even so, the debate in itself is important for our purposes in that it acknowledges the heritage qualities of the Jubilee films and other Topicals and related material.

The cult of the hero

A third way in which heritage discourses are re-worked in cinema in this early period is in the continuation of the ostentatious nineteenth-century cult of the hero. While the 1918 *Nelson* was by no means the first film to dramatise the dutiful and patriotic life and death of a national hero, the cult of Nelson was amongst the strongest of these traditions. A vast range of nineteenth-century representational practices commemorated and reproduced his personality, deeds and death in victory. These practices included paintings, ballads, biographies of all sorts, plays, statues and monuments, and other more fleeting patriotic displays. Nelson, like many others, was represented as the central protagonist of a national and imperial epic. It was then inevitable that cinema should eventually take on fragments from this narrative and related pictorial displays.

In 1897, a song-film called *The Death of Nelson* was produced (or possibly just distributed) by Philip Wolff to celebrate Trafalgar Day (21 October). The title, and the scenes depicted, recall Arthur William Devis's famous painting of the same name (c. 1805). John Braham and S.J. Arnold's ballad, 'The death of Nelson', dating from 1811, and source of the phrase 'for England, home and beauty', is perhaps even more important. The ballad, one of many on a similar theme, subsequently became a nineteenth-century favourite. The idea of the Wolff film was that a singer should perform the ballad while the audience watched the film – a not uncommon mode of presentation in the early period.

Hepworth and Fitzhamon made another film version of the ballad in 1905, the centenary of The Battle of Trafalgar and of Nelson's death. Once again, the film was to be accompanied by a live performance of the song. The film itself was therefore not self-sufficient, but the vehicle for the presentation of another textuality. Also made in this anniversary year was a film of modestly epic proportions for the period, *Incidents in the Life of Lord Nelson*. The title tells all: this was evidently an episodic rather than a continuous narrative, presenting scenes from a familiar story. In 1907 a sound-film called *Nelson's Victory* appeared. This was probably another song-film,

although the song this time was recorded for synchronous reproduction at the film screening.[18]

Apparently early topicals from the turn of the century showed the Trafalgar Day decorations and celebrations in Trafalgar Square in London. There were also various films of Nelson's flagship, 'Victory', including one by that name made by Mutoscope and Biograph in 1898. Another Hepworth film, *HMS Powerful Arriving in Portsmouth Harbour* (1899), juxtaposed the historical and the contemporary:

> This photograph ... has for a background Nelson's flagship, the *Victory*, gaily decorated with bunting in honour of the homecoming of the modern war vessel. The *Powerful* is bringing home those heroes who fought so well and so successfully at Ladysmith ...[19]

A very similar image closes the 1918 *Nelson*, with a modern iron-clad battleship passing in front of the *Victory*. Both films thus stress the continuity between past and present.

Numerous literary, theatrical, pictorial, monumental, and filmic celebrations of the life and death of Nelson are quite self-consciously on display in the 1918 film, which was made as part of the war effort. The ways in which these various representations and the broader cultural practices that supported them are re-worked for the cinema on this occasion are typical of the heritage film. *Nelson* is in effect a spectacular showcase for a whole range of heritage properties. The book that the Admiral gives to the boy in an early scene could well be Robert Southey's classic 1813 *Life of Nelson*, much re-printed, including in educational editions. The film also reproduces several well-known paintings. Along with period architecture, furniture and fittings, and 'typically English' landscapes, they are as much on display in the film as the hero himself. The list could continue.

Literary adaptation

The fourth way in which early films engaged with heritage discourses was by adapting established classics of the national literature and drama. As we have already noted, such adaptations began as early as the 1890s. They were particularly important in the period after

1895

1911 or 1912, when they played a key role in the revival of British film production. Costume dramas, period films, and films with prestigious and/or popular literary sources were frequently the vehicles for significant innovations in the development of British cinema from as early as the turn of the century. Such films often ushered in significant developments in length, extravagance of production values, bids for authenticity, cost, marketing techniques, even the use of colour.

R.W. Paul's *Scrooge, or Marley's Ghost* was one of two Dickens adaptations he made in late 1901 for the Christmas market. It came in at an impressive 160 feet and thirteen scenes, already nearly three times as long as another Dickens fragment he had presented three years earlier.[20] Dickens, of course, was both popular and respectable. Other popular English melodramas worth noting include the first of many adaptations of *East Lynne*, made in 1902 with a length of 500 feet. Hepworth produced a very tasteful 880-foot version of *Alice in Wonderland* in 1903, with sixteen scenes of much pictorial interest. The source for the images was Sir John Tenniel's illustrations, a fact that contemporary publicity stressed as a matter of great authenticity.[21]

According to Denis Gifford, the first British one-reel feature was another Hepworth production, *Dick Turpin's Ride to York* (1000 feet, 1906).[22] This time the source was the well-known story of one of the exploits of a hero from the heartland of English popular culture. The first British two-reel feature was Barker's famous 1911 production of *Henry VIII* (2000 feet), which also pioneered the practice of exclusive rentals rather than outright sales of films. The first three-reel feature was an adaptation of Sir Walter Scott's novel, *Rob Roy* (2500 feet, 1911). This suggests that there is room here for the elaboration of an alternative heritage of popular heroes bucking against the English system. (Another such hero would be the infamous nineteenth-century criminal, Charles Peace, subject of several film treatments in this period.) The first of several tasteful Dickens adaptations by Hepworth and Bentley, *Oliver Twist* (3700 feet, 1912), was also the first four-reeler. A Clarendon production of the same year, an adaptation of

R.D. Blackmore's *Lorna Doone* (4300 feet, 1912), was the first British five-reeler.

Several patriotic subjects from this period could also feature in this list of cinematic innovations. One of the more notable films in this category was British and Colonial's dramatisation of one of the great moments of the national history, *The Battle of Waterloo* (1913). This was a big-budget epic, which came in at 4500 feet. Another was Barker's hugely expensive film of the same year, *Sixty Years a Queen*, dramatising the life of Queen Victoria. Contemporary commentaries conceived this very much as an authentic historical reconstruction. It was by all accounts pictorially splendid but under-narrativised, a chronology of public occasions and private moments. Rachael Low compares it to a long, loose topical, a type of filmmaking for which Barker was previously well known.[23] It is worth noting in addition that the Natural Colour Kinematograph Company produced a series of popular historical films in 1911. These vehicles for their colour process sought to exploit the potential of the costume drama for colourful *mise-en-scène*.[24]

In the 1910s in particular, many of the longer and more tasteful adaptations and historical subjects tended to be aimed at what we would now call the art-house market. The target audience was thus the respectable middle-class public, more used to visiting the theatre than the cinema. As I noted above, adaptations of classic literature and patriotic costume dramas were central to the relative revival of British production in the early 1910s. They were also an integral part of the simultaneous bid to move upmarket, to establish an aura of respectability around cinema, to cultivate a middle-class quality cinema. Such developments are comparable to the work of Films D'Art and Pathé in France, and Vitagraph in the USA, although the British films appear a few years later than those in France and the USA.

Some of the most important British productions in this respect are the several adaptations of Shakespeare films of the early 1910s, most of them records of (aspects of) contemporary stage versions. These include a series made by F.R. Benson in 1911, of which his *Richard III* is a good example. Its theatrical

1895

origins are only too clear, the stage set and playing area clearly visible as such, the actors clearly performing as for a live audience according to the theatrical conventions for which Benson was well known in the period. Despite its relative length, the film includes only key scenes from the Shakespeare text and without some prior knowledge it is extremely difficult to follow the story. The camera remains fixed and at a distance throughout the film, thus capturing the full pictorial glory of the costumes and grouping of characters in the many set-piece theatrical tableaux, but hardly narrating the story. For these reasons, many historians have dismissed the film as a primitive throwback to a now outmoded form of cinema.[25]

The various Hepworth–Bentley adaptations of Dickens' novels have attracted similar accusations.[26] Like most of the Hepworth productions of the period, these were deliberately tasteful and restrained rather than sensationalist. They were also quite self-consciously conceived as English films, over against the various imports of the period. The 1913 version of *David Copperfield* is a good example. This is a long film (six reels), and includes a great deal of story material. Even so, it still does not run with the narrative fluency and energy of comparable American productions of the period – or even some British films. Again, there is a sense that the narrative motor is outside the text, and that you have to know the story in advance in order fully to appreciate it. On the other hand, there are a great many informative intertitles which function almost as chapter headings. The plot remains highly episodic, with its pictorial values stressed over its narrative values. The producers also aimed at authenticity of location and adaptation, and overall the film gives the impression of displaying scenes from a familiar novel.

Clearly many of these longer quality films of the 1910s from *Richard III*, via *David Copperfield* to *Nelson*, are much more heavily narrativised than films of the previous decade. At the same time, it should be clear, too, that they are still heavily dependent on the attractionist aesthetic of display. The films still display the attractions of the source text, for a knowledgeable and knowing spectator. I would, however, argue that this is insufficient grounds for dismissing such cinema as impoverished, primitive or outdated. On the contrary, it seems to me that the attractionist mode is an ideal form for the display of heritage properties, whether they are landscapes, buildings, royal processions or classic novels. This is a different cinema, not a primitive cinema. It is a cinema that displays indigenous cultural traditions for the pleasure of an imaginary national audience. It is a cinema that we should think of – as contemporary commentators did – as a distinctive and respectable national cinema.

The repertoire of heritage discourses and representational practices mobilised by British films in the first decades of cinema history played an important part in the subsequent development of British cinema. The repertoire remains familiar, but it has not always found the favour of critics and historians. Such filmmaking embodies a particular combination of tradition and modernity. This combination was however very much at odds with the modernist appreciation of film that gained such a strong foothold in British intellectual film culture from the late 1920s. Revisionist histories of British cinema 'before Hitchcock' need always to claw their way back past the moment of The Film Society, *Close-Up* and Rotha's *The Film Till Now*...[27]

Notes

1.   See Patrick Wright, *On Living in an Old Country: The National Past in Contemporary Britain* (London: Verso, 1985), 48ff.

2.   See *Waving the Flag: Constructing a National Cinema in Britain* (Oxford: Clarendon Press, 1995), especially Chapter 3; and 'Re-presenting the National Past: Nostalgia and Pastiche in the Heritage Film', in Lester Friedman (ed), *Fires Were Started: British Cinema and Thatcherism* (Minneapolis: University of Minnesota Press and London: UCL Press, 1993), 109–129. The present paper is itself

adapted from my forthcoming *English Heritage, English Cinema*, to be published by Oxford University Press.

3. 'The Cinema of Attractions: Early Film, its Spectator and the Avant-garde', in Thomas Elsaesser with Adam Barker (eds), *Early Cinema: Space, Frame, Narrative* (London: BFI, 1990), 56–62.

4. See my 'The Heritage Film and British Cinema', in Higson (ed), *Dissolving Views: Key Writings on British Cinema* (London: Cassell, 1996), 232– 248.

5. *On Comin' Thro' the Rye*, see Higson, *Waving the Flag*, ch. 3; on *Nelson*, see Higson, 'The Victorious Re-cycling of National History: *Nelson*', in Karel Dibbets and Bert Hogenkamp (eds), *Film and the First World War* (Amsterdam: Amsterdam University Press, 1995), 108–115.

6. See Luke McKernan, 'Beerbohm Tree's *King John* Re-discovered: the First Shakespeare Film, September 1899', *Shakespeare Bulletin* (Winter 1993): 35–36; and 'Further Notes on Beerbohm Tree's *King John*', *Shakespeare Bulletin* (Spring 1993): 49–50.

7. Barnes, *The Rise of Cinema in Great Britain*, vol. 2 of *The Beginnings of Cinema in England 1894–1901* (London: Bishopsgate Press, 1983), 7; see also 178ff.

8. *The Era* (24 July 1897): 16, quoted in Barnes, *op. cit.*, 193.

9. *Ibid.*, 198.

10. Quoted in Barnes, *op. cit.*, 241.

11. *The Pleasures of the Past* (London: Collins, 1989); and 'The Context, Performance and Meaning of Ritual: the British Monarchy and the "Invention of Tradition", c. 1870–1977', in Eric Hobsbawm and Terence Ranger (eds), *The Invention of Tradition* (Cambridge: Cambridge University Press, 1983).

12. *The Strand Magazine*, vol. 12 (July–December, 1896), George Newnes (ed) (London: George Newnes, 1896), 139, 137.

13. Frederick A. Talbot, *Moving Pictures: How They Are Made and Worked* (London: William Heinemann, 1912), 117.

14. Hepworth Catalogue (1903): 14, quoted in John Barnes, *Filming the Boer War*, vol. 4 of *The Beginnings of Cinema in England 1894–1901* (London: Bishopsgate, 1992), 205.

15. Hepworth Catalogue (1903): 14, quoted in *ibid.*, 206.

16. *The Era* (24 July 1897): 16, quoted in Barnes, *The Rise of Cinema*, 193.

17. See e.g. Talbot, *op. cit.*, 330.

18. See entries 01149 and 01807 in Denis Gifford, *The British Film Catalogue 1895–1970: A Guide to Entertainment Films* (Newton Abbot: David and Charles, 1973).

19. Hepworth Catalogue, entry 101 (1903): 21, quoted in John Barnes, *The Beginnings of Cinema in England 1894–1901*, vol. 5: 1900 (Exeter: University of Exeter Press, 1997): 158.

20. Lengths of films here and subsequently are taken from Gifford, *op. cit.*

21. See Hepworth Manufacturing Company Catalogue (1906): 55.

22. Gifford, *op. cit.*, entry 01287; subsequent references to 'firsts' are also derived from Gifford.

23. *The History of the British Film, 1906–1914* (London: George Allen and Unwin, 1949), 202.

24. See Gifford, *op. cit.*

25. See e.g. Low, *op. cit.*, 224ff; for additional accounts of this and other Shakespeare films of the period, see Robert Hamilton Ball, *Shakespeare on Silent Film* (London: George Allen and Unwin, 1968), 84–88 and 322–333; John Collick, *Shakespeare, Cinema and Society* (Manchester: Manchester University Press, 1989), 42–46; and Luke McKernan and Olwen Terris (eds), *Walking Shadows: Shakespeare in the National Film and Television Archive* (London: BFI, Publishing, 1994), 136. I should also like to acknowledge the pioneering research of Jonathan Burrows, for his Ph. D. on British film acting in the 1910s and 1920s, at the University of East Anglia.

26. See again Low, *op. cit.*, 236ff.

27. The Film Society was established in London in 1925; the journal *Close-Up* was published between 1927 and 1933; the first edition of Paul Rotha's *The Film Till Now* was published in 1930; see Higson, *Waving the Flag*, 13ff.

'Animated Geography': Early Cinema at the American Museum of Natural History

Alison Griffiths

Department of Cinema Studies, New York University, 721 Broadway, 6th Floor, New York, NY 10003, USA

THE ETHNOGRAPHIC PROMISE of motion pictures was strikingly prefigured in a 1853 review of Lord Byron's play *Sardanapalus* in *Lloyd's Weekly* of London. The costumes and set design of the play were based on Assyrian artifacts recently acquired by the British Museum and, according to the anonymous reviewer:

> ... that one performance gave us a better insight into the manners and habits of the Assyrians than a whole lifetime has enabled us to acquire of the French. It was a grand lesson of animated geography; and the more curious as being the animated geography of a nation that is dead.[1]

As a popular object lesson in exotic ethnography, *Sardanapalus* illustrates the longevity of debates about the efficacy of distinct modes of ethnographic representation. Indeed, the trafficking between popular ethnographic spectacle and scientific models and institutions of anthropological knowledge which characterised this mid-nineteenth-century theatrical production forecasts the contested place of

ethnographic filmmaking within anthropology and popular culture some 60 years later.[2] Likewise, the reviewer's appreciation of Byron's play as a form of 'animated geography' prefigures the mobilised gaze of early ethnographic cinema in which spectators could travel vicariously to exotic locales. I will examine in this essay some of the efforts to reconcile the conflicting values of anthropological rigour, visual spectacle, and popular pleasures as they were played out in a preeminent American scientific and public institution, the American Museum of Natural History (AMNH) in New York City (Fig. 1), and analyse one of the earliest uses of moving pictures within American anthropological fieldwork. While an examination of internal documents reveals no discussion of the role of motion pictures within the Museum before 1908, by 1914 the field correspondence and published work of Museum anthropologist Pliny Earl Goddard displayed growing sensitivity towards film's promise and limitations as an ethnographic recording device.[3] Goddard's interest in film remained exceptional within both the Museum and the larger US anthropological community of the time, how-

1895

ever, and the paucity of professional debate on the use of moving pictures for ethnographic data collection suggests that anthropologists were reluctant to incorporate moving pictures into their arsenal of fieldwork research techniques. This lack of interest in cinema as a tool of ethnographic inscription is somewhat surprising, since, as film historian Lisa Cartwright has argued, many nineteenth-century American and European scientists from other fields regarded the cinematic devices introduced by the Lumières, Edison, and others not so much as new inventions but as more sophisticated extensions of Marey's and Muybridge's photographic apparatuses which had already seen widespread scientific applications.[4] French physician Félix-Louis Regnault, for example, utilised Marey's *fusil photographique* to obtain chronophotographs (serial photographs) of West Africans participating in the Exposition Ethnographique de l'Afrique Occidentale in Paris in 1895 and one of the rare early applications of motion pictures in anthropological fieldwork involved British anthropologist Alfred Cort Haddon's use of the camera during an anthropological expedition to the Torres Straits three years later in 1898.[5]

However, despite the exceptional efforts of a few anthropologists and cinema's intellectual ties to nineteenth-century scientific culture, most professionally-trained anthropologists within the fledgling discipline were cool to the adoption of film as a scientific apparatus. Two reasons may be proposed. The first involves both the specific phenomenological features of motion picture spectatorship, as well as the medium's associations with popular entertainments such as phantasmagoric and erotogenic representations of the human figure, associations which clashed with anthropology's claims for scientific legitimacy. The second area of institutional resistance stemmed from the daunting logistical and financial challenges confronting anthropologists using motion pictures in the field. Intemperate climates, remote topographies, highly flammable film stock, and technical inexperience all discouraged anthropologists from exploiting motion pictures on ethnographic expeditions. In this regard, motion

Manhattan Square, AS IT IS

pictures proved more resistant to adoption by anthropologists in the field than contemporaneous mechanical recording devices such as the photograph and the phonograph.[6]

Given this general indifference toward cinema among anthropologists, it is not surprising to find a lack of consensus at the American Museum of Natural History regarding the role of motion pictures in Museum-sponsored anthropological expeditions or in its public programmes; instead, film became enmeshed within long-standing debates about popularised forms of museum display such as the illustrated lecture and the human life group, an exhibit form which featured plaster cast mannequins of native peoples set before illusionistically-rendered dioramas. The sometimes testy exchanges between Museum officials and guest speakers employing film in their invited lectures, along with the challenge of integrating Museum-sponsored anthropological field footage into public programmes, illuminate wider professional attitudes towards moving pictures during the period. Moreover, the complex interactions among Museum staff, visiting lecturers, and anthropologists corresponding with the Museum from the field provide compelling evidence of the unstable and contentious nature of film as a transmitter of

Fig. 1. *The American Museum of Natural History and Manhattan Square, 1878. The arrival of the elevated train helped boost attendance at the Museum. [Neg. no. 471. Courtesy Department of Library Services, American Museum of Natural History.]*

anthropological knowledge and the interdependence of anthropology and popular culture within the institution.

This essay examines two applications of moving pictures by the American Museum of Natural History between 1909 and 1914. The first concerned a series of lecture-screenings by guest speakers who either rented commercial films for the occasion or used their own footage as visual aids in their presentations; the second involved the Museum as motion picture producer, including sponsoring the 1912 expeditionary filmmaking of Howard McCormick, commissioned by the Museum to conduct research on the Hopi in preparation for an AMNH life group, as well as the field cinematography of Museum staff anthropologist Pliny Earl Goddard in 1914. Together, these case studies illustrate the institutional negotiation of the demands of scientific education and popular appeal, the nature of film spectatorship at the Museum, and the logistical problems of anthropological field recording. They also demonstrate ways in which the Museum viewed photography and moving pictures not merely as objective representational systems but as technologies capable of making claims and arguments; consequently, these technologies were subject to a disciplinary regime within the Museum that sought to ensure that potential threats to perceived scientific objectivity and veracity were swiftly contained.

Moving pictures and the illustrated lecture

Given the small number of films regularly exhibited at the American Museum of Natural History before 1914, decisions concerning funding, suitability of material, and editorial control over the use of film by guest speakers in the Museum's public programmes were made on a case-by-case basis. In arranging a lecture by Dr. Hugh Smith of the United States Bureau of Fisheries in December 1913, Museum Director Frederick A. Lucas instructed the lecturer regarding how much and which portions of the rented film shot by Museum scientist Roy Chapman Andrews could be used:

We understand that these motion pictures

give an excellent idea of some of the life of the Pribilof Islands, including seals, sea lions, reindeer and natives. We would wish to use probably not more than 2,600 feet of the film; for instance, we would not care for the skinning of the seals, portions of the film that duplicate over other sections, or parts that are not especially good.[7]

The casual listing of 'natives' along with the regional wildlife suggests that Museum film policy made few distinctions between films with ethnographic content and those that focused exclusively on zoology or botany. There is no specific discussion of the representation of indigenous peoples in lecturer correspondence or in internal Museum documents, despite the fact that from the lecture titles alone, it would seem that a significant number of films with ethnographic content were exhibited at the AMNH between 1908 and 1915.[8]

If the use of moving pictures within the Museum's public lectures was not addressed in internal memoranda before 1908, subsequent Museum-lecturer correspondence refers repeatedly to disputes over the suitability of specific film sequences for Museum audiences. For example, in 1912 AMNH President Osborn advised lecturer Frank E. Kleinschmidt that in future presentations of his lecture 'Hunting Big Game with a Cinematograph in Alaska and Siberia' he should 'omit the [seal] killing and not extend the series [of the polar bear] too long'.[9] Interestingly, a review of the same film in the *Philadelphia Telegraph* from 1912 cited the same polar bear hunt scene as the one the commercial audience was 'most impressed with'. The reviewer continued:

Here the pictures are so nearly perfect that the illusion is quite compelling and one imagines oneself aboard the schooner pursuing the polar bear mother and the cub as they swim along the ice flows, the little fellow with his teeth fixed on the mother's stumpy tail'.[10]

What are we to make, then, of President Osborn's admonishment of Kleinschmidt to censor the same scene which a journalist had singled out as the source of greatest audience

1895

approval? On one level, it suggests the culturally-contingent nature of meaning across the film's distinct exhibition sites, since the responses from Osborn and those reported by the anonymous Philadelphia reviewer are determined in part by the imputed class tastes of their respective audiences at AMNH's Auditorium and at Philadelphia's Garrick Theater. The critic's references to filmic illusionism might also be read as a displacement of the audience's sadistic pleasures in viewing the polar bear and seal hunting scenes. Fearing the prurient appeal of these scenes, Osborn felt duty-bound to register his displeasure with Kleinschmidt and to prohibit such footage from future screenings at the Museum.

The Museum as film exhibitor intervened even more directly and narrowly in the case of lecturer James Barnes and his 1914 film *From Coast to Coast Through Central Africa*, which contained footage from the AMNH-sponsored expedition he undertook with British naturalist Cherry Kearton. Sherwood demanded that Barnes change an intertitle which used the word 'playground' in describing an animal watering hole back to the original intertitle 'African Animals in their Home', because, as Sherwood declared, 'the Museum stands for science and must therefore adhere strictly to facts'.[11] That this seemingly insignificant semantic change elicited such a strong response from Sherwood is symptomatic of the Museum's heightened sensitivity about the use of figurative language in ostensibly scientific presentations, and a more general fear that the popular would contaminate the zoological or the ethnological. As historian Nancy Leys Stepan has argued regarding the use of race and gender analogies in nineteenth-century science, 'one reason for the controversy over metaphor, analogy, and models in science is the intellectually privileged status that science has traditionally enjoyed as the repository of non-metaphorical, empirical, politically neutral, universal knowledge'.[12] J. Hillis Miller's explication of the function of the label or the caption in placing a picture 'back within the context of some diachronic narrative', may also be relevant here; while not wholly opposed to the use of illustration in public lectures, Osborn seems to share Miller's concern that illustration 'to some degree interferes with [a] text', and, in this case, with science's own master narrative of truth and objectivity.[13] Thus, every editorial change Osborn was able to impose upon visiting lecturers represented a small victory of science against other belief systems and the dissociation of the Museum from some of the undesirable popular associations of moving pictures.

The Museum's efforts to police the language of motion picture intertitles and to eliminate specific film segments are merely two examples of the extreme measures Sherwood and Osborn took to regulate the use of motion pictures at the Museum in the teens. In another context, Sherwood wrote to Lee Keedick, self-described 'Manager of the World's Most Celebrated Lecturers', suggesting that in children's presentations at the Museum, lecturers should show lantern slides of each exhibit before screening moving pictures. As late as 1919, Osborn wrote Sherwood insisting that either a taxidermy specimen, a slide of a Museum habitat group (a synthetic construction of a natural habitat containing preserved specimens of fauna and flora), or a photograph of the group should be displayed in order to 'connect moving pictures with the serious side of zoology'.[14] In 1920, Osborn felt compelled to admonish Sherwood that 'the educational must not be swallowed up by the popular aspect of our lectures'.[15] That the Museum wanted *some* spectacle is evident from the institution's ongoing efforts to popularise its exhibits – the large numbers of diorama life groups and taxidermy specimens installed during this period are testimony to this shift – although unlike permanent exhibits, which could be designed according to scientific principles and contextualised via labels, moving pictures rented from commercial exchanges presented a different set of problems.

The fearful prospect that the seductive illusionism of the moving image would undermine more scholarly aims thus threatened the precarious equilibrium between science and spectacle Osborn strove to maintain in the Museum's public displays and lectures. It is perhaps worth underscoring the

1895

Fig. 2. British lanternist and cinematographer Frank E. Butcher about to embark on another world tour. [Cartoon from The Bioscope, *16 February 1911.]*

invited to appear at the Museum and kept a watchful eye on exactly how moving pictures would be incorporated into the illustrated lecture. Osborn's recommendation that spectators not be permitted to get caught up in the lure of the moving image is thus part of a defensive strategy adopted to minimise the risk of Museum-goers misconstruing the ostensible scientific aims of the lecture.

Osborn's insistence on the use of the static image or object before motion pictures in public lectures also opposes the presumed non-scientificity of illusionistic movement with the reflective qualities of stasis, including a projected still image as an overture to the cinematic projection. Osborn's concern that scientific principles would be undermined or trivialised in the case of unaccompanied moving pictures invokes a hierarchy of visual representation in which stasis is afforded greater scientific exactitude than movement, and a spoken or written text is imbued with more authority than a visual image. In taking away the very thing that vivified filmed zoological and biological studies, Osborn sought to mitigate cinema's distracting kinetic and illusionistic qualities by ensuring that the controlling vocal sanctioning of the speaker would preserve the scientific seriousness of the lecture.

fact that the viewing public at the Museum would have been exposed to a wide array of popular ethnographic imagery at that time, some of it represented in vulgarised form in freak shows, circuses, and vaudeville line-ups, as well as in more salubrious form in commercial motion picture travelogues. The figure of the travel lecturer who filmed native peoples as part of a whirlwind world tour was parodied in a cartoon that appeared in the British trade journal *The Bioscope* in 1910 (Fig. 2), while the appeal of the heroic Western explorer/cameraman/quasi-ethnographer in popular fiction of the 1910s illustrates the interpenetration of the scientific and the popular within quasi-ethnographic filmmaking of the time (Fig. 3). Fearful of the touristic and unscientific connotations of such travelers who frequently wrote to the Museum offering to exhibit their latest travelogue films, Osborn carefully vetted those lecturers

The rented footage exhibited at the Museum during this period served an essentially illustrative function in public lectures, since films were generally exhibited within the context of the lecture presentation. However, in the case of Frank E. Moore's film adaptation of Henry Longfellow's poem *Hiawatha*, a joint presentation by the Museum and the American Scenic and Historic Presentation Society in April 1913, a simultaneous reading of the classic poem during the film projection replaced the traditional lecture format.[16] Though resistant to the use of commercially-produced fiction films, the Museum recognised the utility of exhibiting *Hiawatha* in light of what it saw as the film's ethnographically-redeeming features and educational appeal. Moore had cast Native Americans actors and drawn upon the ethnographic expertise of the Assistant Curator of the Museum's Department of Anthropology, Alanson Skinner (one of the first American anthropologists to specialise in the study of the Cree tribe). Moreover, recalling the 1853 precedent of Byron's play *Sardanapalus*, Moore borrowed Native American costumes and props from the Museum for use in the production.[17] The film was subsequently screened as part of the Museum's Saturday morning children's lecture series in 1913; in the promotional booklet accompanying the series, children were reminded that even if the picture was 'only a legend' and 'not a true Science Story' it was, nevertheless, told by 'real Indians' who took us 'into the deep wild woods to learn many of the animals *Hiawatha* might have known'.[18]

It would thus seem that in assessing the ethnographic value of moving pictures the Museum attempted to rationalise its decision-making policy by arguing that the verisimilitude engendered by Moore's casting of 'real' Indians mitigated against other less scientific criteria such as the fictional form of the film. Such discourses of authenticity and ethnographic 'purity' were also employed as evaluative criteria by Museum employees in the context of ethnographic fieldwork.[19]

Early ethnographic film in the American Southwest: McCormick's 1912 films of Hopi Indians

The first Museum-sponsored expedition to the American Southwest to produce films of native ceremonies and industries took place in the summer and early autumn of 1912. During this expedition, Museum artist Howard McCormick complained that he faced the choice of either making do with good-quality footage of an inauthentic Indian dance, altered for the touristic gaze, or sticking with a badly photographed version of a more pristine, 'uncontaminated' dance.[20] When filming a Snake Dance at Oraiba in August of 1912, McCormick wrote to Goddard complaining that while the light had been 'great', the 'dance was not the real thing as they had snake men acting as antelope men'.[21] Thus McCormick seemed aware of contemporaneous complaints of the deleterious effect of commercial and tourist photographers and filmmakers on native dances and able to differentiate between 'authentic' dances and more

Fig. 3. *Book cover from 1917 showing the adventurer-cameraman braving the wilds of Africa.*

compromised versions aimed at the tourist market. Indeed, camera-toting anthropologists were often not the first to gain access to native communities; other Westerners equipped with still- and moving-picture cameras in search of visually spectacular images of American Indians had frequently preceded them. Adhering to the same protocols as commercial film producers, anthropologists had to negotiate the right to film with the Indians themselves, and often with Reservation Superintendents and the Bureau of American Ethnology, established in 1879 as a clearinghouse for US government research into Native Americans.[22]

Writing in the AMNH's publication the *American Museum Journal* in March 1913, McCormick discussed the negative impact of Indian acculturation on traditional culture and the problems this presented to the ethnographic artist:

> The Hopi have now adopted white man's dress in their daily life. Automobiles carry the mail to within a few miles of the Hopi villages ... and it will soon be necessary for the artist to reconstruct the customs

and habits which may now be seen in their final stage of dissolution.[23]

In commenting on the effects of Western acculturation on Southwest Indian tribes, McCormick conceived of his painting and photography as small attempts to salvage what traces of native culture remained for future generations; acknowledging that there would be little indigenous culture left for an ethnographer to salvage in the near future, McCormick offered artistic reconstruction as the only viable means of piecing together accounts of these people's lives.

McCormick's sensitivity to issues of authenticity may have stemmed from the insistence of his supervisor, staff anthropologist Pliny Goddard, that footage obtained under the auspices of the Department of Anthropology had to be ethnographically accurate. In outlining the Museum's policy on suitable subjects for filming, Goddard encouraged McCormick to procure as many films of Indian industries as

ethnographic film between relatively 'raw' fieldwork footage for an audience of anthropologists, and films that are more obviously constructed for general consumption. Goddard's sensitivity to these differences is remarkable, evidence of a sophisticated grasp of some of the underlying principles of contemporary issues in ethnographic filmmaking. However, it is worth pointing out that McCormick's (and possibly Goddard's) concern about ethnographic truthfulness may have waned over the following months of the expedition, so that by September 1912 McCormick had few qualms admitting to Goddard that as a result of the difficulties he encountered both in trying to procure permission to film the Hopi Snake Dance and cope with the lighting conditions (Snake Dances traditionally took place late in the day), he was now 'ready to shoot the first Snake Dance that show[ed] its head'.[25]

The surviving footage from McCormick's 1912 expedition is an eight minute fragment called *Snake Dance of the Ninth Day* which McCormick filmed at Shipaulovi, Arizona in September 1912 (Fig. 4). The opening intertitle informs us that the dance we are about to see was substituted for the planned dance because of 'the meddling of a Hopi from another village'; consequently, 'the consent of the Snake Priest was withdrawn and the last dance was not secured'.[26] Writing about his experiences of shooting the film, McCormick pointed out that 'the Snake Dance has always been hard to get on account of the lateness of the hour. At Shipaulovi I took the last pictures at 6.45 pm'.[27] Compounding such technical problems were the challenges of obtaining permission to film sacred dances. Tribesmen and women were routinely paid to perform dances for visitors, although on several occasions the offer of money was insufficient compensation for what was considered the sacrilege of performing the dance in front of the camera. For example, McCormick mentioned offering Hopi women $10 for a Butterfly dance, but complained that 'the girls would not dance so we gave up the idea'.[28]

Fig. 4. *Production still of Hopi Snake Dance photographed by Howard McCormick in 1912. During this part of the ceremony, the priests carry snakes in their mouths.* [Courtesy Department of Library Services, American Museum of Natural History.]

he did of Indian ceremonies, because, as Goddard put it: 'I really care as much for the industrial ones as I do for the ceremonies, since other people are inclined to take ceremonies and the films are sure to be in existence somewhere'.[24] However, recognising the popular appeal of ceremonial dances for general Museum audiences, Goddard conceded that 'the ceremonials will be the proper thing for lectures', thereby anticipating the perennial (if contested) distinction made in

Another challenge facing McCormick concerned the limited amount of film stock to which he had access; the Museum had very little money available for the purchase of film

1895

stock – 500 feet cost about $25 in 1912 – and McCormick spent a great deal of time pleading for more film in his correspondence with the Museum. McCormick routinely shot time-consuming native crafts such as blanket weaving or plaque making in 100-foot rolls and complained to Goddard that he found it 'impossible to get the various phases of the dances in less than 50 or 100 feet'.[29] In a subsequent letter, though, McCormick reassured Goddard that with the experience he had now acquired, he thought he could 'take any dance out here with about 200 feet and get the various incidents'.[30] Goddard's lack of appreciation of how much film would be required to shoot a specific event – McCormick had constantly to justify the need for more film stock – indicates his scant technical understanding of the exigencies of shooting film in the field at this stage in the project, although Goddard's appreciation of the practical challenges of field cinematography was undoubtedly deepened when Goddard himself joined McCormick in the Southwest to shoot film of members of the Apache tribe in 1914.

Filming the Apache: Goddard's 1914 ethnographic films

Equipped with an Ensign daylight loading camera and three-inch lens, a panning and tilting tripod, a leather carrying case, six 25-foot rolls and nine 100-foot rolls of Ensign film, Goddard and McCormick set off for Arizona in July of 1914.[31] Goddard's first-hand experience with the challenges facing the ethnographic filmmaker are suggested in his description of one of the earliest films he shot of an Apache woman making a basket; according to Goddard: 'I used 25 feet first and didn't get all I wanted so I put in 100 feet the next time. I hope I didn't cut her head off. I developed a little piece which came out rather poorly'.[32] Goddard was keen to receive feedback on some of the early footage he shipped to the Museum and suggested to his secretary that either Museum taxidermist Carl Akeley, curator George Sherwood, or 'anyone who knows about films' should assess the quality of the footage and offer advice on how it could be improved.[33] His secretary reported to Goddard that Akeley had found the films

'somewhat blurred and lacked "snap" ' and had wondered whether it was 'because of an error in exposure or because of poor developing'.[34]

Perhaps as a result of Goddard's early unsatisfactory attempts to shoot the large spontaneous movements of dancers, he devoted more time to shooting Indian industries such as 'putting sinew on a bow, feathers on an arrow and making and attaching a flint arrow head' and food preparation (chucking and grinding corn) than ceremonial dances, since he felt that it would 'probably be impossible to get dances'.[35] Goddard's pessimism about being able to film dances was based upon both the logistical difficulty of filming unpredictable movement and the problem of gaining access to ceremonies that were restricted to outsiders.[36] The complex interpersonal transactions involved in filming Native American cultural practices was commented upon at some length by Goddard following his attendance at a ceremony involving an adolescent girl that took place over several days in late August 1914. Writing to his secretary, Goddard expressed disappointment at being unable to film the ceremony, but admitted it would have 'produced a panic, probably, and ruined the ceremony'.[37] Deeply affected by the aura of the live event, Goddard settled for a description of the adolescent social dancing; he wrote his secretary that:

> It was really very interesting and beautiful and supplied the feeling and vividness one never really gets from descriptions. I wished many times you could have seen it for it would have repaid you for many weary years spent on the uninteresting side of ethnology.[38]

If, for Goddard, cinema could capture the affect and intensity of the ethnological encounter otherwise lost in the process of translating ethnographic data into written text, it was precisely these qualities which motivated the efforts of AMNH President Osborn to subjugate the aesthetic to the scientific at the Museum; the emotional responses of spectators to exhibits and illustrations could never overwhelm the intended intellectual lesson. Goddard's reference to the 'uninteresting side of ethnology' can also be viewed in the light of the contemporaneous profes-

1895

sional debates between the curatorial and fieldwork responsibilities of the anthropologist. Goddard was unquestionably in favour of the latter, arguing that the 'true subject of ethnology is made up of the habitual movements and activities of a people', data recoverable only through intensive fieldwork observation.[39]

Despite the problems and frustrations encountered in the field, Goddard stated his belief in the ethnographic value of moving pictures in an *American Museum Journal* article written shortly after his return from Arizona:

> The moving-picture camera furnishes an excellent method of making a permanent record of the movements of one or, if properly localised, of several people. This record can be scrutinised in detail for as long a time as is desired and can be viewed repeatedly. It records many things which otherwise would not be made objective, such as the characteristic nervous coordinations and movements of different people.[40]

For Goddard, the camera's mechanical eye could open up a world of ocular phenomena otherwise closed to the unaided senses and, through the unique facility of repeatability, offer the ethnographer access to minute details only detectable upon repeated viewings; as Goddard pointed out: 'When several individuals are engaged in the same undertaking, it becomes impossible for a single observer to follow the movements of each worker'. Goddard criticised written methods of ethnographic data collection, arguing that traditional systems of observing and inscribing native culture ended up '*reducing* such observations to writing'.[41] Goddard suggested that, unlike an observer taking notes of an industrial process such as the making of a flint arrowhead, a moving picture camera could 'observe and record every significant movement involved in the work of a single individual' and, in the case of several individuals performing the same activity, could perform what no single observer could; namely, through a wider shot, capture the entire scene.[42]

Furthermore, while Goddard advised readers

that 'great pains must be taken not to arouse self-consciousness in the subjects being photographed', he nevertheless conceded that a certain amount of 'unavoidable self-consciousness' on the part of the ethnographic subject was unavoidable. This recognition of the inevitable intersubjectivity of the visual anthropologist's encounter with native informant is perhaps the most strikingly contemporary quality of Goddard's text; as an implicit rejection of nineteenth-century claims for the ability of the camera to collect ethnographic data 'uncontaminated' by the subjectivity of the anthropologist, Goddard's essay on ethnographic film demonstrates remarkable sensitivity to the contingencies attending the confrontation between Western image-maker and native peoples.

Given the limited discussion among anthropologists of the early moving picture camera's potential as an ethnographic recording device, Goddard's writing on early ethnographic film is an important record of one of the earliest published articles on ethnographic cinema in the United States. In light of Goddard's not-altogether favourable first impression of using a camera in the field (at several points in his fieldwork letters he refers to the heat of the Southwest buckling the metal lining of the meter, the image being fogged around the edges, and 'considerable' camera vibration), his views are significant because, in spite of his technical inexperience, he was genuinely interested in the possibilities of an ethnographic cinema that would contribute to an understanding of cultural patterning. Four years before his death in 1928, Goddard set out once again to the Southwest, this time to shoot film among the Hopi and Navajo peoples. While these films survive, there is no evidence of any published discussion of them and Goddard's own letters to the Museum from the field relate mainly to practical matters of filmmaking. Thus it is Goddard's 1915 article on 'Motion Picture Records of Indians' which best represents his philosophical and epistemological positions on the role of the motion picture camera within anthropology.

The field correspondence of Pliny Earl Goddard and Howard McCormick and the extant ethnographic footage from McCormick's 1912 expedition are compelling records of the challenges facing scientists and camera operators working with indigenous peoples on reservations. Moreover, Goddard's attempts to negotiate the multifarious factors involved in shooting film in a remote and at times inhospitable environment is testimony to an early instance of ethnographic filmmaking that has been largely overlooked in traditional histories of the genre.[43] However, despite the fact that these films constitute some of the earliest American examples of what may be called ethnographic film, within the context of the American Museum of Natural History the films themselves were largely undifferentiated from other films made by non-anthropologists discussed in this essay. While it is difficult to reconstruct the Museum's precise use of McCormick's film footage from the surviving documentation, Goddard demonstrated few reservations about interpolating the field footage into a range of educational lecture formats.[44] It is also clear that Goddard, as one of the preeminent anthropological authorities on the American Southwest, wished to assume total responsibility for the film's public presentations, although McCormick's role as camera operator was acknowledged in some screenings. It was perhaps inevitable that it was Goddard (the professional anthropologist), rather than McCormick (the artist and cameraman), who typically introduced the films, given the Museum's perennial concern that science not be 'swallowed up' by the artifice and illusion of the moving image. Moreover, the Museum had little problem exhibiting both actuality footage of Native Americans and fictional films featuring Indian characters, albeit in separate lecture-screenings; for example, Frank Moore's fictional *Hiawatha* was screened at the Museum within a month of a Public School's Teacher's special screening of McCormick's Hopi footage. It would seem, then, that the Museum integrated the fieldwork footage of Goddard and McCormick seamlessly into the institution's public screening programme. It would also seem that these films were not used in any special way within the Anthropology Department, and there is no evidence of Goddard analysing his fieldwork footage in the manner outlined in his 1915 article. A clue to the Museum's apparent indifference to the provenance of early ethnographic film lies in the faith of Museum officials in the decisive role of the contextualising remarks of the scientific lecturer to produce the intended meanings for audiences. The scientific credibility of the invited speaker and the physical setting of the Museum itself, with its architecture of scientific reverance and civic uplift, served to neutralise the amateur and/or commercial production contexts of some of the ethnographic films exhibited at the AMNH. In other words, for the Museum to differentiate between the scientific and non-scientific production contexts of the films it exhibited would have drawn undesired attention to the sometimes questionable educational value of films that were, after all, simultaneously available to audiences in commercial theatres. The debates accompanying the emergence of film at institutions such as the American Museum of Natural History therefore serve as evidence of the importance of the context of reception in determining audience meaning in early cinema. These debates can also be useful to historians as one indicator of the complex institutional and professional attitudes towards early ethnographic film, and provide us with a useful vantage point from which to survey the gradual acceptance of ethnographic film as a medium of anthropological knowledge within twentieth century anthropology.

Acknowledgements: My thanks to Belinda Kaye, Archivist in the Department of Anthropology at the AMNH for making available material on Goddard; Tom Baione, Senior Special Collections Librarian, Department of Library Services, AMNH for his assistance with the illustrations; and Antonia Lant and William Boddy for comments on earlier drafts. This essay forms part of a larger investigation into the origins of ethnographic film from the silent film period.

1895

Notes

1. Review of *Sardanapalus* in *Lloyds Weekly Newspaper* (n.d.) cited in Inge Krengel-Strudthoff, 'Archäologie auf der Bühne – das wiedererstandene Ninive: Charles Keans Ausstattung zu *Sardana-palus* von Lord Byron', *Kleine Schriften der Gesellschaft für Theatergeschichte* 31 (1981): 19, in Frederick N. Boherer, 'The Times and Spaces of History: Representation, Assyria, and the British Museum', in Daniel J. Sherman and Irit Rogoff (eds), *Museum Culture: Histories, Discourses, Spectacles* (Minneapolis: University of Minnesota Press, 1994), 215.

2. As a genre of filmmaking and mainstay of visual anthropology, ethnographic film did not attain widespread currency until after the Second World War. There is to this day, much theoretical debate over the precise definition of the term. I am using it in this essay to describe a group of films whose larger ideological premises are, broadly speaking, ethnographic; in other words, films featuring indigenous peoples and/or their cultural practices.

3. For an overview of Goddard's contributions to the field of anthropology, see the obituary/tribute in the AMNH journal *Natural History*, vol. 28, no. 4 (1928): 441–442. Sadly, though not surprisingly, there is no mention of Goddard's experiences using a moving picture camera to record ethnographic material among the Apaches in 1914 and among the Hopi and Zuni in 1924–25.

4. Lisa Cartwright, *Screening the Body: Tracing Medicine's Visual Culture* (Minneapolis: University of Minnesota Press, 1994), 20. For more on the history of photography and anthropology, see Elizabeth Edwards (ed.) *Anthropology and Photography: 1860–1920* (New Haven: Yale University Press, 1992) and Melissa Banta and Curtis M. Hinsley, *From Site to Sight: Anthropology, Photography, and the Power of Imagery* (Cambridge, MA: Peabody Museum Press, 1986).

5. For a detailed analysis of Regnault's chronophotography, see Fatimah Tobing Rony, *The Third Eye: Race, Cinema, and Ethnographic Spectacle* (Durham: Duke University Press, 1996): 21–73.

6. The usefulness of the phonograph as an ethnographic recording device was discussed by J. Walter Fewkes in an 1890 article in *Science*; according to Fewkes: 'The use of the phonograph among the Passamaquoddies has convinced me that the main characteristics of their language can be recorded and permanently preserved, either for study or demonstration, with this instrument. ... In the quiet of his study [the anthropologist] can hear the song repeated over and over again as often as he wishes, and can, so to speak, analyse it, and in that way separate the constituent sounds'. What Fewkes saw in the phonograph was its unique capacity to replay the exact sounds the anthropologist had heard in the field with the same tempo and emotion as the original utterance, something that a transcription of the song or sentence could never achieve. J. Walter Fewkes, 'On the Use of the Phonograph in the Study of the Languages of American Indians', *Science*, vol. XV, no. 378 (2 May 1890): 267–268.

7. Letter to Hugh Smith from Frederick A. Lucas, 1 December 1913 in file #1906–20, Central Archives, Department of Library Services, AMNH, hereafter cited as CA-AMNH.

8. While the precise identification of ethnographic subject matter is complicated by the fact that few of these films are extant, and by the common practice of using stock footage obtained from commercial rental agencies as opposed to titled films to illustrate lectures and talks, the following examples of lecture titles allude to or indicate the presence of native peoples in the films: 'Travels in Europe and the Far East' (Roy Chapman Andrews, 1911); 'Travels in South America' (L. Hussakof, 1911); 'Jungle Scenes in Africa, India, and Borneo' (Cherry Kearton, 1913); 'The Indians of the Southwest: Their Daily Lives and Ceremonies' (Pliny Goddard, 1913); 'Africa, Egypt, Algiers, Interior, South Africa' (Dr. Fisher, 1913); 'The Indians of New York State' (Alanson Skinner, 1913); 'Among the Wild Tribes of the Philippine Islands' (Dean C. Worcester, 1914); 'Mexico and Her People' (Frederick Monson, 1914); and 'Blackfoot Indian Life' (E.M. Deming, 1915).

9. Letter to Frank E. Kleinschmidt from President Osborn, 1 April 1912 in box #903 (Spring Course, 1912), CA-AMNH.

10. Anonymous review in the *Philadelphia Telegraph* (21 May 1912), n/p in Frank E. Kleinschmidt clipping file, Billy Rose Theater Collection, New York Public Library Lincoln Center.

11. Letter to James Barnes from George Sherwood, 27 September 1915 in box #903 (1914–24), CA-AMNH.

12. Nancy Leys Stepan, 'Race and Gender: The Role of Analogy in Science', *Isis* 77 (1986): 261.

13. J. Hillis Miller, *Illustration* (London: Reaktion Books, 1992): 61–62; 102.

14. Letter to Sherwood from President Osborn, 27 December 1918 in box #903 (1914–24), CA-AMNH.

15. Letter to Sherwood from President Osborn, 16 January 1920 in box #903 (1914–24), CA-AMNH.

16. Robert Stuart Pigott was hired to read the poem. Pigott's recollection of reciting the poem was not entirely favourable. Responding to an invitation from Sherwood to read the poem again in a repeat screening of the film (for a fee of $25 and travel expenses) Pigott replied: 'When I gave the reading the first time I was at the disadvantage of using an unedited set of films and no rehearsal depending almost entirely upon my sense of time to keep up with the strange operator. Fortunately, he, or rather they, knew the business and even Mr. Moore said we synchronised perfectly, but the strain on me was more than I care to undergo except in an emergency', letter to Sherwood from Pigott, 8 October 1914, in box #903 (1914–24), CA-AMNH.

17. Items lent to Moore by Anthropology curator Clark Wissler in September 1912 included birch bark vessels and dishes, wooden utensils, decorated mats, wooden flutes, cotton shirts, woven bags, skin bags, beaded girdles, leggings, quivers, moccasins, horse hair headdresses, stone spear points, and arrow points.

18. Description in 'Stories for Children's Members' brochure (21 November 1914), CA-AMNH.

19. For an analysis of how discourses of authenticity determined the construction and reception of films representing Native Americans from the early film period, see Alison Griffiths, 'Science and Spectacle: Native American Representation in Early Cinema', in S. Elizabeth Bird (ed), *Dressing in Feathers: The Construction of the Indian in American Popular Culture* (Boulder: Westview, 1996): 79–95.

20. McCormick traveled to the Southwest in the late summer of 1912 to 'make sketches and obtain other data for the proposed Pueblo [human life] group' at the Museum; along with sculptor Mahonri Young, who was instructed to make no fewer than seven casts of Hopis for the human life group, McCormick was commissioned to make drawings and to supervise the life group's construction on his return to the Museum in the autumn. Before leaving for the Southwest, Goddard wrote McCormick inviting him to shoot film of Native Americans during a three month expedition: 'If you care to provide films for taking moving pictures in the Southwest, we shall be glad to have ... negatives of any of the dances or other ceremonies of the Hopi and also of such industrial processes as the making of baskets, pots, and blankets'. Goddard also made it clear that the Museum had no funds to purchase film stock, but would reimburse McCormick for negative and developing costs, providing McCormick shot no more than 2,000 feet and incurred costs of less than $25. McCormick would also be given a copy of the films he shot. He was given a $500 advance by the Museum and $250 from the Director's fund for additional expenses. Letter to McCormick from Clark Wissler, 15 June 1912; letter from Frederick Lucas to Wissler, 13 June 1912; and letter from Goddard to McCormick, 22 July 1912 all in file #566. Department of Anthropology, AMNH, hereafter cited as DA-AMNH.

21. Letter to Goddard from McCormick, 26 August 1912 in file #566, DA-AMNH.

22. For more on the BAE, see Curtis M. Hinsley, *The Smithsonian and the American Indian: Making a Moral Anthropology in Victorian America* (Washington: Smithsonian Institution Press, 1981), 145–147, 274–285.

23. Howard McCormick, 'The Artist's Southwest', *American Museum Journal*, vol. XIII, no. 3 (March 1913): 125. McCormick's lyrical, nostalgic tone permeates the article: 'These people adjusted so perfectly to their surroundings, furnish for the artist the human interest for his pictures. In their daily life and many ceremonies they reflect the colors of skies, the shapes of the clouds and mesas and fill both with the innumerable supernatural logic': 124–125.

24. Letter to McCormick from Goddard, 2 September 1912 in file #111, DA-AMNH.

25. Letter to Goddard from McCormick, 14 September 1912, in file #566, DA-AMNH.

26. Intertitle that appears in *Hopi Indians of the Southwest* McCormick compilation film (1912–25), housed in Special Collections, Department of Library Services at the AMNH.

27. Letter to Goddard from McCormick, 8 September 1912 in file #566, DA-AMNH.

28. Letter to Goddard from McCormick, 6 September 1912 in file #566, DA-AMNH. During his solo trip to Kean's Canyon, Arizona to shoot moving pictures in the autumn of 1914, McCormick mentioned being prepared to pay $30 for a daylight ceremony of a Yabichai dance which a Mr. Hubbell was hoping to arrange for him. Unfortunately, when McCormick wrote Goddard for permission to pay this amount, Goddard replied that he didn't think the Museum had that kind of money to spend on dances. Letter to McCormick from Goddard, 6 October 1914 in file #566, DA-AMNH.

1895

29. Letter to McCormick from Goddard, 8 September 1912, in file #566, DA-AMNH.

30. In a letter to Goddard, 8 September 1912, McCormick listed the following subjects and film lengths: Hautsella Snake Dance (600 feet); Shipaulovi Snake Dance (500 feet); Basket Weaving at Oraiba (100 feet); Basket Weaving at Mishougouri (100 feet); Navajo Rug Maker (100 feet); Flute Ceremony (400 feet), a total of 1900 out of 2000 feet of film endorsed by the Museum. In file #566, DA-AMNH. None of Goddard's films shot during the 1914 expedition have survived.

31. Goddard rarely mentioned McCormick in his correspondence with Anthropology Department secretary Bella Weitzner, other than occasional references to McCormick's painting studies for Museum habitat groups. When McCormick left for Kean's Canyon, Arizona in September of 1914, he took the moving picture camera with him. Letter to Clark Wissler from Goddard, 13 September 1914 in file #111, DA-AMNH.

32. Letter to Weitzner from Goddard, 14 August 1914, in file #111, DA-AMNH.

33. *Ibid.*

34. Letter to Goddard from Weitzner, 2 September 1914, in file #111, DA-AMNH.

35. Letters to Weitzner from Goddard, 20 and 24 August 1914, in file #111, DA-AMNH.

36. Anthropologists' frustration at having imperfect control over the moving picture apparatus and the profilmic event was noted as early as 1901, when Walter Baldwin Spencer described using a Warwick cinematograph in his 1901 expedition to Central Australia: 'The chief difficulty was that the performers every now and then ran off the ground into the surrounding shrub, returning at uncertain intervals of time, so that now and again, in the expectation of their reappearing, and fearful of missing anything of importance, I ground on and on, securing a record of a good deal of monotonous scenery but very little ceremony', in Walter Baldwin Spencer, *Wanderings in Wild Australia* (London: Macmillan & Co., 1928), 360. For an analysis of Spencer's filmmaking and Alfred Cort Haddon's 1898 expedition to the Torres Straits in which he filmed Mer Islanders and Australian Aborigines, see Alison Griffiths, 'Knowledge and Visuality in Turn of the Century Anthropology: The Early Ethnographic Cinema of Alfred Cort Haddon and Walter Baldwin Spencer', *Visual Anthropology Review*, vol. 12, no. 2 (Fall/Winter 1996/1997): 18–43.

37. Letter to Weitzner from Goddard, 29 August 1914, in file #111, DA-AMNH.

38. *Ibid.*

39. Goddard alludes to this debate in the opening paragraph of his *Museum Journal* article entitled 'Motion Picture Records of Indians: Films that Show the Common Industries of the Apache', vol. V, no. 4 (April 1915): 185.

40. *Ibid.*

41. *Ibid.* Emphasis added.

42. *Ibid.* Goddard also touches upon the contentious issue of ethnographic reconstruction when events, performances or craft-making are performed especially for the camera; Goddard felt that 'in practice it is necessary to have these duties undertaken for the special purpose of photographing them', p. 186.

43. Museum records suggest that Goddard's footage was awaited with excited anticipation by Museum officials such as George Sherwood and Clark Wissler who repeatedly inquired as to when the moving pictures would be ready (letter to McCormick from Goddard, 2 September 1912 in file #566, DA-AMNH).

44. Several special events were hosted at the Museum in the spring of 1913; for example, McCormick's films were exhibited in a special event that took place in February entitled 'The Indians of the Southwest: Their Daily Lives and Ceremonies', while at a meeting of the Monday Club at the Museum in May, two films, 'Ceremonies of the Hopi Indians' and 'Snake Dance of the Hopi Indians' were shown before Goddard's lecture on Southwest native culture.

1895

James Williamson's 'Composed Picture': *Attack on a China Mission – Bluejackets to the Rescue* (1900)

Frank Gray

Curator, South East Film & Video Archive, University of Brighton, 10–11 Pavilion Parade, Brighton, BN2 1RA, UK

THIS STUDY OF JAMES WILLIAMSON's film of 1900, *Attack on a China Mission – Bluejackets to the Rescue*, places it within his development as a filmmaker and considers its political and commercial significance. A multi-shot film, it was not only Williamson's most ambitious work to date but also one of the most sophisticated 'edited' films of its time. It reveals his interest in creating a rescue narrative through the construction of individual shots of dramatic action and unifying them into a plausible whole. Williamson's film demands a contextual reading as the film was inspired by the Boxer Rebellion. This was an international episode which was used by the dominant powers of Europe to define its moral, spiritual and economic superiority in the world.

James Williamson, the Hove Chemist, magic lanternist, photographer and X-ray photo-grapher, began to make animated photographs in 1897. His first catalogue of 1899 listed 60 films, each usually from 60 to 75 feet in length. They were all single shots except for a few notable exceptions – his multi-shot actualities. These were compilation films which consisted of either a number of shots on the same film (an early example of in-camera editing) or separate single shot films, usually of standard length, which could be 'joined' to create what his catalogue called a 'long film'.[1] The subjects were either related views of a single activity or views of different activities taken at the same location. Williamson's compiled 'actualities' did not depict sequential action and no attempt was made to harmonise camera position and framing. They are examples of what Gunning has called the 'anthology format'.[2] The best surviving exemplar of Williamson's work of this type is *Bank Holiday at the Dyke, Brighton* of

1899. It consists of three separate shots, respectively swing boats, merry-go-round and cycle railway. Williamson suggested it could be joined to the 40-foot film of another attraction at the Dyke – *Switchback Railway*.

Williamson's conception of editing in 1899 was still very rudimentary, unlike that of his contemporaries. Robert Paul had produced a 'joiner' as early as 1896 with his Derby films, and his 1898 catalogue sold 'instantaneous film cement' for the purpose of editing both related films together and making a complete programme. By 1899, Paul's trick films were becoming very adventurous and he was beginning to explore multi-shot narratives. Williamson would have known of this work as well as examples of early multi-shot French and American films, and Charles Goodwin Norton's 'edited' actualities of 1898–99. The latter had been processed by G.A. Smith at his 'film factory' in Hove, a site only minutes from Williamson's studio at 55 Western Road, Hove. Williamson would not, however, produce his first edited multi-shot narrative film – *Attack on a China Mission* – until the next year. This four shot film of 230 feet was made in the autumn of 1900 (some sources say November), and came after a summer of inspired filmmaking by Smith, Williamson's friend and counterpart. Smith's films of 1900 – *As Seen Through a Telescope* (3 shots), *Grandma's Reading Glass* (c. 9 shots), *The House That Jack Built* (2 shots) and *Let Me Dream Again* (2 shots) – were radical through their creation of subjective and objective point-of-view shots, dream-time, the employment of reversing and the interpolative use of close-ups. These works, as well as his three shot *The Kiss in the Tunnel* of 1899, were the products of what we can call Smith's laboratory phase. It is in the context of this exciting development of English film form that Williamson conceived and executed *Attack on a China Mission*. Its appearance marks his move from the production of 'non-continuous' to 'continuous' film narratives.

The film was known under two titles in 1901 and 1902. Williamson's advertisement for the film, as found on page x of the January 1901 issue of the *Magic Lantern Journal and Photographic Enlarger*, carried the title, *Attack on a Chinese Mission Station. Bluejackets to the*

Rescue. However in Williamson's Catalogue of September 1902 we find the variant, *Attack on a China Mission. Bluejackets to the Rescue*. [For the convenience of this history, I use the first part of the second title – *Attack on a China Mission*.] Two versions of the films have survived and they are both incomplete. Print number 603653 in the British Film Institute's National Film and Television Archive is the best example at 133 feet.[3] By following the 1902 Williamson catalogue description, it's clear that this print possesses virtually all of shots 2 and 3 but only the last section of shot 1 and the beginning of shot 4 remain. Around 100 feet are missing.

The production details are scant but Florence Williamson's notes, written in the early 1960s, provide us with the basic information.[4] For the location, Williamson had 'rented a derelict house with a large garden, called Ivy Lodge'. This Hove Victorian villa, set within a walled garden, was very suitable for his Boxer drama. Contemporary reports had described the British Legation in Peking as 'a garden of some ten acres, partly occupied by buildings, and surrounded with a high wall of sun-dried clay'.[5] The dense foliage around 'Ivy Lodge' enabled Williamson to keep the everyday life of Hove out of his shots, thereby creating a rough illusion of a Chinese scene. We are to imagine that his Mission Station is an island of European-ness surrounded by the unseen and exotic landscape of China. Florence was cast by her father as the 'young girl'. The 'Missionary' was performed by Ernest Lepard, Manager of the Brighton Alhambra Opera House and Music Hall. This theatre, which had opened in 1888, was on Brighton's seafront in the proximity of the two piers and the largest hotels. It had incorporated animated pictures into its programmes from 1897. A Mr. James played the mounted officer leading the Bluejackets. He was associated with Dupont's Riding School in Hove. It is likely that the Bluejackets were, as Florence claimed, an acrobatic team from the Alhambra as well as members of both the Hove Coast Guard and the Royal Naval Volunteer Reserve. The Hove Coast Guard Station and the Naval School were only a few hundred metres from Ivy Lodge and probably provided the uniforms. The acrobats were required to stage the 'daring' rescue from the balcony in shot 4. Williamson's Boxers were probably also connected to the Alhambra. An act called the 'Six Brothers Luck' had performed at the theatre in early October.

In her notes, Florence Williamson wrote that the film had been *rehearsed*. All of his previous one shot, 'one-minute comedies' had been rehearsed, out of necessity, in order to fit within the temporal and structural constraints, and to ensure that the joke was created. His Boxer film was conceived on a much bigger scale. The cast numbered around 29 (the household: 4, the Boxers: 9, the Bluejackets: 16). Williamson needed to have a clear understanding of the action in relation to the three camera set-ups and be able to convey his dramatic vision to his cast. His Boxer story is structurally very simple.

> Shot 1: Chinese Boxers break into the grounds of the Mission Station.

> Shot 2: The Missionary and his household, surprised by the Boxer attack, begin to take defensive action. He is killed instantly.

> Shot 3: Almost simultaneously, the British Bluejackets arrive at the Station and fire volleys of shots at the intruders.

> Shot 4: The Boxers are overwhelmed and taken prisoner and the Station is saved [Fig. 1].

The film is a chronological arrangement of the four shots with an adequately defined sense of simultaneity and consecutive action occurring across the three edit points (shots 1/2, 2/3, 3/4). We can interpret the use of shot 3 as an early attempt at cross-cutting, interpolated between shots 2 and 4 which were both filmed from the same position. They are linked by the action of the Missionary's wife waving from the balcony to the the approaching Bluejackets. This starts in Shot 2, and is completed at the start of shot 4. In shot 2, she looks to her right which positions the outer gate of the Station through which the Boxers have entered and the Bluejackets will enter. Shot 3, the view of the outer gate from about 20 feet within the grounds, is an approximate reverse angle of shot 1, and the viewer is led to imagine that this position is in the wife's

line of vision from the balcony to the gate. All four shots possess camera positions which view the action at some distance. However, to create a real sense of dramatic urgency for the viewer, Williamson organised shots 3 and 4 in such a way that the action started from the middle distance and proceeded towards the camera and continued out of the picture plane. In shot 3, the sailors form their ranks and fire at the camera, making clear that the Mission and the siege is directly in front of them. After a volley, each rank breaks and runs towards the camera/viewer. In shot 4, the mounted officer rescues the young lady, and carries her towards and past the camera, through the gate which we imagine is behind this viewpoint. Williamson, in both instances, is creating a truly filmic sense of narrative space by placing the camera/viewer in the garden at the moment of this imagined scene. He is introducing the strange, vicarious pleasure of being part of a virtual space. By inventing this garden, Williamson broke with that comfortable, 'theatrical' viewing position which viewed all action from the middle of the stalls.

We can read the four shots as an edited sequence without ellipsis. It can be interpreted as a real-time drama of continuous action, especially in performance when it was accompanied by sympathetic music and a lecturer's narration. This 'live' interpretation would en-

Fig. 1. *Frame enlargement, shot 4,* Attack on a China Mission – Blue- jackets to the Rescue, *James Williamson, 1900. [Courtesy of BFI Stills, Posters and Designs.]*

sure that an audience made sense of the structure, smoothed over the weaknesses of some of the shot transitions, and became emotionally involved and visually intrigued. *Attack on a China Mission* was a new model for film realism as it was founded on naturalistic acting, a real location, and a linear structure.

Williamson's conception of the film's narrative structure conforms very neatly with Todorov's understanding of a common master narrative. This begins with a stable situation (an initial equilibrium: the white Missionary and his household, content and secure in their mission to bring enlightenment to China), then disequilibrium (that force, as depicted by the Boxers, which threatens the original state of affairs) and finally, the reinstatement of equilibrium (the arrival of the Bluejackets, and their success in overcoming the intruders to bring peace and order to the household). In Williamson's drama, the original state cannot be restored since the Missionary has been killed, and the survivors face the trauma of experience. Although a new order is established, it is one which is coextensive with the values that informed the original state of equilibrium. The film, thus, is a rescue narrative with the 'white', Christian family being saved from their persecutors, the Chinese 'Other'. As in fairy tales, the 'young lady', as 'Princess', is literally snatched from danger by an Officer on horseback, the 'Prince'. Williamson's film, with its equilibrium-disequilibrium-equilibrium structure, exemplifies in simplified form what David Bordwell has called the 'canonic story format'.[6]

The most complete version of the film [print no. 603653] concludes with the first part of shot 4 which depicts the arrival of the Bluejackets in the garden. The fact that the film ends at this point can give the (false) impression that Williamson either chose an inconclusive resolution, or that he sought to create an enigmatic ending which left no side victorious. Neither conclusion is correct as the catalogue reveals. Williamson was very clear about the film's ending and its purpose.

The events in China in 1900 informed the making of the film and its reception. Williamson shot *Attack on a China Mission* at the end of a year in which the Boxer Rebellion had overshadowed the on-going Boer War to become the most important international incident of the year. As a text, the film inscribed a discourse which expressed the dominant Western understanding of China and the conflict constructed through newspapers, photographs, illustrations, lantern slides and films.

The Times, in its review of 1900, wrote with great gravity about the 'China Crisis' which had unfolded that year. Speaking from its position as the voice of the British establishment, *The Times* represented the conflict between the Boxers and the 'Powers' as a symbolic and primary conflict between the West and the East:

> ... it is possible that future historians may regard the events which have taken place in China ... as the most important events of the year 1900. Never before have East and West, barbarism and civilisation, the forces of reactionary superstition and the forces of modern enlightenment, been brought into such sharp, sudden, and violent collision. Never before, since civilised States came into existence, has a powerful Empire so openly defied the first principle of international intercourse as to levy war upon the foreign Ministers accredited to it, and to attempt their destruction by arms, by fire, and by starvation. Yet this is what the Chinese Government has done with the immediate result that the Chinese capital has been taken by the joint forces of the civilised Powers, and is now being held by them until the Ministers have obtained such a reparation as shall convince the most ignorant of the Chinese that the hated foreigner has the power and the will to make himself respected.[7]

The success of the Powers (Britain, Germany, Austria, America, France, Italy, Japan and Russia) in capturing Peking and subjugating the Boxers marked the return to order and the 'triumph' of the West. The China narrative conformed to the Todorov tripartite model, and offered Williamson, in the autumn of 1900, a template for the structure of his film.

1. Equilibrium – The narrative commences with the 'benevolent' Powers in China in the late nineteenth century ex-

erting their right to use the country for their own purposes, and encouraging the 'civilising' of the Chinese through their conversion to Christianity;

2. Disequilibrium – The rise of the Boxers, the Chinese republicans, first threatens the Imperial project, and then violently rejects it through acts of terror and war on the legations in Peking, the primary symbol of foreign domination. The latter event occurs in the period from June to August 1900;

3. Equilibrium – The Return to Order. This stage sees the Powers using their armed forces to reclaim their authority in China by liberating the legations in August, and occupying the country.

The narrative of the Boxer Rebellion provided Williamson with a 'closed' text which functioned to present a state of crisis and siege – the attack on the mission and the death of the Missionary – with the subsequent relief provided by the arrival of the Bluejackets and the rescue of the missionary's family and household. We can assume that the majority of the film's viewers would have expressed interest in and drawn comfort from this rescue narrative because of its unique dramatic energy, its prescient representation of the Boxer Rebellion, and its confidence in the West. The film operates as an abstraction of the actual attacks on the Christian communities by the Boxers throughout 1899 and 1900, and the siege and liberation of the legations in Peking from June to August 1900. *Attack on a China Mission*, made after the liberation of Peking, is a mythic and moral distillation, predicated on an understanding of history that resembles Todorov's master narrative model.

The illustrated London periodicals of 1900, with their special supplements and maps, provided an important visual analogue to *The Times*' text-only perspective of events in China, and would have been seen by Williamson and the viewers of his film. The *Black and White Budget* was one of a number of new periodicals which were exploiting the use of photography. Its China coverage began in June with articles covering the 'crisis', diplomatic and military news, and general stories on the characteristics of Chinese life, the latter

providing a stereotyped and racist depiction of the culture. The alleged dangers to 'civilised' society were always present in the *Black and White Budget*'s analysis. Library photographs and illustrations of imagined scenes accompanied the China stories up until the autumn, by which time actual photographs from China were printed. It is interesting to note that the periodical sold lantern slide versions of a sample of its illustrative material.

A significant example of an imagined scene appeared the *Black and White Budget* in early August (Fig. 2). It is an icon for the conflict, created from a contemporary report. Its accompanying caption reads, 'The massacre at Mukden. The Catholic mission at that place was burned, three sisters perished in the flames, and two bishops and two priests were atrociously murdered.'[8] This is a depiction of an attack on Christendom, and the justification for the *Black and White Budget* to be clear that, 'China must be Europeanised',[9] and that, 'if the Christian religion is to be preached successfully in China, the missionaries must be backed by the men they have eventually to fall back upon – Jack Tar and Thomas Atkins'.[10] The connection of this emblem of the 'crisis' to Williamson's film is obvious. The *Black and White Budget* concluded the year with a startling juxtaposition. On page 260, an image of modernity is offered – the leader of one of the Powers, the French President M. Loubet, in a motor-car. In sharp contrast, the drawing on the opposite page,

Fig. 2. *'The massacre at Mukden. The Catholic mission at that place was burned, three sisters perished in the flames, and two bishops and two priests were atrociously murdered.' [Black and White Budget, vol. III, no. 43, 4 (August 1900): 553.]*

1895

"When the dawn comes up like thunder,
Out o' China 'crost the Bay."—Kipling.

—*New York World.*

If Chinamen won't be good.
—*Cleveland Plain Dealer.*

can approach Williamson's film as an expression of this occidental-oriental dialectic.

The King, founded in 1899, was a large format illustrated weekly published by George Newnes, the company which had launched *The Strand* in 1891. With news of the 'massacre' in Peking, *The King* published a collection of cartoons in its edition of 21 July 1900 which conveyed the dominant view of the Powers. These images, taken from a number of sources, offered a succinct and emotive response to what it called 'one of the greatest horrors of modern times':

> 'When the dawn comes up like thunder,
> Out o' China 'crost the Bay – Kipling.'
> (Fig. 3)

China, with its sword dripping with blood, threatens the world. The 'yellow peril', as a result of the Peking 'massacre', has now become a frightening reality.[12]

> 'If Chinamen won't be good.'(Fig. 4)

If Chinamen, as the cartoon declares, have decided not to 'be good' to the West, China must be punished. 'China' stands on the book of 'Civilisation', from which pages have been torn and mutilated. For this desecration, a Chinaman's pig-tail, on which hangs his dream of self-government, is about to be cut by scissors held by 'The Powers'. Such a cut will also sever his sacred link to heaven and eternal life.[13]

> 'Awaiting the News' (Fig. 5)

Civilisation' anxiously stands outside the locked door of 'China', a door with hinges labelled 'superstition' and 'intolerance', and bolted with swords labelled 'anarchy' and 'murder'. Superstition, intolerance, anarchy and murder, these are the characteristics of the Asian foe. Blood seeps from under the door. To the right is a notice which reads, 'Death to all Foreigners', one of the Boxer slogans. The cartoon implies that Civilisation must act in order to end this barbarism. The 'foreigners', with their good and moral values, must break down the door and enter the evil house of China. But it also conveys the painful wait for the Allied troops to arrive in Peking: four weeks separated the announcement of the 'massacre' (14 July) from the relief of the Peking legations (14 August). This cartoon dates from the very start of the period.[14]

depicting the terror and barbarity still found in China, is entitled, 'The Recent Murder of Missionaries on the Upper Yang-Tze'.[11] We

'Retribution!' (Fig. 6)

This full-page cartoon was drawn by Harry Furniss for *The King*. China appears as the Dragon of 'Pekin' with the fangs of a snake, holding in its long-nailed hand a sword which is stabbing prey who are represented as young white women. This is a massacre of the innocents. Liberty, like some Wagnerian goddess, holds a torch which is lighting the way for the rescue party in the distance, a party composed of horrified European soldiers. John Bull is pictured on the right-hand side; 'Retribution' is her cry to the Westerners. Furniss, in his call to arms, makes clear reference to the iconography of 'George and the Dragon', identifying China as the evil monster that must be destroyed on the arrival of the Christian soldiers.[15]

Popular graphics like these cultivated an emotional and moral response to the conflict and helped to establish the climate in which *Attack on a China Mission* was produced and received. Williamson's film was only one of a small genre of China films produced in 1900. They were all informed by the China intertext, and provided exhibitors with a popular expression of the 'Crisis'. From the early summer, film producers in the United States and England produced imagined Chinese incidents. The American 'representations' came from at least two companies. The Lubin Company of Philadelphia exploited the Boxer Rebellion through a series which included *Beheading the Chinese Prisoner* and *Chinese Massacring Christians*. Using sets and models, the Edison Company issued its five shot interpretation of the *Bombardment of Taku Forts by the Allied Fleets*. The English Company, Mitchell and Kenyon, produced four China films in July, including the single shot, *Attack on a Mission Station*. This crude 86-foot film provided Williamson with a simple prototype. It depicts the missionary and his family, the subsequent attack by the Boxers, and the rescue of the family by the British Army. The Warwick Trading Company, the largest English production company, issued a Supplement no. 1 to its catalogue of September 1900 at the end of the year. The Supplement listed three films (nos. 7204, 7205, 7206) under the title, 'Representation of Chinese War Scenes at a Military Tournament'. They were de-

Fig. 5. *'Awaiting the News'*, New York Tribune. [The King, *vol. II, No. 29 (21 July 1900): VII.]*

Awaiting the News.   —*New York Tribu*

scribed as, 'only representations, photographed in France'. I believe that these 'arranged scenes' have not survived but no. 7204 is clearly another variation on the Mission theme. Entitled, *Chinese Attack on a Mission*, this single-shot film of 75 feet depicted the attack and murder of a Missionary by Boxers, and the arrival of the Allied troops. The making of Williamson's more sophisticated film was most likely undertaken between the release of these other two Mission films.

Williamson's immediate marketplace for *Attack on a China Mission* was Brighton, about one mile from his home. This seaside town was one of Britain's most important centres for popular spectacle. Throughout the autumn of 1900, four theatres regularly featured programmes with China material. For three weeks, from 29 October to 17 November, the Grand Concert Hall entertained 'Poole's Royal Myriorama'. This multi-media entertainment offered a 'magnificent series of tableaux, showing all important events in connection with THE BOER WAR ... THE CHINESE CRISIS, Striking view of Pekin, scene of the terrible massacre ... THE BATTLE OF WATERLOO, the entire battle from start to finish ...', and the 'EDISON-POOLE EVENTOGRAPH. The latest and best of all the animated picture machines'.[16] A Mr. William Stuart took the role of 'guide' through what was an entertainment shaped largely by current news stories. The 'American War Biograph' visited the

"THE KING'S" CARTOON.

RETRIBUTION !

Drawn by Harry Furniss.

Fig. 6.
'Retribution!',
Harry Furniss [The
King, vol. II, no. 29
(21 July 1900): 89.]

corporated the 'Edisonograph' as an 'act' into its music hall programme during the autumn. Florence Williamson believed that Williamson's China film was exhibited at the Alhambra, but I have not yet found any evidence for this screening.

The West Pier and its Pavilion was one of Brighton's most popular attractions. It had entertained almost one and a half million visitors in 1899. It was here that Gordon & Co. presented its show, 'Sons of the Empire', in November. Akin to West's 'Our Navy', it illustrated 'the lives of our soldiers and sailors ashore and afloat' through lantern slides and films. The 'Living scenes from AFRICA, CHINA, & c.' were 'fully described by Mr. T. C. Hepworth'.[18] A review of this show from the *Brighton Herald* dealt with the Chinese content:

> A distinct novelty is a scene on the Canton River, with the water alive with Chinese craft, propelled in all manner of quaint ways, by women as well as men; the water looks as crowded as at Henley on a regatta day. A large number of 'composed' pictures are included in the exhibition. Some of these are arranged with much skill and realism, notably an 'attack on a mission station by Boxers'... The pictures have given unmistakable interest to large audiences.[19]

This was the local exhibition context which was articulating the established China narrative. The last-named film is probably either by Williamson or Mitchell and Kenyon. The other films could have come from the Warwick Trading Company as its publications of 1900 listed various generic views of China. None of these related directly to the 'Crisis', but they were made to serve the wider agenda of the China intertext through their incorporation into 'live' performances on the conflict and its meanings. In such instances, the lecturer's spoken narrative would have served as a bridge from the Chinese 'actualities' and the historical fiction of a Mission film to the story of the 'Crisis'. In the advertisement for *Attack on a China Mission*, when it appeared in January 1901, Williamson declared, 'This sensational subject is full of interest and excitement from start to finish, and is everywhere received with great applause'.

venue in December with Boer War scenes. 'Horace Bank's Pictorial Tours' paid two visits to the Aquarium, offering illustrated journeys using both still and moving images. Animated war pictures from the Transvaal and China – the latter described by the *Brighton Herald* as, 'a country which at the present moment is occupying so considerable a share of public attention' – were valued by the local press as a significant and novel part of a show which also contained songs 'illustrated by views' and recitations.[17] The Alhambra, intimately connected to Williamson through its Manager appearing in *Attack on a China Mission*, in-

Williamson designed and placed his film in a commercial context which was devoted to pleasure and national celebration. The loss of the relevant business records makes it impossible to corroborate the filmmaker's very positive understanding of the film's reception. Empirical evidence does suggest, however, that the film was successful because it engaged with an international issue which was already an important feature in popular periodicals and in the theatre. It was irrelevant to the late Victorian audience that Williamson's film was staged in Hove, England, and displayed the Boxers in absurd ceremonial dress. The audience's applause, we can imagine, was for the victory of Empire and Christendom, the defeat of the 'yellow peril', and the wonder of animated photography. Williamson's film, as this study demonstrates, is a meeting point between the histories of Orientalism and early cinema.

Acknowledgements: The author gratefully acknowledges permission from the editors of KINtop to publish the essay in this collection.

Notes

1. To facilitate the process of joining the films together, the catalogue advertised, 'Film Cement. Per bottle, with brush, 1s.' *Williamson's Kinematograph Films, Revised to September 1899*, Emery & Son, Hove, 12 pp. A copy of this catalogue, which was 'lost' for many years, has been located at the Huntley Film Archive, London. George Eastman House holds photographs of both the 1899 and 1902 Williamson catalogues.
2. Tom Gunning, 'The Non-Continuous Style of Early Film' in R. Holman (ed), *Cinema 1900–1906: An Analytical Study* (Brussels: FIAF, 1982), 219–229.
3. Version 1 contains only material from shots 2 and 4. Version 2 is an incomplete four-shot version but shots 1 and 2 are transposed so that 1 follows 2. Print number 603653 'corrects' this fault.
4. The Florence Williamson Notes are in the collection of the South East Film & Video Archive.
5. *The Times* (31 December 1900): p.12.
6. David Bordwell, *Narration in the Fiction Film* (Madison: University of Wisconsin Press, 1985): 35. See also Tzvetan Todorov, *Introduction to Poetics* (Minneapolis: University of Minnesota Press, 1981).
7. *The Times* (31 December 1900): 11.
8. *Black and White Budget*, vol. III, no. 43 (4 August 1900): 553.
9. *Black and White Budget*, vol. III, no. 42 (28 July 1900): 521.
10. *Black and White Budget*, vol. III, no. 42 (28 July 1900): 525.
11. *Black and White Budget*, vol. IV, no. 60 (1 December 1900): 260–261.
12. *The King*, vol. II, no. 29 (21 July 1900): VII.
13. *Ibid.*
14. *Ibid.*
15. *The King*, vol. II, no. 29 (21 July 1900): 89. Furniss (1854–1925) was an established Victorian illustrator who had taken his graphics and topical anecdotes to the music hall stages of Britain, Australia and America in the 1890s. In 1912 he travelled to New York to learn the craft of filmmaking from the Edison Company, and then returned to Hastings where he made a number of films.
16. *Brighton and Hove Guardian* (31 October 1900): 1.
17. *Brighton Herald* (1 December 1900): 3.
18. *Brighton and Hove Guardian* (7 November 1900): 1. T.C. Hepworth was Cecil Hepworth's father.
19. *Brighton Herald* (3 November 1900): 3.

1895

The 'Philopene' Through Gringo Eyes:
The Colonisation of the Philippines in Early American Cinema and other Entertainment Forms, 1898–1904

Clodualdo del Mundo, Jr.

Metro Manila, Philippines

1895

ABOUT TWO WEEKS AFTER Commodore George Dewey's destruction of the Spanish fleet on 1 May 1898, J. Stuart Blackton and Albert Smith produced their film version of *The Battle of Manila Bay*. Shooting on the rooftop of the Vitagraph headquarters in New York, these enterprising partners reconstructed the battle by using cutouts made from photographs of the American and Spanish fleets. They exploded pinches of gunpowder in the enemy 'ships', thus concealing the illusion behind clouds of smoke. This work was sold as an 'original and exclusive' war film.[1]

What does a film like *The Battle of Manila Bay* contribute to our understanding of history?

Do early films like this one have anything to tell us about a particular historical moment? Are they merely cinematographic exercises, the 'baby steps' in the history of cinema? Are they innocent representations? In his essay 'It's Only a Film/ ou La Face du Néant', Pascal Bonitzer says that the early years of cinema are characterised by the absence of the 'look', and thus constitute a period of innocence:

> There was first of all the twenty-odd years during which the cinema was content merely to be the object of viewing, recording phenomena and movements and the sights of the world. When today we see those early films ... we are seeing the varied fruits of a kind of cinematic Eden

where the coldness and sophistication of the look had not yet penetrated. The impression is usually spoken of in terms of freshness and innocence ... A cinema where the only currency was that of gesture, where the viewer's eyes are functioning but not looking.[2]

I wonder if it is at all possible to see without looking? To see gesture, not actions? To see people moving, not characters? To see early cinema as an innocent cinematographic practice?

Marc Ferro, *co-directeur* of *Annales (E.S.C.)*, explores the intersection between cinema and history by reconsidering film as a document, unwinding its possibilities as a source and agent of history. Cinema does not merely reveal a glimpse of the external aspects of a particular historical moment (i.e. appearances of places and people). Cinema as a source reveals the social attitudes and ideological trends of a certain period and, as an agent, cinema can intervene in history through the pretext of telling a story while in the process indoctrinating or glorifying a cause. Ferro's project is to go back to the images:

> We need to study film and see it in relation to the world that produces it. What is our hypothesis? – that film, image or not of reality, documentary or fiction, true story or pure invention, is History. Our postulate? – that what has not occurred (and even what *has* occurred) – beliefs, intentions, human imagination – is as much history as History.[3]

Following Ferro's lead, I reconsider a number of early American films about the Philippines. Such a re-vision of early cinema and other entertainment forms, like the patriotic songs, coon songs, stage plays, naval spectacles, magic lantern and stereopticon slides, that project the seemingly disinterested and innocent look of the period may tell us about the *mentalité* of a recent past in the history of the United States.

***

The Paper Print Collection in the Library of Congress includes films that were recreations of scenes from the Filipino–American War as well as actualities that were shot in the Phil-

ippines. These films were produced by the Edison Manufacturing Company and the American Mutoscope and Biograph Company.[4] Except for one title (*Troop Ships for the Philippines*), the Edison films in the Paper Print Collection that are related to the Filipino-American War are all dramatised scenes (see Table 1).[5]

Table 1. Edison Films in the Paper Print Collection on the Subject of the Philippines

Edison films	Date of Copyright
Troop Ships for the Philippines	22 June 1898
US Troops and Red Cross in the Trenches before Caloocan	5 June 1899
Advance of Kansas Volunteers at Caloocan	5 June 1899
Filipinos Retreat from Trenches	5 June 1899
Rout of the Filipinos	10 June 1899
Capture of Trenches at Candaba	10 June 1899
Col. Funston Swimming the Bagbag River	23 Sept 1899

Table 2. Biograph Films in the Paper Print Collection on the Subject of the Philippines

Biograph films	Date of Photography	Date of Copyright
The Escolta	21 Dec 1899	19 Aug 1903
Unloading Lighters	21 Dec 1899	19 Aug 1903
An Historic Feat	5 Feb 1900	18 Apr 1902
Pack Train	6 Feb 1900	10 Apr 1902
Water Buffalo	1 Mar 1900	19 Aug 1903
25th Infantry	23 Mar 1900	21 May 1902
Aguinaldo's Navy	9 May 1900	18 Apr 1902
Bridge Traffic	14 Aug 1901	23 May 1902
Filipino Cockfight	15 Aug 1901	21 May 1902
The American Soldier in Love and War	9 July 1903	21 July 1903
Battle of Mt. Arayat	n.d.	3 Aug 1903
Filipino Scouts, St. Louis	5 June 1904	17 June 1904

The Biograph films that relate to the Philippines and the Filipino–American War, on the other hand, were photographed mostly in the Philippines (see Table 2). Except for *The American Soldier in Love and War*, these Biograph films could be described as actualities in the Lumière tradition.[6] Some of the Biograph films appeal to the exotic. They are images of everyday scenes, but for the foreigner they must have appeared to be strange places, faces, and practices. *The Escolta* is a

1895

busy street scene showing horse-drawn, two- and four-wheeled *carretelas* as well as horse-drawn trams that once crowded the major thoroughfares criss-crossing on the bridge. *Unloading Lighters* is a scene at the docks. In the foreground, a row of two-wheeled carts drawn by *carabaos* move towards screen left, with a native standing or seated on the cart and controlling the rig; in the background, some bystanders (soldiers?) look on. According to the Biograph catalogue, 'coolie laborers and water buffaloes lend a picturesque aspect to the scene'.[7] *Water Buffalo* shows two-wheeled carts that are drawn by *carabaos*, a scene that is not much different from *Unloading Lighters*. In *A Filipino Cockfight*, a scene in a cockpit shows a young boy holding a fighting cock while an elderly man holds another. In the background, men raise their hands in gestures of betting as the cockfight ensues. The Biograph catalogue describes this film, measuring 24 feet, as 'one of the very best of the Oriental series. The birds are very lively and the battle is carried on as naturally as if no camera was in sight.'[8]

While these scenes display the exoticism of a newfound land, other actualities show something more. Edison's four-shot *Troop Ships for the Philippines* shows a steamship leaving the dock and soldiers on deck waving their hats. In contrast, a Biograph film of small-sized passenger boats crossing the river, 'curious Filipino boats' according to the Biograph catalogue,[9] is entitled *Aguinaldo's Navy*, not quite a subtle way of belittling the enemy. The other Biograph actualities show soldiers marching through a dusty village road (*25th Infantry*), pulling a train of horses across the Agno River (*An Historic Feat*) and, in a panoramic shot, climbing a mountain trail (*Pack Train, Gen. Bell's Expedition*). The treacherous climate and geography are suggested, and the mission seems to be akin to the taming of the wilderness. In *Battle of Mt. Ariat* (Arayat), soldiers on horseback and a few more on foot charge away from the camera towards upper screen left, past haystacks standing in a field; the camera pans left to follow the action, with the mountain looming large in the background. The camera stays in its position, left by the soldiers, without capturing any scene of actual battle. A later

Biograph film, *Filipino Scouts, St. Louis*, displays the tamed natives, as it were, in a high-angle, wide shot, with the conductor, moving spiritedly on the lower edge of the screen, leading a military band; on the upper screen, rows of natives do calisthenics presumably in time with the absent music.[10] I shall go back to the significance of this exposition at St. Louis at the end of this essay.

In contrast to the documentary but ineffectual record of *Battle of Mt. Ariat*, the encounters between the 'Filipinos' and the 'Americans' in the early Edison films are dramatised representations that are undoubtedly fictional. There are interesting patterns in these films that, in my view, are aimed to rouse the patriotic enthusiasm of the American viewers. In the Edison films of these encounters, the running story is defeat for the natives and victory for the invading forces. In *US Troops and Red Cross in the Trenches before Caloocan*, an officer of the American Infantry jumps into a trench, pitches the American flag, and brandishes his sword. The heroic image of the American soldier is unmistakable. More soldiers join the officer in the trench and, after some firing, there is the victorious waving of hats which has become *de rigueur* in these films. When two of the soldiers appear to have been shot, two Red Cross nurses enter screen right to take care of the casualties while the other soldiers exit screen left to attack. At the end of this scene, an American soldier on horseback appears in the background – an image which recurs in several other films.

Advance of Kansas Volunteers at Caloocan is a representation of face-to-face combat between Filipino and American soldiers. The Filipino insurgents advance and shoot toward the camera (and at the spectator); they are repulsed immediately by American soldiers who come in from the position of the camera, entering frame from screen left. In this particular instance, the camera obviously takes the position of the coloniser. An American officer enters from the right side and moves with the other soldiers toward the enemy in the background. The soldier carrying the American flag is shot and the officer immediately picks up the 'old glory'. While the Filipinos run away, the officer waves the flag triumphantly.

Filipinos Retreat from Trenches, Rout of the Filipinos, and *Capture of Trenches at Candaba* are variations on the same theme and, not unexpectedly, their titles suggest the defeat of the enemy. In *Filipinos Retreat from Trenches*, the scene opens with the Filipinos shooting from the trenches toward screen left. The short, lifeless tree trunk with protruding twigs in the background betrays the same location where *US Troops and Red Cross in the Trenches* was shot; only this time, Filipino soldiers are in the trench. Quite interestingly, and quite fantastically, each soldier is armed with a rifle. Some of the Filipinos in the trench fall down, wounded or dead; others retreat and exit screen right. The Americans enter screen left and pursue the insurgents off-screen, driving them out of the contested space. At the end of this scene, an officer on horseback appears in the background. A native soldier who is supposed to be dead or wounded moves to avoid being trampled upon by the horse.

In *Rout of the Filipinos*, the insurgents are forced to retreat in the midst of American gunfire and they exit screen right. Soon, American soldiers, led by the ubiquitous flag carrier, enter screen left. The signs of victory are present – brandishing of the sword by an officer, waving of the hats by the soldiers, and occupation of the central space of the screen.

Capture of Trenches at Candaba is another variation on the same theme of American soldiers overrunning a group of insurgents. There is the usual waving of hats in victory; the officer on horseback makes another appearance, but this time the horse gallops wildly. The officer fails to control the horse and he is about to fall when he is saved by a cut to another take of the shot, this time with the officer in full control of the horse.

Col. Funston Swimming the Bagbag River is unique for its reference to an individual historic character. The river separates the American soldiers in the foreground from the insurgents in the background. Col. Funston quickly removes his uniform and swims toward the opposite shore where the insurgents are. Once on the other side, Col. Funston pulls the rope of the raft that carries a number of soldiers. As the raft nears the other side, the Filipinos run and exit for their lives toward

screen right. An officer on a white horse enters screen left, joining the soldiers who have just reached the other side. The Edison catalogue concludes that the film is 'highly exciting and true to history'.[11] While Col. Funston's swim across the Bagbag River is corroborated by official military reports (he did swim across the river with four other men), the anecdote of the raft happened two days later at another place called the Rio Grande; in this event, Privates Edward White and W.B. Trembley were the heroes.[12] The Edison film here collapses the two events into one and allows Col. Funston to fill the role of the popular hero.[13]

These Edison films unmistakably embody values that one could identify with colonialism. The natives are literally driven out of the screen and the contested space is claimed by the coloniser. Each victorious battle ends with the constant waving of hats, a rousing celebration of adventure and heroism. The flag is pitched at every piece of land that the soldiers subdue and there is always someone to raise it proudly. Moreover, Red Cross nurses take care of the wounded, while the enemy run for their lives, leaving their fallen comrades. Americans wage an orderly war against the disorganised rebels. Quite interestingly, an officer on horseback ends four of these Edison films – *US Troops and Red Cross in the Trenches before Caloocan, Filipinos Retreat from Trenches, Capture of Trenches at Candaba*, and *Col. Funston Swimming the Bagbag River*. Apparently, this was the supreme image of conquest and subjugation.

The only dramatised film in the Biograph list is *The American Soldier in Love and War*. At the time this film was made in 1903, the insurgency had been virtually subdued. During this period, films were relatively longer and stories were told in multiple shots. It is interesting to see how this Biograph film reveals a further stage in the development of American colonisation. Working around the story of a soldier who leaves his sweetheart to fight the war in the Philippines, the film does not dwell on battles but on the peaceful co-existence between coloniser and colonised. The first scene is the heart-rending separation of the two lovers. The distraught white woman waits in the living room; the dashing soldier enters the curtained door on

1895

screen right. After a number of embraces suffused with kisses, the soldier finally breaks from the embrace and exits. He comes back for another kiss and then exits for good. The poor woman goes back to her seat and cries her heart out. In the second scene in which a native man is about to strike the American soldier with a club, a fat native woman intercedes and saves the day for the soldier. The natives in this film, it should be noted, are performed by actors in blackface and who wear black tights and grass skirts, the stereotypical image of the jungle savage. In the third scene, the native woman cares for the wounded soldier. Then, the sweetheart, accompanied by a fatherly-looking gentleman, arrives and rewards the native woman with a necklace. The fatherly-looking gentleman reaches for his breast pocket (to take his wallet?) as the scene ends. Indeed, there is economic advantage in welcoming the American soldier. A peaceful co-existence is made possible within a paternalistic relationship between the coloniser and the colonised.

* * *

At the turn of the century, other American entertainment forms also exploited the topical events of the day. The Spanish–American encounter in Manila provided a wealth of source material for songwriters and composers. 'Brave Dewey and His Men (Down at Manila Bay)' was advertised as 'the running song of the season'.[14] There were two versions of 'The Battle of Manila' – one, a serio-comic song by Ennis and Barnhouse from Oskaloosa, Iowa; another, a number for a brass band by Edward Holst. 'The Hero of Manila Bay' also had two versions – one by Tom J. Quigley for a publisher in Chicago; another by Tony Stanford for a publisher in New York. Stanford's version was advertised as 'The everlasting march song. The Battle of Manila graphically described.'[15] The call to arms which all these patriotic songs seem to embody is captured in this refrain from 'We'll Hold the Philippines' by Harmon and Raab:[16]

> The Yankee Eagle screams,
>   'We'll hold the Philippines,
>   That her people never more
>   may be oppressed';
>
> Our flag shall ever wave,

> to free the true and brave,
>   And our banner shall by noble
>   deeds be bless'd,
>
> Who mutters 'take it down'
>   shall meet the Freeman's frown,
>   And tremble as the sword hand
>   takes the hilt;
>
> The Yankee Eagle screams,
>   'We'll hold the Philippines,
>   Where tyrants reign
>   our Altar shall be built.'

This refrain underscores a common rationale for the war – to subdue the tyrants, to defend and free the oppressed. The liberation of the Philippines from Spanish oppression beclouded the economic and political issues of American expansionism; Harmon and Raab's patriotic song sold the idea of America's noble deed.

There were other patriotic songs inspired by the Filipino–American War in the Philippines, e.g. 'Miss Philopene' and 'It's Only a Portrait of Mother'; the latter was advertised as a 'descriptive story of Love and Duty at Manila'.[17] But, another type of song took up not only the subject of the Philippines, but also the Filipino in particular – the coon songs.[18] Six of the seven titles I have come across address the Filipina. 'Ma Filipina Babe' by Chas. K. Harris was advertised as 'The oddest, cutest and most original coon ballad ever written'.[19] 'My Own Manilla Sue' by Earl C. Way was 'A refined darkey song success, with a contagious rag refrain'.[20] Lask and Hawley produced 'Ma Phillipina Gal'. James Ferdon's 'My Phillipine Queen' was number two of the seven best coon songs of the season published by Zeno Mauvais Music Co. of San Francisco, California.[21] 'Ma Belle of De Philippines' by Edgar Smith and Fred Gagel was sung by Olive Redpath in *Mother Goose*, a production at Weber and Fields' Music Hall. Hurtig and Seaman's Enterprises published 'Philippino Lady', a coon serenade. The only coon song, it appears, that veered away from the Filipina as subject was Irving Jones' 'I Want a Filipino Man', performed by Fay Templeton at Keith's Theatre, New York, 'to three encores nightly', and by Cissie Loftus at Proctor's New York theatres 'to tremendous applause'.[22] 'I Want a Filipino Man' was advertised as an 'up-to-date darkey oddity, coon song hit of the era'.[23]

The reference to the Filipino in the titles of the coon songs indicates two things: firstly, the Filipino was identified with the coloured races; secondly, the prejudice that accompanied this identification imaged the Filipino as an inferior Other. The term Filipino was once used exclusively to name the Españoles-Filipinos or creoles (Spaniards born in the Philippines); then, gradually, the name spread to include Chinese mestizos and urbanised natives who acquired a Hispanised cultural background. Finally, during the Propaganda Movement of the last quarter of the nineteenth century, the term Filipino was used to signal national identity, regardless of economic class or racial origin.[24] The American coon songs gave a different dimension to the identity of the Filipino at the turn of the century. Surely, it was not what the revolutionaries were fighting for; but, then, that was how the Filipino was represented to American audiences.

Aside from songs and films, there were magic lantern and stereopticon slides. Some of the producers and distributors of these slides include the Kleine Optical Company, Stereopticon and Film Exchange, L. Manasse Company, and Sears, Roebuck and Company. Like the motion picture films, these slides cover travel and war scenes – from slides of local structures like 'A Native House', 'Santa Cruz Church', 'A Small-Pox Hospital', to portraits of 'Filipino Mother and Baby' and 'Philippine Fruit Girl', to battle scenes like 'The Victory at Caloocan' and 'The Fall of Manila'. Moreover, not unlike the films, these slides project an image of a weak and inferior people. About the slide of 'A Company of Ingorrote (*sic*) Spearmen', the Sears and Roebuck catalogue underscores, 'If these people were more enlightened and educated, they would realise how foolish it is to oppose our army with such primitive weapons'.[25] It should also be noted that these slides of the American soldiers' 'Deeds of Daring!' and 'Acts of Heroism!' were often accompanied by a lecture that, as a poster of a stereopticon-lecture entertainment announces, 'will interest and inspire every patriotic man, woman and child in our audience'.[26] But the bottom line of this appeal to patriotism is the business that it is designed to generate – 'nearly every one has a near or distant relative or near friend who was in the service, and they will gladly patronise anything that will freshen their memories and throw more light on the subject'.[27]

Naval shows were staged, too. The Spanish-American War became a display of fireworks, 'a magnificent open-air summernight's spectacle' showing the fierce battle in Manila and the annihilation of the entire Spanish fleet.[28] The Madison Square Garden was the site of Imre Kiralfy's 'Great American Naval Spectacle', featuring 'Our Naval Victories' in Cuba and the Philippines.[29] War posters were also produced and sold, some in four colours, like the posters of Dewey in Manila.

Then, there were the stage plays. *Dewey, The Hero of Manila*, a melodrama in four acts, was produced at the Court Theatre in Chicago. 'Dewey' makes a grand appearance at the end 'to release the prisoners and take possession of the Philippines in the name of the United States of America'.[30] *Across the Pacific*, described as 'a scenic melodrama in four acts', was first produced at the Hartford Opera House in Connecticut. A convoluted story of a man's love for his adopted ward, the characters find themselves for one reason or another in the Philippines. After a series of spying and killings, 'Elsie (the ward) declares her love for Capt. Lanier (the "father", now lover) and the story ends in a blaze of glory.'[31] *Manila Bound*, adapted from *Un Voyage en Chine*, was first produced at the Tivoli Opera House in San Francisco. A comedy opera in three acts, the plot is a comedy of remarriage. The couple was married in Europe without the father's blessing. The play shows how the father's consent for the remarriage of his daughter to Capt. Moreland is obtained on the main deck of the USS Wisconsin 'by the subterfuge of taking the whole party to Manila, when they are only sailing around the bay'.[32] In the three plays whose synopses appeared in the *New York Clipper*, the Philippines is used as backdrop for the melodramatic plots.[33] In *Manila Bound*, specifically, the mere mention of 'Manila', not without a tinge of a threat for sure, finally causes the happy turn of events. There are

1895

some common patterns in these plays, e.g. the leading male characters are officers in the US army, figures who perform heroic acts in a land that supposedly needs the saving hand of America. In light of this, the use of the Philippines as setting might have not been innocent at all. The heroism that is obvious in the early films of Edison and Biograph is also highlighted in these plays.

***

The early war films were used as attractions in the diverse programme of a vaudeville show. The exotic scenes of the documentary films and the adventure of the dramatised war scenes provided the vaudeville audience, which was largely middle-class and urban, with an exciting programme. This fascination with topical subjects like war – in moving images – continued to be exploited through 1900–02.[34] Whether or not these mock battles appeared authentic to the vaudeville audience can only be conjectured. (Was the incredible commotion caused by *The Arrival of a Train* a myth?) Perhaps the more useful question is 'Does authenticity matter?' It is with this question in mind that I now turn to an eyewitness account, Joseph Markey's reports to *The Express* in Red Oak, Iowa. Markey, a private in Company M of the 51st Iowa Infantry Volunteers, assumed the role of correspondent for *The Express*. His letters, 'written under adverse circumstances and amid surroundings unadapted to literary effort', were compiled in a book, *From Iowa to the Philippines: A History of Company M, Fifty-First Iowa Infantry Volunteers.*

The amount of detail that Markey includes in his reports naturally is far greater than what an entertainment could provide. The environment that is only suggested by the dusty village road in the Biograph film *25th Infantry* is extensively described by Markey. The tropics, with its climate that the white man considers repulsive, was considered an enemy; but, always, 'the boys never gave up'.[35]

Markey's descriptions of skirmishes and battles differ quite distinctly from the close encounters in the Edison films. The distance between the warring groups was a function of their weapons. Markey, hoping for the more powerful Krags being used by the other com-

panies, complains about the antiquated Springfields of Company M and notes the capability of the insurgents' Mauser rifles:

> The insurgents with the Mauser have some 800 yards the better of us in the matter of range ... Besides this the smokeless powder enables them to hide in trees and bushes and do deadly work without uncovering their position.[36]

The Edison films, on the other hand, hide the illusion of battle under a haze of smoke. How else can a silent cinema that uses one shot for one scene show the burst of rifles?

The reality of war, as always, comes across upon sighting death. Markey's own description of a small incident which he witnessed when General MacArthur had ordered that the bodies of the dead insurgents be displayed at the plaza vividly brings home this reality. While the natives that gathered were 'stoically indifferent', Markey notes a scene that is worthy of any film:

> Two boys, clad in white and evidently sons of a rich planter, were near me. They went hand in hand peering at each swollen and distorted form before them. Near one, a young sergeant of twenty-five, they stopped. Then, with an outburst of tears – still hand in hand – they turned and left amid their suppressed boyish snobs, speaking of their 'Hermano', whom they would never see again. They had found their brother.[37]

A touching incident, indeed, but not enough to trigger an insight in Markey's mind. This attitude, in my view, is an index to Markey's overall perspective on the war in the Philippines. Like the war in the Edison and Biograph films, Markey's war is an adventure. It is the same war that Gen. Funston celebrates in his memoirs as 'a contribution ... to the literature of adventure'.[38] In one skirmish, Markey confesses:

> I know of no sweeter sound than that of your own artillery in battle. There is so much of awful strength and destruction in the sound of artillery; first the sharp report of the gun, the long shrill, sweeping sound of the passing shell and then the dull muffled roar of shrapnel as it bursts.

1895

No wonder it is so terrifying to these 'niggers'.[39]

The adventure of war goes hand in hand with the notion of manifest destiny. Markey exemplifies this destiny in his description of a grove of tropical fruit trees, an hacienda of banana, pineapple, guava, coconut, and mango trees:

> No one accustomed to the flat, low country around Manila could dream of such a country only thirty miles away. It would remind one of an Iowa prairie but for its rich growth of tropical trees in little clumps about the plain or bordering the banks of swift clear streams, which flow from the distant hills to the bay below. One can readily realise the rich possibilities of the splendid valley in the hands of progressive American farmers.[40]

Quite clearly, Markey's reports differ in details but share a way of looking with the Edison and Biograph films. The American soldiers are engaged in an adventure of war against the 'misled insurrectos'; and, against the heroic American 'boys' are portrayed the terrified Filipino 'niggers'. In both representations, American imperialism is clothed in the disguise of manifest destiny and basks in the projected inferiority of the other race.

* * *

In 1904, the Filipinos were made into a major exhibit in the Louisiana Purchase Exposition at St. Louis. Over 1200 natives were transported to the United States. The contingent was composed of a variety of Filipino ethnic groups – Visayans, Moros, Bagobos, Negritos, and Igorots. A Philippine village occupied a 47-acre site around Arrow Head Lake to the southwest of Forest Park. The exhibit highlighted 'dog-eating Igorots and stone-age cannibals'; but, so as not to miss the point of the exposition, the 'savage' was displayed side by side with the disciplined native constabulary that was formed by Philippine Governor William Howard Taft. The Filipino was exposed, studied, and culturally graded. When a few natives died on the site, anthropologists could not help but measure and analyse their brains. Robert Rydell sums up the message of the Philippine exposition:

> Under the primary direction of government-appointed scientists, the reservation affirmed the value of the islands to America's commercial growth and created a scientifically validated impression of Filipinos as racially inferior and incapable of national self-determination in the near future.[41]

The St. Louis World's Fair, Rydell demonstrates convincingly, was not just about the Louisiana Purchase; it was about imperialism. And this imperialist vision, I would add, was foreshadowed by the complex of entertainment forms at the turn of the century. Whether by design or by chance, the popular patriotic songs of the period, the coon songs, the stage plays, the naval spectacles, the magic lantern and stereopticon slides, the posters, and definitely the early films – all this embodied a vision screened through a consciousness of racism and imperialism. In the end, what mattered was not the authenticity of these entertainment forms but the interested look that was far from innocent.

Notes

1. Charles Musser, 'The American Vitagraph, 1897–1901: Survival and and Success in a Competitive Industry', *Film before Griffith*, John L. Fell (ed) (Berkeley: University of California Press, 1983), 33–34.

2. Pascal Bonitzer, 'It's Only a Film/ou La Face du Néant', *Framework*, no. 14: 23.

3. Marc Ferro, *Cinema and History*, Naomi Greene (trans.) (Detroit: Wayne State University Press, 1988), 29.

4. Film catalogues of the period include even more titles that were produced and/or distributed by various companies, such as F.M. Prescott, Selig-Polyscope, Lubin Manufacturing Company, and Sears, Roebuck and Company. One of the F.M. Prescott films, simply labeled *A New Philippine War Film* and measuring 400 feet, is described as 'an amazing spectacle never before reproduced, showing a running fight between the American forces and the savage Filipinos'. The colonised is easily characterised as 'savage' and the film is sold as 'the most realistic film of the late war' (Edison Papers,

Motion Picture Catalogs by American Producers and Distributors, 1894–1908, microfilm ed. (Frederick: University Publications of America, 1984), Reel 1, F-00048.

The theatrical trade paper *New York Clipper* additionally includes Lubin Manufacturing Company advertisements for some Filipino–American War films; however, these films do not survive in the Paper Print Collection. Titles of the Lubin films include *Hoisting of the American Flag at Cavite* (25 June 1898; 286), *Scaling a Fort at Manila* (11 March 1899; 38), *Admiral Dewey's Flagship Olympia in Action at Manila* (22 April 1899; 160), *Capt. Coghlan, One of the Manila Heroes, and Crew of the Raleigh, Reviewed by the President* (6 May 1899; 200), and *Fighting in the Philippines* (10 March 1900; 48). The F.M. Prescott catalogue describes *Hoisting the American Flag at Cavite, Near Manila* as a film 'you have no doubt read in the newspapers concerning this fight, and you can now see it just as it was' (Edison Papers, Reel 1, F-00016). The Selig-Polyscope catalogue describes a similar film of flag-waving, *The American Flag*, thus – '*Old Glory* fluttering in the breeze never fails to rouse an audience to the highest pitch of enthusiasm and is, of course, a splendid film with which to wind up an entertainment' (Edison Papers, Reel 2, I-00035). If the Edison films are any indication, these Lubin films (except perhaps the President's review of the crew of Raleigh) and similar films produced or distributed by other companies could all be staged scenes and could have been shot in the United States. They could possibly have been highly imitative of the existing films since during this period it was commonplace to pirate, imitate and copy each other's work. And Lubin especially was notorious for this practice.

5. The actual dates of the making of these Edison films were not recorded in the Library of Congress. Only the dates of copyright can be ascertained. Compared with the copyright dates of the Biograph actualities that were shot in the Philippines, these Edison copyright dates are suspiciously early, if indeed the films were shot in the Philippines. But, they were not.

6. From April 1899 through November 1911, Biograph made it a practice to record with the dates of copyright, however inconsistently, the dates of photography and the locations of production. This information allows us to verify the date and place of production of each film. The dates of photography of these Biograph films are closer to the dates of copyright of the Edison films. The three- to four-year gap between the dates of copyright of the Edison and Biograph films indicates two possibilities: (a) Biograph was not too concerned about the question of copyright (however, the films that were shot in the US, namely *The American Soldier in Love and War* and *Filipino Scouts, St. Louis*, which were copyrighted in a matter of days after the photography do not support this assumption); (b) the Biograph films were shot in the Philippines but, for some reason (perhaps problems in shipping), copyrights were obtained much later. These dates of photography and copyright, together with an analysis of the internal structures of the films themselves, suggest the authenticity of these films.

7. Edison Papers, *Motion Picture Catalogs by American Producers and Distributors, 1894–1908*, Reel 2, H-00092.

8. *Ibid.*, Reel 2, H-00049. Other relevant Biograph films that are not available in the Paper Print Collection but are listed in the 1902 Biograph catalogue include titles like *Blanco Bridge*, 29 feet, where 'over this famous structure passes most of the traffic of our new capital city in the Philippines'; *Bridge of Spain – Manila*, 54 feet, described as 'The centre of activity in Manila, showing the natives, Chinese coolies, street traffic, etc., well-arranged and interesting'; *Making Manila Rope*, 27 feet, which illustrates 'one of the chief industries of our new possessions taken during the occupation by the American Army'; *Market Place*, 53 feet, 'A panoramic view of the market place of Manila, showing native women with their baskets, various stalls with fruit and fish displayed, and American soldiers patrolling' (Edison Papers, Reel 2, H-00071); *Coolies at Work*, 27 feet, a scene of 'Chinese coolies carrying out the cargo' (Edison Papers, Reel 2, H-00092); and *Manila*, 28 feet, a panoramic view showing the river front from the dock of the port capital (Edison Papers, Reel 2, H-00094).

9. Edison Papers, Reel 2, H-00071.

10. The Biograph catalogue lists other scenes of the Filipino–American War that read like actualities: *Going to the Firing Line*, 28 feet, a scene of soldiers 'starting out from Manila for the front'; *The Call to Arms!*, 53 feet, ' An exciting episode in the Philippine War, Company I, 37th Regiment, Capt. Leo F. Foster'; *In the Field*, 53 feet, described as a 'surprise attack'; *The Train for Angeles*, 27 feet, shows 'how Uncle Sam's soldiers have solved the transportation problem in the Philippines'; *Going into Action*, 53 feet, a scene at Angeles; *An Advance by Rushes*, 26 feet, another film of American soldiers attacking the insurgents; *A Military Inspection*, 27 feet, a market place scene at Angeles; *The 17th*

Infantry, U.S.A., 54 feet, shot at Dagupan, of soldiers returning from a fight; *The Attack on Magalang*, 53 feet, American troops depart from the Cathedral of Magalang after 'The Filipino insurgents have made an unexpected assault upon the town'; *Back from Battle*, 54 feet, the 25th Infantry returns from Mt. Arayat; *Under Armed Escort*, 26 feet, shows an 'ox-train carrying supplies and ammunition'; *On the Advance with Gen. Wheaton*, 54 feet, appears to be another film of American soldiers on the attack – 'The American troops come at full tilt down a narrow path at the foot of a mountain, deploy into the open, and start the engagement'; *Slow but Sure*, 54 feet, displays 'a train of water buffalo at work in the Quartermaster's Department, Manila'; *Into the Wilderness!*, 27 feet, is another scene of Gen. Bell's expedition, coming down the hillside; another version of *Into the Wilderness!*, 54 feet, is a nearer view of the expedition; a third version, 54 feet, shows Bell's 'pack train emerging from the underbrush'; *With the Guns!*, 54 feet, shows the 6th Artillery going into action at La Loma Church; *The 4th Cavalry*, 28 feet, is a scene in Pasay; *A Charge on the Insurgents*, 55 feet, shows Gen. Wheaton's force in action at Calamba; *The Fighting 36th*, 53 feet, taken at Lingayen, shows the regiment that 'killed more insurgents, and covered more territory in the Philippines, than any other regiment in the army'; *A Filipino Town Surprised*, 53 feet, is yet another scene of soldiers charging; *After Aguinaldo*, 54 feet, is about the 4th Cavalry's search for insurgents; *Maj.-Gen. Lloyd Wheaton*, 52 feet, shows a reconnoitering tour from Calamba, the 'Hell Hole of the Philippines'.

Other Biograph actualities cover the departure of American soldiers for the Philippines, like *Fifteenth Infantry, U.S.A.*, 73 feet, taken at Governor's Island, New York, or their return from the colony, like *Heroes of Luzon*, 52 feet, which shows the reception at Pittsburgh of the 10th Pennsylvania volunteers, and *Back from Manila*, 55 feet, which shows 'a regiment of US Regulars, marching through Market Street, San Francisco' (Edison Papers, Reel 2, H-00091–H-00094).

One other film, *What Our Boys Did at Manila*, 62 feet, is a flag raising film that may or may not be documentary; appealing to popular patriotism, the film shows an American sailor as he 'rips down the Spanish flag, nails Old Glory to the staff, and as the breeze carries it out, waves his cap to the cheers of his comrades below' (Edison Papers, Reel 2, H-00085).

11. Edison Papers, Reel 1, G-00059.

12. *The Fighting Twentieth: History and Official Souvenir of the Twentieth Kansas Regiment* (Topeka: Morgan Press, 1899), 37–41. Frederick Funston, *Memories of Two Wars: Cuban and Philippine Experiences* (New York: Scribner, 1914), 273–285.

13. A stereopticon slide from the Sears and Roebuck catalogue, however, is closer to the actual event. 'Funston's Two Volunteers Crossing the River with Line' is a slide of Privates White and Trempbley's heroic act. How the lecture which usually accompanied the stereopticon slide show coloured this heroic event is another question though (Edison Papers, Reel 5, AA-00035).

14. *New York Clipper* (18 June 1898): 270.

15. *New York Clipper* (19 November 1898): 648.

16. *New York Clipper* (20 May 1899): 236.

17. *New York Clipper* (23 December 1899): 905.

18. Coon songs were the basic stock in trade of the early minstrel singers; the importance of this type of song had diminished by the end of the Civil War. However, with the increasing use of syncopation, new coon songs composed in the 1890s were played in ragtime, Eileen Southern, *The Music of Black Americans: A History* (New York: Norton Press, 1971), 314.

19. *New York Clipper* (7 January 1899): 763.

20. *New York Clipper* (17 June 1899): 318.

21. *Ibid.*, 319.

22. *New York Clipper* (25 November 1899): 823.

23. *New York Clipper* (27 January 1900): 1018.

24. Renato Constantino, *The Philippines: A Past Revisited* (Quezon: Tala Publishing Services, 1975), 147–148.

25. Edison Papers, Reel 5, AA-00034.

26. *Ibid.*, Reel 5, AA-00038.

27. *Ibid.*, Reel 5, AA-00107.

28. *New York Clipper* (25 June 1898): 283.

29. *New York Clipper* (17 September 1898): 491.

1895

30. *New York Clipper* (14 January 1899): 769.

31. *New York Clipper* (3 March 1900): 3.

32. *New York Clipper* (21 April 1900): 171.

33. Another opera, *The Manila Beauty*, was advertised in search of a 'solid manager'; nothing more is known about this 'spectacle of war' in three acts. *New York Clipper,* 16 March 1901, 65.

34. Robert C. Allen, 'Vaudeville and Film 1895–1915: A Study in Media Inter-action', (Ph. D. Thesis, University of Iowa, 1977): 136–147.

35. Joseph Markey, *From Iowa to the Philippines: A History of Company M, Fifty-First Iowa Infantry Volunteers* (Red Oak: T. D. Murphy, 1900), 234.

36. *Ibid.,* 212.

37. *Ibid.,* 252.

38. Funston, *Memories of Two Wars: Cuban and Philippine Experiences,* vii.

39. Markey, *From Iowa to the Philippines: A History of Company M, Fifty-First Iowa Infantry Volunteers,* 221–222.

40. *Ibid.,* 218.

41. Robert Rydell, *All the World's a Fair: Visions of Empire at American International Expositions, 1876–1916* (Chicago: University of Chicago Press, 1984), 170.

1895

5

Reconsidering formal histories

1895

Narrative Structure in Early Classical Cinema

Kristin Thompson

Honorary Fellow, Department of Communication Arts, University of Wisconsin, Madison, WI 53713, USA

Enduring notions of narrative proportion in classical filmmaking

THIS ESSAY ON EARLY CLASSICAL filmmaking emerged, paradoxically enough, from a current project on narrative structure in recent Hollywood cinema. This book is intended to cover the era since the mid-1970s. David Bordwell, Janet Staiger, and I ended our earlier study, *The Classical Hollywood Cinema*,[1] with 1960, since by that point the original studio system had largely been broken up. Yet it was our contention that most of the basic principles of classical filmmaking outlived the studio system and are still very much in use. This continuing stability of the classical cinema, and in particular of its narrative structures, underlies my project.

In looking at recent classical narrative, I have examined a number of modern scriptwriting manuals to see what assumptions practitioners have about how Hollywood films should be structured. These manuals differ somewhat from their counterparts in the silent era – books which we drew upon extensively in researching *The Classical Hollywood Cinema*. Manuals of the past 25 years or so tend to be even more uniform in their advice to script-writers. They are also far more explicit and specific in their dictates on how stories should be broken down into parts and how those parts should be proportioned. Virtually every such manual, for example, insists that a film should fall into three so-called acts, and many even give precise timings for when the breaks between these acts should fall.

It occurred to me that some of these principles, so baldly laid out in these manuals, might be of use in looking back to the early classical period when the feature film was being standardised and the continuity filmmaking guidelines were being formulated. Do the carefully-timed proportions of modern scripts derive in any way from practices of the pre-1920 era? If indeed the classical system has been so stable for so many decades, we might expect to find early features displaying at least rough versions of these same divisions within the narrative and at least vaguely similar proportions among the parts.

My hypothesis upon undertaking this study was that early films might well contain at least the germs of the narrative divisions and proportions that have more recently become so very codified and precise. I re-examined about two dozen of the early manuals, looking for terms and concepts that might be somewhat

1895

comparable to those in modern screenwriting guides. I also looked at some early features, segmenting them in order to see if there was any pattern to the timings of the major breaks in the action.

I shall begin with a brief overview of recent Hollywood scripting practice, as revealed in manuals and some major films of the past two decades or so. Then I shall jump back to the pre-1920 era and see what can be learned by looking for comparable structures in much earlier films.

First, however, I should give you a little history of the screenplay manuals themselves, since quite a bit of my evidence will be drawn from them. In the United States, there have been two main eras when such manuals were published. As the early studios regularised and expanded their weekly outputs of short films in the period from 1910 on, they came to depend on freelance submissions of scenarios. Many thousands of such scenarios were submitted, and one of the tasks of the scenario editor at each studio was to read them and buy the few that were of use. During the 1910s and 1920s, dozens of scenario manuals were published to guide the freelancers in their work.

During the early to mid-1910s, these manuals tried to teach writers some basic principles of narrative construction, as well as the newly developed continuity script format.[2] With the rise of features, script format became too complex for most amateur writers, and the studios were establishing writing departments that included specialists in breaking a script down into numbered shots. Even in the late 1910s and early 1920s, however, stories in synopsis form were welcomed by the studios, and a few specialised manuals on how to write photoplay synopses were published.[3]

During the 1920s, the studios expanded their writing departments and spent more money on plays, novels, and other literary works for adaptation. The coming of sound further curtailed the use of freelance stories as the basis for Hollywood films, and the publication of manuals also dropped. About half a dozen appeared during the 1930s, and only about two each over the next three decades.[4]

With the break-up of the studio system, however, the freelance market in scenarios has returned to prominence. Now scriptwriters work through agents, and the stakes are much higher. Whole productions may be cast and financed around a promising synopsis. Consequently the 1970s saw a rise in the number of scriptwriters' manuals, to at least ten for the decade; the 1980s brought forth close to fifty, and several continue to appear each year.

I would like to turn briefly now to the modern scenario manuals and films, in order to see what large-scale structures and proportions they reveal. We can then compare these with the classical feature film before 1920.

Recent ideals of classical narrative construction

In one aspect, scenario manuals of recent years are completely consistent with those of the early period. They inevitably state that a film should have a beginning, a middle, and an end. This is of course, self-evident, but the modern manuals go considerably beyond this bald declaration. As I mentioned earlier, one of the basic assumptions of virtually all modern scenario manuals is that all films should contain three 'acts'.

The most influential proponent of this notion has been Syd Field, whose *Screenplay: The Foundations of Screenwriting* was first published in 1979. Though somewhat simpler than many subsequent manuals, it has remained a sort of bible for the aspiring scriptwriter. In it, Field lays out the basic rules. Act I he calls 'The Beginning', or the 'setup'. It lasts for 30 minutes of a two-hour film and ends with a 'plot point'. This he defines as 'an incident, or event, that hooks into the story and spins it around into another direction'. Act II is 'The Confrontation', containing the conflict that forms the bulk of the story. It ends with another plot point. Since one page of a contemporary script equals one minute of screen time, this new plot point occurs between pages 85 and 90 of a two-hour film. Act III, which Field terms the 'Resolution', occupies pages 90 to 120.[5]

Linda Seger's somewhat more sophisticated *Making a Good Script Great* agrees with Field on the timings. She allots 30 to 35 minutes to

1895

the first act, which she also terms the 'set-up'; the second is the 'development', and runs for 45–60 pages; the third act, or 'resolution' occupies 25–35 pages. Each act ends with what she calls a 'turning point' (as opposed to Field's 'plot point').[6] One more example should show how very formulaic this idea has become. Michael Hauge's *Writing Screenplays that Sell* insists that films *always* have a three-act structure. In a two-hour feature, Act I is the first quarter, or half an hour; the second is half the film, occupying the central hour; the third is also half an hour, in the final quarter of the film.[7]

Hollywood writers and other practitioners have widely adopted this terminology and these assumptions. In interviews actors or directors commonly refer to acts. Ron Bass, who wrote the script for *Rain Man*, describes his working process:

> I just start with a pencil and my three little sheets of paper – acts one, two, and three.
>
> My scenes are broken down on those sheets before I start writing, and I have lots of notes in my notebook keyed to the numbers of those scenes, with different ideas I may get about what's going to go into them. Then, when I begin to write scene twenty-three, for example, I look back at this voluminous notebook and find all the ideas numbered 'twenty-three', get back into what those ideas were, and use them for what I do with that scene.

The resulting script, he declares, is 120 pages long.[8] This idea of three acts, with the central act running about an hour and sandwiched between two half-hour segments, is universal. But do actual films follow such a mechanistic formula?

It turns out that they do to a surprising extent, though one crucial caveat must be added. Although there are some three-act films, I would contend that the majority of recent Hollywood films actually break down into four large-scale parts and an epilogue. (I have not adopted the term 'act', as it seems misleading, since there is seldom an interval between acts, as there is for stage plays.) Most films have a turning point about midway through where some important new premise is set up. That is, what the manuals consider an hour-long second act is usually in fact broken into two halves by an additional turning point.

The reason for the modern feature having four parts rather than three is simply length. I shall be suggesting in my conclusions that the classical film gravitates toward large-scale parts of about 25 to 30 minutes. Except in cases where the set-up creates a very strong situation, an hour-long central section without any major new premises or twists is difficult to maintain. I shall look at some examples in a few moments.

The failure of scriptwriting experts to notice that most modern films have four large parts is puzzling. Syd Field's recent book, *Four Screenplays*, slightly modifies his original simple schema of three acts; he now claims that there is something called a 'midpoint' halfway through the second act (and hence halfway through the film itself). Why this moment should be different from the main turning points is not explained, but at least this shows that Field has realised there is something wrong with the three-act schema.[9] Moreover, most of the other manuals warn aspiring scriptwriters that the second act is long and apt to bog down.

My terms for the five parts of the modern feature derive from those used in the scenario manuals, both of the silent and the recent eras. These are: the set-up, the complicating action, the development, the climax, and the epilogue. The shifts between parts almost always hinge on crucial stages and changes in the goals of the main characters.

From the accompanying table of timings for some modern Hollywood films, it is apparent that several of them fall into four portions quite neatly, with just under half an hour for each part, see Table 1. (The list is in chronological order, since the timings seem to have become increasingly precise over this period. Perhaps as new generations of film-school students have graduated and entered this very competitive field, they have become both more aware of the guidelines and more intent on proving to agents and producers that they can conform to those guidelines.) The numbers of minutes for the parts do not add up

1895

Table 1: Large-scale parts of some modern Hollywood features (timings in min)

Title	Running time	Set-up	Complicating action	Development	Climax	Epilogue
Jaws (1975)	124	22	43	29	26	2
Alien (1979)	117	33	24	27	28	1
The Empire Strikes Back (1980)	124	36	24	24	34	Brief
Tootsie (1982)	115	25	32	21	34	Brief
Back to the Future (1985)	116	27	32	18	30	5
The Silence of the Lambs (1991)	118	27	33	28	23	8
The Bodyguard (1992)	129	31	29	236	23	6
Falling Down (1993)	113	30	30	25	24	3
Jurassic Park (1993)	127	31	60		30	2
Groundhog Day (1993)	101	31	37	16	15	1
Speed (1994)	116	27	66		18	1

exactly to the totals, partly because of credit sequences and partly because of rounding off to the nearest minute. Recent films tend to be around two hours long, with three to five minutes of credits at the end. Thus the prototypical film has four segments of around 28 minutes each, with a two-minute epilogue, plus title and credits.

I shall briefly describe the large-scale structures of a couple of the films on this list, in order to suggest what these parts consist of; both of my examples are considered models of current scriptwriting practice.

In the set-up section of *The Silence of the Lambs* (1991), for example, Clarice Starling has one initial goal: to become an FBI agent and work for Jack Crawford. When Crawford sends her to interview serial killer Hannibal Lecter, the latter mocks her ambitions but gives her a clue concerning the latest serial-killer case the FBI is investigating. When she finds the victim's head in the storage warehouse, it becomes apparent that Lecter is willing to help Clarice solve the case. That ends the set-up portion. Clarice now has a second, more urgent goal: to solve the Buffalo Bill case. As you can see, this initial set of basic premises is complete by 27 minutes into a 118-minute film.

The complicating action begins as Lecter of-

fers to help Clarice with the case in exchange for a transfer to a cell with a view – thus revealing *his* goal. Clarice's involvement in the Buffalo Bill case becomes more suspenseful as a new victim is kidnapped. This section ends with Clarice's false offer of a transfer for Lecter, who in exchange offers her another clue. Thus the complicating action sets up the method by which Clarice will achieve both her goals.

The development begins just over halfway through the film – 60 minutes in. Often the development portion of a film involves obstacles put in the way of the protagonist's achievement of his or her goal. These create delay, and relatively little progress toward the goal may actually occur. In the development section of *The Silence of the Lambs*, Dr. Chilton reveals the FBI's false offer of a transfer and has Lecter taken to a jail in Tennessee. Clarice does finally manage to interview Lecter before his escape, and she gets the vital final clue that he offers. This section of the film ends as she and her roommate figure out the significance of the clue.

This prepares the way for the climax portion of the film. By 'climax' I do not mean simply the final high point, a single scene that resolves the goals and conflicts set in motion earlier. Rather, the climax is that section of the film that follows after everything necessary for the resolution of the plot has been introduced. It includes the steady build up toward that final high point. In *The Silence of the Lambs*, the climax portion begins with Clarice going to Belvedere, Ohio to track down the killer. She still needs to find some clues in the house of the first victim, but these lead her to the killer's home and the final climactic shoot-out. In the epilogue, Clarice receives her degree and a call from Lecter. As Table 1 shows, the epilogue of this film is unusually long. I have included the entire credits sequence, since the final, long take continues throughout it, inviting us to speculate as to what is going on offscreen between Lecter and Dr. Chilten. (Up to the point where the credits begin, the epilogue is three minutes long.)

To take a second example, the set-up in *Back to the Future* (1985) introduces Marty McFly's friendship with the inventor Doc, his problems at school, his girlfriend, and his unhappy family life. When he meets Doc at the shopping mall, the inventor explains how the time machine works. A brief ellipsis follows, as the pair don safety suits. This marks the transition to the complicating action, which begins as Doc prepares to set out into the future but is interrupted by the attack of the Libyan terrorists. After Marty flees and ends up in 1955, he disrupts the events that were to have caused his parents to fall in love. During this section of the film, two crucial goals are set up: Marty must return to the future at the precise moment a bolt of lightning will supply power to the time machine, and he must cause his parents to attend a dance and fall in love. The complicating action ends as Doc states the second goal: 'You stick to your father like glue and make sure he takes her to the dance'. (This occurs just about one hour into the film.)

As in *The Silence of the Lambs*, the development consists mainly of delaying obstacles. Marty encounters a series of problems in trying to bring his parents together at the dance. Finally, however, he devises a plan. He also conceives one additional goal: to try and prevent the Libyans from killing Doc in 1985. The development ends with Marty slipping a warning note into Doc's pocket. The climax section of the film includes all the scenes at the dance and the action scene in which Marty races to start his time machine at the exact moment when the lightning strikes. It also includes the subsequent scene in 1985, at the mall, when Doc successfully eludes the Libyan assassination attempt and finally departs into the future.

The epilogue of *Back to the Future* is also uncharacteristically long. Marty must have time to discover that his pathetic family has been transformed into the ideal Reagan-era middle-class household. Moreover, Doc returns to warn of a crisis going on in Marty's future life, thereby setting up a sequel. (The setting up of sequels has had a major impact on the epilogues of recent Hollywood films. The same was true of *The Silence of the Lambs*.)

Despite the prevalence of films with four major parts, I have found a few films with the three-act structure recommended by the manuals. *Jurassic Park* (1993) is one. Table 1 indicates how very precisely timed the parts are. The set-up ends with the witnessing of the birth of the baby dinosaur and the claim that the dinosaurs cannot breed in the wild. We learn that the baby dinosaur is a velociraptor, the most deadly kind.

The complicating action occupies the central hour of the film, and the action is able to go on so long without a central turning point primarily because so many characters and so many varieties of dinosaurs have been introduced. The narrative can continue for some time without anything new being introduced, simply because it can move among these elements. There is no turning point at the centre of the film – but I should note that the attack of the Tyrannosaurus Rex comes 64 minutes into the film, providing a good example of placing a high moment of the action midway through.

This central portion ends 30 minutes before the epilogue, with the discovery that the raptors are breeding in the wild. The climax then culminates with the battle with the dinosaurs in the visitors centre, and a two-minute epilogue show the main characters leaving the island.

Speed (1994) is another instance of a three-act film. The central action on the bus is quite long and the final sequences relating to the

1895

subway train unusually short – hence the frequent spectator reaction that the subway segment is a letdown after the bus portion. This suggests, I think, another reason why films tend to fall into four portions: shorter major segments are less likely to become noticeably unbalanced in this way.

These brief examples and Table 1 demonstrate, I hope, that recent Hollywood filmmaking has adhered to a model that dictates a careful balance among portions of the narrative.

Early scenario manuals: conceptualising narrative progression

Let us turn now to the questions of whether or not practitioners in the pre-1920 period saw narratives as having some sort of comparable parts and how they thought those parts should be proportioned. There is little standard usage of terminology among the writers of these early manuals – certainly there was far less agreement on terms than there is in modern guides. One manual might speak of the 'complication' as what follows the introduction; another might call that same part the 'situation'. My attempt here will be to see if there is any consistency in the concepts underlying these varied terms.

As in modern screenplay manuals, these early guides inevitably invoke the notion of every narrative as having a beginning, middle, and end, often citing Aristotle by name. For example, J. Arthur Nelson's 1913 guide, *The Photoplay: How to Write. How to Sell*, mentions this concept, then tries to specify what the three parts consist of: 'The photoplay must have a beginning, a middle, and an end. These are technically known as cause, crisis, and *climactic effect, or cause, effect and sequence*.' Nelson likens the plot to the tying and untying of a knot. The tying is created by 'complications', which all good plots include.[10] He then further divides the narrative into parts: 'The outline of the play should comprehend: First, "cause", or beginning; second, development; third, crisis; fourth, climax or effect; fifth denouement or sequence.' He describes how these parts create a forward movement after the first section, the cause:

The Purpose of development is to bring the play closer to a realisation of its crisis, and thence to its climax and sequence. Development, then, should take on all the requisites of a forward movement. In the primary scenes we have the introduction and primary clash of interests. The importance of the issue, and the complications which attend it, will regulate the number of scenes required to make its purpose clear.

The crisis, he adds, is 'the situation which leads directly to the climax'.[11] In this sense, the crisis can perhaps be seen as the first portion of that large-scale portion I have labelled the 'climax'.

Nelson makes no distinction between one-reelers and longer films, but since features were relatively rare in 1913, he probably refers primarily to shorter narratives. The same is presumably true of Henry Albert Phillips, a practicing scenarist who published an important manual, *The Photodrama*, in 1914. There he declared that the 'structure of the play' consisted of 'Introduction, Situation, Crisis and Solution'. Philips' definition of the 'Situation' is worth quoting at some length, for it seems to be comparable to what modern manuals would term a 'plot point' or 'turning point':

Since drama is an artistic process of obtaining striking and gratifying effects upon the emotions of an audience, the situation is the most frequent and positive means to that end. The situation is what lends novelty, fire and brilliance to the progressive units of the play. It places the characters in a galvanic relationship with each other or with their condition or environment. It means the introduction of *the unexpected – either from the point of view of the character or of the audience*. Its introduction marks the beginning of Suspense, and raises the question, What will he do about it? For it means a relationship about which something must be done immediately, and that something is a Crisis. The Situation itself is of short duration but of tremendous power and effect. It succeeds the introductory action, or a sudden revealment to the audience, of which the character may remain in ignorance, or an unlooked-for entry, or an undreamed-of relationship disclosed – that sudden[ly] change the whole aspect of development.[12]

Phillips' idea that the situation raises the question 'What will he do about it?' suggests that it consists of an intense action that may alter the hero's goal or at least introduce a major new set of premises. Hence, it seems to function as what we would now call a turning point.

As films became longer, photoplay advisers became more specific about the film's ideal movement from beginning to end. In 1913, Eustace Hale Ball declared: 'The technical presentation of a two or three reel subject is virtually the same as that of a single reel, except that there should be a proportionate addition to the number of scenes, and dramatic crises'.[13] Some writers equated the individual reel within a feature with the acts of a stage play. Epes Winthrop Sargent explained this idea in 1913. Some studios, he said, released each reel of a multiple-reel film separately and hence wanted them to have self-contained stories. He then described more typical practice:

> The more general demand, however, is for a series of reels with a continuous subject, each reel terminating with a minor climax with the grand climax at the end of the last reel. For this no better example can be given than the play of the stage. At the end of each act there comes a definite stoppage of the action at a point which leaves the audience eager for the continuation. At the end of the first act the villain declares that the heroine shall be his and the curtain falls on this situation, leaving the audience wondering how he is going to bring this to pass. We are eager for the curtain to rise again that we may have our curiosity gratified. At the end of the second act the hero is being led off to jail on a trumped up charge, while the villain takes the heroine off on a yachting cruise very much against her will. This is a pretty state of affairs and we wonder how things are ever going to right themselves after all this mix-up. We know, because we have been to the theatre more than once, that it will all straighten

out in the last act and that the villain will get the worst of it, but the situation is interesting and we wish we were up in the gallery along with the rest of the kids that we might hiss the villain, too.[14]

Sargent uses the term 'situation' in much the way Phillips had, making it a sudden moment that generates suspense and leads to questions in the audience's minds. Recall Phillips' question that results from a Situation: 'What will he do about it?' Here Sargent says the situation at the end of the first act leaves the 'audience wondering how he is going to bring this to pass'. The second act curtain situation makes us 'wonder how things are ever going to right themselves after all this mix-up'. Sargent also offers specific proportions for the parts of the narrative: 'One point to observe is that the minor climaxes or critical moments shall fall every thousand feet. This may bother you at first, but a little practice will show you how to write about so much action to each reel.'[15] In 1915, the year when five-reel features were rapidly becoming the standard basis of film programmes, another scenario manual used the stage-play analogy:

> In a stage play an act is a definite division of the progress of the play. A reel in a multiple-reel subject may be likened to an act. One must be careful to get the whole play sequence right and then to get right the internal sequence of each reel. … one should strive to make each thousand feet of film convey a definite and complete division of the action.[16]

In 1916, Harry R. Durant, head of the scenario department at Famous Plays, drew upon a comparison with magazine fiction in advising aspiring freelancers:

> In writing a five-reel feature plot very much the same procedure might be employed as in planning a five-part magazine serial. Magazine editors and authors know the importance of the 'curtain' at the end of each instalment – the dramatic scene split in two, followed by the usual 'To Be Continued' notice, which rouses the interest of the reader to the extent of purchasing the next issue – and authors should recognise the equal importance of

1895

big scenes and situations in the picture plot.[17]

Note here that Durant refers specifically to a five-part serial as being like a film. Whether or not the comparison was to plays or magazine serials, such advice suggests that from early on, writers of feature-length films were encouraged to divide their narratives into five parts of equal lengths. Each would end on a high point designed to propel viewer expectation and excitement. In practice, as we shall see in examining the large-scale parts of some actual five-reelers, features rarely contained four turning points (or situations or minor climaxes or whatever) in addition to a final climax. Three or four large-scale parts perhaps seemed a better proportion for a running time of roughly 75 minutes. After all a single fifteen-minute reel was half or less the length of a typical act of a stage play.

Indeed, by the late 1910s, the notion of reels as comparable to stage acts was fast disappearing. One of the most respected scenario advisers of the day, Victor Oscar Freeburg, debunked this notion in his important 1918 book, *The Art of Photoplay Making*:

> This difference between the units of attention in a photoplay and in a stage drama has not always been grasped by scenario writers, who have looked upon the reel (a thousand feet of film) as the unit of attention. A reel would, of course, be a unit of attention only when the showing of the reel was followed by a fairly long intermission before the showing of the next reel.[18]

As Freeburg pointed out, however, by this point features were usually shown continuously. Most American theatres would have had two projectors, with no need for a gap for threading the next reel. Spectators would probably not have been aware of reel changes as a significant division within a film, and scenarists actually had little reason to take them into account.

Instead, Freeburg cited Aristotle once more: 'Instead of the terms beginning, middle, and end we prefer to substitute the term premise, complication, and solution'. For him, the premise and solution sections were relatively short, with all the crises, including the climax,

coming within the larger central complication section. Thus Freeburg seems to use the term 'solution' to be the equivalent of a denouement or epilogue. Some manual writers, as we have seen, seem to use 'solution' as including the climax. All seem to be in accord, however, concerning the general principles of narrative progression.

Although Freeburg eschewed the 1000-foot reel as the measure of one major unit of action, he did suggest that the story proceeds in regular parts. He supplied a metaphor not derived from the other arts:

> Let us symbolise the progression of dramatic attention by a loosely hung cable which ascends a hillside rhythmically over a row of posts. The angles, or apexes, of the cable would each represent a crisis, except the highest, which would represent the climactic point of the plot. The most dramatic pictures [i.e. shots] would, of course, coincide with these apexes of the cable. Those pictures which narrate incidents or situations would be on the up curves, since they create suspense. Still lower down on each curve would be the descriptive pictures, pictures which describe environment and character, and thereby lead to the succeeding rise of plot interest. And decorative pictures, pictures with no story interest at all, would be on the lowest points of each curve, or might even come on the down curve immediately after a crisis.[19]

Freeburg's claim that the cable ascends the hillside 'rhythmically' over the poles hints that he considered that the parts of the narrative should be roughly equal in duration, though not measured in 1000-foot lengths.

After 1918, the notion that reels equalled acts or magazine serial episodes largely disappeared, though the basic parts of the feature-film narrative remained roughly the same. For example, William Lord Wright, who wrote a regular scenario advice column in *The Moving Picture News*, wrote in 1922: 'There must be the opening of the story, the building and the plot development; the big situations and the climax; comedy relief and a happy ending'. For a five-reeler, 'there must be no deliberate padding of plot, and yet there must

1895

be minor climaxes in the action as well as one great major climax.[20] Many other manuals give similar pronouncements, but these examples should make the point clear. It was widely assumed that scenarios had to have a series of high points, termed crises or situations or minor climaxes, leading up to one final climax.

Clearly, simply giving a hero a goal and letting him or her struggle against obstacles to achieve it was not a sufficient basis for a feature film. Many one-reelers and even two-reelers were structured with this kind of steadily ascending movement toward a single climax, but the feature could not just be a one-reeler prolonged. As early as 1916, scenarist Marguerite Bertsch insisted that longer films had to be broken into what she termed 'telling scenes':

> Most pictures that run through more than two reels have a plot that resolves itself at first glance into numerous telling scenes; for, unless there are various turns in the plot, the structure follows an upward slant so direct as to allow of no climax to the reel. Then, too, the story that follows one direct crescendo without surprising or interesting fluctuations would make tedious material for a multiple reel subject. At times, such a subject, when delicately handled, will carry successfully through as many as two reels.
>
> As a rule, however, stories falling under this class build up the market of one-reel subjects.[21]

In 1924 Frederick Palmer, head of the most prominent school of scenario writing, summarised the same idea briefly: 'In creating a drama, there must be much more than the mere competition between two individuals for a given point, or toward an eventual goal. Other characters must be introduced, and there must be plot and counter-plot'.[22]

In 1922, Palmer offered a rare suggestion as to how many major parts would make up a feature. He assumed that plots were built when incidents led to situations, which in turn accelerate into crises: 'A [screen]play must have several minor situations. And it must have at least three major situations which grow into crises'.[23] Thus a feature film would have a minimum of three large-scale parts, advice which perhaps is an early version of the modern Hollywood script manual's 'three-act' structure.

Unfortunately, scenario manuals of the silent era do not offer many suggestions as to how the large-scale parts of films were to be proportioned. Unlike their modern counterparts, advice-givers did not offer precise page-lengths for each part or act. They did, however, occasionally specify roughly how to break up a film story into parts. For example, a 1916 scenario manual that still assumed that each reel of a five-reeler should be a separate act, gave this advice:

> In the opening period, that of making known the characters, the location and the general trend of a story may be one-third of a three-act stage play. It is not, however, advisable to use more than one-fifth, the first act of a five-reel photo-drama, for such introductory and preparatory work, though this limitation is not actually imposed.[24]

As we shall see, this allotment of one-fifth of the film to the set-up phase proved not generous enough in practice. Most films used more like the first reel and a half.

In 1917, successful freelance scenarist Maibelle Heikes Justice shared her practical wisdom concerning plot progression:

> The plot or central idea of the drama must never for an instant be forgotten – it reaches like a taut plumb-line directly through the play, no matter how frequently one may vacillate or side-step the main thread of the story on his way, and each scene must be a little stronger in story value than its predecessor, till with the story and action well in hand about two-thirds of the way through, one is over the hill of 'high lights' and must now begin to drive his subject home in a strong and perfectly logical manner toward the final[e] – known as the climax.[25]

Here Justice suggests what I outlined earlier, that the push toward the climax, rather than the climax itself, begins after all other major actions and premises have been introduced. Without resorting to any measurement based on reel length, she assigns the climax portion

1895

to roughly the last third of the film. Again, this accords roughly with the notion of a three-act structure.

One further indication of proportions comes in a 1920 scenario manual by Frances Patterson, which defines the three parts of the narrative as 'the premise, the complication, and the end: In terms of reels the premise usually takes about one reel of continuity. The second, third and fourth reels are devoted to the complication, and the fifth is given over to the solution.'[26] This agrees fairly well with modern scenario manual dictates concerning three acts.

We have seen that modern scriptwriting advisers give writers a guide as to how to proportion their narratives by dictating that a page of a script should, on average, translate into one minute on the screen. The end of the set-up should come about a quarter of the way through, or on about page 30 of a two-hour film. Did silent scriptwriters have comparable guidelines? There is certainly no indication that any formula was articulated so precisely and explicitly during the period. The only reference I have found to the optimum length of continuity scenarios in terms of pages comes in John Emerson and Anita Loos's *How to Write a Photoplay*, published in 1920. This manual, apparently directed as much at aspiring contract writers as at freelancers, is one of the most detailed and explicit descriptions of silent script-writing practice.

At one point Emerson and Loos offer their continuity scenario for *In Search of a Sinner* (a Constance Talmadge film of 1920) as a good model for the length of a typed continuity script for a five-reeler. The script was 76 pages long. Though Emerson and Loos do not go on to make the point, at silent speed, this would work out almost exactly to one page per minute for a 75-minute feature. Whether other authors followed this model is difficult to determine. Still, it may possibly be that the modern guideline of one page per minute is a legacy of this earlier age.

This examination of early scenario advisers' views of large-scale narrative parts and their proportions has suggested that the ideal was a feature with a regular series of rising and falling action. We need now to examine some of the films of this era to see if any more precise patterns emerge.

Large-scale parts in early hollywood features

The second accompanying table (see Table 2) gives a list of examples from the period 1913 to 1921, also in chronological order. These are mostly fairly famous films, with which many readers will no doubt be familiar. I should lay down a few provisos concerning these examples. The timings are from video viewings. Some of the recordings were done at silent speed, some at sound. I have noted if the recording was obviously at sound speed. For my purposes, however, determining the exact authentic silent-era running speed is not particularly relevant. What I am primarily interested in here is the *proportion* of time allotted to each large-scale part.

Nevertheless, one obviously needs to be *very* cautious in coming to any conclusions based on such timings. The status of the original prints is usually dubious. Some of these films are missing footage, such as that brief portion of a scene lost from the last reel of *Alias Jimmy Valentine* (1915) and noted in the Library of Congress's video release. Others may be reissue prints, as seems likely with *The Social Secretary* (1916). Thus I am well aware that my arguments and conclusions here are quite tentative. Still, enough of a pattern emerges across this set of examples that I think one can make some useful hypotheses concerning the number of large-scale parts in early films and the way such parts were proportioned to one another.

Looking at these examples, it becomes immediately apparent that filmmakers seem not to have followed the manuals' advice to break films into large-scale parts according to the reel breaks. Ben Brewster has already analysed *Traffic in Souls* (1913) in detail and concluded that, far from trying to end each reel at a high point or a pause in the action, the filmmakers seem to have attempted to carry the action uninterrupted across the reel breaks.[27]

It is in fact fairly clear that most early features fell into three large-scale parts, usually with a brief epilogue. (For convenience's sake, I

Table 2: Large-scale parts of some early Hollywood features (timings in min)

Title	Running time	Set-up	Complicating action	Development	Climax	Epilogue
Traffic in Souls (1913/6)	71	23	25		19	4
The Avenging Conscience (1914/7)	56	20	19		18	2
The Virginian (1914/5)	54	23	15		16	0.5
The Wishing Ring (1914/5)	45 (sd.)	17	12		15	1
The Italian (1915/6)	60 (sd.)	15	14	16	14	0.5
Alias Jimmy Valentine (1915/5)	65	17	27		19	?
Regeneration (1915/5)	61	19	19		23	0.5
The Social Secretary (1916/5)	62	14	15	18	14	Brief
Male and Female (1919/9)	94	21	26	30	17	2
The Last of the Mohicans (1920/6)	71	18	26		23	4
Miss Lulu Bett (1921/7)	64	22	23		19	1

will call the central portion the 'complicating action'.) Again, the problem with possible missing footage renders it risky to make claims about any one title, but in general, the parts of the films often seem to be roughly proportioned to fall into thirds that do not differ greatly in length. *The Avenging Conscience* (1914) provides a good example. The opening part, or set-up, introduces the romance between the hero and heroine, the disapproval of his uncle, and the Italian who will later blackmail the hero. As the set-up ends, the hero watches the heroine crying disconsolately after having been separated from him. The middle section begins at roughly 20 minutes in, with the title 'The birth of the evil thought'. Clearly this is a major turning point, establishing that the hero's character and goals have changed; this prepares the way for the murder and later madness. In my segmentation of the film, this complicating action ends about 19 minutes later, after the brief scene in which the hero shows the Italian his preparations to escape the detective. After this point, nothing more has to be introduced, and the action builds toward the climactic shoot-out, suicide of the hero, his waking from his dream, and his union with the heroine. A brief epilogue then shows the happy couple as he

reads her some of his writing. The timings suggest that the proportions of the parts are balanced in *The Avenging Conscience* – especially if one combines the climax and epilogue portions which make up the final third of the film.

I shall not describe the large-scale parts of each of these films. I shall mention them for *Alias Jimmy Valentine*, since Tourneur uses an interesting device to mark the parts off quite clearly from each other. The set-up segment deals with Jimmy's life of crime and ends with him in jail. There is a brief, static silhouette shot of Jimmy in his cell, beginning and ending with fades. This shot seems to act as a sort of curtain or pause between parts. The central section then involves Jimmy's reform: his pardon, his growing love for Rose, and his consequent determination to go straight by working in a bank. Once it has been established that Jimmy will not relapse, the film is ready to move into the climax portion. Again Tourneur signals this with a single static shot bracketed by fades: a view of Rose's little sister praying by her bed. She is the one who will precipitate the crisis by getting locked in the bank safe. We can only guess what the film's epilogue would have been like, as the ending is missing. Although the three portions of *Alias Jimmy Valentine* are not divided into anything like equal thirds, it is perhaps notable that the set-up and climax are fairly well balanced on either side of the longer central complicating action.

Even fairly early on it was also possible to make a feature with four major parts and an epilogue. *The Italian* (1915) offers an interesting example, since the original reel breaks are preserved. There are even two of the sorts of titles that originally ended many reels of early features: 'Part four of this picture will be shown in one minute'. This practice resulted from the fact that in the 1910s theatres were still in the process of adding second projectors, and features would sometimes be shown with a short break for threading up the next reel. These breaks were presumably one reason why scenario manuals advised putting a high point at the end of each reel.

Yet *The Italian*, a six-reeler, has no breaks or high points coinciding with the reel ends. The first reel, for example, ends during the intercutting between Beppo and Annette walking in the woods and Gallia and Trudo talking in the house. Reel four ends with a shot of Beppo moving angrily toward the men who have just stolen his money; reel five begins with a shot of a nearby space into which Beppo is moving. This pattern fits in perfectly with what Brewster found with *Traffic in Souls*. In *The Italian*, the major breaks in the action come in the middles of reels.

The four major sections are easy to determine, being clearly separated off with time lapses. The end of the set-up comes when Trudo gives Beppo his ultimatum: 'One year do I give thee, Beppo Donnetti, to win a home for my daughter. Should thou fail, she weds the merchant Gallia.' With the hero's goal established, the action then moves into the complicating action, the journey to America and the accomplishment of the goal. This section ends almost exactly midway through the film, with the wedding. A year passes, and the development then deals with the illness and death of the pair's son. The climax portion traces Beppo's despair, his attempt at revenge on the official who refused to help him, and his change of heart. The epilogue consists of one shot of him by his son's grave.

Conclusion

The typical early feature film was not simply a one-reeler expanded – not, that is, a single build to a climax. Some scenario manuals of the period explicitly made this point. Nor was the feature a string of one-reelers, with a climax exactly timed for each reel's end and a longer one for the finale – despite the common claim of the advisers.

Instead, from early on in the era when features were coming to prominence and the continuity system was being formulated, the better scriptwriters seem to have realised, consciously or unconsciously, that one reel was simply too short to be a really major part of a lengthy narrative. Building up to five or six high points in a film that would last 75 to 90 minutes was apparently just too fast-paced.

Why should this be? The early American cinema quickly became noted for being action-packed. The high points – situations, crises, minor climaxes, or whatever they were called – were universally assumed by the manuals to generate those staples of narrative action, suspense and surprise. Why not jam as many in as possible? I suspect it may be because too much high-pitched action would not allow enough time for other staples of the classical story-telling system: most importantly exposition, motivation, and redundancy, but also humour, romance, motifs, subplots, and the like. A balance needed to be kept between these factors and the strong action. Freeburg's notion of the gentle rhythm of a rising and falling were hints at how that balance could be attained.

Early scenarists achieved balance by splitting their story up into thirds or quarters, with high points or major breaks between them. Modern scenarists are still doing much the same thing, though, as I have suggested, recent films are more likely to contain four than three parts. This makes perfect sense in terms of the differences in length. At silent speed, an early five-reeler would run on average a little under 75 minutes, a six-reeler closer to 85. The ideal feature today is between 110 and 120 minutes long. Rather than using three parts and stretching them all out, Hollywood practitioners have added a fourth segment –

even while apparently thinking that they are still using a three-act structure.

The timing of each part, however, has remained fairly consistent between the two periods in question. Certainly there are difficulties in comparison, given the problems with running times for the early features. Yet it seems possible to suggest very broadly that the ideal length for a large-scale portion of a film is between twenty and thirty minutes in both periods. These ideal proportions might be said to form almost a temporal equivalent of the golden mean for Hollywood storytelling.

This essay has compared the earliest and latest phases of Hollywood feature filmmaking. The next step, of course, is to do similar large-scale segmentations and timings for films of the intervening decades. I suspect that the proportions I have examined here would be present there as well. After all, recent filmmaking practice is not a throwback to early features. It is likely that the narrative principles I have been examining here are simply one more instance of the remarkable stability of classical Hollywood filmmaking.

Notes

1. David Bordwell, Janet Staiger, and Kristin Thompson, *The Classical Hollywood Cinema: Film Style and Mode of Production to 1960* (London: Routledge and Kegan Paul, 1985).
2. Some of the best and most influential of these are Epes Winthrop Sargeant, *Technique of the Photoplay* (New York: Moving Picture World, 1912), issued in two subsequent editions; Howard T. Dimick, *Photoplay Making* (Ridgewood, NJ: The Editor Company, 1915); and Henry Albert Phillips *The Photodrama* (Larchmont, NY: Stanhope-Dodge, 1914).
3. See, for example, A. Van Buren Powell, *The Photoplay Synopsis* (Springfield, Mass: The Home Correspondence School, 1919).
4. Sabine Jarothe and Wolfgang Längsfeld's *The Art of Screenwriting: an International Bibliography of Books on Screenwriting* (Munich: Filmland Press, 1991) provides the basis for a rough count, though it is not complete for the earliest years. I have excluded foreign manuals and those designed for amateurs.
5. Syd Field, *Screenplay: The Foundations of Screenwriting* (New York: Delta, 1979), 8–11.
6. Linda Seger, *Making a Good Script Great* (New York: Dodd. Mead, 1987), 4–5.
7. Michael Hauge, *Writing Screenplays that Sell* (New York: Harper Perennial, 1991), 86–87.
8. Quoted in Karl Schanzer and Thomas Lee Wright, *American Screenwriters* (New York: Avon, 1993), 24–25.
9. See Syd Field, *Four Screenplays: Studies in the American Screenplay* (New York: Dell, 1994), xviii.
10. J. Arthur Nelson, *The Photo-play: How to Write. How to Sell* (Los Angeles: Photoplay, 1913), 76, 95.
11. Nelson, *The Photo-play*, 169–170.
12. Phillips, *The Photodrama*, 167–168.
13. Eustace Hale Ball, *The Art of the Photoplay* (New York: Veritas, 1913), 57–58.
14. Sargent, *Technique of the Photoplay*, 2nd ed., 121–122.
15. Sargent, *Technique of the Photoplay*, 2nd ed., 123.
16. Dimick, *Photoplay Making*, 80–81.
17. Quoted in Capt. Leslie T. Peacocke, *Hints on Photoplay Writing* (Chicago: Photoplay Publishing Company, 1916), 107.
18. Freeburg, *The Art of Photoplay Making*, 234.
19. Freeburg, *The Art of Photoplay Making*, 258–259.
20. William Lord Wright, *Photoplay Writing* (New York: Falk, 1922), 60, 82.
21. Bertsch, *How to Write for Moving Pictures*, 56–57.
22. Frederick Palmer, *Technique of the Photoplay* (Hollywood; Palmer Institute of Authorship, 1924), 97.
23. Frederick Palmer, *Palmer Plan Handbook. Volume One* (Los Angeles, Palmer Photoplay Corporation, 1922), 61.
24. Louis Reeves Harrison, *Screencraft* (New York: Chalmers, 1916), 48.

1895

25. Maibelle Heikes Justice, 'The Photodrama', in Louella O. Parsons, *How to Write for the 'Movies'*, 2nd edn. (Chicago: E. McClurg & Co., 1917), 240–241.

26. Frances Taylor Patterson, *Cinema Craftsmanship: A Book for Photoplaywrights* (New York: Harcourt, Brace and Howe, 1920), 11.

27. Ben Brewster, 'Traffic in Souls: An Experiment in Feature-Length Narrative Construction', *Cinema Journal* 31, 1 (Fall 1991): 37–56.

Magnified Discourse: Screenplays and Censorship in Swedish Cinema of the 1910s

Jan Olsson

Department of Cinema Studies, Stockholm University, 102 51 Stockholm, Sweden

Preliminaries

SWEDISH CINEMA OF THE 1910s is sometimes considered in terms of its stylistic difference to Danish and American cinema, the former allegedly akin to the latter. From this perspective, it may be argued that Swedish films evidence a different practice, foregrounding the pro-filmic realm – lighting, acting style, character placement, deep staging etc. – to downplay the role of editing. John Fullerton's doctoral thesis provides important insights into the mechanics of Swedish cinema from this perspective.[1] What follows are reflections with limited scope, a sort of close-up on close shots and their place in Swedish screen writing practice and censorship discourse with some comparative background notes regarding American cinema.

The material under consideration is, however, very scarce, almost non-existent in terms of footage. Apart from *Ingeborg Holm* (1913), there is only one other surviving film from 1913, a one-reeler. From 1914 and 1915 we have only one film respectively, although the archival situation is somewhat less bleak for subsequent years. *Ingeborg Holm* is, indeed, a film that uses deep staging and restrained acting style, and confines the use of scene dissection to a series of still photograph inserts, some letters, and a bill. Given the almost one-to-one ratio between shots and scenes, Sjöström's film is often contrasted with George Loane Tucker's *Traffic in Souls*, produced in the same year, characterised by its highly developed fast-paced editing, including at least one breathtaking tracking shot, which, as a transitional style, has been contrasted with the European concern for slow-paced but elaborately crafted staging of the 'pro-filmic'.

If the style displayed in *Ingeborg Holm* represents the Swedish – read Swedish Biograph – norm, how long did it prevail? And when did cut-ins, analytic editing, point-of-view shots and shot/reverse-shot structures become options or preferred choices within the Swedish production system?[2]

1895

The concept of 'magnification/enlargement' for close shots can serve as a hub for shedding light on these issues. I will ignore the distinction between close-ups and inserts. It doesn't matter much if a close shot focuses on a face, some other part of a body, or a non-bodily phenomenon so long as such a shot dissects a scene, that is, interrupts the scene's spatio-temporal continuum. Henry A. Phillips made the same point in *The Photodrama* in 1914: 'Technically speaking, all inserted matter is [*sic*] inserts. From a mechanical point of view, the film must be cut in order that captions, printed or inscribed matter, close-views, visions, spoken lines, etc., may be inserted.'[3] Inserts – newspaper headlines, telegrams, letters and the like – were, of course, just as in *Ingeborg Holm*, more numerous then close-ups in transitional cinema. The important and related issue of intertitles (leaders in contemporary terminology) not addressed here is their frequency, placement, and function as narrative vehicles. Some historians would probably even question the exclusive narrative function of intertitles.[4]

Close-ups do not necessarily imply close shots, or extreme close shots. Rather, I use the term to denote a change in shot scale – including that of the cut-in – so marking a departure from the standard long shot. Manuals for screen writing are eloquent on the conceptualisation of this and other style parameters. As Elbert Moore's *Text Book on Writing the Photoplay* put it:

> The term *'close up'* as the words would imply, means that when the picture is being taken, the camera is moved close up to the object and the resulting image, when reflected on the screen, is enlarged in size so as to show the detail which is important. The close up has several divisions ... One is 'the bust'. This means a close up of a character that shows only his bust, or head and shoulders. Another is 'the three-quarters', which shows the character from the waist line up. Then there is the *'the full length'*, in which the character is shown in full length, but close to the camera.[5]

Magnification, as a term designating the spatial enframing of the cut-in from a long shot to a closer view, marks an important change

in the scopic potential of early cinema, if we accept such a monolithic formulation for pre-classical film.

Equating the camera position with diegetic vantage point (i.e. a point of view), which the spectator could share, was not an obvious metapsychological option. The camera, conventionally, was understood to stand in for the eye of the spectator, static and frontal, presenting an ideal view of the entire filmic space with all the players visible in full figure. The audience was affiliated with the display through pro-filmic practices and enframing, but rarely through editing. The actor, on equal footing with the spectator, could meet his/her eyes; they were partners in the same world. Filmic address was one way; from the actor to the spectator/camera. Only after being expelled from the paradise of the attraction world were actors forced to lower their gaze shyly before the camera and retreat into their own 'fishbowl' world. In transitional cinema the direction of address was gradually reversed; cut-ins imaginarily transported the spectator towards the threshold of the diegetic world. Screen writing manuals attest to this change of direction. Close shots were initially described as bringing the players closer to the camera, a reminiscence of earlier practices; later on, they were perceived as moving the camera closer to the players. Only in the second case was point of view an option. In earlier practice, the camera was deemed to occupy a fixed position and actors were drawn or attracted by it to make contact with the spectator. In later practice, it was the diegetic world that was on display; a practice in which the camera was understood to highlight important aspects, to transport the spectator close up. James Slevin, in *On Picture-Play Writing*, says:

> The actual space in which the principal action of the ordinary picture-play takes place is about five or six feet wide and less than ten feet in length. Frequently not even this much space is used, as when the principal characters are brought very close to the camera, and are cut off at the knees or waist.[6]

Louella O. Parsons defines 'Closeup, or Bust' in a glossary section in her *How to Write for the 'Movies'* as, 'Magnifying a scene or figure by bringing the camera closer'.[7] Compare this formulation with my earlier quotation from Moore.

Magnification/enlargement/close-up in discourses of the period cue a perceptual oscillation related to a transformation in the modes of reception between presentation and narration, with narrativised attractions as a transitional middle term or, in current terminology, showing and telling. Close shots are crucial components in the dialectics involved in a cinema of attractions in transition, in a practice transforming gradually into the classical style; a codified system of devices cueing a synthetic or analytic organisation of filmic space. Such a trajectory represents neither a pre-determined path nor a natural outcome. Rather, it reflects a move towards an institutionalised mode grounded in the practices of the industry, and triggered by historical circumstances.

'Magnification', cued by inserts, close-ups and medium close-ups, seemingly dislocating objects and/or persons and making them come closer to the observer, initially conceptualised the changing relation between spectator and diegetic world, and hence upgraded visibility to serve a variety of functions. Cut-ins destroyed the conventional spatial relation, and were perceived, according to many contemporary sources, to put the narration 'on hold', as it were. Spectators were relegated to a process of 'fort/da', an interplay of presence and absence, in the pursuit of retrieving meaning, a procedure which, if not exactly non-legible, doubtlessly violated earlier reading protocols, and hence made the image strange. The fact that many cut-ins were shot with a background different to that of the master shot demonstrates that spatial continuity was not yet a determining principle. Cut-ins or close-ups are, therefore, somewhat misleading terms for such decontextualised shots; magnification/enlargement *is* a more accurate term for a process that transported the spectator elsewhere, since the notion of continuity related to character, not space. An unidentified fragment in the Danish Film Museum even allowed the actress to change costume between the shots.

Enlarged or magnified characters and objects took on grotesque proportions, or appeared mutilated. George C. Pratt gives ample evidence of such response in his selection of texts from the American trade press arguing for 'uniformity of proportions' (*Moving Picture World*, 24 July 1909), criticising shot scales ('Too Near the Camera', *MPW*, 25 March 1911), and complaining about mutilation ('Cutting of the Feet', *MPW*, 6 April 1912). These headlines evidence the perceptual disruption that changes in shot scale induced. Pratt also reprints Dr. Stockton's famous empirical findings (reported in *MPW*, 10 August 1912), and subsequent statistics provided details of films that contained even more shots than Stockton's top titles.[8]

Elbert Moore gives a different account in 1915:

> [T]he *close up* […] centres the attention of the audience on the important detail in question. The eyes of the audience are riveted to the screen, and they must look at it […] Thus, close work, or detail on the screen is admirably adapted for the purpose of gaining *emphasis*.[9]

The complaints, voiced in Pratt's selections from *MPW*, over too many shots, and shot scales that perceptually overwhelmed the spectator, are here read as a narrational strategy that was used to give direction and clarity, in short, emphasis. Such an impression of continuity was, of course, a prerequisite for the eventual success of analytic editing.

With the spectator's gaze centred via camerawork, the characters' looks into the camera were consequently banned. A newspaper report from Swedish Biograph's Lidingö studio, published the same year as Moore's manual, describes the shooting of some scenes in *Landshövdingens Döttrar* (The Governor's Daughters, 1915). The reporter illuminates the then prevalent norm regarding the relation between spectator and camera/screen:

> … Victor Sjöström won admiration for his excellent method of instruction. […] What appeared to be particularly onerous for one of the performing ladies was not being able to receive constant approval in the eyes of Mr. Sjöström. For she doggedly looked at him instead of at her co-actor. That earned her constant reproaches, as she should of course imagine that Mr. Sjöström at the camera represented the

public and you definitely do not fix your eye at the public from the screen.[10]

This passage confirms the assertion that the camera was understood to function as an intermediary providing spectatorial access to a closed diegetic world. Eye contact, associated with the attraction style, had been outlawed from the studio of Swedish Biograph. Let us accept that as one point of departure.

Deprived, in the main, of filmic sources, I have turned to two types of non-filmic discourse to advance further reflection on the status of magnification in Swedish cinema of the 1910s. Censorship records and surviving screenplays bear testimony to the ways in which the device and its functions were conceptualised from two different perspectives: those of the censors (who were historical spectators performing an institutionalised reading practice), and those of the script writers who represented the industry's understanding of its practices. When was the term, 'magnification' replaced by 'close-up'? What functions were assigned to cut-ins?

The censor['s] views

The Swedish censorship body came into effect late 1911 after several years of campaigning. The principal activists suddenly found themselves as official censors with power to regulate the trade. During the initial inspection period, the censors were often generous in apportioning value judgements and comments on the 'censorship cards'. They later became much more circumspect, only specifying a modicum of necessary factual information relating to the description of content and, very laconically, providing reasons for prohibition or a cut. This 'white' discourse (banned films were given a white label; red indicated general admission; yellow indicated entry forbidden to persons under 15 years of age) represents 'non-visible' evidence (since most of the films are lost) from what the censors described as their chamber of horrors. It reflects, of course, the set of criteria of the official censorship ordinance, but is embellished by further comments from the censors. The judgements oscillate between the norms of the ordinance (opinions

that reflect their taste and class-conditioned ideals concerning education and upbringing) and an antipathy towards the world from which the feature films, especially Danish ones, derived their material: modern city life highlighting criminality and depravity.

The struggle against so-called recorded or staged pictures (i.e. fiction films), in favour of images from nature (topicals, scenics, actualities), dominated the censorship campaign. From this standpoint, magnification in film drama came to epitomise everything that should not be seen: spare us the details! As the film medium, according to the censors, was one that should serve an educational function, depictions of crime would, by definition, function as latterday instruction manuals. And as the film experience was considered highly suggestive, there was a close correlation between see, learn, and imitate, at least for young audience members. This thesis was considered proven by a handful of case studies.

The most illuminating deliberation from the censors is represented by Gustaf Berg's article, 'Biograf och censur' (Cinema and Censorship) which appeared in 1912.[11] Berg provides a comprehensive sample of what had been forbidden or cut by the Board of Film Censors. He groups this material in relation to its family resemblance with other forms of entertainment, particularly the gestalt world of the waxworks in which criminal activity, pathology, and abnormality flourished in abundance. The actors in the films have been divested of their waxworks deathmask, he writes, and appear in full action, 'not drawing back from teaching their arts, if so required, in specially extracted and magnified pictures'. The term, 'magnified' occurs on two further occasions in Berg's short text: 'the fear of death staring from his face (now and then magnified!)', and 'the mundane pickpocket's magnified grip on the wallet'.

Berg's comments are one of the first observations on magnification in the Swedish context. He rebukes the exaggerated specificity of magnified shots which function as a sort of manual for criminal activity by virtue of their sheer tangible size on the screen. It is an invasive strategy, he argues, that gives crimi-

1895

nal techniques, immoral acts or horror effects disproportionate attention.

Many of the early censorship cards justified cuts in terms of magnification. For instance the film *En Överrocks Rundresa* (original title *Le Voyage Circulaire d'un Paletot*, Pathé, 1908, – card 3146): 'Shows how a watch theft is performed, in magnified form'. The film was examined in December 1911. Four years later, and vigilance stands unshaken. In a letter to the Stockholm branch office of Pathé Frères (6 December 1915) concerning *A Rose Among the Briars*, censor Berg writes, 'Via the cuts ordered by the Board of Film Censors that remove an ... even more irrelevant element from the main plot – a magnified clip of a revolver scene'.[12] In an essay titled 'Biograf och brott' (Cinema and Crime) dating from 1916, Berg returns to the topic: 'It is of course self-evident that detailed presentation, and then in the form of extricated magnifications, of instructive criminal tricks is absolutely reprehensible'.[13] The emphasis on 'instructive' criminal acts confirms the pedagogical perspective.

The justification given for cuts in Swedish features from the 1910s cover quite a number of magnifications excised in the wake of Berg's statements. Around 1916–17 a shift is apparent in the perception of the nature of the cut-in. Conceptually, 'magnification' becomes associated with supplementary expressions such as 'large-scale picture', 'large picture', and eventually, ' close shot' covering medium-shot, medium-close shot and close-up. The conceptual fluctuation mirrors a new understanding of the function of the cut-in and, also, a higher degree of narrative complexity in their articulation with other shots.

The censors disapproved of magnifications in the following Swedish films:

- Card 5676 *Dödsritten under cirkuskupolen* (The Last Performance, 1912) directed by Georg af Klercker:

  Three cuts in part II:

  '1. magnification of the drawing of poison into the syringe [...]';

- Card 10279 *Börsspekulantens Offer*

(i.e. *För sin kärleks skull* (Her Love's Sake, 1914) directed by Mauritz Stiller:

'Cut in part I of the magnified spiriting away of the banknotes at the bank';

- Card 15622 *Balettprimadonnan* (The Ballet Primadonna, 1916) directed by Mauritz Stiller:

  'At the end of part III, the magnification of the pistol, when the shot goes off, is removed';

- Card 15689 *Vid dödens tröskel* (i.e. *I elfte timmen*, At the Eleventh Hour, 1916) directed by Fritz Magnussen:

  'Cut in part III of the magnification where the gypsies' robbing of Brandt is demonstrated';

- Card 16276 *Den levande mumien* (The Living Mummy, 1917) directed by Fritz Magnussen:

  'Cut in part II of the shooting scene in the attack on Hearn and the first showing (in large scale) of him tied up';

- Card 16616 *Sin egen slav* (His Own Slave, 1917) directed by Konrad Tallroth:

  'Cut in part II of Ibrahim's demonstrative display of the bedroom, including the magnification of Ibrahim standing at the bedroom door, and even the subsequent display of the bedroom';

- Card 16794 *Fru Bonnets Felsteg* (Mrs Bonnet's Slip, 1917) directed by Egil Eide:

  'Cut in part I of the magnification of the theft of money at the café';

- Card 18733 *Berg-Ejvind och hans hustru* (The Outlaw and His Wife, 1918) directed by Victor Sjöström:

  'In act V the close shot [*närbild*] of Arnes with the knife at the rope is cut out'.

The cuts described by the censors primarily

concern exaggerated or spectacular criminal passages in conformity with the various statements of Gustaf Berg.

National Board of Review of Motion Pictures

The Swedish censorship board was a state agency whose decision could only be revoked by the government. After a few years, the industry and the Board got along without much friction, partly due to the government's overruling of all complaints. The New York based reviewers had no official authority, and could only issue recommendations hoping that their pronouncements had an impact on the market. Their seal of approval was sought by producers in the wake of controversy leading to the temporary closing down of Nickelodeons in New York City. In *Weekly Official Bulletin* (*WOB*),[14] published by The National Board of Review of Motion Pictures in New York, the National Board of Review initially, and to a limited extent, shared the Swedish censors' predilection for the term, 'enlargement/magnification'. Such shots are tagged as an unattractive manipulation of filmic discourse, switching narrative into pedagogy. These terms occur, however, far less frequently than in the Swedish context. Apart from proposed cuts, the National Board of Review was happy to propose that offending shots should be trimmed. Their colleagues in Stockholm preferred the scissors:

- *The Post Mistress* (Lux, *WOB*, 1 May 1911):

  'We would ask for the elimination of the enlarged view showing the man taking a wax impression of the lock.'

- *The Temptations of a Great City* (Great Northern, 1 May 1911):

  '[...] the enlarged view showing the man imitating his mother's signature [...]'.

- *The Root of Evil* (Biograph, 1 January 1912):

  'Elimination of the two enlarged views

of the placing of the poison in the glass ...'

- *The Overworked Bookkeeper* (Lubin,1 January 1912):

  'Elimination of the enlarged near view, which now follows the scene in the cell, showing the demented bookkeeper grimacing.'

- *The Flappers and the Nut* (Urbanola, 27 December 1913):

  'Eliminate the enlarged view of the two girls smoking just before the school mistress enters the room.'

- *The Gypsy Gambler* (Kalem, 23 May 1914):

  'Eliminate the enlarged view of the part where the man marks the cards.'

- *A Physical Culture Romance* (Komic, 22 August 1914):

  'Cut out entirely all close up enlargements of the physical culture instructress. We refer to those views where the flexing of the muscles are shown and where the woman's back is exposed.' In this late example the terms are merged.

- *Damaged Goods* (American Film Mfg Comp, 26 September 1914):

  'Reduce to a flash the enlarged view of the two syphilitic infants in the basket.'

The term enlargement was soon replaced with expressions like close view, close-up view, scene in great detail. Instead of expressions like 'enlargement' that were used to designate a fixed distance between the object/character and spectator, or some form of optical tampering or manipulation with the apparatus, we encounter phrases that stress the camera's closeness to the characters. A random example: 'the camera is put up close to the operating table and all the details of the operation are so very plainly in view'.

The degree of closeness had a direct impact on whether something could be shown or not.

If criminal tampering was depicted in long shots instead of being detailed in close shots, the Board was less severe:

A Desperate Chance (Kalem, 4 January 1913):

> 'Elimination of the close view in detail of the man on the train operating and closing the air-brake valve. It has been the custom of the Board to eliminate the close view of scenes showing the tampering with railroad apparatus. Of course, this does not exclude the use of the incident in the picture, but simply its being shown in detail.'

Closeness had a tendency to be read as description or instruction, as in *The Tragedy of the Arena* (Vitagraph, 7 March 1914): 'Eliminate close view of the use of the hypodermic needle, and all close or detailed description of the hypodermic'.

The censorship records from both countries share a common concern for the instructional nature of close shots when such shots show criminal or undesirable aspects or behaviour. The conceptualisations overlap only to a limited degree, reflecting differences, perhaps, in filmmaking between European and American screen practice. Such a polarisation is problematic, however, since both the Swedish censors and their audience were more than familiar with films from the USA.

Historical spectatorship: Artur Möller's account

The lack of more penetrating discussion on stylistic matters in Swedish film reviews during the 1910s, combined with the scarcity of surviving studio records, makes it difficult to be precise on matters of historical spectatorship. One example though: in a series of articles from 1916 titled 'Filmkultur' in a Stockholm morning paper, Artur Möller introduces the second installment with a vivid film description:

> We are in the bedroom of a rentier. He has just fallen asleep with an insouciance that one must term frivolous for the world of the cinema. Then there is a glimpse of a pair of masked villains outside the balcony doors. It's the fearful wrestler 'Bloody Billy' with one of his companions.

The millionaire's awakening is terrifying. He fumbles for a clock on the bedside table, but Bloody Billy twists it out of his hand. And now commences a struggle for life and death which ends with the millionaire being strangled by the two villains. At that point, *the proceedings stop for an instant* to provide an opportunity to regard, in magnification, the dying man's twisted features and his eyes, about to force their way out of their sockets.[15]

This passage is instructive as to the contemporary understanding of the function of magnifications. According to Möller, the narration is frozen while the magnification takes place. Its function is to dramatise grotesquely, to force the spectator into involuntary voyeurism, and to focus on unpleasant and seemingly unmotivated horror. Möller's conception that magnification interrupts the temporal progression of the narrative, provides handsome support for an account of spectatorship focused on displacement in relation to diegetic space.[16] The notion that magnifications halt the smooth flow of the narrative relies on the fixed vantage point of the observer *vis-à-vis* the depicted chain of events, and implicitly takes the naturalistic theatre as its model. Spatial changes dislocate the temporal order, the narrative takes a pause; magnification becomes display. It is this, to us unfamiliar, temporal regime that underpins the censors' reading of magnifications as instruction. Möller's account from 1916 parallels earlier claims from the American trade press reprinted in Pratt.

Screenplays

Surviving Swedish screenplays – irrespective of their relation to lost films – evidence a variety of scenes labeled magnification. I will quote pertinent scenes and briefly comment upon the function of the device in each case.

De Svarta Maskerna (The Black Masks, 1912), directed by Mauritz Stiller, provides an illuminating example when it comes to the interplay between the screenplay's designation and the practice of the censors:

Scene 94. The room in the house opposite

> Adèle is cutting the rope. The man stands with his lantern. Lola and the lieutenant

can now be seen hanging under the rope, clinging to each other as closely as possible. Adèle cuts with the power lent by desperation.

Scene 95. The magnification of the rope (where the hand cuts)

The rope is almost cut through, and starts slowly to break.

Scene 96. A street. Street scene

The motor car with the lieutenant's friend rushes up at tremendous speed.

Scene 97. Magnification of the rope and the hand

(a short scene) Only a few thin strands remain of the rope and they go one by one.

These magnifications fulfil a strongly dramatising function, and the cross cutting underscores the suspense. This mode of utilising the device presupposes economy; highlighting peaks of suspense – sensations – nothing else. The sequence was handled differently in the film; the rope was burned off. It is hardly surprising, however, that the censors – though without mentioning the concept of magnification – removed 'The very greatest part of the assassination attempt involving the burning of the rope'.[17]

A couple of magnifications can also be found in *Kolingens Galoscher* (Kolingen's Galoshes, 1912) directed by Eric Malmberg. These scenes take place in Monte Carlo:

Scene 38. In the casino

In the foreground stands a roulette table surrounded by a lot of people. The stakes are lively. [Also] [i]n the foreground there is a young negro, the son of a reigning negro king. People are gambling wildly, losing, but staking more. In the meantime K. and D. enter and passively follow the gambling for a while. They appear to be very interested, and D. starts to search frantically through his pockets. He turns them inside out and finally discovers a farthing.

Scene 39. Magnification of the hand holding a farthing

Scene 40. Same as scene 38

It is worth pointing out that the magnification has its own scene number; it is not inserted

as an analytic element in the overall scene complex. Here the effect is mainly ironic, with the value of the coin confirming the relation of the outsiders to the principal characters at home in the fashionable milieu. The magnification is both presentational (in that we are permitted to see the coin) and motivated in that the coin, of next to no value, excludes the person, a tramp, from the ambience of the wealthy gambling club.

According to censor card 4619 another magnification was cut from the film, namely, 'The more intimate toilette arrangements in the scene viewed through the telescope'.

Victor Sjöström's *Löjen och Tårar* (Smiles and Tears, 1913) displays two instances of magnification, an optically unvignetted one and a conventional matte printed keyhole shot:

Scene 10. Augusta's room. (evening sunlight)

Augusta enters, followed by Agnes. Augusta shows Agnes how she wants some things arranged. She also shows an expensive necklace that is lying on the dressing table.

'I am warning you, Agnes, to be particularly careful with that case. It contains a very expensive and priceless necklace.'

Agnes curtsies, promises to handle everything with the greatest care. Augusta leaves. Agnes puts things in order and glances inquisitively at the case. She touches the lid, pulls back her hand, repeats the action a couple of times. Finally she opens the lid, looks in surprise, and carefully takes up the necklace. (cont.)

Scene 11. Magnification

Delighted, she looks at the necklace, unbuttons her blouse and folds down the collar so that her neck is revealed. She puts on the necklace. She coquettes in front of the mirror.

Scene 12. Cont. scene 10

She carefully lays the necklace back in its place and resumes her tasks.

The magnification both demonstrates the way in which Agnes breaks her promise, and, at the same time, stages a kind of masquerade since, as bearer of the necklace, Agnes assumes a different role in front of the mirror.

The shot of Agnes, in magnification in the mirror, confounds her position in the social hierarchy as represented in the long shot, so making way for an imaginary projection of her class and sexuality. In short, the magnification is charged with narrative significance.

Gatans Barn (Children of the Street, 1914), directed by Victor Sjöström, also contains a magnification.

Scene 4. Outside a big parish hall

> Some people enter the house. Jenny and Karl enter.

Scene 5. Big hall full of people

> A man at the rostrum delivers a lecture. Jenny and Karl are inside. They sit.

Scene 6. The hall from the other side

> Karl is talking with Jenny – he explains the lecture in more detail – Jenny appears quite uninterested.

Scene 7. Magnification of Jenny and Karl

> Jenny is sleeping – Karl listens to the lecture with strained attention.

Scene 8.Hall as in Scene 5

> Karl notices that Jenny is sleeping – he is disappointed and embarrassed – looks around – wakes her – he says that it is best that they go – she looks at him – both sleepy and as if caught red-handed – they leave.

Here the magnification provides a confirmation of the course of events of the previous shots: Karl involved and Jenny indifferent. The magnification shows a problem in their relationship, details their different interest in the scene. Differences in narrative perspective, articulated in this instance through magnification, are considerable.

A Swedish screenplay co-authored by two Danes introduced the concept of 'close shot'. In the screenplay to Mauritz Stiller's *Hämnaren* (The Avenger, 1915), scripted by Martin Jørgensen and Louis Levy, there are a couple of close shots, one introducing a sort of mindscreen.[18]

Scene 21. A voice from the grave in the church

> The wedding guests have assumed their seats in the church. The bride on her

father's arm and Emanuel accompanied by his mother walk towards the altar where there hangs a large picture of the Virgin Mary and Child. Jacob Kahn has taken his seat in one of the church pews and you can clearly see his pale, burdened face. As Emanuel passes him, Jacob Kahn gives him a piercing stare.

At the altar

The two young people kneel down. The Dean stands in front of the picture of Mary. He asks them if they wish to be joined in holy matrimony. Emanuel stares at the picture of Mary, which suddenly transforms itself in his eyes.

Close shot

of Ester who bears a little child in her arms. Emanuel stands up terrified, stretches out his arms, and shouts:

'No, I belong to another.'

He falls down in a faint. The Dean hastens to his son's help and the bride sinks sobbing into her mother's arms.

This type of vision, where the magnification closes in on a character, gives us access to the mind of the subject; a similar strategy can be found in *Terje Vigen* (A Man There Was, 1917). In *Hämnaren*, Kahn's hypnotic gaze triggers Emanuel's transposition of the image of Mary

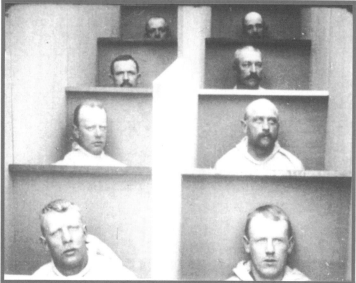

Figs. 2 & 3.
Copyright frame,
Hämnaren, *Mauritz*
Stiller, 1915
[courtesy of
Professor Gösta
Werner].

to his repressed memories of Ester, his abandoned fiancée, now dead. The copyright frames from *Hämnaren* (Figs. 1–3) illustrate an interplay between the close shot and the shot/reverse-shot system.[19]

In *Enslingens hustru* (The Hermit's Wife, 1916), directed by Fritz Magnussen, the magnification is included as a sub-division of a scene:

Scene 24. A corner at the front of the hotel

THE WOMAN hurries around the corner and stands pressed tight against the wall. One now sees that it is Mrs. WILSON.

Almost immediately UNO and EVA come. He has his arm around her waist and they wander slowly past, with eyes only for each other, without suspecting the presence of the spy.

Scene 24. A Magnification

One see Mrs. WILSON's face in magnification. It displays all the torments of jealousy. Her eyes glow in the moonlight and she stares after the departing couple with a vengeful look in her eyes.

Mrs. Wilson's look provides the link between the shots. The 'close-up' of her expression is related to previous and upcoming narrative events: betrayal, jealousy and revenge.

In the screenplay of *Therèse* (Thèrese, 1916), directed by Victor Sjöström, there are comments on the effect of the magnifications in the scene numbering:

'NB! There are two magnifications in scene no. 12, accordingly the next scene becomes no. 16. and not 13.'

Scene 12. An elegantly furnished room

The Detective listens attentively to the concierge's story.

Intertitle:
'... I was awake all night, because there was such a noise going on. At exactly 3 a.m. the lady ran out from his door as though she were hunted – I saw her very well – –'

The concierge talks and the detective listens to him. Suddenly both look towards the window where a woman's face appears. One sees

In magnification Therèse's

face, and the concierge, who recognises her, exclaims:

Intertitle:
'There she is!'

One again sees in

Magnification

the face at the window and it quickly disappears.

The magnification of the face here serves as evidence for the identification of a criminal,

and as confirmation of the concierge's conclusions. The latter's glance is integrated in
the shot as there is no shot/reverse shot pattern
outlined in the screenplay. Preserved copyright frames show that the scenes were staged
differently (Figs. 4 and 5).

In 1916–17 both magnifications and large
shots occur in some screenplays, as in the
instance of Konrad Tallroth's *Sin egen slav*.

Scene 65. Dr. Jussufs's study

> With a gesture the Turk motions the
> young lady to come closer. Struggling
> inwardly, the young marchioness com-
> plies with his summons and sees:

*Scene 66. Large scale shot of an oriental bou-
doir*

> It has multi-coloured harlequin windows.
> It is realistically and tastefully furnished,
> with expensive rugs and low cushions.
> Above the broad, dominating bed rises a
> splendid canopy, from which multi-col-
> oured lamps cast a subdued and veiled
> light over the interior of this temple of
> love. Champagne and glasses stand on a
> low, hammered copper table. And from
> an iron bowl, resting on an antique tripod,
> incense fumes rise into the air.

Scene 67. Dr. Jussuf's study

> The marchioness takes a step back. Her
> eyes glitter with injured pride, indigna-
> tion, and scorn.

In the last example, the screenplay's 'large
scale shot' is linked to the marchioness's un-
willing gaze. That moment, with its mix of
orientalism and sexual desire, was cut because, as the censorship card reveals, of
magnification.

This catalogue of examples from preserved
screenplays shows that shots labeled magnifications fulfilled a multiplicity of narrative
functions beyond the depiction of crime that
the censors focused upon. Magnifications
were enlisted for scene *découpage*, but also
fulfilled rhetorical and figurative functions,
as John Fullerton has emphasised in his thesis. Unfortunately, it is impossible to analyse
the screenplays in relation to the actual films.
The terminology became more complex
around 1916–17, which reflects a number of
other changes, among them longer films, and

an increasing number of shots per reel. The
number of scenes in the screenplays, especially when the increase in their length (as
reported by the censors) is taken into consideration, confirms that the change in
terminology reflects a major transition in
1917:

1912   *Kolingens galoscher* 68 scenes/856 m
1912   *De svarta maskerna* 107 scenes/1096 m
1912   *Ett hemligt giftermål* 49 scenes/754 m

1913   *Säterjäntan* 37 scenes/not finished

Figs. 4 & 5.
*Copyright frame,
Thèrese, Victor
Sjöström, 1915
[courtesy of
Professor Gösta
Werner].*

1895

1913	*Löjen och tårar* 45 scenes/688 m
1913	*Blodets röst* 19 scenes/1826 m
1913	*Ingeborg Holm* 82 scenes/2006 m
1914	*Det röda tornet* 60 scenes/864 m
1914	*Gatans barn* 65 scenes/1103 m
1914	*Hjärtan som mötas* 54 scenes/790 m
1914	*Bröderna* 58 scenes/632 m
1915	*Mästertjuven* 94 scenes/928 m
1915	*Strejken* 74 scenes/1598 m
1915	*Kampen om en Rembrandt* 52 scenes/ 860 m
1916	*Guldspindeln* 79 scenes/1018 m
1916	*På detta numera vanliga sätt* 22 scenes/ 365 m
1916	*Millers dokument* 63 scenes/1061 m
1916	*Hämnaren* 67 scenes/1011 m
1916	*Balettprimadonnan* 75 scenes/1072 m
1916	*I elfte timmen* 79 scenes/691 m
1916	*Enslingens hustru* 82 scenes/910 m
1916	*Thérèse* 100 scenes/1123 m
1917	*Terje Vigen* 110 scenes/1129 m
1917	*Chanson triste* 71 scenes/859 m
1917	*Envar sin egen lyckas smed* 85 scenes/ 988 m
1917	*Skuggan av ett brott* 78 scenes/895 m
1917	*Sin egen slav* 93 scenes/925 m
1917	*Tösen från Stormyrtorpet* 290 scenes/1749
1917	*Allt hämnar sig* 120 scenes/879 m
1917	*Thomas Graals bästa film* 352 scenes/ 1823 m
1917	*Alexander den store* 421 scenes/2018 m
1918	*Berg-Ejvind* 352 scenes/2802 m
1918	*Mästerkatten i stövlar* 438 scenes/2241 m
1919	*Åh, imorgon kväll* 203 scenes/703 m
1919	*Ett farligt frieri* 314 scenes/1339 m
1919	*Synnöve Solbakken* 622 scenes/ 2235 m
1919	*Hans nåds testamente* 351 scenes/1061m
1919	*Herr Arnes pengar* 636 scenes/ 2219 m

The screenwriter's point of view: Oscar Hemberg on The Girl from the Marsh Croft

In an interview given in December 1917, the head of Swedish Biograph's distribution company, Oscar Hemberg, discussed camera technique in what he refers to as the modern film. Hemberg's views are interesting for several reasons, not least because he had written the screenplays for *Hjälte mot sin vilja* (A Hero Against His Will, 1915), *I Kronans kläder* (In the King's Uniform, 1915), and *Bengts nya kärlek* (Bengt's New Love, 1916):

> Film is not just interested in showing a series of pictures. Like other spectacles,

it desires to captivate the observer, develop a specific feeling in him. In this process, technique plays an enormous role – the best directors, such as D.W. Griffith and Thomas H. Ince, are also world famous celebrities. Different lighting arrangements and colour help to underscore the message. Nowadays, they are particularly inventive in the art of switching between long shots and close shots. In *Flickan från Stormyrtorpet* (The Girl from the Marsh Croft, Victor Sjöström, 1917) we witnessed such a construction. First, the entire room is shown – in this instance with a number of people around a coffee table. Then the camera sneaks around and shows a detail here and a detail there, a movement (Selander's thumbs!) and in that way picks out the impressions that a specific event made on those present one by one. Griffith was the first to use the device. The justification he provides is interesting. In the theatre one of course first sees the entire scene – then one observes a detail here and there with the binoculars. Film does exactly the same thing. It focuses the binoculars towards that which is interesting to see. [20]

Hemberg's use of binoculars as a metaphor for the cut-in inscribing an implied point of view, relates back to the optical vignettes of earlier films in which the device was rendered natural by a visual cue: the keyhole, the telescope/binoculars providing narrative linkage. The term, 'magnification' lingered on even when the device had been enlisted for narrative purposes and lacked vignettes. Hemberg locates the visual logic of the scene within the diegesis when he observes that 'the impressions that a specific event made on those present'. And he no longer uses the term, 'magnification' but, instead, 'close shot'. The close shot he describes is not dependent on the external logic of magnifications; its justification is motivated from within the diegesis. That the style employed by Swedish Biograph in 1917 is inspired by American cinema (if one is to believe Hemberg) is interesting information. No less interesting is the use of the terms 'long shot' and 'close shot' to describe stylistic options. Hemberg's description, which applies well to the extant film, has no counterpart in the screenplay: the shot of Selander's thumbs is not specified.

Here terminology is clearly in a transitional phase. The concept of close shot does not exist in the manuscript, but 'magnification' and 'long shot' are used. Large shot corresponds partly to close shot, but the boundary between magnification and large shot is not clear. Of the 108 scenes described in the first act, 15 are described as long shot, 6 as large shot and no less than 42 shots as magnification. The increase in number of magnifications indicate a multiplicity of narrative functions. It is obvious that the non-narrative, presentational, and dramatic functions of the early magnifications have given way to a variety of narrative uses for close-ups. The major process of rethinking that went on at Swedish Biograf concerning style and subject matter to which Hemberg's discussion alludes were the outcome of complex processes intimately related to censorship practices in a broad sense.

A restaurant scene consisting of 75 shots from Mauritz Stiller's 1917 film *Alexander den Store* (Alexander the Great, 1917), discloses a – perhaps surprising – dexterity in classical filmmaking.[21] Spatial relations are firmly established and legible, and a variety of shot scales is used, including close-ups of facial expressions to inscribe character reactions.

The scene employs eyeline matches, shot/reverse shots, cross-cutting, in short, an analytic approach to space and a full mastery of the classical style. The surviving screenplay does not correspond to the actual film, which reminds us to use records and documents with caution. I will not go into a full discussion of the scene, just introduce it for further discussion in other contexts. The film has never figured prominently in scholarship devoted to Mauritz Stiller's career, and it is seldom shown, probably due to the fact that one reel is missing.

The overall paucity of the footage has forced me to deal primarily with secondary sources. The stylistic make-up of Swedish cinema 1910–15 will probably elude us forever; the entire production of the Malmö-based and Copenhagen-oriented Frans Lundberg is dispersed, little remains of the output from minor production companies like Viking Film, and from Swedish Biograph we have only a fraction of their output. What we do have, however, are most of the films from the Hasselblad studio directed by Georg af Klercker between 1915 and 1917. Upcoming studies of his oeuvre, and work in progress on Danish cinema will give us a better framework for assessing the interplay between Swedish and Danish cinema, and their respective relation to the classical style.

Notes

1. John Fullerton, 'The Development of a System of Representation in Swedish Film, 1912–1920, University of East Anglia, 1994.
2. An array of approaches for analysing the functioning of this device and its status in relation to continuity, point-of-view, shot/reverse-shot structures etc., primarily in American and French cinema, has been discussed by scholars like Richard Abel, Ben Brewster, Noël Burch, André Gaudreault, Tom Gunning, Barry Salt, and Kristin Thompson.
3. Henry A. Phillips, *The Photodrama* (New York: Stanhope Dodge Pub. Co., 1914), 54.
4. See John Fullerton, 'Relationen mellan text och bild i en förklassisk svensk film', *Aura. Filmvetenskaplig tidskrift*, 3, 1/2 (1997): 24–65.
5. Elbert Moore, *Text Book on Writing the Photoplay* (Chicago: Elbert Moore, 1915), 150.
6. James Slevin, *On Picture-Play Writing* (Cedar Grove, NJ: Farmer-Smith, 1912), 86.
7. Louella O. Parsons, *How to Write for the 'Movies'* (Chicago: A. C. McClurgh & Co., 1915), 8.
8. George C. Pratt, *Spellbound in Darkness: A History of the Silent Film* (Greenwich: New York Graphic Society, 1973).
9. Elbert Moore, 149.
10. 'Marcelle', *Dagen*, 16 March 1915.
11. *Svensk Tidskrift*, 1912: 111–117. After two years as censor, Gustaf Berg became the head of the Swedish Board of Film Censors in 1914.

1895

12. National Archives of Sweden, Statens Biografbyrås arkiv: *Korrespondens i chefsärenden*, vol. 2, no. 3; the letter is dated 1 March 1916.

13. *Filmbladet*, 2, 3 (1916): 33–34.

14. New York Public Library, Rare Books and Manuscript Division. The first volume covers the period 1911–12, the same period during which the Swedish Board of Film Censors was established. Dates given in this context relate to recommendations published in the *Bulletin*.

15. *Stockholms-Tidningen*, 22 September 1916 (second installment), emphasis added.

16. Noël Burch, *Life to Those Shadows* (London: BFI Publishing 1990), 188ff.

17. See censor card no. 6460.

18. Bruce F. Kawin, *Mindscreen: Bergman, Godard, and First-Person Film* (Princeton: Princeton University Press, 1978).

19. These frames were discovered at the Library of Congress, Washington D.C., by Professor Gösta Werner in the late 1970s. The frame enlargements, now deposited at the Swedish Film Institute, Stockholm, are reproduced with Professor Werner's permission.

20. *Aftonbladet*, 30 December 1917.

21. For frame enlargements, see my paper, 'Förstorade attraktioner, klassiska närbilder: Anteckningar kring ett gränssnitt', *Aura. Filmvetenskaplig tidskrift*, 2, 1/2, 1996: 34–90. See also Bo Florin's recent thesis, *Den nationella stilen: Studier i den svenska filmens guldålder* (Stockholm: Aura förlag, 1997) for an analysis of Swedish films from the late 1910s and early 1920s.

Pictorial Styles of Film Acting in Europe in the 1910s

Ben Brewster and Lea Jacobs

Wisconsin Center for Film and Theater Research, Department of Communication Arts, University of Wisconsin – Madison, WI 53706, USA

ACCORDING TO THE TRADITIONAL AC-COUNT, film acting rapidly departed from the large, stereotyped gestures suited to the scale of the stage and associated with early nineteenth-century theatrical practice, adopting a more modern style which relied upon small, restrained and more 'realistic' gestures and facial expressions better suited to the close framings that the cinema permitted.[1] In an influential recent study of acting styles at Biograph, *Eloquent Gestures*, Roberta Pearson has attempted to trace the eclipse of what she calls the 'histrionic' style, which relied on stereotyped postures and attitudes, in favour of the 'verisimilar' style which aimed to adhere to conventionalised notions of 'real' gesture and action. She argues that by 1912 the verisimilar style had largely replaced the histrionic, at least among the most acclaimed actors at Biograph.[2] In our view, on the contrary, the actor's assumption of stereotyped poses and attitudes was much more important and was important for far longer than this, and other, accounts suggest. In what follows, we begin with a discussion of how gestures and attitudes functioned in nineteenth-century acting traditions, seeking to arrive at a more precise definition of pictorialism in acting. We then turn to the question of how this tradition was taken up within European cinema of the 1910s.[3]

By pictorialism in acting we actually mean a number of styles of acting in which the assumption of poses and attitudes comprised an important part of the actor's technique. This way of thinking about how the actor looked and moved on stage was part of a long-standing theatrical tradition which became pronounced in the mid-eighteenth century and persisted until well into the twentieth. Of course, acting style did not remain invariable throughout this almost two hundred year span, but however acting and staging practices varied, the concern with posing remained central.

It should be noted that our efforts to generalise about an acting tradition that covers such a long time span works against some of the best recent theatre history which has concentrated on reconstructing specific productions, and documenting the activities of particular theatres and companies. Nonetheless we have

1895

been struck by the strong continuities underlying the discourses on acting in this lengthy period, continuities which derive from a vivid concern with the stage picture. The coherence of this tradition is brought out in contrast with present-day acting methods from which it is quite remote. The advent of naturalism, and the new drama of Ibsen, Shaw and Pinero represents a definitive break with the actor's traditional concern with the stage picture (indeed, William Archer's attacks on acting geared to 'picture-poster situations' in the name of the new drama provides some of the best descriptions of the older aesthetic and acting methods). But even if pictorialism begins to appear dated to the most advanced theatre practitioners at the turn of the century, the older tradition did not simply disappear. For example, Delsarte's acting system, which was based on the teaching of poses, was still being taught by Gustave Garcia at the London Academy of Music in the first decade of the twentieth century, and the evidence from film we will adduce later shows that these traditions were still alive a decade later throughout Europe.[4]

We would also like to distinguish what we are calling pictorial styles of acting from pantomime. Although contemporary works on pantomime such as Charles Aubert's *L'Art mimique* of 1901, do include examples and discussion of attitudes, we take pantomime to be more specifically concerned with the substitution of gesture for dialogue.[5] One can find examples of pantomime in silent film, especially in the early years in which actors often resort to it to convey story information. However the practice also came in for criticism, as by Frank Woods in 1909:

> The old pantomime sought to convey ideas by motions as if the persons were deaf and dumb. The natural action of the silent play also entered largely in the development of the plot, but detail ideas were indicated by unnatural movements of the hands. For instance, if an actor desired to indicate to another that he wanted a drink of water he would form his hand in the shape of a cup and go through the motions of drinking. Pantomime of this sort is still seen too often in picture playing, but the tendency is to get

away from it, the idea being that the nearer to actual life the picture can be made to appear the more convincing it must be to the spectators. The modern director of the first class will now avoid the unnatural hand pantomime as much as possible and will indicate the wish for a drink of water, for instance, by having the player do some plausible thing that will convey the desired idea. The player wishing to ask for drink may hand a glass to some one with a natural motion, or he may indicate the water pitcher by a simple movement of the hand, or he may appear to ask a question, which, followed by the fetching of the drink, clearly and reasonably shows what the request has been.[6]

Woods is objecting to pantomime as opposed to stage business as a means of storytelling. And we would agree with Kristin Thompson's assessment that pantomime in this sense does indeed play a much less prominent role in film acting in serious drama by the mid-1910s.[7] However, what we would call pictorial styles of stage acting encompass a much broader range of gesture than this idea of pantomime. Given the resources of the legitimate stage, a character would not have to mime, but could simply ask for a drink of water; she would probably not accompany the request with a marked pose unless the situation called for emphasis, for example, if she was about to put poison in the drink.

The important point, for us, is to move away from the kind of linguistic analogy which posits a one to one relationship between attitudes and speech as is the case in Woods' example where the actor's hand gesture means 'I want a drink'.[8] Poses and attitudes in the general sense which interests us were conventionalised and did carry significance, but they are probably best understood through analogy with the music which always accompanied nineteenth-century popular theatre. Like music, posing was used to underscore dramatic moments, to convey and heighten emotions, to elongate and intensify situations. Poses are best understood therefore, not as a lexicon, but as a way of managing the stage picture, a visual repertoire that was deployed in relation to specific narrative contexts. A given conventionalised pose, for

1895

example an actor placing a hand upon fore-head in despair, needs to be analysed not simply in terms of its conventionalised meaning, but more importantly, in terms of how the gesture is realised and how it fits within the overall visual design of the scene. It is these points which we intend to pursue here: how poses and attitudes functioned as an integral part of an actor's preparation for a role (indeed, of the training of actors in general), and how they provided a means of blocking scenes for individual actors and the ensemble.

The frequency with which actors were enjoined to study statues and paintings, and to practice poses, and the consistent use of illustrative drawings in manuals on acting and oratory stands in sharp contrast with present-day training methods, and helps to signal the degree to which acting was conceived along pictorial lines. To take only one example, from Henry Neville's section on gesture in an 1895 work:

> We term attitude the position adopted at the end of the walk, or when standing still; and this requires very careful study. The elder Kean was so perfect a master of his art that when he first walked on the London stage, and took his position in the centre without speaking a word the audience recognised in him a genius. We may be aided in our selection of appropriate attitudes by attending picture galleries. The painter paints attitudes; his mind is cultivated to record them; they are the significant objects of his art.[9]

Such advice is seconded by the use of illustrations of postures and significant gestures in a range of acting and public speaking manuals. Johannes Jelgerhuis, whose acting manual dates from 1827, is unique in actually having been a painter, and hence able to draw examples of good and bad posture that fit precisely with the text of his lectures, but one also finds illustrations of attitudes in many other sources.[10] Three examples of sitting postures from Jelgerhuis may serve to indicate some of the concerns which dominated this way of thinking about gesture and attitude. Figure 1 illustrates proper attitudes for sitting on a throne (the figure on the left Jelgerhuis claims is copied from a painting by Lairesse, the other

PLATE XIV

PLATE XX

is of his own devising). One of the important points for Jelgerhuis, frequently found in the other manuals as well, is the idea of contrast within the posture. In the case of Fig. 1, note one arm is raised, the other lowered; one of the seated figures has a palm turned outward, contrasted with a palm turned down; one foot is raised, thanks to the stool. The figure in the background is the bad example, an illustration of what happens when the actor drops too low in the chair and the 'opportunity of being graceful is lost'.[11]

Figure 2 illustrates another sitting posture, an illustration of how to collapse at a table in despair. According to Jelgerhuis, position no. 7 (on the right) is all wrong and little can be done to improve it. The legs are badly placed,

Fig. 1. *(above) and* Fig. 2. *(below)*

PLATE XVII

Fig. 3. *(above)* and
Fig. 4. *(below)*

Despair

and the arms are in the same position, which is very bad. Whereas no. 8 has grace and contrast: 'the hand, which lies on the right knee relaxed and hanging down, completes the whole position or posture as a true figure of desperation'.[12]

Figure 3 shows how to be stabbed and die gracefully. Note how the action of falling is divided into distinct poses to avoid what Jelgerhuis calls 'the risk of becoming ridiculous by collapsing in a heap with much noise'.[13]

It is clear from these and many other examples the importance accorded to grace and good

bearing in all dramatic situations, and the way in which actors were encouraged to develop an eye for poses and to analyse their performance in terms of how they would look in each pose. It should be noted however, that some critics argued it was possible to depart from graceful and decorous gesture in the interests of expressiveness. Lessing, for example, argues that as acting, in contradistinction to the plastic arts, is transitory, the actor may permit himself 'the wildness of a Tempesta, the insolence of a Bernini', provided that these attitudes are carefully treated: '[the actor] must not remain in them too long ... must prepare for them gradually by previous movements, and must resolve them again into the general tone of the conventional'.[14]

This comment brings us to the problem of blocking, because it is clear that poses and attitudes were not generally conceived of in isolation, but rather as sequences which helped to organise the movements of actors in the ensemble and in which actors built up to certain attitudes at the high point of scenes.

In a manual written in 1822, Henry Siddons provides a good indication of how a scene could be planned out as a series of attitudes. He discusses a scene from the opera *Alcestis* in which, having already pledged to the gods that she is willing to die in order that her husband may be spared, the queen is overcome by fear, believing that she already hears the underworld shades who have come to take her (Fig. 4). Siddons describes the appropriate attitude of weakness, caused by fear:

> The last attitude of an actress charged with such a part should accompany this expression with a degree of faintness almost approaching to annihilation, with her face averted from the spot whence the terrific sounds are supposed to arise: she should now and then cast a timid and furtive glance, as if fearful of beholding the dreaded spectres: the reversed hands, which she had opposed to them, ought to preserve their former direction; but she should not appear to have force or courage sufficient to give any degree of tension to the muscles, so that, feeble and trembling, they may afterwards drop lifeless by her sides.[15]

Fig. 5. *(above, left),*
Fig. 6 *(above right)*
and **Fig. 7.** *(below)*

However, immediately after this, Alcestis changes her mind and re-iterates her devotion to her husband and her vow in the 'second invocation of the infernal gods' (Fig. 5). In this attitude, 'The countenance of Alcestis should be fixed on the ground, because she is invoking the infernal deities; her body should bend forwards; her step ought to be grand, her arms extend, and each open eye to seem bursting from its orbit: the whole countenance should beam with a species of haggard inspiration.'[16] The problem which Siddons goes on to discuss is how to make the transition from one attitude to the next, how to bind together sentiments and attitudes which are extremely different, and how to motivate the repetition of the musical motif associated with the vow itself. The solution he proposes is to interpose two attitudes in between the first and the second, so as to make the change in the Queen's countenance and posture more gradual. The intermediate postures make use of Parthenia, the Queen's sister. After her expression of fear upon hearing what she imagines to be the shades, the Queen should rest on Parthenia's breast, lifting one arm and drawing it across her forehead 'in the sentiment of the disorder which troubles her soul' (Fig. 6). Then, in response to her sister's tender plea to abandon her vow, the Queen should express displeasure and finally tear herself away from her sister's arms, now ready to re-iterate it (Fig. 7). Siddons concludes:

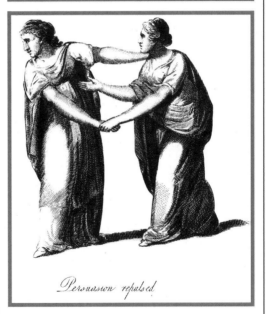

By this means the repetition of this devotion will be found not only perfect, but the hurried leap from one sentiment to the other will be totally avoided; and what, without this prudent precaution, might have appeared a useless ornament or a mere misplaced musical luxury, becomes an admirable and expressive trait in the character of Alcestis.[17]

Fig. 8. *(above) and*
Fig. 9. *(below)*

1895

This is one of the few discussions we have seen of how attitudes could serve as the basis for blocking out a scene, although in Antonio Morrocchesi's *Lezioni di declamazione e d'arte teatrale* there is a similar sequence of plates to illustrate Pylades' false report of Orestes' death to Aegisthus in Alfieri's *Oreste*.[18] Not only the expression of particular emotional states, but also the relation of the poses to the music and the problem of how to make a graceful and logical transition from one pose to the next would have had to be considered. Although they do not approach the clarity of Siddons' directions, we have

found early twentieth-century stage manager's libretti in the Tams-Witmark music library in which it is proposed that the singers be left free to improvise a series of attitudes in tandem with the music in key scenes or arias, indicating the viability and persistence of this way of approaching the problem of staging.[19]

The interest in how actors made the transitions between attitudes is also indicated by Garrick's well-known party piece performed at the salon of Baron d'Holbach in Paris during his visit in 1763–64 in which he poked his head out from behind a screen and illustrated various passions in rapid succession.[20] In about the same period, Lessing also commented on the skill required of an actor who had to 'change from one emotion to another and must make this dumb transition so naturally that the spectator is not carried away by a leap, but by a series of rapid still perceptible gradations'.[21] It seems important to stress the complex effects that could be achieved by modulating attitudes and orchestrating them in series, thereby preparing for the largest and most striking effects. Within film studies this style of acting has often been misunderstood because people have simply looked at the isolated, highly stereotyped poses which are most frequently found reproduced in the acting manuals. But these poses are simply the isolated building blocks of the scene.

In trying to explain how this stage tradition was adapted for film, we have tended to privilege the feature over the one-reel film and European examples over American ones. The one-reel film generally had to have short scenes, and to be acted quickly if all the relevant action was to be conveyed in the requisite 1000-foot length. For example, Frank Woods criticises the final scene of *All on Account of the Milk* (Frank Powell for Biograph, 1910) with the comment: 'The last scene appears to degenerate into farce, and to be acted hastily and with too little dramatic effect, due, perhaps, to the lack of film space'.[22] In general he praises the acting in the film (by Mary Pickford, Arthur Johnson, Mack Sennett and Blanche Sweet) and we assume that the problem of 'film space' to which he refers is the fact that the filmmakers were forced to rush the last scene to insure that the film was the proper length. Even if Woods is wrong in his guess about what happened at the end of this specific film, the comment suggests that he was aware of the lack of 'space' on the reel as a problem for actors. We would argue that it continued to be, and, as compared to the early feature, actors in the one-reel film were given many fewer opportunities to dwell on situations, to hold poses or develop elaborate sequences of them.

The reason for privileging European over American features in an examination of pictorialism in acting has to do with the rapid development of editing techniques in America, and the fact that American films were consistently faster cut than European ones throughout the 1910s.[23] As both Tom Gunning and Roberta Pearson have pointed out, editing often took over functions that had previously been performed by the actor – glance/object cutting, for example, could indicate that a character had seen something without an actor having to strike a pose in reaction to what he supposedly 'saw'.[24] Furthermore, the shorter shot lengths entailed by cross cutting or scene dissection permitted, and indeed required, either a relatively rapid or very reduced acting style. But, given their lengthy takes and tendency to employ deep staging in long shot, European films of this period necessarily relied more upon the actor and the acting ensemble to provide dramatic emphasis.[25] This mode of filmmaking also gave the actor the time to develop elaborate sequences of gestures and poses. European film actors were thus in a relatively better position than their American colleagues to adapt and refine the performance practices associated with pictorial styles in the theatre.

Before proceeding to our example, it is necessary to indicate what constitutes a pose for us. All of the sources we have seen suggest that poses were held for a considerable length of time in the theatre. There are some accounts of actors holding poses for five minutes, which seems implausible, but we would be less inclined to dismiss claims for a length of 20–30 seconds. We have never seen a film actor pause for more than a few seconds (Asta Nielsen holds the record with 18 seconds). Thus, in our efforts to analyse this acting style,

the time of the pause could not be the sole criterion for defining a pose or attitude. Instead we have looked for the following:

(1) There is a slight pause in the actor's movement when the film is viewed at the correct speed of projection;

(2) The actor assumes a stereotyped posture;

(3) The posture expresses the character's interior state or in some other way clearly and directly relates to the dramatic situation;

(4) The posture is systematically iterated and varied by the actor;

Fig. 10. *(above)* and Fig. 11. *(below)*

1895

1895

Fig. 12. *(above)*
and **Fig. 13.** *(below)*

Waiting in the green room after a performance, he sees reflected in the mirror his wife kissing a Count who has come to court her back stage. After a traumatic confrontation with his wife, Daisy returns home and Joe follows sometime later.

> Shot 1. Houlberg is sitting on the settee, her head on her hands on the table. Psilander enters from the rear right, opens the portiere, looks at Houlberg (who does not yet look at him) and stops (Fig. 8).
>
> He staggers slowly down the steps, then comes forward more quickly, crosses to stand between the chair and the settee, with his right hand on the chair back. Only at this point does Houlberg break her pose, raising her head with a start, looking up to apologise (Fig. 9).

With this kind of acting one often finds alternations of poses as in this instance, in which Houlberg, although in the foreground, remains very still to allow attention to be focused on Psilander in the background. Then when he gets to the foreground it is her turn to pose and react. This kind of alternation of poses continues throughout the scene. It is just one illustration of the way that the acting ensemble could direct the spectator's attention, a function which is typically handled by editing or staging in later classical filmmaking:

> Houlberg rises. Psilander steps back, briefly wringing his hands. Without looking at him, she looks down at the table as he leans back towards her, his fist on the table (Fig. 10).

Shot 2. Title: 'Do you love him?'

Shot 3. Cut-in to medium shot. Psilander is in profile left, Houlberg's head is raised. She very slowly nods assent, then wipes tears from her eyes. Psilander looks off front centre vacantly in grief. He puts his hand on his forehead (Fig. 11).

Shot 4. Cut on action (Fig. 12).

Note the return to the same framing as shot 1, the basic framing for the scene. We get the full effect of the pose then, after the cut, in the longer framing. One of the other interesting aspects of this kind of acting is that

(5) The blocking of the actor's movement, or of the acting ensemble, clearly leads up to the pose or leads from one pose to the next.

Obviously frame stills do not 'prove' the existence of an attitude, since they represent no more than 1/16 of a second of the actual time of the performance. Rather, they are used here to facilitate the work of description.

Our example is drawn from the Danish film *Klovnen* (The Clown, A. Sandberg, 1917). At this point in the story, Joe Higgins (Valdemar Psilander) is a well-known and successful clown married to Daisy (Gudrun Houlberg).

because it involves the actor's whole body, films tend to move out of close up or medium shot for moments of greatest dramatic intensity. This happens as this scene builds to a climax:

> Shot 5. Title: 'Then you have only one thing to do; go to him!'

> Shot 6. Houlberg turns quickly to face front left and puts her left hand to her heart (Fig. 13). She leans over to front right in agony while Psilander points listlessly off left (Fig. 14). She tries to face him, raises her arms halfway in appeal, drops them again, turns to face front right, then left again, and passes in front of Psilander and off left slowly. Psilander watches her go, makes a full gesture of appeal off left, raising his hands to head height (Fig. 15). Then he leans back and puts his hands on his head (Fig. 16). He turns to front left, pulls his hands down the sides of his face and leans slightly forward.

In general the gestures get bigger and more extreme as the scene proceeds. Shot 1 utilises the depth of the set with Psilander in extreme long shot. Shot 3 is a medium shot, in which the gestures are scaled down, as in Houlberg's slight nod of the head. By shot 6, however, the actors are making more fully extended gestures with limbs outstretched, as in Houlberg's lean to the right with hand on heart, or Psilander's raising of his arms to head height. It is as if the actors save their biggest gestures for the climax of the scene.

It should also be noted how slow this scene is, at least for our present-day sensibilities. The sense that the pace of the acting is slow is partly a function of the length of the shots (the six shots comprise 2 minutes, 53 seconds assuming a projection rate of 16 frames per second). It is also a function of the tempo of the action, as, for example, in Psilander's pose at the top of the stairs and the slow movement from the background to the foreground in shot 1. Moreover, the gestures and poses adopted by the actors tend to be iterative expressions of grief. This also helps to provide a sense of long duration in the scene, since the succession of poses does not provide us with new information about the characters or

events, but merely a variation on what we already know. The scene is devoted to extending and elaborating upon the situation put in place in the prior scene by Joe's discovery of Daisy's betrayal in the green room. In many ways the scene back at the house is not necessary for the progression of the plot; Daisy decides to leave Joe here, but this could certainly have been suggested in the prior scene. And the acting does not operate to further the action of Daisy leaving, but to delay it – to maintain the situation and exploit its emotional resonances, before the next turn of events. To appreciate this kind of acting, you have to accept and savour this slowness, the

Fig. 14. *(above)* and **Fig. 15.** *(below)*

1895

Fig. 16.

compassed a range of acting styles which incorporated pictorial elements to a greater or lesser degree. These elements included not only gestural soliloquies, but also patterns of alternation which served to focus attention on specific characters or bits of business in ensemble scenes, and strategies for blocking out scenes for two and three actors with appropriate poses and attitudes. This kind of acting became relatively more important in the case of filmmakers who did not pursue the option of shot-based scene construction, that is for most Europeans in the 1910s. Our present-day tendency to see marked pictorialism in acting as 'hammy' or vulgar, our inability to appreciate its grace, sometimes even to understand the ideas emphasised in this way, is a function of the predominance of reduced acting styles made possible by the development of classical editing techniques which have entailed much greater interest in and attention to editing at the expense of the complex pictorial elements within the shot.

way in which sequences of poses and attitudes serve to orchestrate key dramatic moments.

We would emphasise that 1910s cinema en-

Notes

1. In an interview in 1914, D.W. Griffith enunciated one of the earliest versions of this position, arguing that the use of the close up permitted a more 'restrained' style of acting that was 'closer to real life'. See Robert Welsh, 'D.W. Griffith Speaks', *New York Dramatic Mirror* 71, no. 1830 (14 January 1914): 49 and 54; reprinted in George Pratt, *Spellbound in Darkness: A History of the Silent Film* (Greenwich, Conn.: New York Graphic Society, 1966), 110–111. There are many recent variants on this argument, including James Naremore, *Acting in the Cinema* (Berkeley: University of California Press, 1988), 38–39; and Janet Staiger, 'The Eyes Are Really the Focus: Photoplay Acting and Film Form and Style', *Wide Angle* 6, no. 4 (1985): 14–23.

2. Roberta Pearson, *Eloquent Gestures: The Transformation of Performance Style in the Griffith Biograph Films* (Berkeley: University of California Press, 1992).

3. This paper derives from a longer discussion of acting dealing with both European and American film examples in Ben Brewster and Lea Jacobs, *Theatre to Cinema: Stage Pictorialism and the Early Feature Film* (Oxford: Oxford University Press, 1997).

4. For a discussion of Gustav Garcia's textbook *The Actor's Art* based upon Delsarte, see Stephen R. Macht, 'The Origin of the London Academy of Music and Dramatic Art', *Theatre Notebook* 26, no.1 (Autumn 1971): 19–30.

5. Charles Aubert, *L'art mimique suivi d'un traité de la pantomime et du ballet* (Paris: E. Meuriot, 1901).

6. '"Spectator's" Comments', *New York Dramatic Mirror* (13 November 1909): 15; for a similar complaint about pantomime, see C.H. Claudy, 'Too Much Acting', *Moving Picture World* (11 February 1911): 288–289.

7. David Bordwell, Janet Staiger and Kristin Thompson, *The Classical Hollywood Cinema: Film Style and Mode of Production to 1960* (London: Routledge & Kegan Paul, 1985), 189–192.

8. For discussions of posing according to linguistic paradigms, see Pearson, 21–26, and Frank Kessler and Sabine Lenk, '"... levant les bras au ciel, se tapant sur les cuisses": Réflexions sur l'internationalisme du geste dans le cinéma des premiers temps', in *Cinéma sans frontières/Images across Borders, 1895–1918*, Roland Cosandey and François Albèra (eds) (Lausanne/Québec: Payot-Lausanne/Nuit blanche éditeur, 1995).

9. Hugh Campbell, R.F. Brewer and Henry Neville, *Voice, Speech and Gesture: A Practical Handbook*

to the Elocutionary Art, (New York:, 1895; rpt. Granger Index Reprint Series, Books for Libraries Press, 1972), 121.

10. For example, Henry Siddons, *Practical Illustrations of Rhetorical Gesture and Action* (London: Sherwood, Neely and Jones, 1822); and Antonio Morrocchesi, *Lezioni di declamazione e d'arte teatrale* (Florence, 1832). Various acting teachers published their versions of Delsarte's system, with illustrations; one of the most important in America was Genevieve Stebbins, *Delsarte System of Dramatic Expression* (New York: Edgar S. Werner, 1886). For a discussion of Delsarte's influence in England, see Macht.

11. Johannes Jelgerhuis, *Theoretische Lessen over de Gesticulatie en Mimiek* (Amsterdam, 1827; rpt. Uitgeverij Adolf M. Hakkert, 1970), plate number 6; the discussion of this plate is translated in Dene Barnett's useful 'The Performance Practice of Acting: The Eighteenth Century, Part V: Posture and Attitudes', *Theatre Research International* 6, no. 1 (1981): 24–25.

12. Jelgerhuis, plate number 14; the discussion of this plate is translated in Barnett, 28–29.

13. Jelgerhuis, plate number 11; the discussion of this plate is translated in Barnett, 27.

14. Gotthold Ephraim Lessing, *The Hamburg Dramaturgy*, Helen Zimmern (trans) (New York: Dover, 1962; 1769), 19 (from no. 5).

15. Siddons, 347.

16. Siddons, 347–348.

17. Siddons, 348–350.

18. Morrocchesi, 255–257 and fig. 17–38, illustrating his own performance of a speech in act 4, scene 2 of *Oreste* in Vittorio Alfieri, *Tragedie*, Nicola Bruscoli (ed) (Bari: Laterza, 1946), vol. 1, p. 363.

19. The Tams-Witmark music library is the major US clearing house for performance rights for opera, operetta and musical theatre. A collection of libretti and musical parts for material now out of copyright is held at the John Mills Music Library at the University of Wisconsin-Madison. For many productions the holdings include a stage manager's score with staging instructions. The date at which most of these annotations were made cannot be established with certainty, but most of the material in the University of Wisconsin's holdings was acquired by Alfred Tams between the mid-1880's and 1920. The stage manager's guide for Donizetti's *Lucia di Lammermoor* notes that in the aria Lucia sings after her first entrance with her maid in act 1, scene 2, p. 33, 'Lucy should portray the emotion the words express facially and physically with hands and face and especially eyes, and the two girls should come to an agreement as to what they will do on the different phrases; if they have enough interest in the scene to make it go, as far as it rests on their efforts. It is well worth the trial and so we leave it in their hands.' A similar kind of notation is found in the stage manager's guide for Sir Julius Benedict's *The Lily of Killarney*, p. 144, for the scene in which Danny Mann sings an aria about his willingness to kill Eily.

20. For a discussion of this incident and the commentary it provoked on the part of Diderot and others, see John Roach, *The Player's Passion: Studies in the Science of Acting* (Newark: University of Delaware Press, 1985), 111, 127, 138.

21. Lessing, 46.

22. Unsigned review [Frank Woods], 'All on Account of the Milk', *New York Dramatic Mirror* (22 January 1910): 17; rpt. in Anthony Slide (ed), *Selected Film Criticism 1896–1911* (New Jersey: Scarecrow Press, 1982), 4–5. Woods' review of *The Merry Wives of Windsor* (Selig, 1910), *New York Dramatic Mirror* (30 November 1910): 30; rpt. in Slide, 69, makes a similar point: 'The part of Falstaff was adequately taken, although it suffered like all the rest from the necessity of hastening the action to make it fit into the allotted time'.

23. Barry Salt, *Film Style and Technology: History and Analysis* (London: Starword, second edition, 1992), 146–147.

24. Tom Gunning, *D W Griffith and the Origins of American Narrative Film* (Chicago: University of Illinois Press, 1991), 113–114; and Pearson, 63–74.

25. Ben Brewster, 'La mise en scène en profondeur dans les films français de 1900 à 1914' in *Les Premiers ans du cinéma français*, Pierre Guibbert (ed), (Perpignan: Institut Jean Vigo, 1985), 204–217; in English in *Early Cinema: Space, Frame, Narrative*, Thomas Elsaesser with Adam Barker (eds), (London: British Film Institute, 1990), 45–55.

Early German Cinema: A Case for 'Case Studies' or for 'Recasting It All'?

Thomas Elsaesser

Department of Film & Television Studies, University of Amsterdam, Nieuwe Doelenstraat 16, 1012 CP Amsterdam, The Netherlands

Norms and normalisation

WITH THE CENTENARY of the cinema, film studies can look back on two decades of intense interest in early cinema, during which much has been rescued from oblivion and neglect. The initial twenty years of the cinema's history are now firmly established in even the lay audience's mind as a distinct phase and epoch of the movies, neither the childhood of the medium on its way to maturity, nor the naive country-cousin whose presence is an embarrassment to his urban and sophisticated relatives. In fact, so distinct and varied are the phenomena now discussed under the heading early cinema that a discipline almost in its own right has emerged, not entirely congruent with so-called 'revisionist film history', nor as hostile to film theory as an earlier generation of historians whose demand for 'just the facts' would today earn them at best an ironic nickname.[1] This said, it is also true that as our knowledge has grown, so has our ignorance: with new insights come new questions, and problems open up where previously none had been suspected. Quite apart from the work still needing to be done for primary materials to be rescued in archives and films to be restored, there are the baffling questions of colour in early films, for instance, and we could certainly do with a better understanding of 'the sounds of silents': the lecturer, the projection noises, the musical accompaniment, and above all, the many hitherto ignored allusions to sound sources and sound effects in the films themselves.

In the following I want to present a project that has been with me since 1983. It concerns the early German cinema, and more specifically, the first two decades, from 1895 to 1917. The project has a definite time frame, using as its – perhaps slightly too convenient – point of closure the year in which Ufa was founded: for most film historians the date at which it is worth talking about a history of the German cinema. In this respect, I could call it the archaeology of German cinema 'as we know it'. Yet crash-courses for film-historical revisionists like the Pordenone retrospectives must have made experts in almost any field wonder whether they ever knew 'it', and never more so than at the 1990 retrospective devoted to German cinema, whose motto 'Before Caligari' in a double irony both endorsed and contested the received wisdom that up till then made of the early history of German cinema merely a pre-history.

Germany is a particularly blank spot on the map of early cinema, the more noticeable since the 1920s the so-called Expressionist cinema – are so overexposed and have been in the limelight for so long. This has had regrettable consequences, above all the neglect of the basic preconditions for a history: preservation and archiving, securing sources and collecting primary materials. Behind the history of German cinema historiography is the history (or lack of it) of German film archives from the 1930s to the 1980s. Furthermore, insofar as any critical literature exists, it conceptualised German film history mainly as the history of films, and the history of films as primarily that of their production, and the status as authored, self-contained, singular 'works'. This approach is particularly problematic in countries like Germany before 1913 which had been successfully colonised by other filmmaking countries, notably France (Pathé, Gaumont, Eclair), Denmark (Nordisk) and the United States (Vitagraph). At the same time, this type of colonisation has been the fate of most countries in Europe, so that the experience of Germany in the 1910s is fairly paradigmatic for the writing of European film history generally. My title and the juxtaposition implied by it – case studies or recasting it all – is therefore borrowed from the polemical vocabulary of the 'New Film History', especially the essays by Robert C. Allen. In a book review from 1983 he urged film historians to rewrite film history once more, monograph after monograph, case study after case study, not only because the standard histories were wrong in so many details, unreliable and full of gaps, but because most of them were wrongly conceived, so that even where the empirical data was there, the way it was used remained highly dubious.[2]

The first 'revisionist' move was the decision to regard German cinema in a comparative perspective, and to try and understand it in an international context. This may seem self-evident, not least because the legendary Brighton FIAF meeting of 1978 (from which so many film historical initiatives took their cue) had shown how early cinema needed to be studied – both in its film-material as well as historiographical dimension on a broader front, if new insights were to be gained. But German cinema has always been treated differently, making it especially difficult to cast aside the notion that national film history had to be the metaphoric double of political or social history. Film production and motion picture mania already in the early years were such highly international affairs that it was pointless to continue using the idea of a national cinema, without at the same time setting it alongside international developments. Before one could properly study the German cinema, in other words, one had to know the situation at the time in other major film producing nations, such as France, Denmark, Italy and of course the United States, the premise being that Germany might best be understood as a significant variant of the interplay between different film industries, which together constituted something like a norm that in turn could serve as reference point for 'case studies'.

Film history in the 1980s often scored highest when its goal was to infer, test and verify norms, and to these 'normative' perspectives we owe the work of, among others, Noel Burch and Barry Salt, Ben Brewster, Tom Gunning and Charles Musser.[3] When one adds the monumental research enterprise that has examined the origins and stabilisation of the 'mode of production' of classical Hollywood cinema,[4] one realises the rewards of proceeding in this way. My project on Early German Cinema was heavily indebted to these research efforts, and in more practical terms nourished itself from two different sources: the Pordenone Festivals (since 1985), and the annual CineGraph conferences in Hamburg (organised by Hans-Michael Bock since 1988). At the latter events, the international and comparativist perspective of the 'new film history' found an echo in the work of among others, Heide Schlüpmann, Klaus Kreimeier, Corinna Müller and Martin Loiperdinger.

To internationalise early German cinema meant in the first instance to 'normalise' it.

This is evidently a problematic term, given that it seems to announce a certain complacent revisionism, especially suspect when applied to aspects of modern German history. I nonetheless opted for it, because the very suspiciousness about the term may itself be guilty of a certain complacent iconoclasm. Two circumstances in particular make the word 'normalisation' seem apposite. Firstly, the focus was indeed on a cinema that was normal, in the sense of ordinary, popular and widely available, and secondly, this cinema could only be understood within an approach that proceeded – as indicated – in an 'archeological-normative' fashion, given the gaps in our knowledge, and the paucity of primary material that has survived. What remains are fragments, 'bits and pieces', isolated elements of a picture that we can at present only guess at.[5] In this effort, the international debates and comparisons as to what might have been the 'norm(s)' of film style, film production and film reception in the decades, say, leading up to the war were relevant, helping to reconstruct the archaeological object which was early German film from better preserved specimen of the same genus, but from different locations, such as France or the United States.[6]

The trouble with German film history

With this, a third form of 'normalisation' was inevitably set in motion, namely one that put some distance between German film history and the key myths and demonic antinomies so often invoked when discussing it. No other national cinema has been honoured or plagued with as many imaginary histories as that of Germany, whose vanishing points have always been 'catastrophe' and 'redemption', '(self-)deception' and 'enlightenment'. So strong has been the pull of political events, that German film historiography often seemed to lose its bearings faced with the abyss that opened up around Nazism, trying to confront the overtly political (ab-)uses of the cinema by the regime. It was as if the medusa-head called propaganda was blinding several generations of film historians to such an extent that only the mirror-shields called 'film as art' or 'realism' could resist the petrifying stare. Hence the fascination with the

Caligaris, the Mabuses and Nosferatus for subsequent generations: they are, in this constellation, both the highest achievements of film art, but at the same time also (already) the deep chasm of a terror (yet to strike), and thus the mirror-images of a retrospective imagination, which can take fright at its own (anticipatory) prescience, while consoling itself with the knowledge of its own impotence, as it contemplates the disasters it can no longer avert. To put it in slightly less polemical terms: the fact that the cinema in Germany has been perceived, ever since the end of the First World War as above all an ideological-political fact has given rise to a whole number of ideological histories (about the cinema reflecting authoritarian, nationalistic or racist values), as well as ideologies in the guise of history (on behalf of art, of critical realism, of political emancipation). As a result, these histories managed to distance themselves from the ideologies they were attacking only at the price of reproducing these ideologies in inverted or mirrored form, even when trying to establish counter-ideologies.

What, then, is German cinema before the First World War? Mostly, it seems to exist as preparation, premonition and precursor. The Kaiser's passion for the cinematograph makes him the first of a long line of 'Führer' figures and thus a precursor of all the Prussian-military propaganda films around Frederic II – rather than, for instance, the first German film star and a figure out of operetta.[7] *The Student of Prague* from 1913 becomes the premonition of all the *Doppelgänger* and malevolent alteregos, rather than an experiment in cinematic space and film technology using standard Gothic and fairy tale motifs,[8] and Asta Nielsen is the preparation of film as art in Germany, rather than the key figure for introducing and consolidating a crucially different exhibition and marketing strategy, the 'Monopolfilm'.[9] In other words, early German cinema is rarely considered *sui generis*, or as making a contribution to the processes of modernity and modernisation at the turn of the century in one of Europe's most dynamic societies. Instead, here, too, we think we already know what this cinema is about, what its films 'mean', and not unlike the other periods and figures that follow, this 'pre-history' has become a matter of cultural semiotics, a bricolage of meaning-making elements, yielding not so much a history of early German film as testifying to a persistence of German film fantasies.[10] What can then be the task of the film historian? To translate these signs and icons into an ordered procession of fact and figures, of causes and consequences, of actions and agents? Hardly. For what conceivable discursive or chronological space could contain the disparate 'facts' we carry with us about this cinema before 1918?

If the most tempting discursive space to accommodate all these signifiers is that of the nation and its national cinema, then Kracauer, writing around 1946, but distilling reflections formulated in the late 1920s, knew how to resist it as much as he seemed to yield to it. Firmly embedded in his Faustian story, where youthful heroes sell their shadows to the devil, while their souls 'toss between rebellion and submission' is a somewhat less metaphysical construct: the cinema as a social practice, with its target audience the petit-bourgeois male. Thus, it could be argued that the single most influential source (along with Lotte Eisner's *The Haunted Screen*) for 'demonising' German cinema is also the one in whose writings one can find the antidote to the hydra-like growth of German film fantasies, giving us yet another meaning for the term 'normalisation'.[11] Not the major political upheavals, the turning points of history mark this cinema, if one follows Kracauer's logic, but the continuity of the motifs, the genres, the narrative modes – evidence that the mainstay for audiences-appeal and bedrock of popularity remained remarkably similar: by tracing the stereotypes, by refusing to differentiate on aesthetic grounds between art cinema and mainstream, between avantgarde and commercial cinema, Kracauer actually wrote the outlines of a reception history in which the German cinema normalises itself, by 'democatising' its audiences: the adolescent, upwardly mobile young men, and later in the 1920s, the 'little shopgirls at the movies', both groups using the films as mirror-images of their all-too-normal anxieties and desires, with the exception that – as in most European national cinemas – the anxieties (i.e. unhappy endings, gothic and fantasy

genres) seem to prevail over the wish-fulfilments (comedies, adventure genres), but only just ... Looking at the men and women who in the vast majority of the films appear as protagonists, one can indeed say that the German cinema of the 1910s forms a continuum not only with the entertainment cinema of other nations, but with the German entertainment cinema of any other decade, making a *prima facie* case against weighing these films down with too much of the ballast of the German 'Sonderweg' (separate development). Once one grants the historical agenda of reception studies, and approaches the films via the question of audiences, focusing on a cultural studies or gender studies perspective, whatever one's findings, they can at least be put in relation: be it to the theoretical paradigms of 'negotiated reading' and 'stereotyping', or to the norms derived from the aggregate data of comparable national cinemas in France, Britain, Italy or Russia.

On the whole, this is not the way in which early German cinema has been researched in Germany itself, where throughout the 1980s, publications dealing with aspects of film in a historical perspective had begun to appear. Mostly, they amounted to what in my terminology would be 'case studies', usually around a single personality, like Henny Porten or Asta Nielsen, a specific sets of events like the First World War, a physical site like the Babelsberg production facilities or an institution, like the Ufa Studio. On the whole, this 'archeological' work was neither part of an ongoing research project, nor were the resulting books or studies 'film histories' in the sense that I understood them, whether 'old' or 'new'. The activities were for the most part anniversary-driven and museum-sponsored;[12] in other words, they were part of what has been called the heritage culture and nostalgia business. Accordingly, one can roughly categorise these publications in two groups: biographical studies and geographical studies.

Among the biographical studies, the 1980s saw a change insofar as the spate of star memoirs or star biographies began being replaced by more solidly researched monographs on individual directors and personalities (Erich Pommer, Asta Nielsen, Reinhold

1895

Schünzel, Richard Oswald, Joe May, Conrad Veldt, E.A. Dupont, Oskar Messter). The geographical studies, on the other hand, focused above all on the cinema and film culture in particular cities or regions: the first studio-buildings in Berlin, early cinema in a provincial city like Eckernförde or Osnabrück, or film-going in Hamburg, the cinemas of Cologne, Frankfurt as film city in the 1910s, or the cinema comes to East Friesland.[13] Virtually all these studies were event-driven and themselves produced or accompanied events: around anniversaries (750 Years Berlin, the Murnau centenary which encouraged his home town of Bielefeld to sponsor a Murnau society which has now completed a study of local film culture, 75 years Babelsberg, the Ufa anniversary, or as on this occasion, 100 years cinema); around festivals (the regular Berlin Film Festival retrospectives) or around exhibitions, launched out of civic pride, where a local need for prestige released some precious funds for researching cinema history. This does not mean the work that has come out of this conjuncture has not been stimulating and sometimes even pathbreaking. But it is well to keep in mind this structural feature of German film historiography which is not present to the same degree elsewhere. In the United States, for instance, it is difficult to think of Detroit paying tax dollars in order to commission a study of movie-going among its generations of auto-workers, or even New York paying for anything other than promotional literature to advertise the New York Film Board which sells facilities and services to film crews and location units.

The German situation reflects both the intense regionalism of German cultural politics (with Berlin, Hamburg, Munich/Bavaria, Frankfurt, Cologne, Düsseldorf/North-Rhine Westphalia all pursuing their own film-policy) and the fact that film studies in general and film history in particular has only a very weak institutional base in the universities, so that little fundamental research can be undertaken, because the monies available have to be tied to 'representational' events. The same goes for publishers who do not see a 'market', and hence rarely publish major studies, unless, again, an anniversary is tied to it, as was the case for *Die Ufa Story*, a magisterial study to which Klaus Kreimeier devoted a decade of scholarship.[14] There is thus a vicious circle or downward spiral regarding such work, unless the universities can in fact initially support and fund such research, or at least allow film history to be taught, so that film students can constitute the first 'market' for publications, which in turn can encourage people to write such books, knowing that they get published at prices that readers can afford. As a consequence of the event-driven nature of much of this work, it would be unreasonable to expect these case studies to be methodological self-critical, even if such self-reflexivity would seem a *sine qua non* for anyone writing elsewhere within the 'new film history'. The studies also rarely seem to feel the need to be innovative with regards to their research perspectives, even though the empirical material and documentation is often both recalcitrant and riveting, and therefore demanding new ways of organisation and presentation.

The institutional power-structures underpinning film history in Germany are thus crucial in trying to understand what gets worked on and what does not: it determines the themes, the topics, and also the underlying outlook – sometimes at the expense of other, equally plausible or even more urgent priorities. In the absence of university courses or academic conferences, and institutionally driven by varieties of heritage thinking (often called 'the culture of commemoration'), film history found itself in the shadow of the *Historikerstreit*, the historians' quarrel about how to 'historicise' the Nazi regime and the Holocaust. As such, it could be said to have been under the sign of its own kind of 'normalising' German cinema, putting together a version of 'the nation' anxious to stress continuity. Around names, dates, places, regional loyalties, local traditions and family dynasties this practice of film history tried to put Germans on a more friendly, nostalgic or benevolent footing with their own past and popular culture. Obviously, it was not only the cinema that benefited from such retrospection, and obviously, often enough, those commissioned to work on such projects had to navigate split loyalties or conflicts of interest.

Film history: counter-history or counter-factual history

The impasse my project came up against was how to conceive of early German cinema when it seemed to have no evident masterpieces, and no standard versions or 'official' histories other than the politically problematic, but nonetheless indispensible 'heritage histories'. At the same time, no sensible division of labour could establish itself between universities and archives, or between archives and museums, not only because their agendas diverged so drastically, but also because their manner of proceeding violated some of the very ground-rules of the new film history. The theoretical question was therefore: what kind of outlook does one take, once one is neither bound by anniversaries and prestige cultural politics, nor by an interventionist agenda? It also seemed wrong to argue that the German cinema had simply been neglected and overlooked out of ignorance and prejudice, so that it merely needed to be restored it to its rightful place.

Luckily, the impasse was overcome, not least thanks to two studies that were in the making throughout the 1980s, but were published at the beginning of the 1990s. Both were explicitly committed to the 'new film history', both recognised the need to rethink quite radically our approach to early German cinema, by regarding this cinema as not a pre-history, but as possessing a distinct identity: yet their methods as well as their conclusions could not be more different. The first, by Heide Schlüpmann sees itself as a kind of counter-history, drawing as sharp as possible a contrast between Wilhelmine cinema and Weimar cinema, a contrast located in the profound structural changes in their respective 'public spheres', i.e. spectatorship and conditions of reception. Giving a new interpretation of the films, Schlüpmann considers key works across the contemporary debates about audiences and thus succeeds in making this cinema strange, different, and yet familiar, fully justifying her title 'The Uncanny Gaze'.[15] Looked at from the vantage point of Weimar Cinema as a 'patriarchal', 'male' and 'oedipally obsessed' cinema, Wilhelmine cinema for Schlüpmann appears as something like a refuge for a different conception of the body and of femininity, one that offers especially the female spectator a novel form of visual pleasure. Emphasising, extrapolating and identifying the female gaze, she is able to set up a number of films and genres as 'canonical' texts that become a sort of norm, in which the reception by female spectators is both an historical fact and a theoretical requirement. With this, Schlüpmann provides a rich Wilhelmine film culture sourcebook as well as a number of hypotheses that imply, within the terms of a counter-history, something like an attempt to 'recast it all'. By inverting the teleology according to which Wilhelmine cinema was merely a precursor of Weimar, she effectively argues that Wilhelmine cinema is in some sense a 'reaction' to Weimar.

For Schlüpmann then, early German cinema appears in terms of a counter-history, even a sort of counter-factual history, if we consider the female public sphere she outlines and invokes as a virtuality that may never have existed as such 'historically'. With this she could – if she chose to – also counter Barry Salt's objections, by showing that his criteria are elaborated from the vantage point of a 'cinema of narrative integration', i.e. what was to become the classical Hollywood norm, when for her, not only is early German cinema a cinema primarily for women spectators, it conforms also to what Tom Gunning has labelled 'cinema of attractions'.[16] Schlüpmann's other strategy is to define early German cinema around one icon-figure, Asta Nielsen, and to highlight around her films a number of key tropes: mobility of the body ('exteriorised', eloquent body language, in contrast to the repressed, muted body language of Asta Nielsen's counterpart, Henny Porten); Asta Nielsen returns the gaze and thus, according to the paradigm developed by Laura Mulvey, she does not fall under the category of femininity as deployed by classical cinema.[17] Finally, the multiplicity of the spaces Nielsen inhabits transgress boundaries that are at once boundaries of class and status, and also cinematic space. Schlüpmann has, for instance, a particularly sophisticated argument around narration in Nielsen's films. It is as if the cinematic apparatus and her deployment of it made Nielsen the prototype

1895

of the woman who negotiates different social and physical spaces, where nothing seems out of bounds to her, and where there is no area of the represented world she cannot 'penetrate'.[18]

Schlüpmann's history is a counter-history: against the patriarchal linearity of the traditional accounts, she 'goes backwards', and from the rigidity of Weimar cinema's notion of gender and identity she 'reconstructs' Wilhelmine cinema as its opposite. But she also treats the films as incomplete as texts, since implicit in her argument is that only once we 'add' the female spectator as the films' ideal addressee, does the logic of Wilhelmine film production, as well as the narrative logic of each film, become comprehensible. Similarly, what makes her history 'possibilist' or 'counter-factual' is that instead of proceding in a positivist-archival spirit, she is capable of thinking history as also the history of losers – women – thus indicating at least tentatively, that it could have been otherwise, which in turn corresponds to the position of the European or American avant-garde *vis-à-vis* the dominant Hollywood cinema. For these avant gardes also drew from the possibility that the past has been different the hope that the future might one day open up a space where things can be different: the historical utopia of the empire of the female gaze empowers the will to create or carve out that otherness in the present for a future practice. Regarding 'normalisation', Schlüpmann seems to move in the opposite direction from the one taken so far: by declaring the bourgeois-patriarchal cinema of the Weimar Republic with its nationalist ideology as the 'norm' of German cinema, she can play off against it an earlier, freer, more experimental Wilhelmine cinema, which thus appears as the exception. Inversely, the perspective of the losers and the awareness of possible alternatives are part of the archaeologist's gaze on the past, for his/her job is to imagine once more a whole out of mere fragments.

An added advantage of such a film history of the possible is that it obliges one not only to look for gaps and retrieve what has been lost, or to test the pseudo-logical causalities of all those accounts which string together the so-called known facts, in order to give a wholly constructed narrative the semblance of plausibility. It also encourages one to look beyond the confines of the discipline, explore new connections, ask different kinds of questions, and keep the story open-ended, so as to avoid all the retrospective teleologies and hindsight histories that have, as indicated, typified German film history even where it broke new ground. In what sense such a broadly archaeological and counter-factual outlook might lead to a different concept of early German cinema I would like to briefly test by looking at the second of the two studies – though not before specifying my concept of possibilist history. On the whole, I am less interested in what might have been, and instead, would suggest that it is also a matter of asking why something did not happen. In the latter instance, we could speak of a theory of film history around 'the dog that did not bark', after the famous Sherlock Holmes story, in which the fact that the dog had not barked becomes the tell-tale sign that it must have known the burglar.

The dog that did not bark

If we look for the dog that did not bark in early German cinema, we could begin with the question Why did Germany, with its above average interest in living pictures and its potentially huge market apparently not develop a thriving indigenous film production on a sound industrial basis until after the First World War? The traditional answer is that the German bourgeoisie was culturally prejudiced against the cinema, and thus industrialists and finance capital doubted the cinema's long-term prospects and refused to invest. The top-down Ufa-foundation, promoted by the military and the State, according to this version, had to rush in where capital feared to tread. This seems classical 'retrospective teleology' even if for once of an economic rather than ideological kind.

Just how different a starting point has been chosen by Corinna Müller, author of the second study, becomes evident when one realises that her book does not discuss any individual films at all, and in fact sets out to challenge the very distinction attraction/narrative integration which forms the theoretical basis of Schlüpmann's study.[19] A case study rather than a totalising history, Müller's *Frühe deutsche Kinematographie* nonetheless recasts a good deal of early German film history, not least because it convincingly shows that the German cinema of the first two decades, when measured by international criteria, behaved exceedingly 'normal'. Her method is to take the evidence amassed in regional and local studies (principally that of Anne Paech)[20] about exhibitors, about picture houses, programme bills, admission prices, advertising in the local and regional newspapers, thereby referring herself explicitly to the premises and assumptions of the new film history and outlining a framework which makes it possible to develop a causal nexus within which a much more plausible, because immanent and structural reason can be given for why German film production did not take off in the same way as that of Denmark or even France.

For far from being anarchic, haphazard and amateurish (as it had been portrayed) the early German film business followed very distinct patterns and organisational principles – namely those of the variety show and the variety theatre. In particular, two principles typical of variety – the programming policy and its internal structure – survived the variety show as a form of entertainment, remaining in place and exerting a determining influence on the development of fixed site cinemas in Germany. The German film business, in other words, developed just like the American and British one – as an exhibition-led industry whose commodity or product was the short-film based number principle, with editorial control largely in the hands of exhibitors, and it remained so longer than elsewhere (until about 1907). At the same time, this exhibition-led industry used up vast quantities of film, but in cut-throat competition also devalued these films so fast that the profit margins for home producers became so slim that the business sucked in cheap foreign (mainly French) imports. It also meant that German producers supplying this market (such as Oskar Messter) geared their production to a mode of exhibition that made their films virtually inexportable. Thus the very strength of the variety theatre as a business and organisation at the exhibition end, made the German film business, from the production end a disaster, because from that perspective, it was both rigid in its programming and anarchic in its trade and exchange practices, provoking a crisis which Müller vividly describes. By systematically following distributors' advertisements in the trade papers (*Der Kinematograph, Die Lichtbildbühne, Erste Internationale Filmzeitung*) she is able to reconstruct the complicated and costly logic by which German distributors fashioned a new product by restricting and regulating access. In other words, she is able to show how German production takes off, precisely at the point where – like film businesses elsewhere – a means has been found to create and institutionalise an artificial scarcity which to this day characterises both the formation of cinema chains and the practice of exclusivity.

Müller is able to show that only when the so-called Monopolfilm established itself between 1909–12 did the indigenous production sector become profitable again, which often enough was by then in the hands of exhibitors become producers, such as Ludwig Gottschalk, Paul Oliver, Paul Davidson, Martin Dentler. These are the (mostly unsung) pioneers of the German cinema as a business and an industry, and it is thanks to their efforts that we have the extraordinary expansion of filmmaking and experiment around 1913, to which we owe the first flourishing of a specifically German cinema, helping to bring into existence the famous 'Autorenfilm' as well as giving Asta Nielsen her well-deserved national and international fame. For it is only at this point that Asta Nielsen properly comes into the picture, whose success greatly aided the establishment of the Monopolfilm as the dominant business practice. We know that Nielsen is central to early German cinema, but we can now see that the logic acts rather the other way round from how it is traditionally pictured, where the Nielsen films are said to be the breakthrough to screen art, finally freeing the cinema from its commercial constraints.[21] It would be more accurate to say that because of the commercial imperatives of making films more valuable by creating the scarcity called 'monopoly' or 'exclusivity', in order to halt overproduction and thus the collapse of prices and profits, an actress like

1895

Asta Nielsen could attain the fame she did. That the kind of surplus exhibition value she brought to the film-product was not grounded in her films' artistic ambition, but in their universal appeal is usefully demonstrated when one recalls that one of the first successful Monopolfilms on offer for distribution by PAGU, Nielsen's future business partners was not a dramatic film at all, but the Johnson vs Jeffries boxing match from July 1910 in Reno. As in the United States, then, the building of the new commodity 'film' in Germany emerges out of a combination of longer films, restriction of access, the transformation of programming policy, and the building up of picture personalities or 'stars': constants that seem to be the necessary conditions for the 'normalisation' of the film business in most producing nations.

Yet for the pre-war period, Müller lets us see not only what the dog that didn't bark was in early German film, but also that it was something film history might not have been able to read off the films themselves: the German variety theatre, its stars, its economic structures, its programming policy. In all its aspect, it appears to have been a well-organised industry, especially at the exhibitors' level, whose existence provides a missing link and a powerful explanatory tool for the seeming anomaly of Germany's weak production sector. The reason it did not develop before 1911–12 was that the distribution and exhibition market remained essentially unreformed: the numbers principle was not only very sophisticated in its sequence and choice of items, but it was also very rigidly adhered to. This gave the French company Pathé an unbeatable advantage in the German market, because they were the only producer worldwide who could deliver whole programmes, and at costs that undercut most others who only delivered part of the programme. Although a structuring absence, the variety theatre as a near-forgotten entertainment industry emerges, in Müller's study, as a multi-faceted factor that both helped the expansion of 'cinema' and hindered the production of 'films'. It once more indicates that film history and cinema history are not the same and that a national cinema must be more than the sum of the films it might have

produced at a given point in time. Müller does so by utilising the new film history as her conceptual tool, but combines it with material that has arisen out of the archival, antiquarian and perhaps even nostalgic impulses of the new regionalism, whose own 'normalisation' tendencies can now be seen as even more politically ambivalent and historically complex than at first assumed.

Forms of perception and constructions of space

One problem with Müller's work is that she may have taken Douglas Gomery's advice almost too much to heart: her book does not discuss any films, and indeed one does get the feeling that for her type of investigation, 'film viewing is really an inappropriate research method'.[22] Needless to say, I think that film viewing does make a difference, but it certainly requires one to reflect quite carefully how this 'difference' can enter into one's conception of such a history. Perhaps one needs to begin reframing some of the issues, even those which the 'new film history' has bequeathed to us. One has, it seems to me, to define the transitional period, or the moments of transition in two directions or two-dimensionally: concerning the length of film and the changes this brings to the idea of the 'programme' (the numbers principle), and concerning the spectator–screen relationship. These are two interconnected but nonetheless independent variables, which need to be examined separately, and which do indeed require a very careful scrutiny of the films themselves. I want, by way of conclusion, to briefly discuss these dimensions, whose importance for the logic of the films appears not to have been sufficiently explored even by the two studies just discussed.

Two films from the early 1910s raise these issues in exemplary form, if only because their relative directorial anonymity would indicate that one is dealing here with formal features so much taken for granted as to constitute the invisible presence of a 'norm'. Since both films were also quite popular at the time, while today the reasons for this popularity almost wholly elude us, they pose the sort of challenge mentioned earlier: What might film history gain from examining the films them-

1895

selves? Picked more or less at random, the films are two Messter productions, *Richard Wagner* (Carl Froelich/William Wauer, 1913) and *Des Pfarrers Töchterlein* (The Pastor's Daughter, Adolf Gärtner, 1912). In the case of *Richard Wagner* the focus is on film length and what it can tell us about a film's social function and intended audience, while with *Des Pfarrers Töchterlein* the screen-spectator relationship is the point at issue, defining its generic identity as melodrama, but also its sociological value as interpretable document.

Richard Wagner, at a length of 70 minutes, seems at first sight one of the more strangely 'inept' films when judged by our contemporary taste or Barry Salt's evolutionary scale. Slow, choppy, devoid of story-telling skills, its succession of tableaux convey the overwhelming impression of stasis: more an illustrated picture book than a dramatic narrative. Yet given that length correlates directly to the conditions of reception (and the structural changes the early film programme underwent) and thus defines generic identity as well as marketing strategy (the 'Monopolfilm'), the film becomes interesting once we regard it as the solution to a problem we may no longer feel as such, namely of how to tell a longer story within determinate conditions of reception, still dominated by the numbers programme. As to its generic identity, one would expect a film about Richard Wagner to belong to the *Autorenfilm*, aiming at the better-paying middle-class audience, looking for cultural respectability. Yet judging from the publicity material, Richard Wagner appears to have been treated as something of a folk hero, whose fictionalised life belonged less to the (later) genre of the musician's bio-pic than to the oral narratives of youthful rebels and national saviours, like William Tell or Andreas Hofer, about whom Messter had already made a film in 1909. Once one regards *Richard Wagner* under the double aspect of hybrid genre (bridging – like its hero – the cultural divides of 'high' art and 'low' entertainment), and transitional form (in the move to the long feature film), the apparent solecisms and stylistic unevenness turn out to have their own logic. In other words, the argument would be that the 'medium' the film intertextualises is not Wagner's music or his operas, but a popu-

lar literary or semi-literary genre, maybe even fairy tale and myth (one notes, from the advertising, that it played as one of the big Christmas pictures of 1913). *Richard Wagner* was a film made for a mass (family) audience, while at the same time possessing an identity as an *Autorenfilm*, involving a 'name' personality from the arts, which goes to show that the concept of the *Autorenfilm* was a marketing concept before it was a quality concept, or rather, the quality concept was also a marketing concept.[23] What, however, becomes evident only when viewing the film itself is that its narrative structure is heavily marked by the numbers principle, and thus represents a distinct stage within the narrative transformations occasioned by the change in film length. Bearing the variety programme in mind, and recalling the distinctions between the various 'genres' of the short film, one can in *Richard Wagner*, without too much difficulty, recognise a range of spectacle attractions and genres from the pre-1910 international cinema: there is the (British) restaged documentary [in the 1848 revolution scene], the (Danish) detective serial [as Wagner hides in the doorway to escape arrest], the (French) *film d'art* [the encounter between Wagner and Liszt], the (Biograph or Pathé) historical reconstruction [the tableau including Friedrich Nietzsche, where in the USA it would be Lincoln, or Dreyfus in France], and there is even a Méliès-type trick film scene, when Wagner is shown telling the story of Siegfried and the helmet that makes him invisible. As especially this last episode shows, the film takes great care over its narrational procedures, putting in place several narrators, both external and internal, introduced by script and intertitles, themselves referring to different narrational levels, as in the narrative within a narrative, or the insert shot of the warrant for Wagner's arrest.

In this respect, *Richard Wagner* seems more 'sophisticated' than many other films from 1913, while at the same time more 'primitive', although especially among the *Autorenfilm* one finds further examples of films where the numbers principle has survived inside the continuous feature film. The phenomenon was appreciated or remarked upon as such by the reviews, as in the case *Atlantis* (by August

Blom, 1913, after the novel by Gerhart Hauptmann) and *Wo ist Coletti?* (by Max Mack, 1913).[24] The examples illustrate less the old argument about the difficult transition from short to feature length film (the problems of how to generate a longer narrative), and rather indicate how beholden the German cinema still was to the variety theatre as its structural principle, not as a performance mode or a cognitive principle, but as the narrative space by which spectators and films communicated. In other words, key films from 1913, in order to reach a mass audience, practically reinvented for the long *Monopolfilm* a narrative which simulated the short film numbers programme. That this is what the audience wanted and expected is clear from many a contemporary account. As it happens, only intellectuals thought the numbers programme incoherent, and the paradox of 'primitive' and 'sophisticated' film form in *Richard Wagner* directs attention to the fact that the film proposes to the spectator a narrative space which is no longer ours, just as its mode of address to the audience puts the modern audience in a relation to the screen we would no longer label 'cinematic'. Like other films from the 1910s by Asta Nielsen/Urban Gad, Max Mack and Franz Hofer, or Paul von Worringen, Joseph Delmont and William Wauer, the Archimedean point around which film form in Germany seems to turn are the different levels that link audience-space to screen space and structure their registers of reference, be they theatrical, illusionist, performative, documentary, fictional. The relation screen space, audience and self-reference and self-conscious experiment in some of them point to the possible logic that underlies the changes of film length, of distribution and exhibition practices, as well as the cinema's relation to other arts. What in the past has sometimes been thematised, often rather polemically and antagonistically, under the heading of the presumed theatricality of early film, or conversely, the cinema's efforts to break free from theatre to find its own identity, turns out to be part not of a modernist quest for medium-specificity, but belongs to a more fundamental history of modernity in the sphere of representation and public spaces, where the cinema plays its role in the shifting and contradictory development which in urban environments at once fragmented and collectivised the masses into spectators and audiences.

The fact that in early cinema the films imagined their audience to be physically present, while in the later, narrative full-length feature film it was precisely the imaginary viewpoint of the spectator, his or her virtual presence in the representation that became the norm, indicates that what is contrasted is not theatre and cinema, but one kind of cinema with another kind of cinema. This affects quite crucially the way a film can be interpreted, and thus points to a possible interface between reception history, genre study and the formal analysis of individual films. While a reception and genre-directed approach to early German films tends to establish a socio-cultural or socio-pathological profile of Wilhelmine class, caste and status society, perhaps by pointing out the many nannies and officer's sons, or all the middle-aged lovers courting tomboys that could be their daughters, such a one-to-one correlation now seems to miss the crucial dimension. How can one feel confident about interpreting the prevalence of authority figures like the military and the clergy within a political or ideological argument after having given some thought to the interplay of spectator space and screen space in some of these films? My second film example is a case in point. *Des Pfarrers Töchterlein*, an all but forgotten Henny Porten film which in its day was internationally popular,[25] emerges as important precisely to the degree that, in contrast to *Richard Wagner*, it requires and to some extent assumes an imaginary spectator, both cognitively (insofar as narrative comprehension depends on the spectator appreciating an uneven distribution of knowledge among the characters) and perceptually (insofar as the spectator is privileged in sharing the heroine's optical point of view in a crucial scene).

More precisely, *Des Pfarrers Töchterlein* combines both models of spectator-screen relationship in early cinema, that of an audience imagined physically present, and that of an audience both 'present' and 'absent'. In a sense, it makes the conflicts between two modes the very heart of the drama, readable today – in the multiplications of diegetic and

1895

non-diegetic audiences, and the discrepancy between optical and 'moral' point of view – as the *mise-en-abyme* of the historical audience's dilemma. One can speak of a veritable object lesson in teaching a new form of perception and reception, of understanding narrative logic and character motivation psychologically (the hallmark of film melodrama), designed to force the spectator to put him/herself into the place of the protagonist, and no longer understand the protagonist as the (re)presenter of feelings and actions.

Such a reading would suggest almost the opposite of a traditional sociological interpretation in the manner of Kracauer: a major is needed (in, for instance, another forgotten, but 'normatively' useful film, *Die Kinder des Majors*/The Children of the Major) not because he reflects the militarism of Wilhelmine society, but in order to motivate efficiently at the level of story-world a most subtle narrational structure about who knows what, when and about whom, allowing the film to introduce the convention of the duel, and thereby obliging the spectator to experience the situation of the brother seeking satisfaction on behalf of his jilted sister as irresolvable and 'tragically' inevitable.[26] Similarly, the pastor needs to be a pastor in *Des Pfarrers Töchterlein* so that the complex architecture of gazes which culminates and climaxes the film – the daughter witnesses how her father marries the man she loves to the woman for whom he has left her – can actually be physically motivated, creating an explosive dramatic space. In addition, only the 'local' or 'cultural' knowledge of the spectator that this concerns a protestant church, and within the church, the physical location of the altar, gives the film its full (melo-)dramatic pathos, since it stages the conflict as the drama of spaces and gazes. What is significant is the pastor's physical position, seeing his daughter appear in the organ loft at the other end of the altar while the bride and bridegroom, kneeling in front of the altar, are oblivious to the drama unfolding between father and daughter, over their heads and behind their backs. In this film, then, it is the pastor who motivates the church setting, which motivates the space, which in turn allows these complex interchanges of gazes and uneven distribution of knowledge

to be physically embodied. Across the pastor as bearer of multiple significations, a space of suspense and drama is created which no other profession could have conveyed as economically.[27]

These two examples of a reading, informed so evidently by present historical and theoretical preoccupations, once more return one to the question of 'normalisation'. They open up the difficulty of assuming that a historical period not only has a norm, but 'knows itself' (i.e. is self-reflexive, or self-expressive) through this norm by deviating from it. Just as likely, the mirroring, the self-referentiality, the *mises-en-abyme*, and the different types of expressivity and stylisation – but also the shadow of hindsight falling on a pre-history – only help to confirm that in the history of the cinema, as in all history, the phenomena analysed neither 'know themselves' in the terms we know them, nor are they ultimately sufficient unto themselves, as the idea of 'normalisation' misleadingly and ideologically suggests. We therefore, inevitably, have to 'normalise' our own demand for normalisation which is to say, relativise any presumption we might have to 'know' how Wilhelmine society has 'lived' its cinema and represented it to itself.

This, too, would be an aspect of the project of 'normalisation', from a theoretical perspective that includes the possibility that sometimes, in the history of film culture, the dog did not bark, because certain phenomena were taken for granted, whose significance now eludes us. These phenomena demand therefore research that can stay quite close to the ground, as it were, at the regional, local-specific level, but which can also work with films that – like most of the examples in the Amsterdam collection I am myself closest to – are not 'author'ised or canonised in any of the standard film histories. Therefore it should not be surprising that a fair amount of the empirical material drawn on by studies such as the one by Corinna Müller (who builds up the case for a 'normalisation' of the development of early German cinema), comes from just such studies as those which owe their existence to the new kind of local patriotism, the new regionalism or the new 'identity politics' of the heritage industry, problematic

1895

though they might be by belonging to a political normalisation of a wholly abnormal national history. Situated at the opposite end of the spectrum of the international research initiatives leading to the revisionism of 're-casting it all', they nonetheless promote just such a quiet revolution. Alongside Robert C. Allen's battle-cry for a new film history re-written 'monograph after monograph' these studies push also towards the large scale projects, by pointing out, if only unwittingly, how 'normal' it was for the early German cinema to be a case study for an a-typical development. With it, the opposition between 'case study' and 'recasting it all' may itself have to be recast – a task to which this centenary event seems to have applied itself with evident success.

Notes

1. Robert Rosenstone has called it 'the Dragnet School of History: *just the facts Ma'am*', in Robert A. Rosenstone, 'The Future of the Past', in Vivian Sobchack (ed), *The Persistence of History* (New York: Routledge, 1996), 202.

2. Robert C. Allen, 'Archeology of Film History' (review of Larry May's *Screening out the Past*), *Wide Angle*, Spring 1983, and Robert C. Allen/Douglas Gomery, *Film History: Theory and Practice* (New York: Alfred A. Knopf, 1985).

3. Essays by these authors are to be found in Thomas Elsaesser (ed), *Early Cinema: Space, Frame, Narrative* (London: BFI Publishing, 1990).

4. David Bordwell, Janet Staiger and Kristin Thompson, *The Classical Hollywood Cinema: Film Style and Mode of Production to 1960* (London: Routledge and Kegan Paul, 1985).

5. As so often, it turns out that both the print records and film materials are more copious than had been assumed. Some 680 German films from 1895 to 1917 are now documented as having survived, and while this is only a fraction of the output, it still represents a critical mass that is far from ever having been evaluated historically or critically. For a list, see Michael Wedel and Ivo Blom (eds), *German Cinema 1895–1917: A Checklist of Extant Films* (Amsterdam University Press, 1995).

6. The testing ground for this approach was, of course, the Giornate del Cinema Muto, held annually in Pordenone since the mid-1980s. Here, too, the first major revision of early German cinema took place in 1990. See Paolo Cherchi Usai and Lorenzo Codelli (eds), *Before Caligari: German Cinema, 1895–1920* (Pordenone: Edizioni Biblioteca dell'Immagine, 1990).

7. As Martin Loiperdinger has argued in 'The Kaiser's Cinema' in Thomas Elsaesser (ed), *A Second Life: German Cinema's First Decades* (Amsterdam: Amsterdam University Press, 1996), 41–50.

8. See Leon Hunt, '*The Student of Prague*: Division and Codification of Space' in Thomas Elsaesser (ed), *Early Cinema: Space Frame Narrative* (London: British Film Institute, 1990), 389–400.

9. See Peter Lähn, '*Afgrunden* und die deutsche Filmindustrie: Die Entstehung des Monopolfilms' in Manfred Behn (ed), *Schwarzer Traum und Weisse Sklavin* (Munich: text und kritik, 1994), 15–21.

10. Both Siegfried Kracauer's *From Caligari to Hitler* and Lotte Eisner's *The Haunted Screen* announce already in their titles this sense of retrospective teleology and hindsight history.

11. By juxtaposing the demonic creatures, the overreachers and tyrants, the test-tube robots and homunculi on the screen with the audiences in the stalls, Kracauer in *From Caligari to Hitler* might just have had his tongue in his cheek, trying to deflate the allegorical constructions which especially among German emigres in the United States had, since the late 1930s, favoured seeing Hitler as a kind of Mephisto who had stolen the Germans' soul. This was the case of Thomas Mann, especially in his novel *Dr Faustus* (1944).

12. See, among others, Lisa Kosok and Mathilde Jamin (eds), *Viel Vergnügen: Öffentliche Lustbarkeiten im Ruhrgebiet der Jahrhundertwende* (Essen: Ruhrlandmuseum, 1992) or Martin Loiperdinger (ed), *Oskar Messter: Filmpionier der Kaiserzeit* (Basel and Frankfurt: Stroemfeld/Roter Stern, 1994: KINtop Schriften 2). The Berlin Historical Museum ('Preussen im Film', 'Film und der Erste Weltkrieg') and the annual Berlin Film Festival Retrospectives ('Erich Pommer', '75 Jahre Babelsberg') are other institutions regularly commissioning original film historical research.

13. See among others, Michael Hanisch, *Auf den Spuren der Filmgeschichte: Berliner Schauplätze* (Berlin: Henschel, 1991); Wiltrud Hennigsen, *Die Enstehung des Kinos in Münster: Versuch einer Historiographie* (Münster: Hennigsen, 1990); Detlef Hoffmann and Jens Thiele (eds), *Lichtbilder, Lichtspiele.*

1895

Anfänge der Photographie und des Kinos in Ostfriesland (Marburg: Jonas, 1989); Dieter Helmut Warstat, *Frühes Kino in der Kleinstadt* [Eckernförde] (Berlin: Spiess, 1982).

14. *Die Ufa Story* (Munich: Hanser, 1992). Typically, Kreimeier does not have a teaching post, but is a 'free(lance) author', who has had to rely on a publisher's advance to fund his research.

15. Heide Schlüpmann, *Unheimlichkeit des Blicks* (Frankfurt/Basel: Stroemfeld Roter Stern, 1992).

16. See Tom Gunning, 'The Cinema of Attractions', in Elsaesser (ed), *Early Cinema: Space, Frame, Narrative* (London, 1990), 56–62.

17. Laura Mulvey, 'Visual Pleasure and Narrative Cinema', *Screen* 16 (Autumn 1975): 6–18.

18. Heide Schlüpmann, 'Asta Nielsen and Female Narration' in Elsaesser (ed), *A Second Life* (Amsterdam, Amsterdam University Press, 1996), 118–122.

19. Corinna Müller, *Frühe deutsche Kinematographie: Formale, wirtschaftliche und kulturelle Entwicklungen 1907–1912* (Stuttgart and Weimar: Metzler, 1994).

20. Anne Paech, *Kino zwischen Stadt und Land. Geschichte des Kinos in der Provinz: Osnabrück* (Marburg: Jonas, 1985).

21. '[Asta Nielsen's] coming characterised the break-through to art in German film production, which so far had been entirely guided by the ever-growing business possibilities. Today it seems almost grotesque to think that those forces which were aiming at the artistic development of the film in Germany were at first opposed by difficulties almost too great to overcome. These difficulties were caused by the lack of interest in the popular new entertainment-medium shown by the ruling classes, by educated and official circles, who had so far completely overlooked its cultural and educational possibilities.' Hermann Wollenberg, *Fifty Years of German Film* (London: Falcon Press, 1948), 9.

22. Douglas Gomery and Robert C. Allen, *Film History: Theory and Practice* (New York: Alfred A. Knopf, 1985), 38.

23. *Richard Wagner* was made to coincide with the composer's centenary. The project gained wide publicity because of a well-known figure of Berlin musical life, Giuseppe Becce, played the lead. Notoriety was added by the outrageous financial demands made for the music rights by the Bayreuth Wagner estate, which necessitated that the film be performed with a Wagner-ish score. For a fuller discussion of the music in *Richard Wagner*, see Ennio Simeon, 'Guiseppe Becce and *Richard Wagner*: Paradoxes of the first film score', in Elsaesser (ed), *A Second Life*, 219–224.

24. As to the reaction of the critics, see Julius Hart, 'Der Atlantis Film', *Der Tag* (24 December 1913). Reprinted in Fritz Güttinger (ed), *Kein Tag ohne Kino: Die Schriftsteller über den Stummfilm* (Frankfurt: Deutsches Filmmuseum, 1984), 292–293. My thanks to Martin Loiperdinger for drawing attention to this passage.

25. The references to its popularity – over 150 copies sold and one of the rare German export successes of the time – are in George Sadoul, *Histoire générale du cinéma* (Paris: Denoël, 1973), vol. 2, 368.

26. *Die Kinder des Majors* maintains a very complex distribution of knowledge among the character at the same time as it elaborates an involuted temporal structure, again indicative of the efforts made to involve the spectator in an 'inner' drama, as opposed to employing what Noël Burch has called 'external narration' and André Gaudreault has defined as 'monstration'.

27. The situation of the heroine is more convoluted still: one not only imagines the silent cry of Henny Porten on the organ loft, before she collapses, but actually 'hears' it, thanks to the prominence of huge organ pipes framing her tormented look. For illustration of this series of shots, see Thomas Elsaesser, 'Early German Cinema: A Second Life?' in *A Second Life: German Cinema's First Decades*, Thomas Elsaesser (ed) (Amsterdam: Amsterdam University Press, 1996), 36.

1895

Index

1895

1895

1895

1895

1895